LAWRENCE DURRELL

From the Elephant's Back

Collected Essays & Travel Writings

 The University of Alberta Press

Edited and with
an Introduction by
JAMES GIFFORD

Published by

The University of Alberta Press
Ring House 2
Edmonton, Alberta, Canada T6G 2E1
www.uap.ualberta.ca

LIBRARY AND ARCHIVES CANADA
CATALOGUING IN PUBLICATION

Durrell, Lawrence [Essays. Selections]
    From the elephant's back : collected essays &
travel writings / Lawrence Durrell ; edited and
with an introduction by James Gifford ; foreword
by Peter Baldwin.

Includes bibliographical references and index.
Issued in print and electronic formats.
ISBN 978-1-77212-051-6 (pbk.).—
ISBN 978-1-77212-059-2 (epub).—
ISBN 978-1-77212-060-8 (kindle).—
ISBN 978-1-77212-061-5 (PDF)

    I. Gifford, James, 1974–, editor, writer of
introduction II. Title.

PR6007.U76A6 2015   824'.912   C2014-908313-0
                                C2014-908314-9
Index available in print and PDF editions.

First edition, first printing, 2015.
Printed and bound in Canada by Houghton-Boston
Printers, Saskatoon, Saskatchewan.
Copyediting and proofreading by Joanne Muzak.
Indexing by Lindsay Parker.

The University of Alberta Press is committed to
protecting our natural environment. As part of
our efforts, this book is printed on Enviro Paper: it
contains 100% post-consumer recycled fibres and
is acid- and chlorine-free.

The University of Alberta Press gratefully
acknowledges the support received for its
publishing program from The Canada Council
for the Arts. The University of Alberta Press also
gratefully acknowledges the financial support of
the Government of Canada through the Canada
Book Fund (CBF) and the Government of Alberta
through the Alberta Media Fund (AMF) for its
publishing activities.

This book has been published with the help of
a grant from the Canadian Federation for the
Humanities and Social Sciences, through the
Awards to Scholarly Publications Program,
using funds provided by the Social Sciences and
Humanities Research Council of Canada.

Canada   Canada Council   Conseil des Arts
          for the Arts   du Canada

Alberta
Government

Contents

Foreword

A taste or more correctly a passion which once contracted can never be cured.

—JAMES POPE-HENNESSY, *Aspects of Provence*

As for human characters, whether real or invented, there are no such animals. Each psyche is really an ant-hill of opposing predispositions. Personality as something with fixed attributes is an illusion—but a necessary illusion if we are to love!

—LAWRENCE DURRELL, *Balthazar*

THE GENESIS OF THIS COLLECTION took place one weekend over ten years ago when I met with my fellow Durrell enthusiast and collector, Peter Dixon, to talk Durrell and to inspect my extensive but disordered collection of work by and about Lawrence Durrell.

I had been a serious collector (someone who will order a book first then look at the price!) since the late 1970s. I had wandered in and out of second-hand bookshops, raided the catalogues of dealers of "Modern Firsts," plagued Bernard Stone (himself a long time collector, seller, and publisher of Durrell's work from various London bookshop premises), and placed daredevil bids at auctions until I had what might be termed a respectable collection.

If space, the arrival of babies, and indolence stopped me cataloguing the collection, it is still great fun to pull down a banker's box marked simply "Durrell" and see what lies beneath the anonymous cardboard lid. Thus it was that, one winter's day, Peter and I dug into this trove. We pulled out all the copies we could find where Durrell had contributed an occasional piece of writing. I knew there would be a lot, and soon Peter and I were in hot debate as to what should be left out of the collection that I then had in mind and of which this book is the result.

Under cover of darkness, we slipped into the law office where I worked, coaxed the photocopier into life, and spent the next two hours copying all that we had found. Having established a bundle of copies which I felt would provide a fair selection of Durrell's writing in this form, I used my charm and the promise of some pocket money to persuade Janet, one of the secretaries at my office, to prepare a typescript for me.

My plan had been to publish the collection under the imprint of my own Delos Press. In the meantime, Richard Pine, director of the Durrell School of Corfu and author of the most impressive *Lawrence Durrell: The Mindscape*, had provided much encouragement by adding some editorial notes to the copy I had prepared. Richard's support and contribution may have come at a time when my interest would otherwise have flagged, given that the project then seemed beyond the scope of both my finances and competence as an editor.

I also had the benefit of advice and editorial encouragement from Dr. James Gifford of Fairleigh Dickinson University. As well as being aware of his scholarly work, I knew that he was instrumental in the republishing of Durrell's first two novels, *Pied Piper of Lovers* and *Panic Spring*. I am immensely grateful for his efforts.

That this selection of essays has progressed from being "good" to exceptional is entirely down to his work and diligence in finalising and editing the selection now available.

Much of what Durrell wrote as occasional pieces about Provence is readily available elsewhere, such as in the *Spirit of Place* collection. For the most part, the essays reproduced here are reprinted for the first time.

My epigraph from Pope-Hennessy's excellent and evocative book opens with the words, Provence is "a taste." So fiery has my passion been for the work of Lawrence Durrell that I benefited from Larry's munificent encouragement to publish two of his books under my own Delos Press imprint: with Penelope Durrell-Hope, a revised edition of *An Irish Faustus* (1987) and a short text he wrote specially for Delos, *Henri Michaux: The Poet of Supreme Solipsism*. I am ever grateful for the opportunity to have published these books and this collection therefore seems to be the best possible tribute to a writer of such style, inspiration, and imagination.

Salut, Larry.

I am gratified that the following shared my commitment to seeing this collection of writing published: Peter Dixon; Janet King for doing the first typescript; Anthony Astbury for the first proof reading; John Glass for adding his editorial skills; Anthea Morton Saner and her successor Camilla Goslett at Curtis Brown for agreeing to the contractual side; Richard Pine of the Durrell School of Corfu for editorial guidance; Penelope and John Hope for offering their wisdom and inspiration; Brewster Chamberlin for checking the chronology I prepared to assist my work on the project; and Tony Rudolf for perfecting my weak translations from the French when only versions in that language are available.

Finally, and most importantly, to Françoise Kestsman Durrell who, as Durrell's literary executor, so promptly agreed to this publication when first mooted as a Delos Press book.

Peter Baldwin
Moseley, Birmingham, England
November 2014

Acknowledgements

I COULD NOT HAVE COMPLETED THIS COLLECTION without a
good deal of help from many people. Peter Baldwin first envisioned
this collection for Delos Press, which has produced many fine editions.
I have benefited from much correspondence with Peter as well as a
detailed conversation in Stratford-Upon-Avon in 2009 with regard to
the changes to the project. In the same year, Fairleigh Dickinson
University supported two weeks of research in Oxford where I completed
the majority of the revisions to the manuscript. The staff of the Bodleian
Library were extremely helpful with locating several otherwise overlooked works by Durrell, including many of his minor works from the
1930s and 1940s, some of which were added to the collection initially
envisioned. I am thankful for their efficient assistance as well as for
providing a working environment that was highly productive. Although
the drafted comments Richard Pine and I created for the Delos Press
edition were abandoned, my discussions with Richard were of great
use and undoubtedly influenced my approach here. I was also fortu-
nate to enjoy two weeks in residence at the Durrell School of Corfu in
2010 at the invitation of University of Iowa's Overseas Writer's Workshop,
during which I completed a good deal of the annotations to the new
additions made in Oxford.

   With regard to this volume's revisions to the accepted critical interpretations of Durrell's notion of the Heraldic Universe, I am in the debt
of the Special Collections librarians at the University of Victoria. They
first introduced me to the Henry Miller–Herbert Read correspondence,

which significantly reoriented my understanding of Durrell's critical context. This was compounded by the Read–Henry Treece correspondence, and the Read–George Woodcock letters, a published copy of which was very generously given to me. The manuscripts for all three items are held in the McPherson Library at the University of Victoria. Members of the International Lawrence Durrell Society have also given me great support through their listserv and as colleagues and friends. In particular, I would like to acknowledge the fine feedback I have received from Charles Sligh, Michael Haag, William Leigh Godshalk, Anne Zahlan, James Clawson, and Pamela Francis.

For the opportunity to teach several of these shorter works, and thereby develop a sense of what annotations would be most congenial to a typical undergraduate reader, I am indebted to my students from 2005 to 2011 at the University of Lethbridge, the University of Victoria, Fairleigh Dickinson University, and Simon Fraser University. Graduate students at the University of Iowa and Simon Fraser University have also helped with feedback on lectures that discussed several of the critical interventions I have attempted here. I am also indebted to Joanne Muzak for her astonishingly keen eye as an editor and generous critical acumen.

James Gifford
Vancouver
November 2014

Introduction

THIS COLLECTION HAS A STRAIGHTFORWARD AMBITION: to redirect the interpretive perspective that readers bring to Lawrence Durrell's literary works by returning their attention to his short prose. This includes three main areas for critical intervention: reconsidering Durrell's political postures over time, reassessing his position in English literature as a Late Modernist, and addressing the role of the poignant suffering surrounding the Second World War in his travel writing. For both "scholarly" and "pleasure" readers, these new perspectives on his texts alter our approach to Durrell's more famous works, mainly his novels and travel books, which continue to attract a wide audience. A century after his birth, such reconsideration is increasingly necessary. And Durrell's works are increasingly necessary to that century's understanding of itself.

In each of the three areas I have outlined, much literary baggage has accumulated over time, and, as a consequence, most readers find it difficult to approach Durrell without preconceived interpretive notions. He is most often presented as an imperialist author belonging to no definite generation or movement, whose works evoke a tourist's dream of the orientalist and philhellenic luxuriance of the Eastern Mediterranean. We need little prompting to regard Durrell's works through such a tinted glass. In a more general sense relating to that first paradigmatic approach—his political positions over time— Durrell is known for his literary activity at the end of empire, writing such works as *Bitter Lemons* and *The Alexandria Quartet* in the immediate aftermath of the Enosis struggle on Cyprus and the Suez Crisis in Egypt. This has led to his works being associated with other late imperial prose writers and works, such as Paul Scott's *Raj Quartet* and Doris Lessing's *The Golden Notebook*. What this perspective masks is Durrell's Indian childhood, his troubled position as an imperial subject, and his close ties to several anti-authoritarian-cum-anarchist figures in tandem with his lifelong anti-Marxism. Durrell's short prose presents a politicized author very much unlike the popular image constructed from the accumulated veneers of many years of critical thought, much of which grew out of the decolonization process that erupted in 1956, the same year as Durrell wrote *Justine*. At a minimum, we uncover a far more politically complex author than we are typically compelled to find when first reading *The Alexandria Quartet*. This other Lawrence Durrell more clearly relates to the major literary achievements of other writers from the same time period.

In the works gathered here, we find the character-defining aesthetic ponderings of the young Lawrence Durrell who was about to begin a series of publications in such venues as George Woodcock's wartime magazine *NOW*, Robert Duncan's *Experimental Review*, George Leite's *Circle* (also with Kenneth Rexroth and Duncan), and Alex Comfort's *New Road*; all four were expressly anarchist periodicals edited by self-identifying anarchist poets. The first was published by Freedom Press and the last by Grey Walls Press, which bound itself closely to the anarchist New Apocalypse movement and produced *Seven*, which Durrell also repeatedly published in and promoted.[1] Immediately prior, he appeared in the Oxford student poetry journal *Kingdom Come*, which was the rebirth of the short-lived *Bolero*—both were edited by John Waller (succeeded by New Apocalypse poets) who had dabbled significantly with anti-authoritarian politics and fostered the network of poets that would reassemble with Durrell in North Africa during the Second World War. Duncan twice published Durrell in *Experimental Review* and reviewed Henry Miller in it, noting, "Politically he has no politics. Having come at last into the real world he is an anarchist. Anyone reading over the foregoing passage will see clearly why the Marxist surrealists are afraid of Miller" (79). At the same time, Duncan was repeatedly attempting to publish Durrell's surrealist *Asylum in the Snow* under the same conceptual revision to Surrealism, though it took him seven years to accomplish it—and the book was finally published by Circle in 1947.

This Lawrence Durrell comes as a surprise to early twenty-first-century readers. This angry young man of the 1940s gives an unanticipated voice to anti-authoritarian visions of poetic inspiration in "Ideas About Poems" and "The Heraldic Universe,"[2] both of which are in this collection and originate in his correspondence with Henry Miller about Herbert Read and Surrealism. Both Read and Miller, again, self-identified as anarchist writers,[3] and the vision Miller fostered shaped Durrell's developing sense of his poetics in the 1930s and 1940s. Recontextualized, Durrell's production of an open text that is dependent on the reader's independent interpretive ventures and individual creativity forces a contemporary reader to examine the potential politics of such an aesthetic vision. If the text thrusts interpretive independence on the reader for a highly personal vision, does this "Personalist" concept imply a politics?[4] More to the point, how is Durrell's "personal" stance akin to or different from the Personalist movement that grew among his colleagues at the same moment in Britain, and which also rebutted T.S. Eliot's impersonal theory of poetry? It is also tempting to ask if Durrell's early "heraldic" notions of creativity influenced the ambiguity and reader-imminent interpretations we are given in *The Alexandria Quartet*, whether they appear as "Workpoints" in *The Alexandria Quartet* that allow the reader to continue the narrative or as an unreliable narrator whom the reader cannot trust to provide meaning. In any case, the traditionally understood notion of Durrell's Heraldic Universe as a mental state of being is insufficient for the context revealed by its publishing history and associations.

As I have shown elsewhere, the descriptions of the Heraldic Universe that Durrell articulates in the works gathered in this collection derive directly from his partnership with Miller in a correspondence with Read that concerned communism and anarchism ("Anarchist" 61–63). This relationship between aesthetics and politics has been overlooked entirely in previous scholarship. In reaction to the copy of Read's speech from the 1936 London International Surrealist Exhibition, a speech that Miller sent to Durrell with Read's letter, Durrell responded, "This manifesto would be a lot clearer if these brave young revolutionaries started by defining what they mean by art. To begin with, they seem to mean Marx" (Durrell and Miller 18). Read concludes his uncharacteristically pro-communist speech with the statement that Surrealism only succeeds "in the degree to which it leads to revolutionary actions" (8) and "work[s] for the transformation of this imperfect world" (13). To this, Durrell responded directly: "A definition of the word surrealism, please" and "I firmly believe in the ideals of cementing reality with the dream, but I do not believe the rest of this stuff. That the artist must be a socialist, for example. That he wants to transform the world. (He wants to transform men.)" (Durrell and Miller 18). It was only in this immediate context, for which Miller had established his anarchist vision in contrast to the communist perspective endorsed by Surrealism, that Durrell offered his first articulation of the Heraldic Universe just a few lines later in the same letter: "Listen, Miller, what I feel about it, is this…What I propose to do, with all deadly solemnity, is to create my HERALDIC UNIVERSE quite alone. The foundation is being quietly laid" (18). In this context, Durrell's subsequent anti-rationalist and autonomous articulation of the Heraldic Universe in *Personal Landscape*, collected in this volume, takes on a new tone: "Describing, logic limits. Its law is causality.…Poetry by an associative approach transcends its own syntax in order not to describe but to be the cause of apprehension in others: Transcending logic it invades a realm where unreason reigns" ("Heraldic," this volume 103). Durrell's other aesthetic comments for the journal, "Ideas About Poems," draw on further loaded terms gesturing to the anarchist New Apocalypse's Personalist movement, "The poet is interested in the Personal aspect.…

That is the only explanation for *Personal Landscape* now" (this volume 99). John Waller, who edited *Bolero* and *Kingdom Come* in Oxford and was published by Durrell in *Personal Landscape*, stated the relation succinctly: "Durrell is likely to found no school. (Indeed the best poetry of 1940 onwards may come to be known as that of brilliant individuals rather than of groups and tendencies.)" (179).

However, this anti-authoritarian component of Durrell's early works came to a head in 1948, shortly after a rapid flurry of publications and attempted publications by anarchist presses and periodicals as well as projects by other authors that he supported through the same literary circle.[5] In 1949, Durrell relocated to Yugoslavia, and in this new place, his anti-Marxist position was reshaped and intensified. The humanist and anti-Marxist elements of the anarchism envisioned by Miller in works like "An Open Letter to Surrealists Everywhere" took on, for Durrell, a conservative tenor after his sequential postings to Belgrade and then Cyprus, the former of which he regarded as proof of the impoverished outcomes of authoritarian communism. As Durrell wrote to his dear friend Theodore Stephanides while serving in Belgrade in 1949, in a letter taken up by Andrew Hammond as a demonstration of Durrell's confirmed conservatism,

> *There is little news except that what I have seen here has turned me firmly reactionary and Tory: the blank dead end which labour leads towards seems to be this machine state, with its censored press, its long marching columns of political prisoners guarded by tommy guns. Philistinism, puritanism and cruelty. Luckily the whole edifice has begun to crumble, and one has the pleasurable job of aiding and abetting.* (Durrell, *Spirit* 101; Hammond 49)

However, like most of Durrell's comments on his reactionary nature, hyperbole and irony play a significant role. Durrell's immediately previous letter to Stephanides shows a much different context and a far more qualified position:

Conditions are rather gloomy here—almost mid-war conditions,
overcrowding, poverty: As for Communism—my dear Theodore a
short visit here is enough to make one decide that Capitalism is worth
fighting for. Black as it might be, with all its bloodstains, it is less
gloomy and arid and hopeless than this inert and ghastly police state.
(Durrell, *Spirit* 100)

This is hardly unqualified conservatism. Moreover, while he did not
consider it as bad as Yugoslavia under Tito, Durrell's capitalism remains
black and bloodstained, and by 1974 he intimately bound money to
merde (*Monsieur* 141) through "Marx's great analysis of our culture or
the Freudian analysis of absolute value as based on infantile attitudes
to excrement. Gold and excrement" (141). A kindred irony appears in
another of Durrell's often quoted comments in a late-in-life interview:
"I'm conservative, I'm reactionary and right wing" (Green 23; Pine,
Lawrence 393–94; Calotychos 185). Richard Pine quotes from a portion
of Peter Green's interview, Vangelis Calotychos quotes Pine to demonstrate Durrell's right-wing position, and from this context, Marilyn Adler
Papayanis contends, "Durrell's...reactionary politics [are] an important
component of his ethics of expatriation" (41). However, this overlooks
the irony and contextual poignancy of Durrell's original statement in
its original context. When Green asked, "Were you, or are you, romantic
about Greece?" (23), Durrell offered a pointed response:

Yes. I think super-starry-eyed in a sense....Remember that neither
my father nor mother had ever seen England....I was already under
the shadow of the myth of the British raj....But I've been progressively
disgusted with our double-facedness in politics over situations like
the Greek situation. Remember I've worked as an official in Cyprus
on that disgusting situation which was entirely engineered by us, do
you see....And, as I say, I've never got over the fact of feeling ashamed
that bits of the Parthenon are lying about. I refused a CMG[6] on those
grounds, though I didn't make an issue of it, and I don't want to—I'm

conservative, I'm reactionary and right wing—so I don't want to
embarrass anybody. But the reason I make a polite bow-out of the
whole thing was that I didn't want to be decorated by people who had
bits of the Parthenon lying about in their backyard; and are too
shabby not to send the biggest battleship…immediately back to the
Greeks with it…to thank them for our existence. (Green 23)

Like his qualified siding with capitalism over communism, for Durrell
to reject the legitimacy of British Hellenic holdings in the British
Museum and the Elgin Marbles is hardly reactionary and points to the
irony in his political positions as well as his express disputation with
British colonialism. It is equally difficult to read Durrell's full comments
as pro-imperial. Moreover, this comment was made at the height of
the administration of Margaret Thatcher's Conservative government
in 1987, and it discusses Durrell's experiences during Sir Anthony Eden's
and Harold Macmillan's Conservative governments in 1957 (which
explains the fluctuations between present and past tenses in Durrell's
language above). The interpretive simplicity that Papayanis finds
would now seem deeply blurred. The trouble for the reader here is
how to hold in creative tension, perhaps even a defining tension,
Durrell's lengthy anti-authoritarian ties and anti-Marxist beliefs, both
of which seem to have a significant role in the aesthetic structure of
his works, in conjunction with his service to the British government.
Durrell's comments remained measured even after he was redefined as
a British non-patrial without the right to enter or settle in Britain without
a visa, a fact that "thickens" this tension. Moreover, we must ask
whether or not the existing political interpretations of Durrell's works
are sufficient for the breadth of this creative tension.

This problem surfaces again in Durrell's travel narrative of Yugoslavia,
"Family Portrait," as well as in his discussions of Sadat-era Egypt and
the communist experiences of his friend Gostan Zarian. All three
pieces adamantly reject Marxist forms of government that arose from
Soviet Russia as well as Soviet influences abroad. They also postdate

Durrell's last publications among the anarchist presses and periodicals. However, in all three, Durrell's vision returns to the village, everyday life, the materials of rural living, and resistance to exploitative labour and class. It is surprising to find an anti-Marxist position adopted that nonetheless questions rural–urban tensions and the transformation of traditional ways of life by the introduction of technology and new forms of organization—both quintessential Marxists areas of attention. To be more exact, it is only if we fail to account for Durrell's previous anti-authoritarian affiliations and quietist interests that his rustic, utopian anti-Marxism is surprising. This combination has confused much previous scholarship, which either casts Durrell as a reactionary Tory or as an elitist artist without regard for the conditions of labour and life. Both are oversimplifications that this collection aims to trouble.

Durrell's only expressly political musings in this collection appear in "No Clue to Living," in which he was invited to consider the role of the artist in contemporary society. Juxtaposed against the activist and formerly communist authors in the series of articles organized by Stephen Spender, Durrell's stance that the public ought to form its own individual opinions without relying on the authority of artists, politicians, or other figureheads is shockingly anti-authoritarian in the comparison. In contrast to the earnest protestations of the other authors involved in the project, Durrell contends, "it is very doubtful whether [the artist] has anything to say which could be more original than the other pronouncements by public figures, for apart from his art he is just an ordinary fellow like everyone else, subject to the same bloody flux of rash opinion" (this volume 37–38). The phrase, "he is just an ordinary fellow like everyone else" is the leveling force that puts the reading public on par with presidents and popes (37), and to which a poet dare not lecture or opinionate. The poet clearly retains opinions but his public is taught self-reliance without relying on opinionated poets for leadership. The result is much akin to Miller's anarchist revision to the authoritarian communism of the Surrealists. Rather than the notion of an artist's authority as a "public opinionator"

(37), which "leads the masses to identify themselves with movie stars and megalomaniacs like Hitler and Mussolini," Miller proposed to abandon leadership because "I am fatuous enough to believe that in living my own life in my own way I am more apt to give life to others" ("Open" 157). Despite the appearance of "No Clue to Living" after Durrell's years in Yugoslavia and the cementing of his anti-Marxist beliefs, Durrell's rejection of "that ineradicable predisposition to legislate for the man next door" demonstrates his desire to emphasize the "limitations of Time, on whose slippery surface neither kings nor empires nor dictators could find more than a precarious and temporary purchase" ("No Clue," this volume 41, 42–43). Doomed kings, empires, and dictators make a striking combination for an author who was a royal subject, servant of empire, and recent resident in Péron's Argentina and Tito's Yugoslavia. It is difficult to recognize in this Durrell the same man described by biographers and critics as a reactionary,[7] although the complex relations among these differing positions certainly enrich our approach to his major novels and the troubled politics of his travel writings. One immediately thinks of Durrell's comments on T.S. Eliot, who when accused by Durrell of being too interested in esoteric material to be Anglican, responded by saying, "Perhaps they haven't found out about me yet?" (this volume 265).

As a Late Modernist, Durrell is also difficult to pin down to a single category. His generation came into its artistic strength after the blossoming of the Auden generation and the outbreak of the Second World War. Although Durrell had already begun to publish innovative works that significantly influenced the network of writers around him, accession to editorial authority and cultural acceptance as the avant-garde did not follow—the High Modernists had attained the former while the Auden poets had become synonymous with the avant-garde until the 1950s. The generation immediately following was largely dispersed by the war or fragmented by distance from the major artistic and publishing centres. This left a gap in the received literary histories until the Movement poets, the Angry Young Men, and the Beats. Yet a significant difference from Auden's sphere of influence appears in Durrell's literary criticism included in this volume.[8] Readers will note the extent of the allusions by Durrell to the works of the High Modernists as well as his desire to recontextualize these works and to resist their influence—Harold Bloom's strong poet struggling through a misprision of his progenitors seems overtly the case here. Durrell's vision of C.P. Cavafy is tied to his resistance to T.S. Eliot, and the two counterpoise each other in several ways. Durrell's attachment to Henry Miller betrays a similar function when he reinterprets Miller's *Hamlet* correspondence with Michael Fraenkel in order to dispute Eliot's influential "Hamlet and His Problems."

Similar tensions arise in Durrell's greatly overlooked comments on Ezra Pound in "Enigma Variations," a work that gives shape to the myriad allusions to Pound across Durrell's works as well as to the specific moment in his career at which it appeared. In this collection, Eliot tell us that the young Durrell "dismiss[ed] Ezra Pound in a phrase" ("Other," this volume 261), yet his influence clearly lingers, and Durrell admits, "I have always loved the early Pound and no writer of my generation can fail to acknowledge the debt he owes to so brilliant an innovator" ("Enigma," this volume 237). At the same moment as Durrell was reviewing Pound's *Section: Rock-Drill de los Cantares LXXXV–XCV*, he was also engaged in the major literary work of his own career. In 1957, he had completed *Justine* and was at work on the remainder of *The Alexandria Quartet*. This specific moment is crucial since it shows the conjoining of Durrell's curious politics, his allegiances to his predecessors, and his desire to revise their strong influence. Pound was notoriously incarcerated in St. Elizabeths Hospital after an insanity plea, which secured him from treason charges and potential execution following from his support for fascism and radio broadcasts for Mussolini during World War II. Yet Pound's literary origins began with a great deal of contact with the anarchist press, albeit of a form heavily influenced by Max Stirner: *The Egoist*. Durrell, after finishing *Justine*, revised the conclusion of the novel to directly allude to the conclusion of Pound's first Canto, and this allusive recontextualization is deeply anti-authoritarian in nature, which rebuilds a specific conceptualization of Ezra Pound.

In a renunciation of the author's authority, Durrell "refer[s] the reader to a blank page in order to throw him back upon his own resources—which is where every reader ultimately belongs" (*Alexandria* 307). This was a technique Durrell discussed in his novel *Balthazar* in 1958 but only realized in 1962 when he added it to his revised 1957 novel *Justine* while revising all the books in this series for omnibus publication as *The Alexandria Quartet*. The reader finds "everything*" given an endnote, which in turn directs the reader to the blank ending of the novel (*Alexandria* 195–96, 203). The reader is led into a collaborative development of meaning with the text rather than receiving meaning from the artist, priest, or political leadership—as the narrator states in the closing of the novel, "I no longer wish to coerce anyone, to make promises, to think of life in terms of compacts, resolutions, covenants. It will be up to [my reader] to interpret my silence according to her own needs and desires" (195). His reader is made to actively grapple with the text and make something of it rather than passively receive it. Moreover, the anti-authoritarian component of this "wish" is difficult to overlook, especially since the conflagration of such coercion, promises, compacts, resolutions, covenants is also the conclusion of Durrell's next novel series, *The Revolt of Aphrodite*.

However, this rejection of authority in "everything*" integrates a new finale for the novel when "Does not everything depend on our interpretation of the silence around us?" in the original is extended with the annotation and a repetition of the famous final words of Pound's Canto as a subsequent sentence: "So that…" (195). In effect, Durrell recuperates the Pound of his youth after reviewing the Pound of his maturity, whom he finds lacking, and this recuperation through the misprision of the strong poet (in Bloom's sense) reasserts a version of Pound more in line with Durrell's vision from the 1930s and 1940s. This tension over the literary baggage of strong predecessors calls out for a critical reassessment of Durrell's work as a Late Modernist carrying the agon of Modernism well beyond the mid-point of the century.

For my third area of critical intervention, the reader will also find a different form of travel writing in this collection. While Durrell obviously used the short travel essay as a genre that could produce significant income, his works have been generally "tidied" by a variety of editors, in large part to avoid the discomforts of writing about beautiful locations in the aftermath of violent struggles. Durrell's travel works here have been unavailable since their initial publication, some for more than seventy years. Scholars are already aware of how Durrell's book *Reflections on a Marine Venus* was heavily edited by the poet and editor Anne Ridler in order to minimize its inclusion of war references and suffering for a post-war British readership (Roessel, "'Cut'" 64–77). "The Island of the Rose" and "Letter in the Sofa" appear without such cuts, the latter of which is clearly meant to charm a specific audience yet still includes discomfiting references to the Holocaust and the extent of destruction endured by the communities of Rhodes even while emphasizing the poignant or melancholy happiness such locations dually afford.

Moreover, Durrell's relationship with many homes becomes evident in these materials. In an autobiographical turn, the titular essay "From the Elephant's Back" sets his childhood as a subject of empire in relief against the homelessness he felt when he was returned to the centre of empire: his Indian childhood and his adolescent migration to London. This theme opens Durrell's first major work of prose fiction, his 1935 novel *Pied Piper of Lovers*, and its importance to his thinking brought about its autobiographical return in this 1982 essay. The potential for a new vision is articulated in both works. The first casts Durrell's semi-autobiographical protagonist as racially Anglo-Indian and hence as a reconciliation between Mother Indian and Father England; the second finds an avatar of Durrell's childhood, very much like his fictional character Walsh in the novel, befriending a juvenile elephant. Although the relations of empire mark the elephant's servant status in Durrell's lecture, it is important that both Durrell and the elephant are "children," and their interactions appear to be mutually beneficial. Durrell's uncle, in this narrative, shot the elephant's parent that went mad and attacked a village.

The natural association for this autobiographical story, especially by 1982 when Durrell included it in his essay, is George Orwell's famous essay "Shooting an Elephant."[9] For Orwell, the servant of empire who shoots the elephant is constrained just as much by the expectations of the indigenous population as he is by his duties to empire, even if as an individual he rejects the social conditions into which he is placed. Yet Orwell's essay casts the elephant as the British Empire itself, brought low by its own servant fulfilling the unwished duties of an imperial subject, ultimately leading to a *Titanic*-like rise and fall in the close to the work:

> An enormous senility seemed to have settled upon him. One could have imagined him thousands of years old. I fired again into the same spot. At the second shot he did not collapse but climbed with desperate slowness to his feet and stood weakly upright...I fired a third time...But in falling he seemed for a moment to rise, for as his hind legs collapsed beneath him he seemed to tower upwards like a huge rock toppling, his trunk reaching skywards like a tree. He trumpeted, for the first and only time. And then down he came, his belly towards me, with a crash that seemed to shake the ground even where I lay.
> (154–55)

For Orwell, the relations among the colonials, the Indians, and the elephant are antagonistic and inextricably caught in dynamics of power, control, and social position. The collapse of the elephant, rising for a final trumpet, is the recognition Orwell had previously lacked: "I did not even know that the British Empire is dying" (149). Durrell's contrast, which avoids empire and focuses on individual relations, could not differ more:

One of the shot elephants had left a small child behind, and this
was to become my playmate during my stay. It was called Sadu. It
was an apprentice elephant learning its duties with a couple of trained
grown-up females. But as yet it was not very big or strong; so it took
me to practise upon. It had learned to say salaam, *to pick up money*
from the ground, and was now learning how to hoist a man on to its
back. A grown man would have been too heavy, so Sadu was told
to practise with me. This he did with pleasure. They hold out their
trunk curled up at the end like a human hand; you put your foot into
it and presto you are raised in the air, and placed securely on the
animal's back, between those two fantastic ears, the signs of super-
normal spirituality, they say. They have a singular floating walk,
a little humorous, like a drunken Irishman....But the proverb says
that whoever sees the world from the back of an elephant learns
the secrets of the jungle and becomes a seer. I had to be content
to become a poet. (this volume 3–4)

For Durrell's vision, the elephant becomes a partner while both are
children and playmates unaware of the training to which they are
being subjected. Moreover, while the elephant grants the gifts that
allow Durrell to become a poet, its walk "like a drunken Irishman"
signals Durrell's most frequently used escape from being identified
as British and a royal subject—his dubious claim to Irish ancestry.
The elephant and the child are a part of each other, and hence both
are reflections of Durrell himself. Perhaps more importantly, both
resist the politics of the conflicting governmental bodies and material
conditions in which they find themselves constituted as subjects.

This childhood experience of India, which fostered his first literary
work and shaped the rest of his career of alienation from Britain, is
reflected in Durrell's approach to other homes, most notably the
Mediterranean and Greece. "Helene and Philhellene" anticipates the
critical vision articulated by Edmund Keeley in *Inventing Paradise* and
by David Roessel in *In Byron's Shadow*. It shows Durrell again revising

the literary influences that shaped his interactions with others such that the historical desire for ancient Greece, which so blinded the vision of the Romantics and Victorians (and arguably a great many of the High Modernists), is displaced by a recognition of the Modern Greece that cannot be ignored, and also the historical desire is also displaced by the recognition of the rich culture that Classicism can inspire one to overlook. Durrell's argument for the virtues of a contemporary vision is strikingly prescient and sets us to reconsider his frequently presented colonial attitudes toward Greece:

> "Hellas" is written rather than "Greece" in order first of all to point the difference between the Philhellene of yesterday and the Philhellene of today—for up to almost the present generation the passionate bias of the English writer and scholar has been towards the classical world. In a sense Greece has represented to him, in terms of landscape and climate, the flowering of an education....But the classical bias has had its defects no less than its virtues. It has tended to blindfold the traveller to the reality of contemporary Greece. (this volume 107)

For Durrell, thinking back to his young adulthood and happy years on Corfu, this contemporary vision demonstrates the transformation of the Romantic vision of a Classical Hellas into a modern vision of Greece, which has been documented by Roessel. For Roessel, "With contemporary notions of dancing Zorbas and Shirley Valentines with or without bikini tops, we might forget that before the late 1930s almost no one went to Greece to find their inner selves. This is the Greece that Miller and Durrell began to construct" (*In Byron's* 6). Durrell's frame is Modern Greek literature, and in his view the quasi-parental relationship to Byron and imperial power remains, but with the significant recognition that Greek authors have transformed and surpassed this restriction: "not only has our Philhellenism undergone a radical change for the better but...the modern Greek has become more than worthy of the admiration that was too often in the past reserved for his ancestors" (this volume 117). The paternalism has not yet vanished, but the recognition of new vitality and the occluding restrictions of an imperialist vantage point are major shifts for this period. Such reconsiderations of Greece as home appear across Durrell's other works in this volume, whether it is his desire to dote on Corfu or his hesitations over Cyprus, an island wounded deeply by imperialism, and which in turn wounded Durrell deeply. Again, the position as a subject of empire shapes the vision Durrell can conjure, but it is by this time most assuredly a vision of contemporary rather than ancient Greece, and that shift is still worth noting, even as we question the difficulties of Durrell's conflicted politics.

In only these three approaches—Durrell's politics, his position as a Late Modernist, and the often-censored poignancy of his writings of place—we find that attention to Durrell's short prose creates a greatly transformed understanding of Durrell as an author and, as a consequence, a radically new way of re-reading his major works. If, in reading Durrell's charming works collected here, the reader develops a startlingly new or at the least refreshed way of engaging with the major novel sequences or with Durrell's overlooked poetry, then the purpose of this collection will be amply served.

THIS EDITION

This collection was first envisioned by Peter Baldwin as a volume to be produced by Delos Press, which has specialized in fine editions. At his invitation, Richard Pine and I prepared a series of very brief comments on each piece to provide a précis for the unfamiliar reader or to point out one or two of the potentially confusing references to which Durrell is prone. The contents of this original volume, and the nature of its editorial comments, were significantly different from those brought together here. Yet this was the genesis of the project, and it remains a significant influence. This project was unfortunately abandoned due to the demands of the financial crisis of 2008, which has impacted small press endeavours in a number of ways worldwide.

While a letterpress edition with marbled wrappers has advantages, and I greatly value the few beautiful Delos editions my shelves afford, the wider availability of this edition and its scholarly nature has led to extensive revisions.

This present volume developed, phoenix-like, from this earlier vision, albeit without any dramatic flames or burning of manuscripts. I have both expanded and contracted the contents, trimming some initially intended works while integrating others that had not been previously considered, and stitching still others together for a future volume on Durrell's creative process. This also led to a new sequence and series of divisions between the various works. Durrell's fascinating discussions of the relations between the visual arts and writing must remain for another project, as does much of his literary criticism and short creative prose. However, the most significant transformation has been to the nature of the volume and its aims, specifically the audience and purpose it envisions. It has shifted from a fine press printing with only very brief and unobtrusive contextual materials to a full critical edition with a scholarly apparatus, detailed annotations, and bibliography. This new vision necessitated changes not only to the selected works, such that those of a more scholarly orientation were retained to a higher degree than others, but also to the order and structure of the work.

In general, I have left Durrell's idiosyncratic grammar untouched, although spellings have been standardized. Where more than one edition of a work previously exists, changes to paragraph breaks are common. This is particularly true for works that appeared in the press. In these instances where variants exist, I have selected those paragraph breaks that seemed most congenial to reading in a book, as opposed to a news column. With regard to other variants, I have generally preferred the first publication, especially when the latter was prepared without significant, documented editorial oversight from Durrell. For Durrell's UNESCO lectures on Shakespeare, which have appeared in print only in a French translation, I have attempted to remain faithful to the original English typescripts, even though they are not as editorially polished as the subsequent French publication. The problems of translating Durrell's prose back into English created too many variants that were surely editorial in nature. To compensate, I have silently corrected the missing punctuation and frequent spelling errors of the draft manuscripts. In these works, I have added or altered punctuation to add clarity where a spoken reading would certainly have avoided misinterpretations through emphasis and pauses.

For the final selection of materials, I have limited myself to works not otherwise accessible and particularly those that appeared in exceedingly rare publications or that exist only in typescript. This has meant excluding materials that would make natural pairings with those included here, such as Durrell's successful surrealist prose pair "Asylum in the Snow" and "Zero," as well as his useful comments on Henry Miller in the Introduction to *The Best of Henry Miller*.

NOTES

1. This is a thorny publication history, and the scarcity of copies has led to a general oversight from scholars. The Freedom Press is the most important anarchist press in the United Kingdom, founded by Peter Kropotkin and Charlotte Wilson in 1886. To give a sense of its position, in 1945, four of its editors were arrested for their pacifism and subversion of military service following the 1944 government raid of the press. This led to the famous formation of the Freedom Defence Committee by Herbert Read, George Orwell, George Woodcock, Alex Comfort, and Osbert Sitwell, among others. Two years later, in 1947, Durrell published his "Elegy on the Closing of the French Brothels" in Woodcock's NOW, printed by Freedom Press ("Elegy" 30–32). Durrell first began to publish with Robert Duncan in 1940 when Duncan lived in an anarchist commune in Woodstock, New York, but he had already written in 1938 to support the journal *Phoenix*, published by James Cooney on the same commune, saying, "*Phoenix* is surely the most fertile effort…in literature for some time now" (Orend, *Henry* 49). Duncan published the largest collection of Durrell's poetry (in a periodical) in 1940 and repeatedly attempted to republish "Asylum in the Snow" while also beginning to typeset an

edition of *The Black Book*. The latter two were advertised but fell through due to financial limitations; they were revived when Duncan relocated to Berkeley, CA, where he entered another anarchist group with Kenneth Rexroth and George Leite. This group then published more of Durrell's works in their anarchist journal *Circle* in 1946, published a book edition of *Zero* and *Asylum in the Snow: Two Excursions into Reality* in 1947, and advertised a completed edition of *The Black Book* for sale, though this appears to have vanished, very likely due to potential obscenity charges. Henry Miller claimed to have read the proofs for the book (*Letters of Henry* 122), and Durrell's contract for it has survived. Alex Comfort, best known for writing *The Joy of Sex*, was another prominent anarchist figure who corresponded with Durrell while he was in Egypt and included his work in his anarchist journal *New Road* in 1944. Durrell and Miller also corresponded about him as an anarchist writer. Grey Walls published *New Road* and had previously printed *Seven*, which included (and was edited and printed by) many of the poets who subsequently led the New Apocalypse movement, which was also expressly anarchist. Previous scholars have not noticed this publishing history, and it casts Durrell's 1930s and 1940s works in a radically different context than has been traditionally accepted. Nonetheless, Durrell only briefly endorsed Cooney, rejecting him after Cooney turned down Durrell's poetry (Orend, *Henry* 50), and John Waller recalls him attacking the Apocalypse Movement late in the war (177). Durrell's positions are far from straightforward.

2. In 1960, Durrell described his 1938 novel *The Black Book* as the work of "an angry young man of the 30s" (Durrell, "Preface" 9), which casts him in distinction from the Angry Young Men of the 1950s who were known for their working-class origins and social realism.

3. Read's anarchism and anarchist writings are widely recognized. Miller's are not, but anarchism is nonetheless explicit and a major component of his works, ranging from his admiration of and correspondence with Emma Goldman to his speaking for the Industrial Workers of the World (IWW) and numerous written endorsements of anarchism. For more information on Miller's Anarchism, see Orend, "Fucking" (44–77) and Gifford, "Surrealism's" (36–64).

4. In this, I am drawing on Durrell's ties to the "Personalism" movement in British literature. For a detailed account, see Gifford, *Personal Modernisms*.

5. For instance, Durrell helped to send Albert Cossery's novel *Men God Forgot* from Egypt for publication in California by Circle Editions, which derived from an anarchist reading circle in Berkeley. Durrell's *Zero* and *Asylum in the Snow* appeared through the same press, and he signed a contract for it to produce *The Black Book*, though this failed to reach distribution and may not have been

printed. Both works had gone through previous attempts at publication by anarchist groups in New York.

6. CMG is the abbreviation for Companion of the Order of St. Michael and St. George.

7. For instance, see Pine's *Lawrence Durrell: The Mindscape* (393) or Herbrechter's discussions of reactionary politics throughout *Lawrence Durrell, Postmodernism and the Ethics of Alterity*.

8. As Fiona Tomkinson has noted, Durrell's poetry still shows significant influence from Auden (117–32), and his 1939 "Poem in Space and Time" (later "The Prayer Wheel") is a direct answer to Auden's famous 1937 poem "Lullaby."

9. Durrell and Orwell also traded letters in *The New English Weekly* over the periodical *The Booster*, which Orwell saw as a return to the kind of magazine of the 1920s (such as BLAST, *The Egoist*, or *The Little Review*). Orwell's objection was to the inefficacy of such avant-garde work in the face of the looming Second World War, and Durrell's rebuttal was fierce. Nonetheless, both authors appear to have borrowed from each other's novels at the same time as well—Orwell lifting a situation from *Pied Piper of Lovers* for his *Keep the Aspidistra Flying* (to which Durrell refers in his rebuttal in *The New English Weekly*), and Durrell repaying in kind by subverting Orwell's novel in *Panic Spring* (Gifford, "Editor's Preface" vii–ix). Nevertheless, Durrell wrote to Orwell from Yugoslavia expressing his admiration for *Nineteen Eighty-Four*.

From the
Elephant's
Back

1982

THIS IS THE FIRST TIME that I have ventured to accept an invitation
to lecture in France, in French, and I am happy that it should be here
in Paris, at the Centre Pompidou.[1] It is a suitable place to discuss the
theory and the practice of fiction in relation to myself, and moreover
in a language which prides itself on being able to make fine distinctions.

The invitation reached me at a suitable moment also, for I was
between two instalments of a new constellation of novels, and pondering
on its form;[2] I thought that the act of turning my notions into French
might help me to realise them more clearly and thus help me to explain,
if not to excuse, the direction taken by my writing. I have nothing very
esoteric to propound, no views about the novel which would justify an
excursion into such disciplines as are offered by the newest sciences,
like linguistics, for example.[3] That would be too sophisticated. At the
worst I might confess to using my Freud as a compass, for psychoanalysis has brought us real treasures of observation and insight which we
should not neglect. Of course it does not go far enough, but then
nothing does!

I would prefer to present my case in terms of biography, for my
thinking is coloured by the fact that I am a colonial, an Anglo-Indian,[4]

born into that strange world of which the only great poem is the novel *Kim* by Kipling.[5] I was brought up in its shadow, and like its author I was sent to England to be educated. The juxtaposition of the two types of consciousness was extraordinary and created, I think, an ambivalence of vision which was to both help and hinder me as a writer. At times I felt more Asiatic than European, at times the opposite; at times I felt like a white negro thinking in pidgin![6]

At first one hatches books, stories, poems, as they arrive, with pleasure and surprise, and quite without guarantees, as one produces babies. It is only after five or ten years that one starts to recognise a family resemblance—the blue eye, the characteristic nose—which give a specific character to the whole. One begins to trace an inner coherence which relates all these separate parts into a system of ideas or a philosophy of life of a distinctive kind. In this way one's author grows his unique personality and assumes himself, just as a child does. In my case, India was just as important to me as England was. I reacted creatively to both styles of vision, and I often criticised both tartly, perhaps unjustly even, for it was difficult to match such opposing attributes and to make something coherent of the lessons they taught me. One part of me has remained a child of the jungle, ever mindful of the various small initiations which an Indian childhood imposes. I have seen the Rope Trick when I was ten, and distinctly felt the hypnotic power of the conjuror over us as we sat round him in a circle.[7] I have been followed from tree-top to tree-top by sportive monkeys which pelted me with nuts and stones. Their anger made them very accurate and I was glad I wore the stout pith helmet of my father, made of cork about two inches thick—better than a modern crash-helmet! I have seen a cobra fight a mongoose, I have seen the peak of Everest from the foot of my bed in a gaunt dormitory in Darjeeling! My first language was Hindi. And so on![8]

My family came to India before the great Indian Mutiny,[9] so that neither my father nor my mother had seen England or experienced the English at home.[10] We were virgin. My father was an engineer at an epoch when we were building the great railway system which now secures the postal system and is a life-line which helps in cases of famine or flood.[11] The family ramified throughout India, in the police, the military, the functionaries, the technocrats. But we were real Anglo-Indians, we spoke the languages of the places, and one of my uncles and a cousin became known as translators of Buddhist texts.[12] But what of my elephant?

One of my uncles was a district Commissioner in Bihar, that is to say a sort of Prefect in charge of a land area as large as two or three French departments. He had many duties including that of shooting elephants when, as often happened then, they went mad and attacked villages.[13] Also tigers and rhinoceroses. But the elephants caused him the most regret. My father wished me to learn to shoot and sent me to visit him—he lived in a strange sinister rambling house in Ranchi,[14] with a large garden full of animals. I arrived at dusk to find it empty— everyone was away on a picnic. I walked round this empty house with interest for I had heard stories of this great hunter among my uncles. But I had not been prepared for the dozen or so skulls of fully grown elephants which lined the back verandah. They were huge and grave, like a Greek chorus. Why had he put them there?

During the week, when I went on my first shoot with him, I was able to interrogate him. He said that he thought that the mad elephants developed a sort of brain tumour, and that when he shot one he had the head cut off and examined. Then the sun bleached away the flesh and you were left with this big beautiful skull. I was struck by the word "beautiful." He said it twice. But this was not all. One of the shot elephants had left a small child behind, and this was to become my playmate during my stay. It was called Sadu.[15] It was an apprentice elephant learning its duties with a couple of trained grown-up females. But as yet it was not very big or strong; so it took me to practise upon. It had learned to say *salaam*, to pick up money from the ground, and was now learning how to hoist a man on to its back. A grown man would have been too heavy, so Sadu was told to practise with me. This he did with pleasure. They hold out their trunk curled up at the end like a human hand; you put your foot into it and presto you are raised in the air, and placed securely on the animal's back, between those two fantastic ears, the signs of supernormal spirituality, they say. They have a singular floating walk, a little humorous, like a drunken Irishman; elephants are great comics. But the proverb says that whoever sees the world from the back of an elephant learns the secrets of the jungle and becomes a seer. I had to be content to become a poet, but it was enough for one life.[16]

I am often asked if I was not marked by India. Obviously, to live in a country where the whole population, both civil and ecclesiastical was trying implacably to seek a fulcrum of repose at the heart of reality, a country where people were living alongside nature and not in tangence to it, gives off a very powerful flavour, permeating the air. On the other hand, what I was learning at school taught me that one should not become too resigned to the behaviour of nature. Famines and floods and epidemics should and could be resisted by science. So our lives ran counter to the life of passivity which was the Indian way. Who is right? Even now the problem dogs India—can one expect to have pure drinking water and modern clinics without losing the Mantras? We were too cocksure about the matter, and gloried in the perfections of Victorian science. I remember a great savant announcing that all the secrets of the universe had been discovered and that only a few insignificant details remained to be worked out! By the time I was sixteen the whole of this scientific edifice had been undermined and was ready to crash down in ruins. Strange that there is no word for the Greek "hubris" in English or French.

I went to school at Darjeeling with the Jesuits, though we were given a strictly secular and not religious instruction. We were about forty Protestants, Taoists, Indians, and so on. So I can say I was brought up by Jesuits, though only as an out-patient so to speak! They were very fine men, preaching by example alone, and they were impressive as indeed their religion is. But what a paradox these black figures presented in the purity of such landscapes, in the purity of these huge clouds sailing everywhere like humble spaceships. Christian prayers in all that smiling silence where the lamas walked—always secure and serene—upon the high road outside the school. It was the main road from Tibet to the plains, and they passed all the time—heading for the two great Indian religious universities in the plains. Often in my dreams I hear the squeak of their little prayer wheels—a scientific device of great cunning, worthy rather of mechanists who believed that prayers can be said by a computer—another unresolved problem of our age! In America people will soon be born from computers, some people believe, while newly-invented prayer wheels work off a torch battery and save energy for better things. Does a prayer wheel know that it is performing an act of merit in revolving? One wonders.

But meanwhile I had said goodbye to my elephant Sadu and my father had obtained a new job in the hills. It was to maintain a small mountain railway, the one that runs in the most precipitous fashion, sometimes upon gradients of one in three, up the rampart of Himalayan foothills until it arrives at Darjeeling, the terminus; after which, mules and horses carry the traveller onwards into Tibet.[17] My father was a true Victorian and his attitude to science was, in the anthropological sense, religious. Moreover he had inherited some ten new little elephants made of steel which he adored. They were sturdy and very beautiful as you will see, and marvellous workers. They were in fact the logical positivist's version of Sadu. They really merited our adoration, and the first time we wound up the cliff-faces of the mountains we realised that they were not toys but as massively powerful as tug-boats. They had no names, but I called them all Sadu. This little locomotive was so simple! It was a *cocotte-minute*, a pressure cooker on wheels. How had nobody thought of it before? The track ran through landscapes of dreams—just as the abandoned railway lines of the Gard, near where I live in the south of France, along which I walk and reflect also.[18] Except that you had the snows and the mists always opening and closing upon sheer precipices. It was an uncanny world of strangely conflicting emanations in feeling, thought, atmosphere. You smelt Tibet!

It was of course a dramatic wrench to leave India, but I was optimistic and eager to see this marvellous distant paradise upon which we had all depended morally for so long. It was known as "Home" which was very touching. I knew that it was better than heaven, because I had been told that everything British was better than everything foreign. I felt as pleased as a Jew, belonging to the chosen race,[19] and I was eager to affront the problems with good grace. Luckily too my school, after a year in London, was a most beautiful public school in Canterbury, whose architecture and atmosphere resembled very closely the school I had quitted in Darjeeling.[20]

I gave no great trouble though I was rather neurotic and so a bad student; but I played games well and boxed so that my life was not rendered miserable like that of weaker boys.[21] I made good friends, and the masters, like the Jesuits, were honest and lively and most competent. My French master for example on learning that I wanted to learn French and become a writer immediately took a subscription to *Le Monde* for me—the weekly literary pages. So every week I had this foreign paper. This kindly and delightful man was mad about France and French literature and encouraged my interest. His name was Mr. Hollingsworth—I found it the other day among my papers. I believe he is still alive. It's a pleasure to thank him publicly in French for he taught me my first words of the language.[22]

But yes, it was a grave wrench leaving Sadu.

There were compensations, the most important being the language and literature, which now became my passport and in which I performed my apprentice duties. My father hoped I would become a senior functionary and return to India, no longer a *petit bourgeois* but a great man with an expensive dinner jacket![23] I was not against the idea, but I said I wished to be a writer. He said it was okay but that I must go to Oxford first. His view was that all writers should go to Oxford where they made very influential friends who helped them to become successful afterwards. Perhaps this was not so silly as it then seemed. But he had read in the paper that Bernard Shaw had three Rolls-Royces and Kipling two[24]—he wanted me to enjoy this sort of success; but I wanted a typewriter and, if such a thing had been possible, an elephant.

I got the typewriter for Christmas, and a complete Shakespeare. My father was a real gentleman in the basic sense and I regret he has not lived to read the fan-mail my books have brought me over the years.

I started to write like everyone else, without having anything special to say. I never thought of my work as particularly original—it was a tessellation of other men's ideas filtered through my vision. But when I began to learn my job I knew that I was part of a splendid tradition and I hoped to do as well as my forerunners. But as I came to read them I realised just how stable their Victorian world had been and how unstable mine had become, how precarious and unsettling the new metaphysics was. What a gap stretched between *Robinson Crusoe*— the last novel of human isolation without loss of identity, without alienation—and Kafka's *Castle* in which the new sensibility had been mercilessly exposed to view.[25] The new departures in scientific thought had unsettled and indeed had even ruptured both syntax and serial order; the signal of course had long been given, as when Rimbaud wrote *Je est un Autre* and when Laforgue echoed him with *Je m'ennui Natale*.[26]

The stable ego of fiction had disintegrated—Lawrence says so in his letters;[27] in every sector the basic propositions of theoretical physics had come under fire and some of these factors were of concern to poets—such as that one could not observe a field without disturbing it, so that all objective judgement was qualified. We had been taught to believe in the existence of absolute objective Truth—which would be revealed when analysis had gone far enough. But the new ideas made truth seem highly provisional and subject to scale and context. The Indians had always said that the notion of matter was an illusion, and *voilà* we had begun to find that this was becoming scientific fact. Not only physics—philosophy and psychology were also in an impasse, thanks to Freud. He had deciphered *Hamlet* at last,[28] and we now knew his madness to be our own. Both the outside world and the inner one had been quite transformed by these ideas. Of course long ago the Indians had told us that the notion of the discrete and separate ego was also an illusion—perhaps a dangerous one. Under the probings of Freud and Co. it had all but disintegrated already! Here again the Asiatics seemed to be right. Hamlet's father's ghost had emerged once more upon the stage.

I am simplifying this matter now, and of course when I was twenty I had not fully grasped it in detail. Now I see that the fashionable critical notion of "two cultures" is a misconceived one.[29] All the great poets who took the European spirit as a responsibility were fully abreast of this crisis. Valéry studied mathematics, Eliot was familiar with the precepts of Patanjali, Rilke, and Yeats also; while in the greatest of them, Fernando Pessoa, we find a lucid exposition of the crisis which led to so many hysterical symptoms like DADA and Surrealism, to mention only two.[30]

This for me was a great problem as I felt that I needed some sort of classical frame upon which to expose the tapestry which I wanted to weave. I did not know whether I could use some of the by-products of this crisis and use them as if they were classical unities. The disintegration of the stable ego, the subject-object relationship, the poetic sickness of syntax which made modern poetry so like the effusions of talented schizophrenics…Could I make myself a classical backcloth out of the by-products of relativity?

The worst was that there was nobody with whom I could discuss such matters; they did not interest people, and I knew no poets. Had I been less of a fool, had I passed my exams and gone to Oxford, things would have been different. But I didn't. I was like a cat taken and left miles from home—I was really trying to find my way back to India. It was not clear of course, but now I see it was really that. It led me to become a European to begin with—at eighteen I was footloose in

Europe. My father gave me some money to spend on books and travel.[31] It was not much: I travelled like a poor student, with a rucksack. How marvellous it was! I discovered Greece at twenty-one.[32]

In this country I discovered the Ancient Greek philosophers like Heraclitus[33] and discovered their Indian parentage, for there was hardly one who had not studied his philosophy in India. I was half way home, and to celebrate this I wrote the *Black Book*.[34] I was influenced by surrealism but not convinced theoretically.[35] It did not really touch my deeper preoccupation with form, and the rupture of form by science. Forms in the novel since Proust had become circular, as if they were trying to darn the hole. Time or memory now extended into infinity. We had believed that the history of man began with Adam and Eve, but the new geology extended time immeasurably. We thought that the *Iliad* was a folklore poem; Schliemann uncovered the remains of Troy and proved it a reality.[36] After Freud it was not possible again to write *Hamlet*. The universe had become a huge incomprehensible machine from which the only philosophy to be drawn was one of cosmic pointlessness.

And man? His coherence and self-possession had become dispersed and tarnished by doubts about his identity. Was he simply a succession of states, like an old movie?[37] Once more one thought of the Indian notions about human identity...

It seemed to me that if I could somehow touch all this in a novel it would need stereoscopic vision and stereophonic sound, not to mention jump-cutting like a modern film. The matter would be the ordinary old-fashioned matter of novels, people and situations and quotidian problems—but all seen through this new angle of vision. I was much helped in these ideas by Wyndham Lewis's book *Time and Western Man*.[38] He was the only English intellectual who was actively interested in these ideas which were fermenting in Europe at the time. It is very hard to interest the English writer in ideas.[39]

I went to live in Greece, a very dangerous course for a young writer, as it cut me off from literary life in London altogether;[40] I had met nobody, neither editors nor publishers nor other writers—which is the normal way to begin a career in letters. But I needed this country very badly in order to hatch the eggs I wanted to lay. In those days Greece was, from the European point of view, not only primitive and dangerous, but a long way away. So much so that when first my poems received any notice I was treated as an English "Gaugin" in an article by Derek Stanford![41] Now everyone has visited this beautiful, modern, prosperous little country.

At first I was very much alone, but in a few years I acquired, by a series of pure flukes, a number of uncles or godfathers or whatever you may call them; benevolent spirits to guide my path, to judge my work. I was electrified when they told me that I had something more than juvenile promise. I am so vain that the more I am praised the better I work. These great men, some of whom were then unknown, gave me the necessary encouragement to persevere. What luck! I discovered that T.S. Eliot was my editor; among other uncles I had Henry Miller, George Seferis, George Katsimbalis the Colossus of Maroussi, and Theodore Stephanides the great savant, doctor, astronomer, biologist, cancerologist—everything![42] I could not have hoped for such a circle of acquaintance had I gone on living in suburban London. And at twenty-two years of age! I was not too stupid not to recognise the importance of these friendships. Among them was one aunt, the delectable Anaïs Nin.[43] I shall never forget that when I arrived in Paris a couple then completely unknown came to the station to meet me and praise me for the *Black Book*—Anaïs Nin and Henry Miller! They brought me as a gift, Otto Rank's *Art and Artist*, right there to the station. We went to the Café Dôme for a drink.[44]

Paris as usual was humming with ideas, like a beehive, and here at last I found people with whom I could discuss these ideas—albeit in the shadow of the swastika, for the war had almost arrived. Yet the portrait I had sketched of our intellectual predicament proved to be accurate—both the outside world, the world of matter, and the inside world, the world of the self, had been completely transformed by advances in science. As for atomic physics, the very language used today to try and describe the debris of the atom—for it has disintegrated into some two hundred sub-particles—is taken from Joyce and reminds one of Lewis Carroll. As the particles become increasingly diminutive in size and enigmatic in function a kind of literary hysteria set in; the smallest so far have been christened "quarks," a word borrowed from Joyce. A quark has three forms: "up," "down," and "strange." This is not all. They have another quality which the same looking-glass minds have christened "charm." Finally, to complicate the picture further, they must be considered as either "top" or "bottom" and to have yet another quality called "spin." The first DADA manifesto[45] is nothing to this extraordinary parade of scientific categories borrowed from literature! Poor Joyce! Even though his Finnegan,[46] a real curiosity of literature, is really a potentially protracted pun! The important thing for me was the dissolution of the fiction of the stable discrete ego. Despite the apparent originality of Freud's discoveries, the majority of his ideas had been anticipated years before by another Viennese doctor whose work, while popular, did not cause the same sort of revolution. His name was Von Feuchtersleben.[47] We see I think from this that each great man is really a syndicate of several other great men. He matches and accords dissimilar views and finds a new synthesis from old ideas. He is a joiner and harmoniser more than an inventor. There is no need to go further with this sort of exposition; the question was this: could such material influence literary form, and provide a sort of frame? It was certainly more topical and more typically modern than so much which the modern novel was treating.

I began to dream of a sort of novel-as-apparatus (*un roman-appareil*) which one could use as a historic or poetic "conscience," as portable as a pocket-compass! I did not wish (even had I ever had the talent) to build a word-cathedral like Joyce; you must be a dispossessed Catholic for that. I wanted to build something like a cave-cooperative with perhaps Dionysus as manager![48]

It was years before I dared to begin on such a book and, meanwhile, I went into training for the big fight by learning how to write. I wrote in many different styles and on many topics. I felt that not only the world was coming to an end but also language—for the new visual age had begun to arrive. I felt that one day we should communicate in grunts like black jazzmen! I was too pessimistic I now see, but nevertheless the trend is still apparent. But side by side with this merely scientific interest I was also reading the *Upanishads* translated by Yeats,[49] and discovering the Chinese philosophers who one day would teach me their magic, which is the art of manipulating the inevitable! What seemed evident to me was that all disciplines, all styles, were gradually moving closer to each other, whether East and West, or simply mysticism and logic. It has not gone as fast or as far as I expected but already in this contemporary world the trend has become a marked one.

I am not sure, but I think there is a faint hope of a great synthesis which will conjoin all fields of thought, however apparently dissimilar, making them interpenetrate, inter-fertilise.[50] This is the sense in which it is worth being a poet. We must learn from such doctor-mystics as Groddeck[51] to treat the whole of reality as a symptom!

I went back to Greece to wait for the coming of the expected war. I took Miller with me for a holiday.[52] In this Greek island one felt very strongly that ancient Greece had its roots in Egypt, whence India. For my part I also had one foot in Vienna, so to speak, with Freud and Jung and Groddeck.[53] I began to see what becoming a European meant!

While I was wondering about this, the Germans made a useful contribution to my thinking by chasing me all the way down Greece, into Crete, and thence into Egypt.[54] I would have been too lazy to visit Alexandria myself—I was not interested in Egypt, I was happy in Greece. But in Alexandria I found myself at the cradle from which the whole of our civilisation had sprung. The roots of all our theologies as well as the roots of mathematics and physics had been hatched here. The first measurements of the earth—something as exciting as going to the moon—had been made here. Between Plotinus, Philo, and Euclid[55] all aspects of human thought had been enriched here. It was the ideal frame for a book which might try, in a modest way, to touch the contemporary reality. It was impertinent, I suppose, to invoke the

Gods, like Einstein[56] and Freud, but that was the way I saw things, and I was quite pleased when in the book[57] I saw the stereo effects, and the slight bending of time and space—like Einsteinian space being curved!

The success was astonishing and very pleasing; I was amply rewarded for the thought and reflection which had gone into the book.

Nothing has changed today in the world picture, but what is apparent is that the two metaphysics, Eastern and Western, are moving steadily together and given time will meet in many essential fields. Numen and phenomenon were made to be complimentaries and not opposites. It is so obvious that this is happening that I decided two years ago to celebrate this marriage, which I foresaw, by making a small group of novels, interlaced and interdependent based on the five-power system of the Buddhist psychology—the five aggregates, so to speak.[58] A five-part book, independent but linked in a new way, a somewhat haphazard way, but occupied with much the same material as the last. One's experience of life is very limited. In this book I proposed to return to India—to move from the four dimensions to the five skandas.[59] The old stable ego had already gone, reality has realised itself there, so to speak. In a sense all my new people are aspects of one great person, age, culture. I would like to make a metaphor for the human condition as we are living it now. I have dug sideways also to make a tunnel back into the *Quartet*, for part of the action of this new novel takes place in Egypt, and one meets characters and places from the old *Quartet*, but they are not named. But passionate fans—*les fervents*—will recognise them. I like to think that there is a family feeling about my books and here and there a character from an early book may stray into a later book without warning. I like this sort of continuity which hints at an inner progression from the *Black Book* onwards. I need two more years for the last three books. I am not of course sure that my idea will work, but if it does I will have two floating structures, poems of celebration drawn from the East and the West. Imagine two Calder-mobiles.[60] After that I shall be happy to retire. I have a few things more to say about the destiny of woman, the fate of the world, and the second law of thermodynamics—the law of divine entropy. I would like to say them as an Indian this time!

Time and causality have very much preoccupied our age, and science has so much overflowed into the field of artistic creation that it has provided new forms, new moulds for the fiery magma. Proust, Joyce were both time-intoxicated artists, soaked in history and the historic consciousness. They were hunting for the *Nunc Stans*,[61] the permanent Now of the philosopher.

Often, effects and causes seem not to be joined, not to depend on each other, when it is simply that the distance is too great to discern the connection. Yet they are.

Once upon a time, Aristotle, who only pronounced upon nature when he was sure of the truth of his statements, asserted, "*Natura non Facit Saltus*,"[62] thus upholding the unbroken chain of causality. "*Nature does not do Anything in Jumps*." It moved in orderly process, link by link, respecting a perfect determinism—that is how he saw it. Then after two thousand years Darwin timidly, haltingly puts down in his private notebook a tentative repudiation of this flat assertion. He writes, "One species does not *change* into another, it does so at one blow, *per saltum*."[63] The jump! It was a treacherous thought to harbour, for it compromised the rigid determinism of the pure Aristotelian thought. Nature could jump, nature could, if she wanted, syncopate! Quanta!

I like to compare these two views of reality in symbolic terms by imagining the contrast between a European cathedral and an Asiatic pagoda; my own word-pagoda is to have five faces. But the cathedral is built like a boat or a bird; you have to enter it to reach its centre of gravity which is the altar which an Asiatic would see as a sort of telephone booth. By putting in the right coin (prayer) one could contact God, the presiding personage or principle, and bargain with him. The altar is the bar or the counter at which the transaction takes place, where your soul is tested for its qualities and defects. Heaven and Hell are the two possibilities which are offered to it; bliss or eternal anguish.

It is a very simple and brutal view of the human option; moreover among the extreme dangers or sins is human sexuality. Well, the cathedral seems to have had its day. Once they were prayer-factories generating good behaviour and a kindly disposition towards men; now they seem like out of work computers. The belief in Christian prayer has been very much eroded. It seems to have been replaced by a communal will to unhappiness which I think we can read into our architecture which breathes confinement, regimentation, heralds of insanity. If this goes on, within a short time it will be hard to decide whether a building is a residence or a barrack or a factory or an insane asylum...They are getting to look so alike.

By contrast to this attitude, the five skanda pagoda mind, which has begun to enjoy a great vogue, is perhaps equally full of traps though for us it seems to represent a blissfully calm view of reality. This is because it seems to offer a relief from materialist thought. The non-ego attitude is its ideal, and its science emphasizes the insubstantiality of matter, and posits a kind of energy over mass state of mind which perhaps is what Einstein really meant, for he was as deeply religious in a pantheistic way as Newton![64]

I am trying to move in my selfish and hesitating way from the fourth dimension to the five skanda view, using the same old equipment of the domestic novel, as a kaleidoscope uses the same bits of glass for different patterns. I would like to try and use the by-products of Asiatic philosophy as I tried in the Quartet to use the by-products of relativity philosophy. I think the new form I am chasing will be less schematic and more floating, to fit the oriental notion of reality; slowly already some of the characters who only exist in the imagination of the others, are coming on to the stage to compromise the orthodox ideas of "reality." I wonder if it will work satisfactorily, and produce a group of books which satisfy as an organic whole? In this new Asiatic domain the passport is the "mandala" (which Jung kept finding in the unconscious of his patients!). It's a sort of cardiogram of the human being's destiny. My cast is more or less the same—the two women blonde and dark, two clowns, lovers, poets, warriors, monks, villains, and seers.[65] The old stuff of fiction and Christmas pantomime, under different names. Looked at in this way one should ask oneself not if they are "real" but if they are "true"; that is to say true to this prismatic poetic reality. A single individual's experience of people and places is extraordinarily limited, and if he is an artist he feels forced to accept these limitations and do his best within them. But certain sharp contrasts of a formal kind will impose themselves; the moving staircase of the "linear" progression will be replaced by something closer to the "flying carpet" of the fairy tales. And people? They will be spare parts of one another from the cosmic point of view, though quite real and discrete from a worldly, novelistic point of view.[66] Underneath the action will, I hope, be the Asiatic notion of a world renewed afresh with each thought; therefore, man as a Total Newcomer to each moment of time. It will need readers indulgent to this rather sphinx-like way of thinking; but then the "real" reader has always known that he or she must read between the lines. That is where the truth hides itself. Process in scientific terms is irreversible, though not in Asiatic, while truth as such is ambivalent. The sages appear to have co-opted it successfully for use as a pivot, so that it gives cosmic balance to the human animal. It would be a wonderful thing to feel that, having paid my respects to Europe and its relativity principle in the *Quartet*, I could now, as my star is sinking, touch my forelock to the Indian view of life. I would like to plant this *Quintet* at the point of tangent between these two cultural principles, so that it could be fruitful as well as entertaining.

In conclusion it is worth stressing that the abstract symbols one uses in a disquisition of this kind—words like "relativity" or "Tao" or "matter" or "Maya" are to be regarded as road signs which indicate the destiny and direction of the intellectual traffic. They are not absolutes. I imagine that the sage considers them to be simply the paint rags upon which the artist wipes his brushes once the painting is complete. We must not let philosophy become a self-caressing machine.

NOTES

1. Durrell first delivered this paper in French as a lecture on April 1, 1981 at Centre Georges Pompidou, a major library and exhibition gallery in the Beaubourg area of Paris. He only subsequently published the English version in James Meary Tambimuttu's *Poetry London–New York* and *Apple Magazine*. A significant variant of the lecture is available in typescript in English at the Bibliothèque Lawrence Durrell at the Université Paris Ouest, Nanterre.

2. These first two volumes of *The Avignon Quintet*, which was so titled posthumously, are *Monsieur or The Prince of Darkness* and *Livia or Buried Alive*. Durrell considered the formal issues in these two books quite a bit, and he was particularly concerned with form while beginning *Livia* just after having finished *Monsieur*. He attempted to revise *Monsieur* to address his new ideas but could not, and the variant first chapter of *Livia* shows these formal ideas clearly (Gifford and Stevens 173–93).

3. This critique distinguishes Durrell's lecture from the then popular seminars of Jacques Lacan (1901–1981) who was tied to the "linguistic turn" in modern literary critical theory, and whom Durrell derogates in his "Endpapers and Inklings" by writing, "As for Lacan—what a frenzy of ignoble parody, rhetoric of self-aggrandisement!" (90). It may also be a general turn away from the "linguistic turn" itself, though this is unlikely given Durrell's other interests.

4. Since his youth, Durrell self-identified as Anglo-Indian, most famously so in his letters to Henry Miller, in which he clarified, "I enclose a photograph to prove that I am NOT a Greek, but a pure Anglo-Irish-Indian ASH BLOND" (Durrell and Miller 30). Durrell's Irish background is disputed, but he was born in India, and in 1968 was redefined as a British non-patrial without the right to enter or settle in Britain without a visa. This was due to the amendment to the Commonwealth Immigrants Act in 1962, which aimed to curb immigration from India, Pakistan, and the West Indies.

5. Durrell's 1935 novel *Pied Piper of Lovers* resembles Rudyard Kipling's (1865–1936) 1901 novel, *Kim*.

6. This is very likely a reference to Norman Mailer's 1957 essay "The White Negro: Superficial Reflections on the Hipster," alluding to Durrell's time in the 1930s playing jazz and failing to fit into English culture.

7. The Indian Rope Trick began as a hoax in 1890 but was developed as stage magic. Versions range from a rope standing up in the air, which a child or assistant would then climb and descend, through to a child climbing the rope, disappearing, his limbs falling to the ground, and then being reassembled. The hoax

was revealed in 2004 in Peter Lamont's *The Rise of the Indian Rope Trick*. If Durrell had seen the trick in the 1920s, it would have been stage magic deriving from the 1890 hoax.

8. While these are both exaggeration, Durrell does use Hindi and Urdu in his first novel, *Pied Piper of Lovers*. Everest was not visible, but he could have seen Kanchenjunga from the dormitory (MacNiven 40).

9. This is a reference to the Indian Rebellion of 1857, which is also called India's First War of Independence.

10. Durrell's paternal great-grandfather moved to India aged eighteen, and his maternal great-grandmother was born there. Both his parents and all his siblings were born in India, and neither parent had visited Britain before sending him there for his education, aged eleven.

11. Durrell's father, Lawrence Samuel Durrell, was a significant railway engineer (MacNiven 1–26).

12. Similar claims are made about Durrell's character Mountolive in *The Alexandria Quartet*.

13. This sets Durrell's works in comparison to George Orwell's "Shooting an Elephant" and invites contrasting readings of their views on empire and government. This is especially so if the elephant is regarded in both texts as a symbol for the British Empire's demise. Durrell and Orwell sparred in the English press and appeared to have borrowed from each other in their novels. Orwell discusses Durrell's *The Black Book* in the second publication of "Inside the Whale," and the two shared several friends, such as George Woodcock and Henry Miller, though Durrell's sympathies for anti-authoritarian politics (as with Woodcock and Miller's overt anarchism) could not easily relate to Orwell's socialism.

14. Ranchi was a significant industrial and military town southeast of Delhi, near to West Bengal. MacNiven identifies this uncle as William Henry Durrell (46).

15. In contrast with Orwell's imperial elephant in "Shooting an Elephant," Durrell's Sadu becomes a partner rather than a threat or "White Man's Burden."

16. Durrell's comparison of the poet and the seer is akin to his good friend G.S. Fraser's "Ideas About Poetry VI" in the journal Durrell co-edited in Egypt, *Personal Landscape*: "All poems written or unwritten exist. I don't mean a platonic but a biological existence. Their relation to their written form is the relation of the model to its portrait. The special ability of the poet is to see them: that's why the poets are sometimes called seers" (2).

17. Lawrence Samuel Durrell tended to several rail lines, but this is likely the Darjeeling Himalayan Railway, well-known as the "toy train" for it small, powerful engines.

18. These railways provide the opening scenes for both *Monsieur* and *Quinx*, the first and final novels of Durrell's *Avignon Quintet*, which he was writing at the same time as this piece.

19. Durrell's ties to Judaism are complex. His second and third wives were both Jewish and Zionist, and he wrote a series of pro-Israeli, Zionist works prior to 1967–1968, after which his attitudes appear to have changed.

20. St. Joseph's College, North Point, Darjeeling.

21. Durrell's alter ego, Walsh, in *Pied Piper of Lovers* has these traits and punches well (26, 82, 122).

22. Durrell includes a scene such as this in *Pied Piper of Lovers* involving Abel, the French master (126). As MacNiven points out, "Larry's memory failed him—*Le Monde* did not commence publication until 1944—yet he did rise from 13th out of 16 in French to first place in his form" (63).

23. Durrell refers on several occasions to the importance of colonial and diplomatic dress. Donald Kaczvinsky has detailed this element of ornamentalism ("Memlik's" 93–118).

24. George Bernard Shaw (1856–1950) and Rudyard Kipling (1865–1936) were both significant influences on Durrell. His "Bromo Bombastes" is a rebuttal of Shaw, whom he engaged in a brief correspondence, and his *Pied Piper of Lovers* shows a significant influence from Kipling.

25. *Robinson Crusoe* is an important novel at the beginning of the novelistic tradition in English, published by Daniel Defoe (c. 1659–1731) in 1719. Franz Kafka's (1883–1924) existential novel *The Castle* was published posthumously in 1926.

26. Durrell refers to both poets and works elsewhere as well, notably in his poem "Je est un autre."

27. From the mid-1930s onward, D.H. Lawrence's June 15, 1914 letter to Edward Garnett held special significance to Durrell:

> You mustn't look in my novel for the old stable ego of the character. There is another ego, according to whose action the individual is unrecognisable, and passes through, as it were, allotropic states which it needs a deeper sense than any we've been used to exercise, to discover are states of the same single radically-unchanged element. (Like as diamond and coal are the same pure single element of carbon. The ordinary novel would trace the history of the diamond—but I say "diamond, what! This is carbon." And my diamond might be coal or soot, and my theme is carbon.)
> (Lawrence, *Letters* 183)

Lawrence's use of the term "allotropic" derives from two footnotes in F.W.H. Myers's *Human Personality and Its Survival of Bodily Death* (Gibbons 338–41), and it is this "'subliminal self' which represents 'our central and abiding being'" (Gibbons 339). Also see Durrell's 1936 letter to Alan Thomas, in which he claims, "it is a qualitative difference in which I blow the Lawrentian trumpet. I [know?] my own kind, I haven't begun. Beside Lawrence, beside Miller, beside Blake. Yes, I am humble, I have hardly started. BUT I AM ON THE SAME TRAM" (Spirit 50).

28. This mention of Hamlet is likely in reference to Ernest Jones's (1879–1958) article "The Oedipus-Complex as an Explanation of Hamlet's Mystery," which was expanded and later published as a book, Hamlet and Oedipus. Both versions developed in response to Sigmund Freud's (1856–1939) comments on wish fulfilment and what would become the Oedipal drama in relation to Freud's comments on Hamlet in his The Interpretation of Dreams.

29. See C.P. Snow's The Two Cultures, which is based on his 1959 Cambridge lecture "The Two Cultures and the Scientific Revolution." In this famous work, he articulates the disjunctions between scholarship in the humanities and the sciences arguing for a synthesis of the two.

30. To some degree, this is an exaggeration, but Paul Valéry was indeed strongly interested in the sciences and mathematics, both of which receive significantly more attention in his Cahiers than poetry. T.S. Eliot learned of Patanjali from James Haughton Woods and his Yoga System of Patanjali while a graduate student at Harvard and insisted this was a valuable part of his studies (Eliot, Letters 109); W.B. Yeats wrote the introduction to Patanjali and Purohit Swami's Aphorisms of Yoga for Faber & Faber's 1938 edition, and Patanjali influenced his poetic works (Marsh 15–18); Rainer Maria Rilke is less clear but is frequently quoted in literature relating to Patanjali; and Pessoa's "lucid exposition" could be any number of his essays from 1917 through the 1920s, though possibly his intended introduction to a translation of Alvaro de Campos's Ultimatum.

31. This was Durrell's inheritance (aged sixteen) after his father's death in 1928. His first trips to France date from the same period.

32. Durrell first moved to Greece to reside on Corfu in 1935, when he was twenty-three, though his good friend George Wilkinson was writing to him from Greece a year earlier.

33. Heraclitus (c. 535–475) was an obscure Greek philosopher from Asia Minor who is famous for harmonizing opposites and emphasizing mutability and continual change.

34. All of Durrell's first three novels refer to India, though Pied Piper of Lovers (written in England in 1934–1935 but edited and proofed on Corfu) does so most

overtly. *The Black Book* was Durrell's first major literary work, published in 1938 but first drafted in 1935 concomitant with editing *Pied Piper of Lovers*.

35. Although Durrell was devoted to the psychoanalytic component of automatism in Surrealism, he was opposed to its communist components and social theorizing. His role in distinguishing between surrealist methods against Surrealism's politics was important to English Surrealism in the later 1930s and 1940s as well as to the New Apocalypse movement. Durrell's comment in the proceeding sentence that Surrealism "did not really touch my deeper preoccupation with form" is a quintessentially New Apocalyptic sense of the movement as "a post-surrealist Romantic Movement...[that] believes in the functions of form" (Schimanski and Treece 14). This component is intimately tied to their anarchist notion of Personalism, which developed from their ties to Herbert Read, and it in turn reflects Read's correspondence with Miller on the subject at the time. James Keery notes that Durrell's "involvement in the Apocalypse movement is documented in [John] Goodland's papers" and Durrell was included in the drafting of the New Apocalypse's manifesto in Leeds in December 1938 (884, 882). The December 1938 drafting would coincide with his visit to London in the same year and the final issue of *Delta*, which he co-edited with David Gascoyne, who was also heavily tied to the New Apocalypse and wrote the first guide to Surrealism in English in 1935.

36. Heinrich Schliemann, an archaeologist, first identified the location of Troy in his attempt to demonstrate that Homer's *Iliad* referred to historical events. While this is still a topic of much dispute, Schliemann's views were influential.

37. Durrell was particularly fond of this simile as a dismissal of "the discrete human personality" (*Justine* 196), and Pursewarden asks, "Are people...continuously themselves, or simply over and over again so fast that they give the illusion of continuous features?" (196).

38. Lewis's 1927 book, in which he critiques the main exponents of Modernism while also attacking several of their philosophical origins or counterparts, such as Henri Bergson's and Alfred North Whitehead's notions of time or duration.

39. Durrell later wrote an introduction, in French only, for the French edition of Lewis's novel *Tarr* (567–68).

40. While Durrell did move from London to Corfu in 1935, this break is not entirely true. From 1935 until his flight to Egypt as a refugee following the German invasion of Greece, he remained in regular contact with T.S. Eliot, Dylan Thomas, David Gascoyne, and a number of other London- and Paris-based writers, and he visited London twice and met with many of them. While in Greece, he also had

significant contact with other writers, including Theodore Stephanides (a significant translator of Modern Greek poetry) and the Nobel Laureate George Seferis.

41. See Stanford's "Lawrence Durrell" (123–35), first published in his *The Freedom of Poetry* in 1945, and reprinted in *The World of Lawrence Durrell* in 1962.

42. Eliot (1888–1965) was Durrell's editor at Faber & Faber as well as his friend; he is one of the defining poetic voices of Modernism. Henry Miller (1891–1980) was a major American novelist and Durrell's closest literary friend, which led to their correspondence from 1935 until Miller's death. Seferis (1900–1971) was the Nobel Prize winning Greek poet who influenced Durrell's sense of Greek Modernism, as well as his professional interaction with Durrell as a diplomat. They continued to have a friendly correspondence even after Durrell's service to the British on Cyprus. Katsimbalis (1899–1978) was a major translator and bibliographer for Greek literature and was the titular colossus in Henry Miller's travel narrative of Greece prior to World War I, *The Colossus of Maroussi*. Stephanides was a dear friend to the Durrell family after their meeting on Corfu in 1935. He appears as a character in books by both Lawrence and Gerald Durrell but was also a significant translator of Greek poetry, a writer in his own right, and a significant scientist who published major works in botany and on the microscope, and had studied directly under Marie Curie.

43. Nin (1903–1977) was a French novelist who wrote in English but was known mainly for her famous diaries and erotica. She was a dear friend and companion to Henry Miller, through whom she knew Durrell.

44. This would have been August 1937 when Durrell travelled from Corfu to Paris with his first wife, Nancy. As MacNiven notes, Nin's recollection differs, and she records meeting the Durrells a day or two later (166). Durrell's notebooks of this month, including his drafts for "The Death of General Uncebunke," contain several passages drawn from Rank's (1884–1939) book on psychoanalysis and artistic creation, *Art and Artist* (1932). Rank edited the successive revisions to Freud's *The Interpretations of Dream*, was Freud's protégé until a public disagreement between the two in 1926, and he was close to both Miller and Nin in Paris and New York.

45. Hugo Ball recited the first manifesto in 1916, but Tristan Tzara wrote what is regarded as the first DADA manifesto in 1918. DADA was a movement that influenced much creative activity and Surrealism in particular.

46. James Joyce's (1882–1941) major Modernist novel and last work was *Finnegans Wake* (1939), which is densely allusive and linguistically complex to the point of being nearly unreadable to some.

47. Baron Ernst von Feuchtersleben (1806–1849) developed the terminology of "psychosis" later used by Freud, and the text is likely *The Principles of Medical Psychology*, published in 1845 and translated into English in 1847.

48. Durrell's differences from Joyce here are notable, in particular given his anti-authoritarian tendencies and sympathy for anarchists such as Henry Miller (Gifford, "Anarchist" 57–71). Durrell's flippancy may be misleading for an otherwise serious distinction.

49. W.B. Yeats and Shri Purohit Swami's *The Ten Principal Upanishads*, first published in 1937, the same time Durrell was writing *The Black Book*.

50. This same terminology appears in Durrell's *Avignon Quintet* (693) from the same period as this lecture.

51. Georg Groddeck (1866–1934) was a German analyst and doctor who wrote extensively on psychosomatic illness and gave Freud the terminology for the Id, the unconscious, in his typology of the mind. Durrell was significantly influenced by Groddeck's works and used his cases as fodder for plots. See Durrell's essay on Groddeck in this volume.

52. Miller's recollections of this trip are published in *The Colossus of Maroussi* and *Reflections on Greece*. A letter from Durrell concludes the former book.

53. Durrell had a short correspondence with Carl Jung (1875–1961) in which he discussed Groddeck's work; this correspondence is held in the Durrell Collection of Southern Illinois University, Carbondale.

54. Durrell often played down the desperation of this situation. After being evacuated to Athens from Corfu, where he was involved in producing anti-fascist propaganda, he was moved by the British Council to Kalamata, from whence he fled by a small caïque overnight on April 22, 1941 to Crete when the Germans invaded, and from Crete to Egypt on April 30 as a refugee. MacNiven discusses this period (226–31), as does Stephanides (75–85).

55. Plotinus (204–270) and Philo (20 BCE–50 CE) were important metaphysical philosophers. Euclid (3rd century BCE) is the creator of modern Euclidean Geometry. All three were active in Alexandria. Alexandria housed the greatest library of the time and was renowned as a centre for learning and the arts.

56. Albert Einstein (1879–1959) was the most influential physicist of the twentieth century. He and Sigmund Freud co-authored *Why War?* in 1939, and Durrell used his theory of relativity metaphorically in *The Alexandria Quartet*.

57. This "book" is *Justine*, the first of *The Alexandria Quartet*. *Justine* begins with two quotations from Freud and the Marquis de Sade. The second volume, *Balthazar*, integrates an opening note that mentions Einstein, and this is developed into an introductory note for the revised omnibus edition of all four volumes. Durrell

refs to Einstein several times in interviews about *The Alexandria Quartet* but generally described this as a purely metaphorical approach.

58. The book series described here was completed three years later and collected posthumously in 1992 as *The Avignon Quintet*, though Durrell generally described it as his *Avignon Quincunx*.

59. In Buddhist philosophy, the skandhas are five aggregates that give rise to the false notion of the ego or self. Suffering is alleviated by practising detachment from the skandhas.

60. Though now associated only with nurseries, mobiles were invented by Alexander Calder, an American sculptor, in 1931 as kinetic art and are associated with the works of Marcel Duchamp, Morton Feldman, and Frank Zappa.

61. Eternity in the present tense, a notion of eternity in which past and future are caught only in the Now. St. Augustine emphasized the *nunc stans*, though Durrell likely came to the concept via Schopenhauer.

62. As Durrell repeats, this is literally, "Nature does not do anything in jumps." Though attributed to Aristotle, the phrase first appears in this context in Carl Linnaeus's 1751 *Philosophia Botanica* and was subsequently taken up by Charles Darwin.

63. This is slightly misquoted, perhaps from memory. Darwin wrote in his *Beagle* notebook in 1837, after returning to London, "so must we believe ancient ones: not *gradual* change or degeneration. from circumstances, if one species does change into another it must be per saltum [sic]" (50).

64. Sir Isaac Newton (1643–1727) was a major mathematician and scientist as well as an alchemist and occult theorist. Newton was deeply religious, but Einstein made his rejection of any personal god or religiosity clear, though he held a quasi-religious awe for the structure of the world.

65. Durrell does employ such pairs, as in Melissa and Justine or Justine and Clea, Scobie and Pombal, Darley and Arnauti, Darley and Pursewarden, and so forth in *The Alexandria Quartet*. Similar pairs or doubles appear in virtually all of his fictional works.

66. The same language subsequently appears in *The Avignon Quintet* when Durrell's protagonist intends to write "a book full of spare parts of other books, of characters left over from other lives, all circulating in each other's bloodstreams.... Be ye members of one another" (693).

Personal Positions

A Letter from
the Land of the Gods

1939

Dear Potocki:[1]

IT WON'T MISREPRESENT the reality of my enthusiasm for your
work if I tell you that though I don't always like what you think, yet I
do always admire and subscribe to what you *are*. There is such bright-
ness and warmth in your prose, and so much leisurely and wicked
humour that I defy anyone not to be interested and delighted by it;
there are good royal colours here, and I love the self-possession which
makes each thrust—like a good fencer's lunge—seem absolutely effort-
less. Power to your long right arm!

   To be a poet is to be religious: and to be religious is to be, in some
way, a royalist. Is it not so? And if for me your admiration for the
Fascists seems a little excessive it is only because I feel that if the Left
are wrong today the Right are not right enough for me. I don't want
to barter the religion of the royal part of men for an inferior sort of
totemism. And every man who feels the same will be more interested
in your writing than in the prodigious squeaking and chirping that
goes up from the leftist barnyards.

   Damn reservations ultimately: they are the critic's drink—literary
Wincarnis[2] with every issue of a paper instead of wine. I like men—
not aggregates and contentions; and I admire the way you stand firm

27

and speak because what you say is worth listening to. I respect the King in you and I respect the king in all men[3]—that is what I mean, I think; and this undercuts all dogma, which is after all only a man-made roughage.

A King for all of us then: and the king in each of us. Would you accept that as a toast?

Sincerely,
Lawrence Durrell

NOTES

1. Count Geoffrey Potocki de Montalk (1903–1997) was a poet and pamphleteer who claimed the Polish throne. He was born in New Zealand but relocated to London in 1926. He was imprisoned for obscenity for six months in Wormwood Scrubs Prison. He produced the right-wing periodical *The Right Review* from 1936 to 1973 and supported the fascists and royalists, regarding them as better than the Bolsheviks. See Stephanie de Montalk's *Unquiet World: The Life of Count Geoffrey Potocki de Montalk*. Durrell knew Potocki and his brother well during his life in London around the Fitzroy Tavern. They first met in 1933 just after Potocki had been imprisoned for libel (MacNiven 83–84).

2. Literally, "Meat Wine." By this time, Wincarnis was a brand name for a tonic wine popular in the British colonies.

3. In the context of Durrell's publications in the anarchist press and interactions with several anarchist authors, the politics of this statement are not casual.

Airgraph on Refugee Poets in Africa

1944

Dear Tambi,[1]

EGYPT WOULD BE INTERESTING if it were really the beginning of Africa; but it is an ante-room, a limbo. In this soft corrupting plenty, nothing very much is possible. The Nile flows like dirty coffee under the solid English bridges. The country steams humidly—a sort of tropical Holland, with no hills anywhere to lift one's eyes to. The people have given up long ago—have lapsed back into hopelessness, venality, frustration. Outside the towns forever the sterile desert preserves its ancient cultures with clinical care. Dust-storms herald the spring; and summer comes in on such a wave of damp that the blood vessels in the body feel swollen and full of water. If one wrote poems here they could only be like marrows, or pumpkins—or like the huge pulpy Egyptian moon which rises like a sore every now and then on this fleshy sky.

Nevertheless, shiftless refugees that we are, living in furnished rooms, something is being done.[2] Of the foreigners still working I think only the Greeks have claim to notice. News from Athens comes in little driblets—but the latest news tells us that the Athenian poets are still at work; and readers of Henry Miller's *Colossus of Maroussi* will perhaps be glad to hear that the Colossus himself is still alive, and still wonderfully talking.[3]

But more interesting still is the fact that two Greek poets of more than local importance are with us in the Middle East. One of them, Seferis, has already been published in English translation, and on his journey across Africa he has continued to build up his personal mythology into poems of all kinds. He is the first Greek poet to write a limerick, and his notebooks are covered with Learish[4] little sketches.[5] For him exile is really a sort of martyrdom; he is not a dramatic poet who can exteriorise himself in his verse, nor is he an empty Alexandrine interested in form and colour. Under his rather artless choice and treatment of themes there is a sharp metaphysical struggle going on—which makes him largely incomprehensible to the Greeks, for whom the personal struggle in the European sense does not exist. By this I mean that the modern Greek critic would be likely to prefer D'Annunzio to Dante;[6] poetry that evokes and exclaims to poetry that says something tightly and categorically. Seferis always talks: he never groans and exclaims and points; nor is he seduced by mere music.

All morning we hunted about round the castle,
Starting from the shadowy side where the sea
Was green without radiance—breast of the slain peacock—
And received us like time itself without gaps in it.
The veins of rock came downwards from above,
Ribbed vine, naked and many branched, enlivening
The utterance of the water, like the eye following them
Struggling to escape the wearisome swing,
Losing strength bit by bit.
From the sun's direction a long beach wide open,
And the light shining jewels on the huge walls.
No living thing, the wild doves having gone,
And the King of Asini, for whom we'd searched two years
Unknown and forgotten even by Homer.
Only one word in the Iliad and this uncertain
Like a sepulture mask of gold.

You touch it—remember the echo? Hollow in light
Like the dry jars in the dug earth:
And the same echo in the sea with our oars:
The King of Asini, a void beneath the mask,
Always with us, always with us, under a name
   Ασίνη τε Ασίνη τε
   and his children statues,
His desires the beat of wings and the wind
In the space between his meditations and
His ships anchored in an invisible harbour.
Under the mask a void.

Behind the huge eyes, curled lips, curved hair
In relief on the gold lid of our existence;
A point of shade which travels like a fish
You see it in the peaceful morning of the ocean,
A void always with us...
(The King of Asini)[7]

The evocation is always personal and immediate in Seferis; his choice of imagery deliberately simple and pure in transcribing the Greek landscape where rock, wave, light, and water present themselves as mythological ideograms rather than material things.

And the poet leisurely looking at the stone, wondering
Among these broken lines and edges,
The points and hollowness and curves
Surely exist
Here where the passing rains meet wind and the decay,
Of those who diminished so strangely in our lives
Who remained wave-shadows and thoughts within the
   limitlessness of the sea...
(The King of Asini)

These fragments from a longish poem give an idea—though only an idea—of Seferis's range and tone of voice. He is difficult to translate, and my Greek is not good: but what is difficult to render in English is the limpid way he manipulates his symbols. As a poet he is difficult not because he is allusive so much as because he depends on the association of words in their context—and of course the profoundest words in Greek carry overtones unmatched by their equivalent in any European language. "Under the mask a void" is a line thousands of years older and riper in Greek than it is in English.

Apart from Seferis there is only, as far as I can see, one other poet at work who is worth a wider circulation than the Modern Greek tongue allows. This is a woman—Elie Papadimitriou.[8] Last year in Cairo in a refugee hotel appropriately named the Lunar Park[9] I discovered this intriguing and solitary authoress who had escaped from Greece with a suitcase full of short stories and one long poem called "Anatolia." She had been working on the latter for some seven years, and it had remained unfinished; since then it has been published in a limited edition in Cairo, and has, of course, passed completely unnoticed by the neo-Hellenist quacks who are only interested in new translations of Byron. "Anatolia" is a sort of "Anabasis"—but written in demotic Greek and with a Chaucerian narrative-sense. It is a shadow-play in which recitatives are put into the mouths of various traditional characters of modern Greece. The theme is the Asia Minor disaster;[10] and the treatment is eloquently simple and bare. It is certainly the most important big poem to appear of recent years in Greek, and we are determined that the English shall have a translation of it some time this year.

How did the women find time to hang
From balcony to balcony the banners
That when the sun rose Smyrna was ready to take sail
With all her canvas on?

From the barges the troops land.
In heavy equipment. The slabs of the wharves
Split, and hearts at each leap delight.
First come the men of the island, from
Happy villages in Samos, Chios, Mytilini;
The first called up as green conscripts
For an archipelago division; but war
Had given them curling moustaches
Pointed at the tips like wings...
Then the Cretan soldiery:
The swaying of their hips
And the straightness of their necks
Causes the balconies around us to melt.
Roses are sprinkled on them
And the bishop in his golden stole—
O Chrysostom, doomed to martyrdom—
Stands on a cart to bless them,
And his tears stream down.
The soldiers stoop to gather the roses
And stop their gun-barrels with them....[11]

The transition from narrative to reflection is managed with complete smoothness by the voices, and the whole poem has the quality of "speaking voice," which gathers intensity for each recitative; "Anatolia" has what novelists admire so much—"canvas." It is like a superbly cut film of the whole tragedy of Anatolia, where so much Greek blood was spilt. And, of course, being written now, when the new tragedy of Greece burns darker every day, it is charged with overtones of the present. Perhaps it could only be finished now when emotions of the hour match it perfectly. Or like "past grief which expresses the present."[12] This is a recitative for the mad boy who succeeds in escaping back to Greece.

When I stood at the tip of the cape
Everything was complete, fingernails in proper number
But no name whatsoever to condense me
So when you speak to me stand a bit to the side;
I too stand aside
And talk in a low voice…

THE WOMEN

There let us pitch our tents;
Let us not go further from those islands
That look out towards Anatolia;
Their accents and their sailing craft resemble
Like next-of-kin standing near the dead.
All this was no channel but a doorstep,
Bays where we slept suddenly lost
And where to go? Are we wanted anywhere?
We are not one or two washed away
But a sinful forest cut down.
The clear night is swamped
By the grief of one cow
When its little calf is weaned from it.
How can it contain the grief of so many partings?
Will covered streets ever be empty of weeping?
Will a shadow ever fall undisputed?

These fragments are translated by Elie Papadimitriou herself, who is at present busy on relief work in Palestine.[13] I cannot tell whether they give an idea of the greatness of her poem. At any rate, they are an advertisement that something good has been done here; they help to keep us alive in this awful country which lies like a partly-conscious human being, dying of an internal bleeding.

Yours,
Larry Durrell

NOTES

1. James Meary Tambimuttu (1915–1983) was the editor of *Poetry London*. Durrell had already published Tambi's works (as he was known to most friends) in *Delta*. Tambimuttu's Poetry London imprint published Durrell's novel *Cefalû* (also published as *The Dark Labyrinth*), and through Durrell's influence Henry Miller's *The Cosmological Eye* and Elizabeth Smart's *By Grand Central Station I Sat Down and Wept*. Also see "Poets under the Bed" in this volume.

2. As is evidenced in Stephanides's *Autumn Gleanings*, this is no exaggeration: "I learnt of Lawrence and Nancy's whereabouts—they were staying temporarily at the Luna Park Hotel, a rather ramshackle place that the authorities had requisitioned to house British refugees from German-invaded Europe....He had managed to get away in a small *caïque* crowded with other refugees, just one day before the entry of the Germans....In its overcrowded state, the *caïque* would founder if even a moderate storm arose....The Durrells, were pounced on by the military authorities and interned in a concentration camp where they were even more overcrowded than in the Luna Park Hotel. This was done routinely as a precaution to prevent German agents from being smuggled into Egypt together with the genuine refugees" (78–79).

3. George Katsimbalis was the titular colossus to Henry Miller's travel narrative of his time in Greece immediately prior to World War II, *The Colossus of Maroussi*.

4. Edward Lear (1812–1888), in whom Durrell had an ongoing interest, in part based on their common residence on Corfu, though Lear predates Durrell significantly. Lear was accomplished as both a writer and visual artist.

5. Durrell's letters to Seferis, now held in the Gennadius Library in Athens, also contain dozens of Learish sketches and frequently quasi-pornographic limericks. Durrell published Seferis's comments on limericks and such in *Personal*

Landscape while in Egypt and while Seferis was in the Greek government in exile in Pretoria, South Africa ("Letter" 10).

6.   Gabriele d'Annunzio (1863–1938) was an Italian poet who is also seen as the forerunner to fascism under Mussolini. The contrast is between a poetry concerned with aesthetics or a primarily propagandist poetry.

7.   This translation is Durrell's own and differs substantially from that published in *Personal Landscape* in 1944 (Seferis, "King" 9–10), which was possibly by Seferis himself or most likely Bernard Spencer.

8.   Papadimitriou was an active and outspoken Marxist as well as an agitator against Turkey's actions in 1922 against the Greek population of Smyrna. Durrell's poem "In Europe" is dedicated, as Bowen notes, somewhat dangerously to her (Bowen 49), and Durrell continued to promote her in his letters to T.S. Eliot (354).

9.   This is corroborated as "Luna Park" by Stephanides's account in *Autumn Gleanings* (79). Luna Park was largely a location for refugees arriving from Greece following the 1941 German invasion.

10. In 1922, following on the defeat of the Greek army, Turkish forces removed the Greek population from Smyrna extremely rapidly in an act has been varyingly described as ethnic cleansing and as defensive. In either case, Durrell's sympathies here fall to the Greeks who feel the loss of the home of Homer to a non-Greek population and language. Population exchanges between the two countries followed shortly after 1922. Even Ernest Hemingway's *In Our Times* emphasizes this event in the opening and closing to his volume of primarily American-based short stories.

11. A variant translation of the fragment of Papadimitriou's "Anatolia: Second Recitative" published in *Personal Landscape* (3–4).

12. This description is quite close to Seferis's argument comparing T.S. Eliot and C.P. Cavafy (121–61), though this was not translated into English and published by Rex Warner until several years after this article. For a discussion of how Durrell appropriated Seferis's comparison to develop a new approach to allusion, see Gifford, "Hellenism/Modernism" (82–97).

13. Olivia Manning translated Papadimitriou at this time, and she also housed Durrell's first wife Nancy when she fled Egypt to Palestine, mainly for safety but also in part to end her marriage. Durrell attempted flights to Palestine to reconcile, but these were not endorsed, and the tensions of the situation seem to expand beyond the Durrells' marital discord. Nonetheless, Durrell continued to promote both Papadimitriou and Manning.

No Clue
to Living

1960

ONE SUPPOSES THAT THE ARTIST as a public Opinionator only grew
up with the social conscience—with Dickens, Tolstoy, and Dostoevsky.[1]
He became an accusing finger pointed at the wrongs of society as well
as something of a soul-consultant for his correspondents. Out of this
change of preoccupation grew the truly extraordinary phenomenon
of his daily postbag today; apart from the begging letters, which doubtless formed a part of Shakespeare's fan-mail as well, there come hundreds
of letters asking him to take up public positions on every conceivable
matter from the fate of Irish horses or homosexuals to the rights and
wrongs of nuclear warfare and theosophy.[2] It is clear that what is
expected of him is to operate as a hardened committee man, appear
on boards, advise and comment on public affairs—in short to add his
mite to the flood of opinionation which is slopping over the world,
obscuring the inner world of values which once he was supposed to
sift within himself before expressing his findings in a work of art—
poems, paintings, plays. Today they want his message in capsule form.
It is, of course, very flattering to see his epigram printed in *Sayings of
Today* beside a message from the Pope and one from Mr. Eisenhower.[3]
But it is very doubtful whether he has anything to say which could be
more original than the other pronouncements by public figures, for
apart from his art he is just an ordinary fellow like everyone else,

subject to the same bloody flux of rash opinion, just as eager to lose a friend rather than forgo a jest.

Yet in some obscure way readers and editors believe that he may have something up his sleeve which will help them to formulate a new way of arranging the world or society; at the worst some sort of tranquilliser which will help alleviate the sleepless pangs of the world conscience. Has he? It is very much to be doubted that he has, outside the world of his artistic formulations where the one constant message (of all artists at all times) remains exactly the same as it always was: and will do until the nature of the work of art is understood and embodied in a way of life, when it will cease to become necessary. This, of course, presupposes that society will enter the poet's kingdom and realise its life fully. But, goodness me, it does not look likely to the artist wrestling with a ten-page questionnaire about the UNESCO Conference on Basic English.[4] How Basic can one really get? We accuse our enemies of double-thinking;[5] but what nature of self-deception would be necessary to invent a word like humane-killer?

No, the artist is not really to be blamed if his laughter is slightly cracked, slightly off-key. Nor does his laugh indicate a flippant attitude to the world of today. He admits that we are in an age of profound crisis. The position of humanity today resembled until recently that of Caryl Chessman,[6] under sentence of death and simply living from reprieve to reprieve, albeit in comfortable prison quarters and denied neither food nor books nor ink and paper. Nobody knows for how long.[7] The opinionators, too, are quite ready to sign petitions and organize meetings, and to these the artist is supposed to contribute his ration of right-feeling and right-thinking. The times are out of joint. A technocratic society is swallowing the individual.

Somehow the artist is expected to find an answer to this situation and to express it in such a way as to make it agreeable to print and palatable to read for the man in the street (the sleeping artist among us). I would like to question whether this is really a proper function for him or not; nor do I mean the word "proper" to be taken in the moral sense—but is this the field in which he can make the greatest contribution? A gaggle of artists round a table busily discussing the human crisis in our culture does not look very different from a Politburo of uncultivated and unshaven peasants discussing how to ameliorate the living standard of a backward province.

The trouble seems to me to be in the act of opinionation itself—because fundamentally when we address ourselves to the enjoyable task of rearranging the world into a juster and more equitable pattern we never consider ourselves as taking part in the plan. We are outside it somehow, directing the operation: *the other fellow must change his ways.* Thinking so directed cannot help but end in a magic formula which argues ill for somebody else's freedom.[8] I deduce this from making a brief survey of my own sinking-fund of opinionations which I trot out in conversation for the sheer fun of the thing. Perhaps a better artist would have learnt to shut up more. I still have not—excuse the *moi haïssable*:[9] there is no other way to tackle these things except from a personal point of view. I must honestly confess to discovering exactly the same quantity of idiocy, bigotry, confusion, and rashness that I am so disgusted to find in the opinions expressed by my own friends. In myself I find this rather a delightful trait, in others I find it most unsound. This is possibly common to all of us?

In this field of idle ratiocination one does, of course, come across bright solutions to the world problem. I can think of several—to abolish all news media, journals, films, books, for a period of ten years. Let no one have anything but word-of-mouth news from the village for a long time. I have tried this on myself and can testify to the extremely bene-ficial effect it has on one. To live in a Greek island with no radio, no newspaper, for a year at a time is a marvellous experience. Energy was saved which could be devoted to private inquiry and the practice of becoming more oneself;[10] I even try the same thing today, for where I live there is no radio, no television, and the papers arrive ten days late. This is a great blessing. It makes it impossible to get worked up about the crises they record—for by the time I read about them they will already have been replaced by others. They come to me, these crises, with the time-lag of distant stars. In this way I strive to keep the milk of opinionation from boiling over. But I have noticed one thing about crises; they perpetually reproduce themselves, there is never any lack of them. Is it possible that man himself is the secret source of manufacture, that the psychosomatic elders of the future will place crises of opinionation in the scale of self-manufactured illnesses—acne of the world soul? It seems likely. Nevertheless, selfish as it may seem, I am spared all the anguish of the opinionator by arriving too late at the denunciation-point. I would always be denouncing the wrong crisis otherwise.

To what point should I try to keep abreast of our crises so that I am always ready with a piece of packaged self-aggrandisement in the form of an opinion? I do not honestly know. But I cannot help feeling that if our crises are conditioned by lack of understanding and good feeling among human beings, no amount of hortatory lecturing will ever add up to a contribution. You get closer to your fellow man, paradoxically enough, by trying to get closer to yourself.[11] We talk with terror of brain-washing—but what of this vast flood of brain-bashing which sweeps the world? And even brain-washing presupposes brains to wash. There seem to me to be very few about. And whether our daily journalism is any better or worse than the methods used to extract confessions in police states is questionable. Can anyone calculate the effect upon human souls of being subjected to an exclusive diet of *Pravda* or the *Daily Mirror*?[12] Perhaps we should talk of a soul-washing rather than a brain-washing; but in this field, too, there are bigots ready with exclusive world-views and questionable techniques for use on children. But perhaps this is simply indicative of my own weakness in opinionizing. I have closely studied several types of government, from democratic, fascist to marxist; in each it seemed to me that the limiting factor could be traced to the region of blank opinionation. Any of them could have become the ideal State if…But I will not dare to finish the sentence, for the answer is known to everyone from the greatest artist to the smallest retail grocer. Here we come up against that ineradicable predisposition to legislate for the man next door.[13] Is the fault perhaps rather in our stars than in ourselves? I would hesitate to answer this dogmatically, living as I do in the country of Nostradamus![14]

But the problem of commitment remains—or at least this is what the world, and very often the artist, maintains. But here again, speaking purely for the artist, I would say that one cannot create and remain uncommitted. To opinion, yes. But the act of laying pen to paper, brush to canvas, is an act of mystical participation in the common world to which we all belong. An unfamiliar corner of it, perhaps, to most men; sometimes (to opinionators-in-ordinary) even a distasteful one; but nevertheless what emerges from the resolution of selves, if it can be called art, of whatever scale of magnitude, is a direct contribution to the health of the human psyche and as such a restorative, a cordial which makes it better able to recuperate its forces against those of destruction. This is not, of course, to be numbered among the artist's conscious intentions. It is a by-product of the work. The artist is only concerned with the pure act of self-penetration, of self-disentanglement when he addresses his paper or canvas. But his audiences (those who get his wavelength, so to speak) get his message not in a formulated manner but as a vicarious intuition of a hitherto concealed part of their own natures. Those who want the message packaged are those whose self-intuitions are in need of practice. This is where our education should be helpful—but is it?

In my view (here we go!) it does little or nothing because it is not oriented around a cosmology or a religion. Music, Divination, Prayer, Sacrifice, Mathematics—how one envies the comprehensiveness of the Greek pattern, with each branch closely linked to the next, each complementing and silhouetting the next. One only has to meet a physicist in the street to notice the pale shrunken soul of the man sprouting behind his eyeglasses. Everything, including the ataxic walk and the twitching, gives away the secret of his imbalance; he is fundamentally doing something meaningless because it is unrelated. Then turn to his spastic brother the artist, clothed in his homespun uniform and decorated by a fern-like spread of beard. He is no less revelatory in his weird habits. (Since television came in beards are going out, but corduroys do not show.) And what is he doing? Painting abstracts which are not half as fascinating as the purely utilitarian shapes of crystals under a microscope. He feels that his function is somehow unrelated, so he takes refuge from the world in this extraordinary activity, the explanations of which appear punctually every week in the press or on television, confided to professional appreciators who can really sling a pot of culture in the public's face.

Is it possible that the answer...I am indulging myself again. But is it possible that given time (as indeed *space*, for another crisis is the cancerous multiplication of races in this present decade: I must remember to give orders to have this process arrested at once): given time enough, it seems clear to me that science could lead us back to the central cosmological preoccupations of religion, and actually reinvigorate what one might call (I don't like the words) "a religious view" of things based on the masses of new information we have acquired in the past fifty years and which is lying idle, stored in the great lumber rooms of the learned journals? This could also be a possibility, for I believe that science and religion are now within hailing distance, though churches and governments are trying to row in the opposite direction.

But all these long term speculations, you will murmur restlessly... they are all very well, but they add nothing helpful to the current crisis. Instead of these vague formulations about a future which we may never see, can you not say something concrete about the present? What, in sum, can the artist do?

I'm afraid nothing—but I utter the word with cheerfulness. From the very beginning of recorded history our world has been apparently in the same disturbed and racked condition. Every attempt at a humane or rational order is subject to limitations of Time, on whose slippery surface neither kings nor empires nor dictators could find more than a precarious and temporary purchase.[15]

Is the artist, then, only a messenger of despair, can he say nothing? He can only say what his predecessors have said in their various dialects and voices. It is a magnificent prospect that he can offer. There remains, until the very last moment, the great Choice, the great act of affirmation. Raising his cracked and somewhat sardonic voice in every generation he utters the same, and by now somewhat shop soiled, truth: Choose![16]

This is not very helpful, I know. But we must take into account the limited field of operation of even the greatest artist. He is only a conveyer of the good news, the herald who plays his part among the other actors on the stage. Feeble in everything but these intuitions of possible miracles which lie buried and unrealised in every human psyche, and out of which one could pattern the real cloth-of-gold fabric of a possible Way.[17] What is lacking then? Nothing but the simplest ingredients, but apparently rarer than uranium or cobalt. It is too tiresome to list them—besides it is unnecessary, for any retail grocer could tick them off on his fingers for you.

And can the artist offer no clue to living? Alas, no; his public does that for him.[18]

NOTES

1. Durrell republished this piece several times in minor variants, which indicates its importance. The numerous political references suggest the work is akin to Orwell's "Politics and the English Language" as it relates to Durrell's oeuvre. Charles Dickens (1812–1870), Leo Tolstoy (1828–1910), and Fyodor Dostoyevsky (1821–1881) are widely known for the social critiques undertaken in their works. Given Durrell's anti-authoritarian postures in this essay, it is worth noting that Tolstoy was a major anarcho-pacifist thinker, and Dostoyevsky is frequently tied to anarchist concepts.

2. As peculiar as this combination sounds, Durrell collected precisely these letters in his unpublished typescript, "Price of Glory: Gleanings From a Writer's In-Tray." This is held in the Morris Library, Southern Illinois University, Carbondale.

3. Dwight D. Eisenhower (1890–1969) was president of the United States from 1953 to 1961. The pope at the time was Pope John XIII.

4. Durrell wrote "Two Poems in Basic English" (141–144) in 1946, which predates the UNESCO conference.

5. A direct reference to George Orwell. Durrell read Orwell's *Nineteen Eighty-Four*, in which double-think is a method for social control, in 1949 and wrote to Orwell to express his admiration for the novel in the same year. The two authors had previously disputed their differing positions openly (Gifford, "Editor's Preface" viii-ix), so Durrell's admiration and echoing of Orwell again in *The Revolt of Aphrodite* would appear genuine. Durrell, like most readers, regarded *Nineteen Eighty-Four* as an anti-Stalinist work, despite the use of dollars and atomic weapons by Big Brother's regime; the Soviets did not acquire atomic weapons until after the novel's publication. However, Durrell's own *Revolt of Aphrodite* contains a similar critique of corporatism and cultural hegemony.

6. Chessman (1921–1960) was a famous California convict who was executed after publishing four books he wrote while on death row. Calls for clemency were highly publicized. During his ten years on death row, Chessman received stays of execution, including one during his actual execution in a gas chamber, which would have stalled his execution had the caller not initially dialled a wrong number.

7. Like Chessman's uncertain stays of execution, this was a time of great uncertainty based on the possibility of nuclear war. It would, however, be anachronistic to read this in light of the subsequent Bay of Pigs Invasion or the Cuban Missile Crisis, although later publications of this article in the 1960s would have aroused that association.

8. The use of the term "magic" here is akin to Raymond Williams's in "Advertising: The Magic System," which was published two months later in *The New Statesman*. They may share a common source.

9. A tradition in French criticism to avoid "the hated I" of the first person singular. Durrell's shift from "a better artist" to "I" is marked here as a refusal of the "society that is swallowing the individual" two paragraphs above. This same pattern from "one" to "I" repeats numerous times in the remainder of the essay, the subsequent paragraph in particular, as a way to emphasize the individual rather than obfuscate him or her.

10. This emphasis on the tension between the individual and the group is also continued in Durrell's next major novel series, *The Revolt of Aphrodite*.

11. Durrell's close friend, Henry Miller, articulates a similar position in his anarchist essay "An Open Letter to Surrealists Everywhere," a text that Durrell admired. In contradiction of Paul Éluard's notion of the Socialist Brotherhood of Man, Miller argues, "The brotherhood of man is a permanent delusion common to the idealists everywhere in all epochs: it is the reduction of the principle of individuation to the least common denominator of intelligibility. It is what leads the masses to identify themselves with movie stars and megalomaniacs like Hitler and Mussolini. It is what prevents them from reading and appreciating and being influenced by and creating in turn such poetry as Paul Eluard gives us" (152). To this, he adds, "I am fatuous enough to believe that in living my own life in my own way I am more apt to give life to others" (157).

12. *Pravda* was a leading newspaper of the Soviet Union and an official organ of the Central Committee of the Communist Party. *The Daily Mirror* was the largest selling newspaper in the United Kingdom at the time and generally promoted a Labour and working-class perspective. Much like his later *The Revolt of Aphrodite*, Durrell's indictment is of the nature of mass media in general as a degradation of the individual, regardless of the media's left or right political affiliation.

13. Apart from left or right affiliation, Durrell's discomfort is with the unavoidably authoritarian nature of government in general or the state itself. This is akin to the anarchist position of many of Durrell's poetic colleagues, as well Antonio Gramsci's concept of cultural hegemony, which was first translated into English by the Scottish poet Hamish Henderson, whom Durrell had known in Egypt during the Second World War.

14. Durrell lived in Sommières at this time, less than one hundred kilometres from Nostradamus's birthplace and the universities where he studied. Henry Miller also refers to Nostradamus twice in his letters to Durrell in 1959 while in France (Durrell, *Durrell–Miller* 343, 363).

15. Notably, these descriptions apply to governments but not to artists or individuals.

16. This is the quandary in which Durrell leaves his readers at the end of each of his major novel sequences. *The Alexandria Quartet* ends with uncertainty just as *Justine* ends with an ambivalent resolution according to the reader's own wants and needs; *The Revolt of Aphrodite* ends with an abolition of contractual obligation in a corporate world; and *The Avignon Quintet* ends with a total reversion to meta-fiction. In all three cases, the reader (and not the author nor critic) is left in an unresolved moment of personal engagement and choice.

17. Durrell refers to "cloth-of-gold" in *The Alexandria Quartet* as well, and he would still have been completing the novel series at this time. Cloth of gold is typically silk wrapped with gold and used as the weft in woven fabric. The "Way" is the Tao, and this sentence combines it with the Western ecclesiastic sense of the cloth as used in church services and for royalty (Psalms 45:13–14). Ray Morrison details Durrell's Taoist interests (446–50).

18. An allusion to the French Symbolist author Villiers de L'Isle-Adam (1838–1889) and his play *Axël*: "Vivre? les serviteurs feront cela pour nous" ("as for living, our servants will do that for us"). Both W.B. Yeats and Friedrich Nietzsche frequently quoted this specific passage, and the work also supplied the title for Edmund Wilson's major study of Modernist literature *Axel's Castle*.

This Magnetic, Bedevilled Island That Tugs at My Heart

1974

THE CYPRUS SITUATION has been likened to a hedgehog wearing a coat full of prickles—too many for his own good.[1]

It is certainly the most obstinate of Mediterranean problems, and, moreover, the issue that divides Greek and Turk has not changed since the very beginning. Once more we have a manifestation of the Greek desire for Enosis,[2] union with Greece, this time in the unfortunate form of a military intrigue which misfired—as anybody could have foreseen it would.

But, of course, Cyprus means something more personal to me, for I was not just a Briton, I was a Cypriote by residence and choice, living in the island with my small daughter.[3] Its peace and happiness was as vital to me as it was to any Greek or Turk, and I still feel the island tugging at my heart.

Behind the politics and the bloodshed I always seem to hear the rumble of surf on Aphrodite's beach, Paphos, always see the sunset, exploding over the Abbey of Bellapais, where the old Tree of Idleness[4] hid nightingales in its leaves all summer long. In the real sense it is what is at stake—the peace of this magnetic island and the happiness of its inhabitants, of whom I was one. Is it too much to hope for? Must the lemons remain always bitter?

That time around, when it was the British who were alleged to be obstructing union with Greece, some compromise was sought to meet the case and the result was the Cyprus Republic under Archbishop Makarios.

Truth to tell, this hybrid political animal managed to work quite well for a decade before the EOKA[5] intriguers, aided by Athens, managed to plunge the island into chaos once more. This was largely due to the astute and deft governorship of the Archbishop who for this long period of time had been riding the tiger of Enosis as nobody else could. The minority of fanatics has always wanted to take the law into its own hands and President Makarios[6] had been running considerable personal danger in trying to hold them down.

He is no less patriotic than the next Greek but he hates bloodshed and faction and he sees that the Cyprus situation can only be settled by a decent compromise. If he had been forced to store arms in the kitchen cupboard it was not the Turks that bothered him so much as his own compatriots. The result of years of intrigue and agitation is now before our eyes to see.

It seems really extraordinary that two small communities, 454,000 Greeks and 106,000 Turks, cannot manage to live in peace in this island paradise. The conflicting claims have often been discussed in a search for a compromise but the real stumbling block is the Greeks' refusal to give up the dream of Enosis, and one of course can quite understand them.

Ethnologically the island is Greek. Aphrodite was washed up in Paphos, and the Cyprus variety of ancient Greek is the oldest known. The majority of inhabitants are Greek and the product of a Greek culture and education. The religion is Orthodox and for the Greeks today it seems unthinkable that union with Greece should not be envisaged even if they have to wait fifty years for it. The Republic of Cyprus temporized on this issue but we have a right to respect the Greek case.

But what of the Turkish? Well, there are no poetical, ethnological, or historic reasons to be invoked by the Turkish position. It is purely strategic and quite straightforward.

The island is too close to Turkey and the Turks would prefer to see it neutralized. Also, the Turks in the island have always claimed that they were being discriminated against. And they have shown a desire to be ruled by something a little more liberal than the Greek-oriented administration. One can respect their point of view, also, remembering that they are Moslems, and that counts for something.

But that this tragic situation should have blown up just at the present moment is terribly unlucky not only for Cyprus but for Greece as a whole, which has just welcomed back the new-old Premier, Constantine Caramanlis,[7] whose Government could be easily overturned on an issue as burning as this one. Surely everything must be done to see that he stays in.

He has hardly begun to liberalize the country and restore a true democracy. He is a careful, thoughtful, and forceful man and certainly the wisest Greek politician since Premier Sophocles Venizelos.[8] Ironically, too, he is the architect of the Cyprus Republic and the man who created a warm rapprochement with Turkey. Yet here he is also riding the tiger of Enosis.

The talks in Geneva appear to be in deadlock and one senses why, for if the Turks are granted the sort of autonomy in the island which they seek, bang might go to the old dream of Enosis and the man in the street in Athens would take that very hard indeed.

The real problem is to try to do justice to Moslem feelings without wounding or stifling Orthodox ones. If an answer cannot be found, we will have to go back to first base.

Curiously enough the Soviet solution—a return to a republic under Makarios—may be the only one still acceptable to the two factions.

After all, the Turks of Cyprus have had ten years of Makarios's rule and they know he is, when all is said and done, a man of peace, and, of course, he has the enormous prestige of being a religious leader.

If, therefore, no compromise is possible, why not return to the old principle which has worked so far? With Caramanlis at the wheel in Athens one could be sure of a fairly peaceful policy instead of one which inflamed the hotheads of EOKA in this astonishingly unlucky island.

The republic has, after all, worked once. Under Makarios it might work again, and we must not forget that the Republic of Cyprus was stable owing to the fact of banking in the City of London, and it would be a pity to throw everything overboard unless one found a better solution to a hedgehog of a problem.

NOTES

1. This article was first published in the *Daily Mail* on August 22, 1974. It was retitled the next day in the *New York Times*, "Must the Lemons Remain Bitter?" This alternate title demonstrates the kinships between this piece and Durrell's travel book, *Bitter Lemons*, which describes his years living on Cyprus during the struggle for Enosis (union). This title, from the *Daily Mail* publication, also connects with Durrell's earlier draft of a novel, *The Magnetic Island*. See Shelley Cox (45–57). I have generally retained the paragraph formatting of the later printing and have eliminated the paragraph headings of the first, which are most likely editorial additions by the *Daily Mail*.

2. The Cypriot struggle for unification with Greece and independence from British rule, which was fought by EOKA (National Organization of Cypriot Fighters) using armed conflict from 1955 to 1959. In 1974, Makarios was overthrown in a coup, and Turkey invaded after failing to secure British support for an intervention. Turkey remains on the island.

3. Sappho Durrell (1951–1985), born from his second marriage to Eve Cohen.

4. This is both a chapter and location in Durrell's book *Bitter Lemons*, which is set during his life on Cyprus, as well as the title of his poetry collection and poem *The Tree of Idleness*.

5. EOKA is the acronym for Εθνική Οργάνωσις Κυπρίων Αγωνιστών (National Organization of Cypriot Fighters).

6. Makarios III (1913–1977), Archbishop of Cyprus and its first president. He was archbishop and enormously influential during the Enosis struggle, and he negotiated the resolution in 1960, which lasted until the Athens-supported coup.

7. Caramanlis was a former prime minister of Greece who went into self-imposed exile after losing the election in 1963. He won the first election after the end of

the Junta in 1974. Originally, Kanellopolous was supported as the interim prime minister to lead the country to elections, and Durrell had tutored him in English during the Greek Government in Exile during World War II.

8. Venizelos (1894–1964) was an extraordinarily important Greek politician. He was prime minister during the Greek Government in Exile during World War II and had led the Centre Union party. Durrell is tactfully balancing his praise between socialist and conservative forces.

Lamas in a
French Forest

1984

WHEN THE HOLY MEN FLED from Tibet in 1950 they sought to follow their Buddhist faith in the west. Some of them found a home in a strange monastery in Burgundy. This is their story.

Just before winter sets in I like to indulge in a journey, a ramble with a friend about an unfamiliar corner of France. It is usually the end of October—the first skirls of snow have settled in the mountains and the first winter thunderstorms have come and gone. The tourists have fled, but there are often spells of good weather until Christmas. Though the little hotels are empty, the food is still ambrosial—after all, this is France.

It was on one of these rambles, a few years ago, that I discovered the Château de Plaige, a Buddhist centre in the heart of the Morvan mountains, near Dijon. It was the oddest happening. Only that afternoon we had been talking about the poetry of Mila Repa,[1] the Tibetan hermit-poet. Suddenly we were riveted by the unmistakable sight of a couple of lamas walking down a country road in the snow laughing their heads off. There was no sign of any habitation—it was as if they had been dropped from the clouds.

Bemused, we stopped to talk to them, finding to our relief that one of them spoke French. He pointed towards the deeper woods, indicating where the château they had come from lay hidden. Obviously thinking that we sought instruction, he urged us to go there and we obeyed without a word.

It was rather an odd château, more like an overgrown seventeenth-century manor house which had had funny conical towers added to it at the start of this century—altogether whimsical and appropriate to its present use. Beside it stood a great white stupa, or Buddhist statue, looking rather like a hippopotamus at its prayers.

A symbol of the so-called "awakened state," it is a strange emblem of a faraway land to find in the misty vales and woods of Morvan.

We were received courteously and invited to participate in a short service. Then, over tea and sweet cakes, the forty-two-year-old Tibetan in charge of the monastery, Lama Sherab, answered our questions. He explained that the version of Buddhism expounded at Plaige was derived from the inspiration of none other than Mila Repa himself. It seemed a lucky omen and it made my first contact with Plaige a memorable one.

Until the fall of Tibet, Buddhism was a plant of slow growth in the west, though there was much sympathy with the oriental point of view and it had been given some intellectual respectability by famous writers such as Aldous Huxley and Somerset Maugham.[2] But the Chinese invasion of Tibet produced a radical change, something like the fall of Constantinople:[3] for the holy men and the priests were forced to fly into India, taking with them the jealously guarded holy texts of their faith. Suddenly we found ourselves overwhelmed not only by the documents (it would have taken us another 200 or 300 years to get our hands upon all this important documentation), but by the very presence of the religious leaders themselves. New centres and agencies for the study and practice of Buddhism sprang up of which several hundred are listed in the directory of the London Buddhist journal, *The Middle Way*.[4]

Plaige was bought in 1974 by Buddhist adherents and was among the first of these new institutions. It was offered as a teaching centre to the Venerable Kalou Rinpotché,[5] a renamed master of higher insight. He named it Kagu-Ling and dedicated it to the central work of his life and creed. Plaige was to be a centre of repose, study, and meditation, and Kalou Rinpotché proposed to run it on exactly the same lines as the larger seminary over which he now presides in Darjeeling.

The abbot, now over eighty, visits Plaige several times a year and is always on hand during the principal ceremonies. But the day-to-day running is confided to three of his most cherished and trusted lamas, among whom the expansive and jovial Lama Sherab rules, because of the excellent knowledge of French he has acquired after ten years in the country.

As the establishment has gradually expanded over the years, a whole cluster of little chalets has grown up in the surrounding woods. The château offers its novices the means to practise the tough withdrawal period of initiation which lasts three years, three months, and three days.

Accommodation at Plaige is limited to about thirty resident lamas and novices, but people often come and lodge in the village to spend a few days of study and meditation at the centre.

A Tibetan lamasery encourages visitors even if they do not attend services; in Plaige many local people like to have picnics with their children in the grounds. In fact anybody can just arrive at the château and ask for instruction—there are courses dealing with every stage of Buddhist realisation, classes in yoga and meditation, and even simple language courses in Tibetan. But the religious services, also open to all, are the most important part.

A similar Buddhist centre, called Kagyu Samyé Ling, presided over by the same teachers, exists in Dumfriesshire in Scotland. The two communities keep in close touch, despite the language difference, and British novices often do a stint at the French centre.

On my first visit, Plaige, like other Buddhist centres, was suffering from lack of space. According to Lama Sherab the plan was to build a temple as a centre of assembly and welcome, a chapter house and a lecture hall.

"Plaige is growing out of its limits," he said. "The temple is the pet notion of our spiritual master, Kalou Rinpotché, who has been dreaming about it for some time." And Lama Sherab added: "Whatever he dreams up there in Darjeeling tends to come true, either here or in Scotland."

More than a year later Lama Sherab appeared on my doorstep in Provence in the depths of winter. He had come to ask me if I would consider helping to raise funds for the temple. The basic structural work had been done but they had run out of funds to complete the project.

I agreed and formed a small committee with my brother Gerald and two French writers.[6] Together we plotted a few fund-raising gambits, the most successful being our lotus wall inside the temple itself: each person who gave money was encouraged to plant a lotus leaf or flower which would bear the name of a loved one.

Last autumn I returned to Plaige to see what progress had been made on the temple. The chosen design was the inspiration of the Abbot: an exact copy of the Temple of Samyé, the first Buddhist temple to be built in Tibet during the eighth century. All the heavy construction work on the building was complete, but the decoration and colour still had to be added. It stood there looking rather forlorn but so eloquent—like the skeleton of some prehistoric animal.

My visit coincided with a three-day "coming-out" party for twenty new Western lamas, ten women and ten men; their initiation was complete and they were due to emerge the next day. The ceremonies were being attended by lamas from several countries, including the United States and the UK. Kalou Rinpotché was there for the occasion. Though at first he seemed very old and as frail as a gnat, the energy which poured out of him was closer to that of a vivid little dragonfly. He hardly seemed to breathe; he never gestured. But he was every-where, and so was his compassionate smile of welcome, so typically Tibetan.

There was a distinctly festive air: friends and relations had come to greet the novices and swap the traditional white scarves of congratulation.

Lama Sherab was quite adamant that the three-year incubation period was not too long. "It's not long enough to make either a surgeon or a violinist. It's simply the initial contact with all the muddle and mix up and distortion of the psyche. But it's the first grasp or inkling. If successful then it's a point of departure out of which one can develop a new sort of life-pattern."

Nevertheless, toughness and resolution are essential qualities for the novice. Another young Buddhist felt that three years was just the right length of time. "It's decisive, why don't you try it?" he said. The Tibetans themselves obviously do not think the retreat is onerous. The pamphlet which describes the activities of the château refers to it as "delicious." But it also emphasises that Buddhism takes work, effort, and diligence.

At the ceremony, as well as a few French boys and girls who had taken the plunge into the Dharmic life, there were two couples, one American and one Canadian, and an English lama called Alasdair MacGeach. Having done welfare work, chiefly in India among the poorest communities, he saw this European retreat as a refresher course, a welcome breath of air after the torrid heats of India. Soon he would be returning there, after a short visit to England. The Canadian couple described with warmth and humour the sacrifices they had made to pay their way and become members of the little community—no job had been too humble for them to take on if it answered their purpose.

The scene in the forest in the early morning was strange and moving. The initiates emerged pale and exhausted from their long vigils, to be greeted by the roaring and blaring of Tibetan horns, the gnashing of gongs—a strange barbaric orchestra of salutation to be heard in a French forest at the crack of dawn. Then followed the ceremonial procession round the grounds of the château and the religious offices in the old shrine room which marked the re-entry of the novices into the ordinary world. Some were to stay on at the château; others were to travel or work elsewhere. The celebratory air of these

Buddhist services was striking—there seemed nothing penitential or gloom-laden about them. It was as if the spectre of original sin had been laid to rest.

Perhaps the feeling of ease and ampleness about Plaige was due to the Tibetan view of reality with its accompanying belief in human reincarnation: what you cannot achieve in this life you can attend to in the next.

The Karmarpa, one of the great Tibetan doctors of divinity who had a share in the founding and expanding the work of Plaige, had recently died.

In discussing the loss with Lama Sherab I was told that before his death the Karmarpa had left the most precise instructions as to where and when he would be reborn. I supposed it would be a generation or more before this happened. "Not at all," said the lama. "In a couple of years or so. With so much to be done, why waste time?"

NOTES

1. Jetsun Milarepa (1052–1135) is one of the most famous Tibetan yogis and poets.
2. Huxley (1894–1963) was a British novelist best known for *Brave New World*, though he wrote many highly successful works. Maugham (1874–1965) wrote in many genres but is best known for his semi-autobiographical novel *Of Human Bondage*.
3. Durrell's comparison is bold and marks his pro-Tibet and pro-Greece position. China first invaded Tibet in 1950. The Fall of Constantinople refers to the 1453 conquest of the capital of the Christian Byzantine Empire by the Islamic Ottoman Empire, modern Turkey, which renamed it Istanbul. Referring to the city using the Greek name recalls the attempt in 1922 by Greece to reclaim the city, which failed and led to the Asia Minor Catastrophe.
4. The quarterly journal began in 1943, replacing *Buddhism in England*, which began in 1926. *The Middle Way* is still published.
5. Rinpotché (1904–1989) was the modern holder of Shangpa Kagyu lineage. He taught extensively in Europe and North America after being forced into exile from Tibet.

6. Although Durrell is modest here, this was a fairly extensive campaign, and Durrell wrote giving his support to a variety of French government officials, including the president and minister of culture (MacNiven 660–61).

Ideas about Literature

The Prince and Hamlet

A Diagnosis

1937

> *Englishmen have always, in spite of the national anthem, been slaves.*
> —from a letter to Henry Miller[1]

THE CRITICS, FOR INSTANCE.[2] One cannot help thinking as one reads them, that criticism is a trade which deals with inessentials: with artifice and not art. For the joy of art is in its privacy, in its exclusiveness. In this Museum the artist is the only one who is really at home; we, as privileged guests, are allowed to wander round it provided we do not touch. And criticism loves to touch, to handle, to analyse, to assess.

The artist retires into his private pandemonium and emerges suddenly with a few scraps—a notebook jotted in a kind of gnomic shorthand: a description of what the critics are forced to call the "life beyond life."[3] His work is a battle to superimpose this private reality on the common reality of men. His battle, in fact, is really to destroy literature pure—the organism on which the critic fattens. When he does fuse the two realities he creates a work of art. He describes his interior world and through his medium, makes it overlap with the world of common or garden reality. Hence the disgust. Because you cannot criticise a world of which the artist is the sole inhabitant. You can only analyse the external reality which you share with him. The internal one is always beyond you.

In our time the critics have almost persuaded us that in order to be sensible to art one must understand it rationally. Whereas it must be obvious to at least twelve or thirteen people that art—the real core of a work of art—does not need to be understood. It is a pure experience, and only needs faith in the prophetic sense. Who can understand, for example, Lawrence's world, or Gauguin's?[4] But it is there as an experience to be partaken of by the butcher, the baker, the candlestick-maker: anyone with the faith to give himself to a new reality without question.

This is important to realise when one reads *Hamlet*. The interior battle which rages suffocatingly as an undercurrent the whole time. It is from the remote battle-front of the self that the artist sends us back his messages, gnomic scribbles, fragments, *which we can never understand*, but which thrill us, pierce us, and remain with us for centuries as a sort of tribal experience. Let us, for once, dispense with its critical literature, not only on the purely agricultural side (Dover Wilson, Harrison,[5] etc.), but also on the side of pure criticism.

Hamlet is a representation of the inner struggle written in terms of the outer one. It is the union of the "dream" and the reality, that Breton[6] mentions. All the critical mouse-traps set to catch the king fail,[7] because up to now, everyone has tried to relate the outer reality (the murder, Ophelia, etc.), to the interior reality. Fail completely, because the inner and outer move along separate planes, and seldom meet. There are two co-existing Hamlets. Or, to be deadly accurate: there is the Prince, and there is Hamlet.

It is this dual growth which has made the moods so incomprehensible; the interplay between the social and the psychic pressure which creates the unique Hamlet: the creature living in a new chronology, the new universe, which we call insanity. Was he mad or did he only pretend he was mad? A century of theorising has not answered.

Hundreds of genial idiots have sifted every line of the play, to no effect. Hamlet was no madder than Shakespeare. In fact it was the new *sanity* which was killing him, and which drove Shakespeare away to his farm in silence, leaving all his work in chaos, unedited, unhonoured, and unsung.

The Age of The Prince was the Elizabethan Age. An Age that poisoned its young men with the humanities and then showed them none. The Prince was society. But the pressure that closed on the personal, the gentle, the malleable *Hamlet*, was the pressure of all circumstance common to all ages. Hamlet is the psyche for ever trying to fight its way out of the armour of the Prince; through the chinks we catch glimpses of this ephemera, in revolt against its social function, resentful, but dying—all the time very quietly and vividly dying. But the real death, the internal quietus was never delivered by Laertes but by Hamlet himself. The real play, in fact, is Hamlet and nothing but Hamlet. The King, the Queen, Horatio, Ophelia—they were all nothing but conventional voices calling him to conventional action—rut, revelry, or sentiment. Most terrifying of all to the dying Elizabethan was the ghost: that representative of the other world who became nothing but a social gramophone, calling for a conventional revenge. "The world is out of joint, O, cursed spite, that ever I was born to put it right!"[8]

The inner Hamlet, when it sees that the ghost, *even the ghost*, is just another social mouthpiece, begins its death, its personal declension. Here you have a loneliness which is only emphasised by the mouthing of the chorus, by the external action—murder, love, revenge. There is your tragedy. For the rest, the insane machinery of the plot, the heroics of Laertes, the sweet stupidity of Ophelia—these are just different flavours of irony which leave nothing but a bitterness in the mouth. Hamlet is dead—Long live the Prince!

Two chronologies: two lives: two separate sanities: two planes of action moving disjointedly along together: and two protagonists who are one. Hamlet and the Prince.

Now this may sound nonsense, but it is not. In order to illustrate it, let anyone turn to the first quarto version of the play.[9] He will find the whole idea laid bare for him with an accuracy the more astonishing because it was unconscious. The long Folio version of *Hamlet*, as we know it, was much too long for presentation on the Elizabethan stage. According to custom it was cut, and in this cut and partly altered version we find the real clue to Hamlet, given to us probably by Shakespeare himself.[10]

His problem was this. To present Hamlet to the public in a *comprehensible* form. But to the public the inner struggle has always been incomprehensible, always will be. But the outer struggle—the material, the social, the ancestral problem—that is another question.

In this Quarto we find a play that the public must have understood and enjoyed with comparative ease. It is a play without any Hamlet. Unerringly the whole of the inner struggle, which clogs the action of the Folio, has been cut away. There is only the Prince. And the Prince is subject to fits of madness in a beautifully comprehensible way. *Everything is explainable without any reference to the phenomenon of genius.*

Now in the long version, the Folio, the whole cast revolves around the central figure of Hamlet. Everything in the play is significant only in its immediate relation to him. The cumulative voices of King, Courtier, Lover, Liar, cajole him to relinquish his inner psyche in favour of a material role on the social stage. *Even the ghost*, that ancestral voice, joins its platitudes to those of Polonius, and cuts him off from supernatural aid. This is the final horror. He cannot call on God, since it is the representative of God who has set him this maniac jig-saw to solve, and added his voice to the voices of society. He is so caught up in the machinery that there is no hope of escape. His death begins at the first appearance of the ghost and ends in the ravings over Ophelia's grave.[11] It is death by what the oceanographers would call "implosion." He is crushed inwards, on to himself.

Then, on the other hand, you have the Quarto, in which any signs of the inner feud are cleverly related to external things, to love, to revenge, to madness. The very structure of the play is altered to diffuse the emphasis which lies on the protagonist. The Queen, for instance. What a superb simplification it was to follow the source-story—to make her unconscious of the murder. How human and sentimental the ghost's request:

Speake to her, Hamlet, for her sex is weake.
Comfort thy mother, Hamlet, thinke on me.[12]

And how delicately the same sentiment is made oblique in the Folio—less immediately emotional. Compare the two scenes. In the Quarto we have suddenly a queen who is a bad man's dupe. But a "good" woman. We have a little development on Horatio as the faithful heart-of-oak dumb-bell. The king becomes rapidly more important as the villain of the piece, and the whole play moves nearer to the accustomed forms of drama: hero, hero's mother, villain, friend of hero, etc. It is a slick piece of work that even the critics would enjoy. But in the Folio? The whole scene is pointed like a pistol at the head of the protagonist. It is all part of the mouse-trap.

There it is, then. We have in the Folio a double existence: the Prince, who takes his place among the other characters—any jack in any pack of cards: and Hamlet, the creature of the void, poisoned in the bud and dying the Bastard Death,[13] with a loneliness and irony never before seen in literature.

Looked at from this point of view, how many iron-cold shades of irony we have to suffer in Hamlet? The real grin of the genius is carved in it. The importunities of Rosencrantz and Guildenstern finally answered by that superb whip crack: "I lack advancement."[14] The desperate attempts at self-revelation before Ophelia. For, after all, her betrayal was the biggest one he had to face. In the Ophelia bits we will find the inner struggle most in evidence, because he was counting on her as an ally. But her stupidity—her persistent belief that it was the outward things which were causing his disease—finally alienated him. She became part of the outer struggle herself, and as such he turned against her. The pity of it was that she died, not for Hamlet, who was worth dying for, but for the Prince.

In the mad scene we have another simplification in the Quarto version. It is made quite clear that it is Polonius's death which has caused her madness by the little verse: "His beard was white as snow!"[15] etc. But in the Folio she does not produce this definite indication of her thoughts until *after* Laertes appears. After her brother *reminds* her, in fact, of her father. Before that she has confused the two deaths: *And seems to be talking about Hamlet.* In the Folio, therefore, even this scene points ambiguously back at Hamlet. In the Quarto it is plain sailing. The poor girl is sent mad with grief at her father's death. It is only too clear.

The last ironic throes of Hamlet's own inner death are at the grave-side. Here the complete disorganisation between the two Hamlets has never been so clear or so fearful. He is called upon, after all, to exhibit his formal sorrow for her death, when in his inner chronology Ophelia is already dead and buried and rejected. And it is this knowledge that produces the terrific outburst, the embarrassing strained shouting over the coffin. But he himself is clear enough about who is speaking from the mask: "Behold it is I, Hamlet the Dane!" This is the death-scene for him, which passes all understanding. One is struck dumb by the humour of his word-duel with Laertes. It has an irony which the Greeks could never have approached.

It has been said that Hamlet is an artistic failure.[16] And this is so, if one can only respect in literature the façade, the architecture, the externals. But no writer of any genius attempted artistic success. That is a myth which only the critics and the mediocrities concentrate on. I commend the Quarto to the attention of such literary grave-diggers.[17] It will please them hugely. The Prince can be explained, weighed, analysed, etc.

But as an epitaph there is one little omission from the Quarto which seems, to me at any rate, full of a profound significance. It is in the phrasing of the love-letter which Polonius reads to the king. It is an indication of how much Hamlet needed Ophelia to understand—to respect his inner struggle. Not that she, sweet, silly little wretch, would have been able to comprehend it—even if a modern critic had written it out for her in his own words.[18] After the scrap of verse in the Quarto we have, simply:

To the beautiful Ophelia: Thine ever most
unhappy Prince Hamlet![19]

And in the Folio something more curious, more significant of the real state of the disease. It was really an epitaph on Shakespeare himself:

O, dear Ophelia, I am ill at these numbers,
I have not art to reckon my groans, but
that I love thee best, O most best believe
it. Thine evermore, dear lady, WHILST
THIS MACHINE IS TO HIM HAMLET.[20]

This is not the voice of the Prince![21]

NOTES

1. This letter was sent early November 1936 (Durrell, *Durrell–Miller* 22). Durrell is playing against the lyrics of "Rule Britannia."
2. Although Durrell was not included in their published correspondence, this work relates closely to Henry Miller and Michael Fraenkel's *Hamlet* letters, published in 1939.

3. From Milton's *Areopagitica*, "a good book is the precious lifeblood of a master spirit, embalmed and treasured up on purpose to a life beyond life" (7).

4. The Modernist author D.H Lawrence (1885–1930) and Post-Impressionist artist Paul Gauguin (1848–1903).

5. J. Dover Wilson (1881–1969) was Regius Professor of English Literature at the University of Edinburgh. He was known largely for his work on Shakespeare and his editorship of the *New Shakespeare* complete works through Cambridge University Press, for which *Hamlet* occupied his greatest attention. Durrell is likely referring to his 1935 book *What Happens in Hamlet*, which is still influential, as well as his 1934 *The Manuscript of Shakespeare's Hamlet*. J.B. Harrison was a professor at Queen's University and was the editor of the Penguin Shakespeare beginning in 1937. He produced a wide range of critical texts on Shakespeare and Elizabethan literature in general, including several critical editions Durrell was likely to have owned, such as Thomas Nashe's *An Elizabethan Journal* (published in three volumes in 1928, 1931, and 1933). Durrell claimed to have read across the whole of Elizabethan literature before moving to Corfu in 1935.

6. André Breton (1896–1966) was the founder of Surrealism, and Durrell's ties to Surrealism and English Surrealism were significant both for his own works and for English Surrealism in general (Gifford, "Surrealism's" 36–64).

7. *The Mousetrap* is the play within the play in *Hamlet* through which Hamlet believes "the play's the thing / Wherein I'll catch the conscience of the King" (II.ii.531–32).

8. Durrell misquotes here, likely from memory: "The time is out of joint, Oh, cursed spite, / That ever I was born to set it right" (I.v.885–86). The same misquotation is ubiquitous in works on Shakespeare.

9. Generally known as the "bad Quarto," Quarto 1 (Q1) is likely a pirated version of the play published in 1603, followed by Quarto 2 (Q2) and Folio 1 (F1). Typically, modern editions of *Hamlet* are based on a compromise between Q2 and F1. At the time, Q1 was generally only available in facsimile and not a modernized text—in general, Durrell's quotations are in the original spelling for Q1 and in modernized spellings for F1.

10. Durrell's argument here is the revision hypothesis, which views Q1 as an early version of the play later revised by Shakespeare (or an actor). This contradicts J. Dover Wilson's 1934 argument in *The Manuscript of Shakespeare's Hamlet*, which is likely why he has already dismissed Wilson's work. Also see Kathleen Irace's Introduction to *The First Quarto of Hamlet* (1–27).

11. *Hamlet* V.i.3471–81.

12. *Hamlet* Q1 xiii.2495–96.

13. A reference to Michael Fraenkel, with whom Henry Miller wrote *Hamlet*, a collection of their correspondence. See Fraenkel's *Bastard Death: The Autobiography of an Idea* (1936).

14. *Hamlet*, F1 III.v.2210.

15. *Hamlet*, F1 IV.v.2945. This line is also in Q1 but lacks the same surrounding materials and removes the verb "His beard as white as snowe" (17.2945).

16. This is Eliot's "Hamlet and His Problems" in which he famously argues, "So far from being Shakespeare's masterpiece, the play is most certainly an artistic failure" (98).

17. This is a dry joke on the grave digger scene in *Hamlet*.

18. "Doubt that in earth is fire, / Doubt that the starres doe moue, / Doubt trueth to be a liar, / But doe not doubt I loue" (Q1 vii.1144–47).

19. The line breaks and modernized spelling are Durrell's own (Q1 vii.1148–49).

20. Capitalization and line breaks are Durrell's own (II.ii.1148–52). Polonius is reading aloud Hamlet's purloined letter, though the identity of the speaker changes between Q1 and Q2/F1. Durrell refers to the same passage again in 1974 in his novel *Monsieur* (205), but he blends the two variants in that instance. He discusses the nature of the word "machine" in this passage again in 1947 in "From a Writer's Journal" (52).

21. It literally both is and is not: the personal Hamlet and not the social figure of the State of Denmark.

Hamlet,
Prince of China

1938

NO ONE WILL PRINT THEM. I'll tell you why.[1] You choose a title
with the word *Hamlet*, and ring an old psychic chord in the cranium.
You excite the critics in your first letter by some real death-rays on
the subjects, immensely profound: then you begin rough-necking and
capering the theme around in your second: AND THEN SUDDENLY
the whole arena shifts round and empties for a duel between you
and Fraenkel.[2] Your last letter is magnificent. MAGNIFICENT. It's
all magnificent, but why kill the book by calling it *Hamlet*? Because
somehow it's so unexpected, this tissue of mirth and magnificence. It's
all Henry Miller, PRINCE OF DENMARK. When I said in a previous
letter that Hamlet's major problems you had solved for yourself, I was
nearer the mark than I realized. You cannot write anything about
Hamlet because the place it occupies in the Heraldic pattern is below
you. There is only going up, not down. This peculiar English Death[3]
which is epitomized in the play is foreign to you. I say foreign, and
I mean by that—*China*. The stratosphere. It was a stratosphere that
Shakespeare inhabited, but only *wrote* about by accident. Your whole
propensity is set towards the recording of the flora and fauna of that
stratosphere. You have penetrated it further, and at a higher level.
This is not Shakespeare's fault. It was the fault of the damning literary
formulae of his age. If he had faced the world as it is now, in which

canon is no longer based on anything, he would have written things greater than you can IMAGINE. But poor fellow, he didn't realize for a moment that what was the important thing was the description of his inner heraldic territory. Only sometimes the malaise shook him, tied him up, and presto, out of the folds fell a genuine bit of heraldry. When I say this I am not patting you on the back for being a better writer than Shakespeare, QUA WRITER. I am saying that you have realized yourself as a man more fully: *also this important thing*…In our age we have reached a point in writing when it is possible for the writer TO BE HIMSELF on paper. It's more than possible. It's inevitable and necessary. But for the Elizabethan writing was separated from living entirely. The self you put on paper then might have a HALL MARK: that is to say, it was recognizable by a few mannerisms, a style of moral thought, etc. But it no more corresponded to the author than Hamlet corresponds to you. The virtue of the Elizabethans was this: their exuberance was so enormous, so volatile, so pest-ridden, so aching and vile and repentant and spew-struck, that here and there, by glorious mistakes, they transcended the canon. But their critical apparatus was interested only in the NARRATION. Was it good Seneca, or wasn't it?

If you look at the state of criticism now, you will find that a whole terminology of MYSTICISM has entered it. Even the critic has been trying to accustom himself to the disturbing factor which all this new ego-writing has brought to light. Lawrence is bad Seneca, Ben Jonson would have said, and meant it. The man can write, but having opinions about oneself is not enough. He lacks art. Off with his head! Now we have timely recognition that each man is entitled to his own reality, interpret it as he wants. THE HERALDIC REALITY.[4] To the Elizabethan all types of experience were easily alloyed, epitomized, and REDUCED TO THE COMMON DENOMINATOR OF THE INTELLIGENCE. Even now there are traces of that heresy about among writers—the flotsam left over from the cheap scientific hogwash of the last century. Fraenkel seems also to be one of these crows. But what you say clearly enough (damn it!), a thing I have been trying to say myself in private, is that there is only one canon: FAITH. Have you the faith to deliver yourself to the inner world of Gauguin, or haven't you? The critics will get there on about five p.m. next Tuesday. It'll be the death of criticism, but their terminology is so full of VOICES OF EXPERIENCE and SPIRITUAL TERRITORIES that they'll have to do something about it…

Yes, I like what Fraenkel says about you being at a critical pass in your writing. I feel that too. The next few years will show me whether you can support the theory of the ego-protagonist indefinitely. I rather think you can't. I was surprised by *Hamlet*, because I thought that it was going to be a sort of opus: but Fraenkel has reduced it a little by introducing personalities. Its value therefore will be documentary. I'm amazed at the Pacific Ocean which you keep in your nib. The fertility. The immensely fructuous energy. The paper seems quite used up when once you have written something on it. That is why I'm impatient. These are letters from high latitudes, but the drama that's coming as yet—the drama that you have up your sleeve—it scares me a bit. But it's coming. I have an idea, that if any man can bust open the void and figure it out in a new dazzling mythology you can. And I have another idea, probably a bit repellant to you—that when you do give us this thing it will be full of a divine *externality*. IT will be a synthesis not only of the self you have explored so devastatingly in your two books, and of which these letters are a pendant, but also of the Chinese figures which you find in the stratosphere: AND THEIR STRUGGLE. It is that titanic war which I feel you are going to offer us; I don't think the others understand properly…But *Hamlet*? *Hamlet* is going to be the title of this drama of yours. *Hamlet* squared, *Hamlet* cubed, *Hamlet* in an atmosphere which gives trigonometry cold fingers and logic blunt thumbs.

I wonder if I am right. It seems clear. Walking about this dead town[5] among the flies, etc. I had a long and fruitful think about that letter of Fraenkel's. Poor fellow, he wants you to end inside a system. Perhaps even the Catholic system. He cannot bear to see such a high trapeze act without safety nets. He identifies himself so closely with your acrobatics that he vomits at each flutter of your tropical parasol. His only act of bravery is to do a clever trick with death. Death, after all—that is simple. It is here on the ground. But a trapeze…Well, this is impertinent and neither here nor there.

What I thought was this: you have been beating forward into this territory alone, quite alone.[6] In order not to go mad, you had to keep yourself with you as company. That self, the basis of your ego-protagonist work, you raised to a square root. It had to be or else you would have gone crazy. But there is a more terrible time coming. I can't imagine what the work will be like. I can't imagine you writing anything greater than you have and are: but there is some intelligence in my bones that now you are getting a grip on the stratosphere: the self, which you used as a defence against the novel terrors of this heraldic universe (as one might use smoked glass to look at the sun[7]), is diffusing itself: it is less necessary. You are looking round and beginning to see the shapes of things. That ultimate battle, which I tremble when I think about, is almost announced. IN IT ALL THAT IS YOU WILL BE SUBJECTED TO THE DRAMA. YOU WILL LOOSE YOUR POWER OVER THE ARMIES—and the result will be those immense mythical figures which will fertilize all our books for centuries…and our minds. I tell you this in confidence. It may be nonsense, but it's what I feel. No artist as yet has reached the peak you have without being exhausted. Reading these letters I can see clearly that far from being exhausted you are refreshed by each new battle. This is because you travel so light, with such a little baggage.

And this brings me back to Hamlet…Shakespeare, Lawrence & Co. have been crippled from the start by being unable to realize themselves. Consequently the final drama, THE HAMLET, when they wrote it, was entangled in their diseases, held down by them. But you, it seems to me, are going into this final contortion with the purest mind we have yet had, by what propitious circumstances social, literary, and personal God only knows. I said PURE. That is why when you begin this *Hamlet* the veil of the temple will be rent in twain, and it's no good asking people like Fraenkel to hand you the meat-axe for the job. My quarrel with your title is this: THE BOOK IS NOT YOUR HAMLET. And it's a pity to waste the title on it, and have to call the real *Hamlet* *Ophelia* or something. It will never be your *Hamlet* because your correspondent finds the axe too heavy to lift. And even if he could lift it, it wouldn't be your *Hamlet*, because that is something you can only do alone, in your own unorganized privacy.

What I say is this: you can write *Hamlet*, but in the book so far you have only written about *Hamlet*. Incidentally I should read *Hamlet* again—because you have the idea that it is purely a drama of the ideal. But there is more to it. Subtract the ideal and you have the framework of your own struggle, every great artist's struggle, stated terribly. The ideal is secondary—though it is the main thing that disfigures Shaxpeer, all Englishmen really. (Englishmen have always been, in spite of the national anthem, slaves).[8] It is this lie which I want to tackle myself in England. Shax made a complete statement of it, but died from it. You, for your part, are going into it as blind as a hooded falcon, and undiseased in this particular way. *There is no chance of a stillbirth...*

When you do your own opus I hope you call it "Hamlet, Prince of China!"

These letters disturb me profoundly. I was awake a long time last night reading them over a few times, carefully, and brooding on the subjects they throw up. Particularly the subject of the artist. I was reading pieces of *Black Spring* and *Tropic of Cancer*,[9] and trying to isolate a few of the megrims that Fraenkel was trying to lay. It seems he has spotted a disease, but diagnosed it wrongly. The rotting cadaver of the idea, forsooth. There is no cadaver. It is not against this idea that the recoil takes place: and if Fraenkel were artist enough to understand what an artist is he would never have made such an elementary mistake. The trouble with him is that, for his purposes, he denies experience: he only admits types of experience. Hence the complaint when a bit of sunshine and a full belly makes you prod him into a piece of writing for a change. But I feel he is right when he says there is yet a battle to be fought. Last night I felt it, but I had no idea what it was. Then a shrewd remark of Nancy's[10] started the fuse going and I was grubbing about among books and notes to try and lay it. The mechanism which Jung calls the guilt-responsibility, which you quoted. The germ of it is in there. I was thinking of Cezanne's fear that society would get the grappins on him: of Gauguin's insistence on what a hell of a fine billiards player he was: of Lawrence fervidly knitting, knitting, and trying to forget *Sons and Lovers*.[11] AND OF YOU EATING! Here are numberless types of the same ambiguous desire on the part of the artist to renounce his destiny. To spit on it. O Lord, if it be thy will, let this cup be taken from me. So that when Fraenkel complains that the first spring day makes you murder the idea he is really saying that no sooner is the larder full than you have the very natural desire to call it a shoemaker's holiday[12] and a fig for Momus.[13] But in your books there are also numerous full larders. You say in big strident tones: I AM A MAN. THAT IS ENOUGH.[14] Because you know that an artist can hardly taste his food, he is so weak with virtue. If it were possible you would like to go on saying I AM A MAN ad lib.—in order to hide the more terrible stage whisper: I AM AN ARTIST: and from there to the ultimate blinding conclusion: I AM GOD!!![15] It is this role which confuses you by its limitless scope. And it is in this area of the soul that that germ of the final thunderclap is breeding.

Therefore I can see more clearly what actuates your disgust for Hamlet. Here is a something which is the reverse of the Miller coin. As a man you are realized: BUT YOU ARE TRYING TO AVOID SEEING CLEARLY THAT YOU ARE SHORTLY TO REALIZE YOURSELF AS AN ARTIST. I MEAN AS GOD. With Shakespeare and the other English it seems that they have only realized themselves imperfectly as men: and consequently that image when projected into the opus (the opus *I am God*) limits the scope of the final cataclysm: because to be God greater than anyone else has been it is first necessary to qualify as a greater MAN than anyone else. THIS IS THE EXACT NATURE OF THAT CHINESE STILL-LIFE I WAS TALKING ABOUT LAST NIGHT. As for Fraenkel, he spends his time trying to be God, but there is no man in his God to represent us. That is what poisons his systems. The trinity—Man, Mind, and Monster—is short by one head: MAN. That is why he pedals vaguely from place to place on that antiquated intellectual bicycle and murmurs sweet nothings about the universal sciences and TRUTH! As a writer I don't think he's realized himself... There are some people who can only realize themselves in the past. This is because they are afraid of death. The fascination of the past is the fascination of those things and people who have conquered, viz., passed thru and experienced DEATH...

These Hamlet letters are going to be very valuable as the log of that ultimate journey: I can feel the first peeled statement breaking from them. If only the issues could be cleared and instead of fighting Fraenkel's obsolete battles for him you had time to concentrate on your own, which is more important, I'd be happier. I was thinking all night about Hamlet, Prince of China, and the colonizing of that empty territory out there, beyond Ararat and the Gobi and Thibet and Ecuador.[16] It tires me, this terrible subject. I have to keep going and having a snack and repeating to myself the magic incantation: I AM A MAN. THAT IS ENOUGH. For me it will be enough, I hope, if I ever am. My ambitions are hedge-hopping and clipped of wing. As for you, you are about to do something NEW. No one as yet has been what you are in the mammalian sense. The question is QUO VADIS?[17] Father and Son in all their glory—there remains only the ghost. YOUR HAMLET'S GHOST. Then, and only then, will it be laid...I am writing this letter extremely solemnly and passionately as a salute to you AS YOU ENTER THE INFERNAL REGIONS.

NOTES

1. "This letter was addressed by Mr. Durrell to Henry Miller regarding the book, *Hamlet*, by Michael Fraenkel and Henry Miller to be published next year." (Durrell's original note). Durrell's letter was originally sent from Corfu in mid-January 1937 (Durrell and Miller 42).

2. Michael Fraenkel (1897–1957) was an American poet and critic who corresponded extensively with Miller.

3. Durrell developed the notion of the English Death in his novel of the same year, *The Black Book*, which Miller would have already read in typescript by this time.

4. Durrell's notion of the Heraldic Universe had already been articulated in his September or October 1936 letter to Miller (dated August in MacNiven's edition), in which the notion is closely aligned with refuting Herbert Read's temporary support for communism during the London International Surrealist Exhibition (Durrell, *Durrell–Miller* 17–19; Miller, "Henry Miller's" 33).

5. Corfu Town, Greece.

6. The language here is very close to Durrell's letter to Miller in which he rebuts Herbert Read's communism in contrast to the anarchism Miller espouses. Only four months earlier Durrell wrote to Miller as an interlocutor in his correspondence with Read: "What I propose to do, with all deadly solemnity, is to create my HERALDIC UNIVERSE quite alone. The foundation of which is being quietly laid. I AM SLOWLY BUT VERY CAREFULLY AND WITHOUT ANY CONSCIOUS THOUGHT DESTROYING TIME" (Durrell, *Durrell–Miller* 18).

7. Durrell later uses a similar phrase to finish his "The Heraldic Universe," which appears in this volume (103–05).

8. Durrell makes the same comment, alluding to Thomas Arne's "Rule Britannia," in "The Prince and Hamlet: A Diagnosis" (this volume 63–71).

9. Miller published his novel *Tropic of Cancer* in 1934 and the follow-up collection of short prose *Black Spring* in 1936.

10. Nancy Hodgkin, née Myers, Durrell's first wife.

11. D.H. Lawrence's novel *Sons and Lovers*, perhaps his best novel.

12. A year earlier, Durrell alluded to Thomas Dekker's Elizabethan play of 1599, *The Shoemaker's Holiday* (Durrell, *Panic* 17).

13. Thomas Lodge's (1558–1625) satirical prose work of 1595.

14. The structure of this phrase, and its repetition in the final paragraph, are akin to Durrell's alter ego's realization on the final page of *Pied Piper of Lovers* that "I know something, though, that's very startling—absolute mental dynamite. That is: 'I am, and quite soon I will not be.' Isn't that enough?" (253).

15. The same phrase appears at the opening of Durrell's short story "Zero" published a year after this essay (8).

16. Durrell uses the same notion of colonizing death nearly forty years later in his novel *Monsieur*: "Even death has its own precise texture, and the big philosophers have always entered into the image of the world it exemplifies while still alive, so to become one with it while their hearts were still beating. They colonised it" (21).

17. Latin: "Where are you going?" The phrase is primarily in the Christian tradition, John 13:36, "Simon Peter said unto him, Lord, whither goest thou? Jesus answered him, Whither I go, thou canst not follow me now; but thou shalt follow me afterwards." The phrase was also the title of a famous historical novel, *Quo Vadis: A Narrative in the Time of Nero*, by Henryk Sienkiewicz, who won the Nobel Prize in Literature in 1905.

Prospero's Isle
To Caliban

1939

TO THE ELIZABETHAN, travel abroad was a good deal more than a luxury or a pleasure; it was the duty of the nobleman as well as his right. The age was inevitably an age of gentlemen made conscious of their gentility by the rising power of the middle classes. Throughout the Tudor age the power of the landed nobles had been slowly but relentlessly clipped; under Elizabeth the process of centralization was carried on; and by the time James came to the throne the subjection was more or less complete. By then titles were for sale and the trespassing plutocrat could measure nobility against his bank-book. Already in the shining nineties the decay of nobility was being bitterly lamented, while the carpet knight had already arrived on the scene; Shakespeare himself, remember, joined in the unseemly scramble for arms and quarterings—the *Non Sans Droit* on his shield has a pleasantly defensive ring! As for the wild crowd of literary men—the gingerbread heroes of the pamphlet world like Nashe and Greene[1]— they never lost an opportunity of adding the dignity *Gent* to their title-pages; whatever their behaviour was like, their extraction, they gave the world to understand, was unquestionable.

All this has a certain bearing on the question of Shakespeare's problematical travels; his own testimony shows that, had the chance ever come to him, he would have been man enough of the age to take it.

He wondered that your lordship
Would suffer him to spend his youth at home,
While other men, of slender reputation,
Put forth their sons to seek preferment out
Some to the wars, to try their fortunes there;
Some to discover islands far away;
Some to studious universities.
For any or for all these exercises
He said that Proteus your son was meet,
And did request me to importune you
To let him spend his time no more at home,
Which would be great impeachment to his age
In having known no travel in his youth.[2]

Apart from the pure *snobism*, however, which forced men of slender reputation to put forth their sons, there were purely literary and cultural criteria prevailing; there was the immense cultural accent placed upon the antique works and the countries in which they had been hatched. The English language was still apologetic about itself. The courtier could be witty in several languages; and learned in two or three. Here is the sententious Mr. Howell on the subject; a Welshman with the inevitable bias for Wales, his writings reflect him as a typical mannered arbiter of fashionable travel—the touring gentleman's gentleman.

"*Amongst other peoples of the earth,*" says he, "*Islanders seem most in need of foreign travel, for they being cut off (as it were) from the rest of the citizens of the world, have not those obvious accesses, and contiguity of situation, and other advantages of society, to mingle with those more refined nations, whom Learning and Knowledge did since urbanize and polish.*"[3]

The Elizabethan was more than willing to be urbanized and polished; he was avid for it. His whole literature took its formal impetus from exotic models; no paper war could be fought which did not invoke the Classical ghosts of literature at least twice a page. Antiquity was the universal provider. Quite half the writers strangled themselves and their work by an application to foreign manners and tongues; more than half did the grand tour, even if it was on foot like Munday.[4] A few managed to do it in the grand manner, like Sir Thomas Unton,[5] who walked across France with an umbrella, preceded by a menial who announced him with a flourish outside the gates of each town they passed through.

Whether Shakespeare was among those who travelled nobody knows; the critics who detected a "heightened colouring" in *Lucrece* which might perhaps indicate a visit abroad, do not tell us precisely what sort of travel-colouring was native to the Elizabethan mind. One thing is certain: it was in no way scenic or pastoral, but antiquarian rather and provincial—as anyone who opens Coryat[6] can see for himself. The olive and cypress were symbols of the contemporary poetic thought—not testimonies of quickened eyesight or unfamiliar landscapes. They were borrowed direct from Virgil and the rest. No. The reigning marvels were of a different order. Urban mannerisms, forms of dress, and curious machines—those were the exciting items which touring *parvenus* like Coryat jumped at. This eccentric and delightful courtier whose passion for walking landed him finally in India (where he died), never fails to sacrifice scenery for marvels of architecture or mechanics. Almost his only piece of natural travel-writing as we (the descendants of Borrow) know it today is his description of a channel-crossing, which took him seven hours and ended only when *"I had varnished the exterior parts of the ship with the excremental ebullitions of my tumultuous stomach, as desiring to satiate the gormandising paunches of the hungry haddocks."*[7] Between his infectious bouts of buffoonery we get occasional glimpses of towns and manners—but it is always the eye of the courtier at work, the vision of the townee traveller. It is fairly certain from all this that the literary colouring which we should expect to find in the writers of the time is usually absent; like awed antiquaries they pursued their dutiful tours, but brought back what one would least expect of them—urban memoranda instead of novelty in landscapes.

In the case of Shakespeare, who is to be certain? A great number of his plays were written into foreign settings; but this argues for a possible unfamiliarity with the continent. The sea-coast of Bohemia has become a critical chestnut; it is used as proof positive that he did not know what he was talking about. Yet the mistake was lifted direct from Greene, as was the plot of the play.[8]

In the criticism of the day no very great emphasis has been laid on the Venetian plays: the plays whose setting was concerned with the domains of the Venetian Republic. It is perhaps a subject that lacks interest for those whose scholarship is not speculative but factual. Yet I would like to point out that Venice was, to all intents and purposes, the boundary of the known Europe, and as such would be a possible *dramatic* boundary which the Elizabethan would not trespass. This has a certain relation to what I am about to write on the subject of *The Tempest*. Howell remarks, "How the Signory of Venice is the greatest rampart of Christendome against the Turk by sea."[9] Venice at that time owned a large portion of what today is Greece—notably the Ionian islands which still have so many legacies of this great occupation. Read any of the Elizabethan travel-books and you will notice the air of unfamiliarity which enters them once they move beyond the confines of the Venetian republic. It is the "Great Turk's Land" which looms up then: unfamiliar, religiously alien, obscure. It has the same ring as the word "Muscovy." It was to the Elizabethan what *Prester John*[10] was to the medieval man: as unreal and exciting as Mandeville's quaint bestiary. My point here is simply that *dramatically* the subject was too exotic for great treatment. Shakespeare stops short at Cyprus, where a frontier battle was fought against the hideous Ottoman. The travellers penetrated deeper—Sandys, Lithgow, Coryat, Fynes Moryson[11]—the list is a formidable one. But the geographical boundaries of Venice were good enough for Shakespeare; *Othello* at Cyprus, *Measure for*

Measure pitched in Sicily, *Anthony and Cleopatra* further south in Arta, *The Merchant of Venice* in the great capital city of the Republic which was the marvel and enjoyment of every traveller. These are not the only plays whose setting is Neapolitan; but these are the plays whose impulse and interest is Venetian; today we should say "Dalmatian."

The Barbary coast[12] was a dangerous and indented coast-line swarming with armed pirates—a large portion of whom, by the way, were English. The Venetian State papers in the British Museum which deal with the Ionian Islands bristle with the names of English robbers, whose capabilities for loot were quite equal to those of the Turk himself. The great sea-lines of the Republic were continually nibbled for plunder by the pirates, operating from the islands north and south of Corfu. By Shakespeare's time there were still maritime difficulties with these seafaring vagabonds. Argosies of merchandise were lost and written off the sheets; thus Shylock on the Rialto.

Ships are but boards, Sailors but
men: there be Land Rats and Water Rats:
Water thieves and Land thieves: I mean
Pirates.[13]

In the Venetian plays (the last of which, as I hope to demonstrate, being *The Tempest*) there is a connection which argues for a geographical familiarity; perhaps not personal, but second hand. There is no proof that Shakespeare knew the Ionian from his own personal experience. Both the Rome and Athens of the fustian plays become anonymous classical localities; and the few dim touches in *A Midsummer Night's Dream* do not carry us much further south than Dulwich; to argue for a greater verisimilitude with regard to Verona, Padua, Vienna, would also be of little use. The detail of *Anthony and Cleopatra* is from Plutarch; and there is only one Grecian touch. It is when Anthony says:

Is it not strange, Camidius,
That from Tarentum and Brundisium,
He could so quickly cut the Ionian Sea
And take in Toryne?[14]

The battle of *Actium* itself does not afford a single clue to locality; yet the place-names are bandied about with a familiarity which may well be bookish. Anthony's desire to live "a private man in Athens" (a desire shared most ardently by the writer) does not indicate an Athens any newer than classical. Greece itself was very largely unknown; the mainland at any rate. There was a caravan route across Greece to Asia Minor, which Howell recommends as an alternative route to the Ionian one (the better known). But the sad plight of Greece then evokes the following note:

Here he (the traveller) may ruthfully observe how that great
country, which used to be the source of all speculative knowledge,
as also of policy and prowess, is now overwhelmed with barbarism
and ignorance, with slavery and abjection of spirit. He will admire
how the whole people are degenerated both in their hearts and
heads, from the ancient courage and knowledge they were so cried
up for in former ages.[15]

Yet he mentions that the pure Greek spirit must be sought among the mountains, among the "Epirotiques."[16]

This argues a certain degree of thoroughness in Howell's investigations; Welshman though he was, it did not prevent him from making a few excellent observations on the language of the Greek mainland and the islands. *"There is also,"* he says, *"a mongrel dialect composed of Italian and French, and some Spanish words also in it, which they call Franco, that is used in many of the islands of the Aegean sea: and it is the ordinary speech of commerce 'twixt Christians, Jews, Turks and Greeks in the Levant."*[17] To the best of my knowledge this dialect still persists in the Venetian private language of the Ionian Jews of today. *"Nor,"* adds the untiring Howell, *"is some vulgar Greek so far adulterated and eloignated from the true Greek, for there is yet in some places of the Morea true Greek spoken."*[18] He adds that until quite recently in Italy herself, as in Calabria and Apulia, the Liturgy was in Greek. This seems to demonstrate a very close and accurate knowledge of the Ionian on the part of an Englishman.

It will be fairly apparent by now that in dealing with *The Tempest* I am about to put forth a theory which involves Venice. The island which Shakespeare had in mind is almost certainly an Ionian island. The colouring was not West Indian—if only because the West Indies were too remotely and fancifully new to offer him a sound *conceptual* basis. Venice was the boundary of the poetic imagination; and in searching for an imaginary island he chose one of the Venetian islands.

This is not to say that a marmoset or two did not creep in amongst the pieces of Southern *décor*—the machinery of Ariel. Herein lay his concession to modernity as the Elizabethan knew it. The West Indies would have been a difficult setting for a cast of Neapolitan noblemen, bound home for Naples; more likely Zante or Corfu; most likely a dim backwash of memory blending the two from the tales of a travelling merchant. Is there any evidence? Coryat certainly touched Zante. William Webbe[19] was lugged up through the Seven Isles by his misfortunes at sea. Lithgow, more useful still, reports the steady importation of currants from Zante to England, "where some liquorish lips forsooth can now hardly digest Bread, Pasties, Broth and bag puddings without these currants."[20] It will be seen from this that the trade was no small one; and if one needs testimony that the name Zante was familiar to Londoners of that time, it is only necessary to turn to the *Ortho-Epia Gallica* of John Eliot.[21] This is a quaint phrasebook for French students, which is made up of descriptive dialogues. I imagine that the scope of its reference would be restricted to the topical and immediate in Elizabethan London. Yet even here we find Zante mentioned:

Is the Fleet returned from Bourdis?
You hear no news of the Tripoli and
Zante ships?[22]

It is surely not unlikely that the storm which broke up the Naples-bound fleet carried them past the heel of Italy into the Ionian Sea.

It would do no harm to examine the text of the play itself, and see whether there are any geographical hints as to its situation. The reference to the "*still-vext Bermoothes*" has been pounced upon as an indication of a familiarity with Sylvester Jourdain's *Discovery of the Bermudas*;[23] but the actual context shows that the locality is used to indicate the speed of Ariel, who could be sent from Prospero's island as far as Bermuda for dew; Bermuda, then, being a place incredibly far from the island. Thus Ariel:

Safely in harbour
Is the King's ship, in the deep nook where once
Thou call'dst me up at midnight to fetch dew
From the still-vext Bermoothes, there she's hid.[24]

I suggest that Shakespeare was influenced by the tales he had been told by some Ionian merchant; some friendly gossip on the London exchange who swapped salt-water yarns for tobacco or ale. From such a person he would have heard of the incomparable and exquisite island of Corcyra (now Corfu); the amount of philological talent which has been exhausted in trying to find a source for the name Sycorax might well have been saved. For Corcyra in anagram gives one almost Sycorax.

Caliban's curse, too, is special to a land where the sirocco[25] is the worst kind of weather. "*A south-west blow on ye,*" he screams, "*and blister ye all o'er.*"[26] Merchants plying from Zante would have encountered this pestilent Levantine wind.

But this is not all; certain small items among the "qualities of the isle" have a Grecian flavour. Both Corcyra and Zante were famous for the "brine-pits" which Caliban mentions; indeed the Venetian salt-pans in the south of Corfu still exist and salt is still extracted from them. Something more than coincidence perhaps prompts the remark of the castaway Antonio:

What impossible matter will he make easy next?[27]

Sebastian's answer is this:

I think he will carry this island home in his pocket and give it to his son for an apple.[28]

As a matter of fact Corcyra was presented to a Venetian in 1259, as a dowry; it is an extraordinary enough present even for those times—an island forty miles long and eight broad. Manfred, King of Sicily, became the owner of it by marrying the daughter of Michael II of Epirus.

Something of these matters I have no doubt was talked over and jumbled with other foreign colours in Shakespeare's mind. Just as the gossip of Dowland[29] gave him the vague outlines of Elsinore for Hamlet, so the chatter of some Ionian merchant gave him a sea of islands, in which he could choose for himself a site for Prospero.

Thy turfy mountains where live nibbling sheep,
And flat medes thatched with clover, them to keep
Thy banks with pioned and with twilled brims,
Which spungy April at her best betrims
To make cold nymphs chaste crowns; and thy broom-groves
Whose shadow the dismissed Bachelor loves,
Being lass-lorn: thy pole-clipped vineyard
And thy sea-marge sterile and rocky-hard.[30]

There is another point which has caused a certain amount of contention among the wise.

"Though woulds't give me," says Caliban,
"Water with berries in't."[31]

The ghost of Fynes Moryson is here invoked to prove that coffee
is the suggested drink. But there is a peculiarly national drink which
answers the case much better. It is made of cherry jam, of which
a spoonful is mixed in cold water. There seems to be no reason to
doubt that this was the drink which our anonymous merchant told
Shakespeare about. When he came to write *The Tempest* there existed
in his mind the flavour of these names and facts; so that Prospero's
island is really a mixture of Zante and Corcyra.

Here I would like to explain that I am aware of the symbolic prop-
erties of the isle; I am aware that *The Tempest* is really a lucid parable
which touches the island of the heart's desire; and that in pressing
for a reference to Corfu I am animated only by a most fervent Ionian
patriotism. It has not been my intention to drive nails into the coffin
of legitimate criticism—the graveyard property of others. But there *do*
seem analogies worth mentioning; and they *do* point with tolerable
conviction to Corcyra (already celebrated by Homer in the *Odyssey*).
There remains one conjecture more which will perhaps serve to drive
home my argument.

The most famous of the patron saints among the Seven Islands is
St. Spiridian. A synoptic history of his life, covering the period of his
early adventures, would make exciting reading. Born a Cypriot in the
third century or thereabouts, he was destined to become Corcyrean by
posthumous adoption. Dead, buried, forgotten, the body of the good
bishop of Tremythous in Cyprus (for such was he) was only rediscovered a hundred and one years after his death. From the grave exhaled a
powerful scent of spices, which drew attention to the saint. The body,
once recovered, began to perform miracles no less miraculous than
its subsequent adventures and travels. From Constantinople through
Macedonia he travelled, always under the protection of well-wishing
believers; he arrived in Corcyra about the year 1456. His adoption was

spontaneous—by the consent of both parties; for subsequent history shows the saint to have been a stout miracle worker against the Turks, who were at the time ravaging the coasts of the island. I will not give a detailed account of the argosies he sank, nor the number of times he saved the island from famine by side-tracking convoys of food bound for other ports and impelling their captains to put into Corfu harbour. It is sufficient to say that sailors have always been the children of St. Spiridian; their safety has always depended, and still depends, on his spiritual seamanship. In honour of him children are named Spiro (which is fairly near to Prospero). I defy anyone to travel for a day in Greece, among the islands, without encountering several Spiros. In the Ionian you will scarcely ever see a ship without its little eikon of the saint; it will generally depict him coaxing a storm, a mildly Byzantine and benevolent figure in a cloud. Any such eikon could be used to illustrate *The Tempest*. The likeness between the good saint and Prospero is fairly close. I like to think that in St. Spiridian we have here the original wonder-worker, saint, good man, whom Prospero so much resembles. Those who had travelled in the Ionian (and I hope I have made it clear that many a Londoner of the day did so) could not help hearing of the wonder-working saint; it is even possible that some forsook St. George, whose saving graces are lacking in the spectacular and generous; in favour of this little Ionian saint, whose mummified body is still carried round the Esplanade during festivals, lolling upright in his red sedan-chair. That Prospero, the courtly necromancer of the isle, should be second cousin by conversation, as it were, is not such a frivolous idea as it might seem. His powers over the creatures of the island are no stronger (and no less strong) than the power which St. Spiridian exercises over the hearts and minds of the Corcyreans. There is a certain poetic justice about these matters. The concerns of a saint and a poet in this case converge upon a point of virtue and benevolence; for *The Tempest* is the most lucidly Taoist of the plays, and the most fitting ending to the great wild cycle of comedies and tragedies. It is pleasant to think that these islands became entangled with the dream of the old English poet; influencing him, as they had influenced Homer so many years before. And then: the renunciation of Prospero! Concealed behind this fantasy surely there is a clear statement of the artistic problem—the problem which finds expression in Faust, in the Abbey Theleme of Rabelais[32] (which is only another Prospero's isle): the problem, I make so bold as to say, which the great artist shares with the saint. Here is the pure statement of the case—for all who have ears to hear.[33] Prospero's last words are a beatitude.

> *By now my charms are all o'erthrown,*
> *And what strength I have's mine own,*
> *Which is most faint: now 'tis true*
> *I must be here confined by you*
> *Or sent to Naples: Let me not*
> *Since I have my Dukedome got,*
> *And pardoned the deceiver, dwell*
> *In this bare island by your spell;*
> *But release me from my bands*
> *With the help of your good hands:*
> *Gentle breath of yours, my sails*
> *Must fill, or else my project fails,*
> *Which was to please: Now I want*
> *Spirits to enforce, Arts to enchant:*
> *And my ending is despair,*
> *Unless I be relieved by prayer,*
> *Which pierces so that it assaults*
> *Mercy itself and frees all faults.*[34]

The magician's renunciation of his power is one of the most profound things in Shakespeare; he puts himself at the mercy of the elements which he has learned so painfully how to control. Perhaps Prospero in these lines shows that he had discovered the paradox in things; he had discovered that he who comes down to earth finds himself nearest to heaven.

It is a lesson which all magicians must learn sooner or later: whether they be saints or poets.

SOURCES

Ortho-Epia Gallica by John Eliot, 1593

Instruction for Forreine Travel by J. Howell, 1642

Travel-Diary of Fynes Moryson, 1617

Coryat's Crudities by Tom Coryat, 1611

William Webbe, Hys Travels, 1604

Painful Peregrinations, etc., by William Lithgow, 1614

A Synoptic History of Corfu, with an account of a Famous Patron Saint by Dr. Theodore Stephanides, Corfu, 1938

NOTES

1. Thomas Nashe (1567–1601) and Robert Greene (1558–1592) were English playwrights, and both were involved in extensive pamphleteering campaigns, ranging from religious to artistic and satiric topics.

2. Shakespeare's *Two Gentlemen of Verona* I.iii.307.

3. James Howell (1594–1666) was a Welsh writer, and Durrell is referring to his 1642 book *Instructions for Forrainne Travell* (13).

4. Anthony Munday (1553–1633) was a dramatist who collaborated with Shakespeare on the play *Sir Thomas More*. He was known for his Italianate interests and for having taken the Grand Tour of Europe on foot beginning in 1578, which led to his *The English Romayne Lyfe* in 1582.

5. Unton (–1553) was knighted at the coronation of Anne Boleyn in 1533. Durrell appears to be inventing this history since Unton pre-dates the use of the umbrella, per se, in England.

6. Thomas Coryat (1577–1617) is known for this travel writings, mainly *Coryat's Crudities Hastily Gobbled up in Five Months Travels in France, Italy, &c* and *Coryats*

Crambe, or His Coleworte Twice Sodden (1611), both set in Europe, and his Mediterranean, Persian, and Indian letters in *Greetings from the Court of the Great Mogul* (1616).

7. Coryat, *Coryat's Crudities* (1). Durrell's personal copy of this volume is the two-volume edition by James MacLehose and Sons with Macmillan, 1905, held in the Morris Library, Southern Illinois University, Carbondale.

8. This is a longstanding critical debate, beginning with Ben Jonson pointing out that there was no seacoast. Dozens of critical works had debated this problem and noted that Robert Greene's play *Pandosto: The Triumph of Time*, Shakespeare's source, used the seacoast of Sicily, though it also uses the Isle of Delphos.

9. Howell 45.

10. A mythical king ruling over a lost Christian nation in the Orient.

11. George Sandys (1577–1644), William Lithgow (1582–1645), Coryat, and Fynes Moryson (1566–1630) were all Elizabethan travellers and writers.

12. The coast of North Africa.

13. Shakespeare, *The Merchant of Venice* I.iii.346–48.

14. III.vii.1883–86.

15. Howell 83.

16. Howell 50.

17. Howell 53.

18. Howell 56.

19. Webbe (1568–1591) was a well-known English critic and translator at the time. Durrell's source is uncertain, and little is known of Webbe.

20. As previously, Durrell's source is unknown, but this passage is quoted in Thomas Secombe's *The Age of Shakespeare (1579–1631)* (208), as is the previous quotation from Howell (206).

21. Eliot published this work in Latin in 1593. Durrell may have learned of it through F. Yates's 1931 article "The Importance of John Eliot's *Ortho-Epia Gallica*" (419–30), and he is certainly referring to the reprinting of Eliot's work in extract form in English in 1928 as *The Parlement of Pratlers*, edited by Jack Lindsay, which bears the subtitle *A Book on the Corect Pronunciation of the French Language*.

22. Eliot, *The Parlement of Pratlers*, n. pag.

23. Jourdain's pamphlet was first published in 1610 and is frequently referred to in attempts to date Shakespeare's *The Tempest*.

24. *The Tempest* I.ii.345–48. This passage is often modernized to "still-vexed Bermudas."

25. A wind on the Mediterranean from the Sahara desert.

26. *The Tempest* I.ii.461–62.

27. *The Tempest* II.i.762.
28. *The Tempest* II.i.763–64.
29. John Dowland (1563–1626) was a famous composer and lutenist who also had patronage from Denmark at the time of *Hamlet*'s first performance. The speculation is that Dowland could have offered information about Denmark and Elsinore at the time.
30. *The Tempest* II.i.1720–27.
31. *The Tempest* I.ii.472–73.
32. Christopher Marlowe's (1564–1963) play *Doctor Faustus* (1594). The Abbey Thélème appears in the first portion of François Rabelais's (1494–1553) *Gargantua and Pantaguel*.
33. Matthew 11:15, "He that hath ears to hear, let him hear." Durrell plays off this same passage repeatedly in his contemporary short story "Asylum in the Snow."
34. *The Tempest* Epilogue, 2321–39.

Ideas About
Poems
1942

1. Neither poet nor public is really interested in the poem itself but in aspects of it.
2. The poet is interested in the Personal aspect: the poem as an aspect of himself.
3. The public is interested in the Vicarious aspect; that is to say "the universal application," which is an illusion that grows round a poem once the logical meaning is clear and the syntax ceases to puzzle.
4. This is why good poems get written despite bad poets and why bad publics often choose right.

MEANWHILE.

the poem itself is there all the time. The sum of these aspects, it is quite different to what the poet and the public imagine it to be. Like a child or a climate it is quite outside us and our theories don't affect it in any way. Just as climate must be endured and children kept amused, the poem as a Fact must be dressed up sometimes and sent to the Zoo—to get rid of it. It is part of the ritual of endurance merely. That is the only explanation for *Personal Landscape* now.[1] People say that writing Poetry is one of the only non-Gadarene occupations left—but this is only another theory or aspect. Poems are Facts, and if they don't speak for themselves it's because they were born without tongues.

NOTE

1. This short piece appeared at the beginning of the first issue of *Personal Landscape*, the periodical edited in Cairo during World War II by Durrell, Robin Fedden, and Bernard Spencer. Each subsequent issue included an "Ideas About Poems" segment that personalized rather than politicized poetry, despite their proximity to, and the immediate threat of, the war. The kindred terminology of "Ideas About Poems" to the "Attitudes" about Personalism adopted by the New Apocalypse poets in the following year, 1943, is suggestive. G.S. Fraser, who contributed to *Personal Landscape* and was a friend to the three editors, was also an important contributor to the original New Apocalypse anthologies in London in the preceding years. The personalist nature of both groups appears anti-authoritarian in the same manner as Herbert Read's notion of the politics of the unpolitical.

Ideas About Poems II

The schizophrene, the cyclothyme,
Pass from the droll to the sublime.
Coming of epileptoid stock
They tell the time without a clock.

NONSENSE IS NEVER JUST NONSENSE; it is more like good sense
with all the logic removed. At its highest point poetry makes use of
nonsense in order to indicate a level of experience beyond the causality
principle. You don't quicken or laugh at nonsense because it is complete
non-sense; but because you detect its resemblance to sense.

Logic, syntax, is a causal instrument, inadequate for the task of
describing the whole of reality. Poems don't describe, but they are
sounding-boards which enable the alert consciousness to pick up the
reverberations of the extra-causal reality for itself.

Poems are negatives; hold them up to a clean surface of daylight and
you get an apprehension of grace. The words carry in them complete
submerged poems; as you read your memory goes down like the loud
pedal of a piano, and all tribal, personal, associations begin to rever-
berate. Poems are blueprints. They are not buildings but they enable
you to build for yourself. Serious nonsense and funny nonsense are of
the same order: both overreach causality and open a dimension

independent of logic but quite real. Shakespear and Lear are twins who do not dress alike. Serious nonsense and comical nonsense have a common origin, and an uncommon expression.

Nothing is lost, sweet self
Nothing is ever lost.
The spoken word
Is not exhausted but can be heard.
Music that stains the silence remains,
O! echo is everywhere the unbeckonable bird![1]

NOTE

1.   This stanza is later modified to become Durrell's poem "Echo" (1943).

The Heraldic Universe

1942

Logic tries to describe the world; but it is never found adequate for the task. Logic is not really an instrument: merely a method.

Describing, logic limits. Its law is causality.

Poetry by an associative approach transcends its own syntax in order not to describe but to be the cause of apprehension in others:

Transcending logic it invades a realm where unreason reigns, and where the relations between ideas are sympathetic and mysterious— affective—rather than causal, objective, substitutional.[1]

I call this The Heraldic Universe,[2] because in Heraldry the object is used in an emotive and affective sense—statically to body forth or utter: not as a victim of description.

The Heraldic Universe is that territory of experience in which the symbol exists—as opposed to the emblem or badge, which are the children of algebra and substitution.

It is not a "state of mind" but a continuous self-subsisting plane of reality towards which the spiritual self of man is trying to reach out through various media: artists like antennae boring into the unknown through music or paint or words, suddenly strike this Universe where for every object in the known world there exists an ideogram.[3]

Since words are inadequate they can only render all this negatively— by an oblique method.

"Art" then is only the smoked glass through which we can look at the dangerous sun.[4]

NOTES

1. The New Apocalypse revised its manifesto to adopt a position of anarchist "Personalism" the following year and used a similar description that rebuffs allusions to T.S. Eliot's impersonal theory of poetry in "Tradition and the Individual Talent": "[the artist's] own personality must transmute the artistic materials presented to it, must give form and life where none had existed before" and "Does the artist search for a completion, a pattern, a purpose in the world about him...? Does he use his creative personality to bring about such a pattern...? If he does, he is a Personalist artist" (Treece 217, 219).

2. Although Durrell first noted his Heraldic ideas in print in 1938, this short piece is his first published work on his notion of the Heraldic Universe. The concept itself first appeared in his letters to Henry Miller in 1936: "What I propose to do, with all deadly solemnity, is to create my Heraldic Universe quite alone...I am slowly but very carefully and without any conscious thought destroying time" (Durrell and Miller 18). See Pine's detailed discussion in *Lawrence Durrell: The Mindscape* as well as Lee Lemon's "Durrell, Derrida, and the Heraldic Universe" (62–69). The term "Heraldic Universe" is also political in nature via its relationship to the anarchism of Herbert Read and Miller, and the letter in which it first appeared is a largely unrecognized point-by-point response to Read's work on Surrealism and communism (Gifford, "Anarchist" 61–63).

3. Durrell is likely thinking of Ezra Pound's notion of the Chinese language as ideo-grammic and as an ideal for poetic work.

4. Durrell previously used a similar phrase to describe the Heraldic Universe in his January 1937 letter to Henry Miller (later published as an essay, "Hamlet, Prince of China," in 1938), which is included in this volume (73–81).

Hellene and
Philhellene

1949

THE INFLUENCE OF HELLAS upon our own literature is a theme of
sufficient interest today to tempt the skill of the essayist bold enough
to face its implications fully; bold enough moreover to assess that
influence in the terms of the new literature which the modern Greek
is attempting so obstinately to forge from the popular tongue. "Hellas"
is written rather than "Greece" in order first of all to point the difference between the Philhellene of yesterday and the Philhellene of
today—for up to almost the present generation the passionate bias of
the English writer and scholar has been towards the classical world.
In a sense Greece has represented to him, in terms of landscape and
climate, the flowering of an education. Those unmanageable verbs,
those murderous moods and tenses, the quicksand of Attic syntax—
they all seemed to fall into place to justify themselves against the
Greek landscape. But the classical bias has had its defects no less than
its virtues. It has tended to blindfold the traveller to the reality of
contemporary Greece.[1] Wrapped like a mummy in his classical associations, he has been tempted to dismiss the Greeks of today with
contempt. This attitude of neglect has remained a constant almost
since the time when William Lithgow[2] visited Greece in the course of
his painful but often amusing peregrinations. It is difficult perhaps to
say exactly why and exactly when it changed.

Trelawny has recorded Shelley's[3] emotions on being taken aboard a dirty Greek caïque at Leghorn. "As you are writing a poem *Hellas*, about the modern Greeks," said Trelawny, not without a certain sly humour,

> *would it not be as well to take a look at them? I hear their shrill nasal voices and should like to know if you can trace in the language or lineaments of these Greeks of the 19th century A.D. the faintest resemblance to the lofty and sublime spirits who lived in the fourth century B.C. An English merchant who has dealings with them told me he thought these modern Greeks were if judged by their actions a cross between the Jews and the Gypsies.*[4]

It was a difficult question to put to a Philhellene of Shelley's kind. Yet it was a point well worth trying to clear up. Reluctantly the poet of freedom was dragged aboard the vessel to stand in the midst of her "chattering and irascible crew.... They squatted about the decks in small knots, shrieking, gesticulating, smoking, eating, and gambling like savages." Trelawny watched Shelley's face as the poet stood among them. "Does this realize your idea of Hellenism, Shelley?" he asked at last.[5]

"No. But it does of Hell," replied the poet in hollow tones anxious to escape back into fancy and leave the cold facts to take care of themselves. But Trelawny had not yet finished. They visited the captain in his cabin, where a "flaming gaudy daub of a saint" looked down at them in the light of the spirit-lamp which burned before him. The saint was San Spiridione[6]—which suggests that the vessel was a caïque of Corfu. Shelley made a few desultory attempts to interest the captain in the Greek revolution. The captain was against the whole idea, he discovered to his horror, because it was interfering with trade. "Come away," gasped Shelley, at last, dragging his burly companion by the arm, "there is not a drop of the old Hellenic blood here. These are not the men to rekindle the ancient Greek fire; their souls are extinguished by traffic and superstition."[7]

It is a pity that he did not live to qualify his opinions in the light of the events of 1940.[8] Yet in a sense the moral growth and awakening of modern Greece has been due as much to Byron and Shelley as to the help of those powers concerned purely with political considerations of territorial freedom. With their passionate restatement of classical values and their hatred of tyranny they struck a chord in the Greek heart which echoes on even today; a chord which not even political misunderstandings can ever silence. It was Byron, it was Shelley, who morally re-armed the defeated and disunited little nation. And though the part the former played in the War of Independence is not without certain comic opera elements of an unheroic kind (Byron's procrastinations, his uniforms, his irritation with the Greeks for being un-Homeric), the Greeks owe English poets and poetry a great debt. And they are deeply conscious of the fact. To the Greek peasant of today every Englishman is in some sort a great-grandchild of the famous Byron, and he reaps in terms of friendship and hospitality the love and reverence that the poet himself did not live to enjoy. Yet there is no doubt that Byron shared some of Shelley's opinions about the modern Greeks. He shared much of the despondency and gloom which his fellow-poet felt when brought face to face with a jabbering Corfiot ship's crew. It is clear then that both poets had their eyes very firmly bandaged by the classics they had studied. Byron, it is true, knew and loved Greece. He had even troubled to learn Romaic[9] during his Athenian stay. "Byron formed his opinion of the inhabitants of this planet from books," says Trelawny acidly, and goes on to add: "Personally he knew as little about them as if he belonged to some other."[10] The charge is a harsh one but it contains the elements of truth. Yet what distinguishes the writings of Trelawny from those of the two poets is precisely a sense of human values. Trelawny judged human beings according to the terms of a large and very comprehensive experience of men and affairs. He does not whitewash the character or behaviour of the Greeks, yet he is the only one who came to be on terms of intimate friendship with them, and whose record and evaluation of their character rings absolutely true. While he was sensible of the poetic and historic values of the day, he did not diminish the war-like virtues of the Greeks he knew by measuring them against the mythical picture-book Hellene. This perhaps accounts for the soundness of his judgements and the simple honesty with which he records them.

The later Victorians interested themselves in the Klephtic ballads of Greece which so strongly resemble our Scots Border ballads; the anthropological works of Sir James Frazer and Tylor[11] stimulated the inquiry into modern Greek folklore so ably conducted by Sir Rennell Rodd and G.F. Abbott[12] about the turn of the century. By laying bare the framework of modern Greek superstition, these two scholars succeeded in tracing with accuracy and force the direct connection existing between the customs of ancient and modern Greek. Their laboratory was the peasant tongue, the peasant calendar, the whole complex of contemporary belief in Greece; and in the light of their findings the classical ancestry of much that is modern in Greece became clear. The bandages of prejudice and misconception were withdrawn. The classical scholar began to find himself no longer at sea in modern Greece, but very much at home. His equipment was no longer an obstruction but an aid to his quickened sensibility. He found points of reference everywhere in terms of myth and history and manners; such a rediscovery of Greece added immediately to his pleasure in wine, food, and landscape. The sentimentalist in him, at any rate, rediscovered a historic sanction which could now be applied to retzina, ikons, and State lotteries no less than to ancient Greek sculpture. The range of literary evocation had widened. He began to understand fully how different his Greece—the Greece of today—was from the Greece of Byron and Shelley.

But if the scholar's Philhellenism has modified itself within the last two generations, no less of a change can be found among the writers and travellers who have visited Greece, or written books about it. Virginia Woolf, for example, in her essay "On Not Knowing Greek,"[13] wonders whether Greek literature is not for us simply "a summer's day imagined in the heart of a northern winter."[14] The question was well worth asking, and to some extent it has been already answered by poets like Mr. Rex Warner[15] and Mr. Louis MacNeice,[16] who have given us ancient Greek dramas retranslated into English. We have begun to see the Greeks as something more than Homeric silhouettes. Even Homer has changed in the light of new translations by T.E. Lawrence and Mr. E.V. Rieu.[17] He has moved closer within the range of common familiarity, closer to the common reader.

It would be a rewarding task to attempt a sketch of modern Greek literature from 1821 in order to try to establish whether there are signs that Greek writing has begun to assume a European, instead of a purely national, validity. No literature, to begin with, has depended upon purely linguistic questions to quite the same extent, and if we mark the emergence of Dionysios Solomos and Calvos[18] during the War of Independence as the first birthday of modern Greek poetry, we should not forget how immense their problems were.

The sterility and darkness which lie over the later Byzantine period are a historical commonplace. Four centuries of Turkish rule all but extinguished the Greek spirit, however, and today it seems clear that had it not been for the monk and the bandit the emergence of a new literature might have been delayed perhaps for centuries. It was this unholy alliance that kept the face of the Greek peasants turned towards their ancestors, kept them alive to the responsibilities of their culture. Such literature as there was flowered in the folk-song, while the flavour and ambience of the mother-tongue were preserved in the Church services that the townsman so often heard gabbled out by the illiterate Greek priests.

A Greek poet of the time of Byron was confronted by much the same sort of problem as an early Elizabethan. He was doubtful about the *propriety* of writing in so vulgar a medium as demotic.[19] He suffered also from the critic and the literary reactionary, who decried his happiest attempts in the popular idiom and told him he was un-Greek to attempt such works. It was almost as if the pedantries of Gabriel Harvey[20] were being re-stated. The popular tongue had yet to win its spurs. Critical taste and conservatism set up barriers around the poet, and it is possible that he would never have conquered them had he not recognized his creature kinship with the border ballads, the lovely clearly woven poetry of the peasant folk, the spells and riddles, the acrostics and marriage songs of the islands and the hills. It is directly from this oral poetic tradition that the poetry of Dionysios Solomos springs.

> And still today I'm here on Friday, Saturday.
> Sunday I'll say good-bye and go to the wilderness,
> To the flocks of the nightingales and the fat shadows,
> To lay me down at ease and gather an hour's sleep,
> To listen to the nightingale's songs and the birds' plaints:
> How they all curse the eagle who carries off their young:
>   "May you gnaw off your own talons, O eagle your own claws,
>   For snatching away my mate from out of my arms,
>   The one that I held in my arms and so sweetly kissed."
> (Macedonian Folk-song)[21]

The funeral and marriage songs of the peasant had been flowing on for centuries like an underground river, with their rare wealth of symbolism and the spontaneous purity of their poetic form. The poet whose sensibility was not deadened by literary prejudice found in the folk-poetry of the country a stockpot of imagery and symbol upon which to draw at will. The Greek, like the Elizabethan, chose freedom rather than bondage.

Solomos was the first major poet to draw boldly upon this fund of riches; but to its influence he added both the personal accent of a great poet and a flavour of European intellectual sophistication, for beyond the very real and ardent nationalism of his work lies a metaphysical preoccupation with the nature of human values—a preoccupation generally foreign to peasant and pastoral poetic traditions, and which must be admitted as a part of the European heritage. Folk-poetry is not founded upon the struggles of the individual *ego* as the poetry of Solomos is; it expresses the feelings and beliefs of a community. But in Solomos (though what he said represented the common spirit and voice) the relation of the poet to his public has changed. Solomos has become symbolic as an individual; a *personal* expression of the common voice.[22]

For Solomos, then, the liberation of Greece was something deeper than a romantic fanfaronade; he, a Greek educated largely in Italy (a Greek, moreover, who had to relearn his mother language before he was able to write poetry in it) saw the implications of the whole pattern. He saw that behind the question of territorial freedom for Greece, the question of political balance, lay the whole unexplored question of human freedom itself, the quintessence of the idea of liberation. This was something which embraced the whole area of the individual human soul—a personal and religious question as much as a national one. It is precisely this that distinguishes his voice from that of any other poet before him. His great poem, *The Free Besieged*,[23] is set up as solidly as a monument, as clearly as a marker, to indicate the exact point at which Greece became once more part of that European tradition which she herself had nourished from ancient times. Byron could wish for no finer monument to his self-sacrifice than the works of Solomos. The Greek poet, living in Xante, was able to see the clouds of smoke and to feel the ground tremble under the Turkish cannonade as the Turks closed in on the town. In that strange, unfinished poem, *The Woman of Xante*, which was found untitled among his papers long after his death, he describes the scene with all the freshness of an eyewitness. The refugees, who had crowded into Xante, had become public beggars for alms, though they were not schooled to it. But hunger drove them out into the open street, conquering their shame. The poet follows them to the seashore:

1. *And I followed the women of Missolonghi, they lay down upon the sand, and I kept behind a hedge and watched.*
2. *And each one of them put her hand to her breast and took out what she had gathered, and they collected it all in a pile.*
3. *Then one of them spread out a hand to touch the shore. "My Sisters" she shouted aloud.*
4. *"Listen and see whether you ever felt such an earthquake as now strikes Missolonghi. Perhaps we are winning, or perhaps the town is falling...who can say?"*
5. *And inside me I heard a tremendous disturbance, and the spirit of Missolonghi suddenly took possession of me...*
6. *And I raised my eyes to heaven to pray with all the warmth of my spirit when I saw, lit by a wheel of perpetual sparks, a woman with a lyre in her hand, who hovered in the air above the smoke of battle.*
7. *I hardly had time to wonder at her robe as black as a hare's blood and at her eyes and so on...when the woman stood still in the smoke and watched.*
8. *She spread out her fingers upon the lyre and I beard her sing.*
   i. *Since daybreak I've taken*
   ii. *The road of the sun,*
   iii. *A lyre at my back*
   iv. *From one shoulder hangs down*
   v. *From where daylight broke*
   vi. *To where darkness came on.*[24]

The scattered mass of notes and chapter-headings which compose this, the last of Solomos's works, was only given to the public in 1927.

It was impossible that the new spirit of Greece should not press other poets also into its service as vehicles of expression. With the name of Solomos should be bracketed that of a lesser poet, but one whose taut metaphysical verses also breathed a European spirit. Calvos, like Solomos, owed much to his education in Italy, and perhaps more to a long residence in England, where he twice married, and where he was buried. His great *Ode to Death* has been translated and published among the papers of that gifted young Greek poet Capetanakis, whose own untimely death in 1944 was a serious loss both to English and Greek letters, since he wrote in both languages with equal felicity.[25]

Greek poetry between 1890 and 1920 was dominated by the voice of two other poets of European stature. Perhaps only the difficulty of the language has kept the English-speaking peoples unaware of Palamas and Kavaphis[26] as poets of magnitude and force. It may be that neither poet has yet inspired a translator brave and accomplished enough to render him in English, though a number of essayists, Professor Bowra, Mr. E.M. Forster, and Mr. Robert Liddell,[27] have drawn attention to the powers and beauties of Kavaphis, and Mr. Liddell has also published more than one translation distinguished by lucidity and feeling. But it is doubtful whether an English translator will ever quite manage to capture the wry, almost banal exactness of Kavaphis's poems, many of which are constructed like short stories and depend on situation as much as poetic accent.

His most famous pieces like *Ithaca, The Coming of the Barbarians*, and *The City*,[28] have been attempted by numerous hands but so far without the full measure of success that these remarkable produc-tions deserve. Kavaphis himself was an Alexandrian and his work has some of that calm grace, that exhausted repose which suggest the refinements of the Museum, with more than a touch of orientalism. But to this eastern note of licence, of richness (which appears most markedly in his magnificent love-poems) he adds the more sophisti-cated preoccupations of a twentieth-century man. Some of his work would be considered displeasing by puritans, for much of the subject-matter belongs to the untranslated portions of the Greek anthology.[29] But in no other Greek writer does passionate experience contribute so finely to the structure, the shape, the very grain of what he expresses. In him we find experience completely digested and transmuted. He is not a painter of emotions merely, but a great ironic critic of life.

His simplest poems are deceptive in the way that all really profound writings are deceptive; the fabric of the writing is painfully simple. Everything is in the flavour and taste of the word chosen, and the experience recorded. How will it ever be possible to render him in English?

FAR AWAY

I would like to put a memory on record...
It has faded by this time...as if nothing remains of it...
It lies far away back in my salad days.

Skin as if made from the petals of jasmine...
That remembered August—(was it August?)—
One evening it was...I can scarcely recall the eyes...
They were blue I think...yes blue, a sapphire blue.[30]

His death in 1933, and the death of Palamas late in the war, set a term to the Greek poetry of the early twentieth century; though Palamas enjoyed a priority in reputation due perhaps to a longer working life.

Of those poets who are still living and producing the undoubted senior is Mr. Anghelos Sikelianos,[31] whose passionate and flamboyant writing marks him as a national poet in the direct line of descent from Solomos and Palamas. In 1942 his little group of *Akritan Songs*, which were widely circulated by the underground movement, struck a chord that is still echoing in Greece, and set a seal upon his reputation as Greece's greatest living poet.

Mr. George Seferis, born in 1900, occupies a position which, at the risk of over-simplification, might be described as analogous to that of Mr. T.S. Eliot in England.[32] The publication of his *The Turning Point* in 1931 brought a new influence and a new voice to Greek verse. The reception of this poem was marked by criticism reminiscent of that which greeted *The Waste Land* in 1922. Critics complained of obscurity.

But Palamas, the old poet, himself described this first fruit of a new talent as a real turning-point in Greek literature. Since then Mr. Seferis has added to his reputation with further volumes of verse and has achieved the well merited distinction of translation into both French and English. His technique derives from the same French sources as those of Mr. Eliot,[33] and this accounts for a superficial resemblance in manner; but by temperament Mr. Seferis is contemplative rather than mystical, and sensual instead of puritanical. His poems render admirably the taste and touch of common things, the warmth of sunlight, the perfume of flowers. The ambience of his poetry is the ambience of the Greek landscape, with its warm ringing tones or light, its islands like primitive sculptures, its statues and cypresses. Mr. Seferis is a national poet only in the sense that he is absolutely Greek.

> *Sleep like the green leaves of a tree wrapped you round.*
> *Like a tree you breathed in the calm light,*
> *In the lucent source I discovered your form:*
> *Eyelids shut, eyelashes brushing the water.*
> *My fingers in the smooth grass found your fingers,*
> *For an instant lay on the pulse,*
> *Sensible of the heart's pain in another place.*[34]

Enough has been said to indicate that not only has our Philhellenism undergone a radical change for the better but that the modern Greek has become more than worthy of the admiration that was too often in the past reserved for his ancestors. The poetic tradition indicates clearly that Greek literature is struggling out of the swaddling-clothes of purely political or national aspiration towards a universal validity, a European significance. The span from Solomos to Mr. Seferis is a little over one hundred years; yet those who measure the growth of a national consciousness not in terms of politics or economics but in terms of literature will be able to see, even within this small span, the evolution of a national temperament through the influence of its poets, Greece has turned her face towards Europe; and in the darker moments when political affairs and misunderstandings appear to separate us and make us despondent about the future of Greece, we do well to remember how nobly the Greek poets have carried the flame lit for them by the English poets of 1820. It would gladden the boyish heart of Shelley, and the sad heart of Byron, if they could return to witness it.

NOTES

1. A similar interpretation is taken up by David Roessel in *In Byron's Shadow* and Edmund Keeley's *Inventing Paradise*, both of which discuss Durrell's philhellenic works.

2. Lithgow (1582–1645) was a Scottish poet and travel writer who extensively travelled the Mediterranean and Levant.

3. Edward John Trelawny (1792–1881) was a writer and friend to Percy Bysshe Shelley (1792–1822) and Lord Byron, both of whose funerals he arranged. All three are famous philhellenes, and both Trelawny and Byron were in the Greek War of Independence.

4. Trelawny 56.

5. Trelawny 56–57.

6. The Italianate form of Saint Spiridon, the patron saint of Corfu.

7. Trelawny 57.

8. The remarkable Greek resistance to fascist Italian and German invasions during World War II, which continued throughout the war, perhaps most famously on Crete, despite extreme repercussions.

9. The account of Byron learning the Romaic dialect from Marmaratouri (his tutor and a leader of Greek patriots) while in Athens derives from the compilation of Byron's writings in *The Life, Writings, Opinions and Times of the Right Hon. George Gordon Noel Byron, Lord Byron* (129). Also see Byron's various translations of Romaic songs and "Don Juan," CLXI–CLXV. Romaic is simply Modern Greek, which would have been largely unconsidered by Byron's contemporaries.

10. Trelawny 137. These comments are preceded by Trelawny's quotation of "His life was one long war with self-sought foes" from *Childe Harold*.

11. Edward Burnett Tylor (1832–1917) was, like Frazer, a founding figure in social anthropology. He is best known for *Primitive Culture* and *Anthropology*. He was the first professor of anthropology at the University of Oxford, whereas Frazer was at Cambridge.

12. Durrell also mentions Rodd in his 1947 piece "From a Winter Journal," two years prior to "Hellene and Philhellene." Abbott (1874–1947) was a war correspondent and anthropologist. Abbott frequently discussed folklore in his works, but Durrell is likely referring to his 1903 book *Macedonian Folk-Lore*, for which Cambridge University sent him to Greece and Macedonia.

13. Woolf (1882–1941) was a major British Modernist novelist. Durrell only mentions her works intermittently, though his library held in the Morris Library includes an unusual copy of Woolf's *A Cockney's Farming Experiences* in its 1972 limited printing. Woolf's full sentiment is important here: "Back and back we are drawn to steep ourselves in what, perhaps, is only an image of the reality, not the reality itself, a summer's day imagined in the heart of a northern winter. Chief among these sources of glamour and perhaps misunderstanding is the language. We can never hope to get the whole fling of a sentence in Greek as we do in English....First there is the compactness of the expression. Shelley takes twenty-one words in English to translate thirteen words of Greek" (35).

14. Woolf 35.

15. Warner (1905–1986) was a British writer, known for his translations from Greek, whom Durrell knew well. Durrell's co-translation of *The King of Asine and Other Poems* with Bernard Spencer and Nanos Valaorotis was given an introduction by Warner (1948). Durrell borrowed from Warner's translation of Xenephon's *The Anabasis* (*The Persian Expedition* in the contemporary Penguin edition, which is Warner's) for Nessim's historical dreams in the first book of *The Alexandria Quartet* (143–56). This was first noticed by William Leigh Godshalk.

16. MacNeice (1907–1963) was a major poet in the Auden circle. Durrell is referring to his 1936 translation of *The Agamemnon of Aeschylus*, published by Faber & Faber.

17. T.E. Lawrence's (1888–1935) 1932 translation of *The Odyssey* for Oxford University Press and Rieu's (1887–1972) 1946 translation of the same for Penguin, which led to his founding and editorship of Penguin Classics.

18. Solomos (1798–1857) is most famous as a poet for writing "Hymn to Liberty" that became the Greek national anthem. He also lived on Corfu, not far from where Durrell first stayed. Andreas Kalvos (1792–1869) was, like Solomos, a major Greek poet born on Zakynthos and who settled on Corfu where he became the director of the Ionian Academy.

19. Greek was divided within "Romaic" or Modern Greek between Demotica and Katharevousa, the former being the spoken language and the latter a mid-point between the ancient and modern language. Durrell was fluent in Demotic Greek and translated Emmanuel Royidis's *Pope Joan* from Katharevousa, though Panaiotis Gerontopolous has argued Durrell relied on T.D. Kriton's 1935 English translation of *Papissa Joanna*. Katharevousa was often presented as the appropriate language for written literature.

20. Harvey (1545–1630) is most famous for his public dispute with Thomas Nashe and his "pedantic" attempts to impose Latin meter and iambic hexameter on English poetry.

21. This appears to be Durrell's own translation.

22. This article is close in time to Durrell's editorship of *Personal Landscape* and its politics of the unpolitical as well as the Personalist movement in the New Apocalypse and New Romanticist movements in Britain. Durrell's emphasis of the term here calls up this broader contemporary context.

23. Solomos's major work, which exists in a variety of unfinished states. A complete performance in Greek was delivered in May 2010 at the Durrell School of Corfu. Durrell may have also known of it through his good friend Stephanides, who translated Greek poetry of this period and adapted some of Solomos's works (Stephanides 113–14).

24. Durrell's own translation.

25. Durrell may be developing this from Edith Sitwell's "The Poetry of Capetanakis."

26. Kostis Palamas (1859–1943) was a major Greek poet, wrote the Olympic Hymn, and was closely involved with the Athenian Academy. Several of C.P. Cavafy's (Kavaphis) poems were translated by Durrell. Cavafy appears frequently as a reference throughout *The Alexandria Quartet* and was translated in *Personal Landscape*, which Durrell co-edited from 1942 to 1945.

27. Cecil Maurice Bowra (1898–1971) was a classicist and professor of poetry at the University of Oxford who championed Cavafy's works. Bowra was known for his homosexuality and erudition equally. E.M. Forster (1879–1970) knew Cavafy while in Alexandria, corresponded with him, and promoted his works' publication in English translation. Liddell (1908–1992) was a poet and novelist who wrote the first English biography of Cavafy; he was also good friends with Durrell, published several works in *Personal Landscape*, and had escaped to North Africa with Olivia Manning. See his "A Note on Cavafy" in particular (9–10). Much of the Durrell–Liddell correspondence is held in the Gennadius Library, Athens.

28. Durrell translated "The City" in *The Alexandria Quartet* (201–02) as well as other Cavafy poems (882–84). Also see his "A Cavafy Find," which contains further translations.

29. This is an allusion to his homosexuality.

30. Durrell's own translation. This poem has also been translated as "Far Back."

31. Sikelianos (1884–1951) was a major Modern Greek poet whom Durrell translated only three years earlier in *Six Poems From the Greek of Sikelianos and Seferis* (1946).

32. Seferis (1900–1971) was the defining voice of Greek poetry in the twentieth century, a Nobel Laureate for Literature, and gave his first translations of Eliot's *The Waste Land* into Greek in 1936 (Keeley 214–26). Durrell first met Seferis in the mid 1930s and they formed a friendship that lasted until Seferis's death, despite popular opinion that they had abandoned their friendship after Durrell's service on Cyprus.

33. Both poets were strongly influenced by the French poet Jules Laforgue (1860–1887).

34. The fifteenth section of Seferis's epic poem "Mythistorema," in Durrell's translation. Notably, the "myth-history" became the subtitle to the Greek translation of the first book of Durrell's *Alexandria Quartet*, *Justine: Mythistorema*.

A Cavafy Find

1956

AN INTERESTING DISCOVERY of three hitherto unknown poems by the Alexandrian poet C.P. Cavafy has recently been discussed in the pages of *Cyprus Letters* by the scholar A. Indianos.[1] These poems were unearthed from an old scrapbook in the possession of the Countess Chariclea Jerome Valieri, who lives in Cyprus, and who is the daughter of Cavafy's brother, Aristides.[2] They are the earliest known work of the Alexandrian master, and while they are not equal to the work of his maturity, they show, despite the conventional lyrical form in which they are written, touches of the true Cavafian irony and actuality: the way, for instance, in which he discusses emotions in terms of simple humble objects "the cheap cretonne dress" and the "cheap bracelets on her arms." The word "cheap" he always uses with emotion to offset the values these shopworn objects, bodies, ears, hands, eyes, etc., represent in the eyes of the lover who invests them with his own feelings. Indeed all the grandeur of Cavafy lies in this patient, loving, miserly way of looking at objects[3] and events—reinfecting memory time and time again with the passionate actuality of something that has disturbed him—so that the resulting vibration in words become significant and powerful, and the poem as a whole comes over. Lovers of his verse will be interested in these early examples. Even though, perhaps, in their English versions, they lose something of their natural strength.

MY FRIENDS, WHEN I WAS IN LOVE[4]

My friends, when I was in love,
It was many years ago
I did not share the same earth
With other mortal beings.

Lyrical was my turn of mind
And though so often deceptive
It gave me happiness
Abounding life and warmth

Whatever the eye took in
Was rich in beauty,
The palace of my love
A nest appeared to me

A cheap cretonne dress
The one she used to wear
I swear when first I saw it
Seemed of the finest silk

The two cheap bracelets
She wore on her wrists
Seemed to me precious stones
Adorning some great lady

On her head she wore
Mountain flowers—
The loveliest of all bouquets
They seemed to me.

Smooth the walks we took
Together arm in arm,
Nor thorn or brambles there,
Or if there were earth hid them

Today the orator and the sage
Cannot move me half as much
As a single sign from her did
In those old days

My friends when I was in love
It was many years ago
I did not share the same earth
With other mortal beings.

FLOWERS OF MAY

All the Year's flowers blossom in May,
But of them all Youth is the loveliest,
But how soon it fades, never to come back;
Only the flowers always adorn the ground.

All the Year's flowers blossom in May,
The same ones, but my eyes don't see them,
And other hands put them in other bosoms,
Spring comes and ebbs, but no two springs alike
The sweets of each are different.

All the Year's flowers blossom in May,
But they do not always wait upon our happiness,
The same flowers give joy and bitterness,
Growing on graves we mourn for,
Adorning the scented fields.

Again May comes, and the flowers rise,
But it is difficult to see her from the window,
And the pane dwindles, diminishes, disappears.
The mournful eye grows dim and cannot see,
Our tired limbs can no longer hold us up.

This year the flowers are not for us,
Other springs now crown us with their blossoms;
The past comes surging back,
Beloved shades stoop down and beckon us
Lull the starved heart asleep.

DOUNYA GOUZELI
(The loveliest woman in the world)

The mirror does not lie: what I see is true
There is no one lovelier anywhere than I.
Glittering diamonds of eyes,
Lips verging on corals,
A double line of pearls for teeth,
My body is graceful, my legs admired,
Hands and neck of milk, and hair of spun silk,
But alas what is the good of it all?

Inside this loathed enclosed harem
Who on earth can look upon my beauty?
Only hostile rivals or horrible eunuchs
Poisoning me with looks, my blood freezes
When my terrible husband comes to me.
My prophet, my Lord forgive me if
My sad heart cries "If only I were a Christian."

If I became a Christian I should be free
Show myself freely to one and all,
For men to admire and girls to envy.
All would agree that Nature could not make
Another like me; passing in my coach
The streets of Istanbul would fill
With crowds admiring me.

NOTES

1. Antonis C. Indianos (1899–1968) co-founded *Cypriot Letters*, which ran from 1934 to 1956. He corresponded widely with Greek and English writers, and Durrell would surely have known of his public support as a lawyer for EOKA during the Enosis struggle on Cyprus at this time. He translated both Ezra Pound and T.S. Eliot into Greek.

2. Aristedes Cavafy (1853–1902).

3. As many scholars have noted, Durrell repeatedly uses objects to express emotional content, in particular in the closing scenes of novels, such as the various detritus gestured to at the end of *Justine* and *Bitter Lemons*, both written during the same year as this article. Robert Duncan noticed this Durrell's poetry, which he published in two issues of *Experimental Review*, and echoed in his own tribute "An Ark for Lawrence Durrell" (11), which was first published in the January issue of the same journal.

4. The following translations are Durrell's own. He first began to translated Cavafy with his good friend Stephanides while living on Corfu. In 1939, their translation of "The Barbarians" (Waiting for the Barbarians) appeared in *The New English Weekly* (MacNiven 242).

A Real Heart
Transplant
into English

1973

THE ARRIVAL OF Edmund Keeley and Philip Sherrard[1] on the Modern
Greek translation scene marks quite a definite and definitive stage
of a process; the excellence of their work is really worthy of recognition by the Greek Government. Thanks to them we can now say that
we "have" Seferis and Cavafy in English, and in versions not likely to
be superseded; one hopes that they will continue this triumphal work
and give us a Sikelianos and an Elytis.[2] The volume under review is,
as might be expected, thoughtful, respectful to the great poet and
felicitous in its choice of phrasing—with perhaps one small reserva-
tion about a few Americanisms like "to show up" and "show business,"
which the old poet himself might have found too slangy. But then this
is an American book for American readers, and this observation may
not be worth raising.

It is instructive to see how the greatness of Cavafy has slowly
become accepted. He was first recognised for what he was, a great
original, by E.M. Forster during World War I; and some of his poems
(translated I think by Valasopoulos) found their way into an essay in
Pharos and Pharillon.[3] It was only the very first stage. Since then, translations have succeeded one another like the stages of an etching:[4]

now one feels that a final stage has been reached in the work of these two gifted men, Keeley and Sherrard. It is a real heart-transplant into English of the great Alexandrian love-poet and voluptuary. (Perhaps this is the place to signal the excellence of a small monograph on the poet by Peter Bien, published by Columbia University Press in 1964.[5] It is a model of what such essays should be.)

When first I reached Athens, four decades ago, I was given a selection of Modern Greek poets translated into English by George Katsimbalis and Theodore Stephanides (personages later to figure as characters in books by Henry Miller and my brother Gerald[6]), with a preface by John Drinkwater.[7] It was here that I first came upon the Alexandrian poet; but later, and indeed over many years, I grew more and more familiar with him, since I had him read to me, expounded to me, translated for me and with me by not only the two above mentioned friends but also by Nanos Valaoritis,[8] George Seferis, and others.

Naturally we all boldly tried our hand at translating Modern Greek poetry in those days—Bernard Spencer, Robin Fedden, and myself. While my own Greek was rudimentary and has unfortunately remained so, I really felt I possessed the essence of these Greek poets because I had worked on them and had had them fed to me by these gifted Athenian friends. Later in the day came other translators who really knew their Greek, like Rex Warner, who captured the choice austerities of Seferis, his great friend, in earlier versions; then Robert Liddell, who did some Cavafy with great distinction. I think Lady Smart also tried her hand at Cavafy. And so on right down the years with each version spreading the deserved celebrity of this great poet.[9]

I once earned a mild protest from Seferis for running some of my rather idiosyncratic versions of Cavafy into the *Alexandria Quartet*; he felt I had taken liberties. So I had. But he accepted my defence— namely that Cavafy was not "real." He was simply a character in a fiction in whose name I had borrowed some poems from a real man.[10] I have had a large number of letters since asking me if the "old poet of the city" really existed or not. I myself arrived in Alexandria eight years after Cavafy's death, but the town was still full of memories of him, and of course very many friends of his were alive still and happy to speak about him. So I felt my way into the Alexandrian scene through him, in a manner of speaking: I already knew his work well, but here I was able to situate it clearly in its demographic context. It helped me to estimate his greatness.

During much of this period his excellence was only recognised by the good poets and critics of Greece—not as yet by the poetry-reading public in general, and certainly not by the *bien pensants*[11] of Athens. In part this was due to his frank love-poems about homosexuality. But these poems were not vulgar or crude; they were the poems of a patrician, full of dignity and eloquence even though the scenario, so to speak, might have been based on a meeting in a brothel. He is the greatest love-poet of our time in my view.

There was a second factor which played a role—a subtle kind of disharmony of attitude between the Athens temperament and the Alexandrian. In Alexandria one was born into five languages; one was sophisticated; one was rich, inevitably educated in Paris or London or Berlin (often all three): one rather tended to come it over the poor provincial rowdy Greeks of the mainland with their barbarous politics and bustling vulgarity. Athens tended to frown on modernity also and preferred to stick to safe national poets like Palamas.

Seferis had to work like a dog to argue some sense into the native Athenian headpiece, and only after years of much foreign praise did he himself manage to attain general public recognition for his own fine poems. But he of course was as worldly, sophisticated, and much travelled as Cavafy—he was just like an Alexandrian. So he perfectly understood the position of a poet like Cavafy. The Hellenistic poet of Alexandria was writing for all Europe. Athens did not know it until long afterward. And the city of Alexandria was as much his theme as Dublin was Joyce's theme; he has left us an incomparable study of its *moeurs*, its atmospheres, its history, its greatness.[12]

He has now at last fallen upon translators who can do full justice to his wry melodious poems, glinting with insight as if from veins of mica. He is lucky too to have editors as brilliant as Savidis[13] in Athens whose handsome new editions of his favourite poet have now reached the general public. Indeed we are all indebted to so much fine, scrupulous, and sensitive work. The school deserves a whole holiday.

NOTES

1. Keeley has gone on to write about Durrell in detail in his *Inventing Paradise: The Greek Journey, 1937–47*. Sherrard (1922–1995) was a major British translator of Modern Greek literature. Both knew many of the authors they translated or wrote about personally.

2. Angelos Sikelianos (1884–1951) was a major Greek poet aligned with both anti-authoritarian and surrealist movements. Odysseas Elytis (1911–1996) was an equally prominent Greek Modernist poet. Durrell was deeply familiar with both of their works.

3. Forster's (1879–1970) role in having these translations appear in *The Criterion* is an important factor in the spread of Cavafy's fame. Durrell used Forster's *Pharos and Pharillon* as well as his *Alexandria: A History and a Guide* during this time in Egypt and while writing *The Alexandria Quartet*.

4. This contention was disputed by W.H. Auden in his letter to the editor responding to Durrell's article, in which he reminds his readers of his own Introduction to Rae Dalven's translations (Auden 427).

5. Bien's *Constantine Cavafy* was a part of Columbia's Essays on Modern Writers series. It was formally published in January of 1965.

6. Miller's *The Colossus of Maroussi* features both, and Gerald Durrell's *My Family and Other Animals* famously depicts Stephanides, though in a frequently fictional form.

7. This book is Kastimbalis and Stephanides's 1930 collection *Some Modern Greek Poets*.

8. Valaoritis (1921–) is an important Greek writer and was both a friend to and co-translator with Durrell, which he has described in detail (46–56).

9. Rex Warner's Seferis translations followed after Durrell's joint translations in 1948 with Bernard Spencer and Nanos Valaoritis, *The King of Asine and Other Poems*, which itself came after Durrell's own translations of Seferis and Sikelianos as *Six Poems From the Greek of Sekilianos and Seferis*, though it was not published until he was residing on Rhodes in 1946. Durrell corresponded with

Liddell before the two were evacuated to Egypt, and he retained a strong friendship with him. Liddell wrote the influential first English biography of Cavafy and includes a Cavafy figure in his Alexandrian novel, *Unreal City*, which precedes Durrell's *Alexandria Quartet*. Amy Smart's "The Poetry of Cavafy," was published as Amy Nimr and appeared in Durrell's co-edited journal *Personal Landscape* in Cairo in 1945 (14–20). It contains several translations, as does the journal's print run as a whole. Smart's correspondence from Durrell is now held at the McMaster University Library, Hamilton, ON.

10. Durrell's translations of Cavafy appear several times in *The Alexandria Quartet*, most prominently at the end of *Justine*, which also contains a variant of one of these translations completed by a character. Durrell translated Cavafy a number of times. See Anthony Hirst's "'The Old Poet of the City': Cavafy in Darley's Alexandria" (69–94).

11. Literally "good minded" but implying a conservative or orthodox viewpoint.

12. This is something of a self-allusion here to Durrell's first notebooks for *The Alexandria Quartet*, which he later integrated into the final form of the novel as the novel *Moeurs* written by the character Arnauti.

13. George Savidis (1929–1995) was a professor of Greek literature at Harvard University and the Artistotle University of Thessaloniki as well as an important editor and critic.

Introduction to
Wordsworth

1973

THE PROBLEM OF WORDSWORTH THE POET has always been
bedevilled by the double image of the man—created, one supposes,
by himself, though it has been suggested that it was the work of
Hartley Coleridge[1] when he observed: "What a mighty genius is the
poet Wordsworth! What a dull proser is W.W. Esqre of Rydal Mount,
Distributor of Stamps and brother to the Revnd, the Master of Trinity."[2]
At any rate Hartley (who had inherited much of his father's vivacity of
mind and bright insight) was the first to set up the double Wordsworth,
and all subsequent critics have accepted the same point of departure
easily enough. It finds its way into most critical estimates of the poet's
work, even today. Throughout the twenties and thirties the two
Wordsworths were a convenient cockshy for satirists. Was it not
Squire?—it was either he or Shanks—who published the following
lines in the *London Mercury*.

> *Two voices are there. One is loud and deep,*
> *And one is of an old half-witted sheep,*
> *And Wordsworth, both are thine...*[3]

But it can be made into a persuasive case only by those who have
not been faced (as the present editor has been) with the sum total of

135

Wordsworth's work to read at one blow—supplemented by a comprehensive and sensitive biography of the man.[4] This procedure is guaranteed to surprise one, for the case of Wordsworth becomes more intricate and less clear-cut than it would be convenient to believe; he remained the same man, operating on all the different levels, completely undivided. His political principles were as much part of him as his poetic ones or his religious attitudes and beliefs, and the poetry (the best and the worst) overshadows all these activities, by turn lyrical, didactic, elegaic or hortatory. For the first time one realises how all-of-a-piece the work is, and how in the back of the poet's own mind, all the parts constituted fragments from a single huge work of autobiographical confession[5]—a depiction of the growth of a poet's mind and sensibility.

It was a tremendously ambitious undertaking just to be Mr. William Wordsworth, and to be aware of his vocation and his poetic responsibilities towards it; and it is marvellous to see with what fortitude and in what exemplary degree he managed to discharge them over such a long and truthful life—he died at the age of eighty. Studied in this way he cannot help but grow in stature rather than diminish. Everything—even his less successful work—becomes significant and enriching. Every detail adds, once one sees the character of the man with any clearness.

Wordsworth almost more than any other English poet enjoyed a sense of inner confirmation—the mysterious sense of election to poetry as a whole way of life. He realised too that one cannot condescend to nature—one must work for it like a monk over a missal which he will not live to see finished. He felt he was hunting for what was most itself in nature, the poised and limpid truth of reality. Poetry was his lariat. So that what might, by ignorant or prejudiced critics, be represented as being in some parts the unpolished maunderings of some neurotic sectary, given to introspection, turns out when seen as a whole, as a lifestyle, to which the writing was a mere appendix, a mere illustration—turns out to be one of the most determined, thoughtful, pure, and disinterested attempts by any poet since Milton to purge and mature a human intuition by the practice of poetry, using the direct vision of the natural world as both touchstone and lodestar. The furniture of his universe was nature in all its multiplicity—not a pack of moral attributes or a clique of allegorical figures.

Wordsworth was a man from the craggy north, a blunt man full of psychic obstinacy. He set himself to see nature as a whole, as something more than the sum of its parts. He was celebrating those mysterious "visitations" of which he speaks—flashes of blinding intuition which gave him glimpses of something like process itself at work....There was to be no nonsense about this task, to which he had been called by the deepest part of his own nature. He pitched his work beyond the reach of the contemporary "poetical" style and made it low-toned, mono-chrome in tinge. Though in no way a moralist, he seems to have felt that if one sought and found Truth one would insensibly find goodness there, for they were part of the same animal. And ultimate goodness came from an intuition which had fulfilled itself in its commerce with mother nature: poetry was simply the outward and visible sign of such a search. The originality and magnitude of such a venture for such a man lay in the fact that it carefully side-stepped a dogmatic theology in an age when it was almost impossible to do so comfortably, particu-larly for a man of his birth and background, and in the circumstances imposed by the society of his time and place.

Indeed, when one reflects on his life, one is astonished at the pitfalls he managed to escape; his birth was into a background of parsons, dons, prosperous lawyers, mariners. Minor gentry one might say, which is to suggest a certain level of refinement and culture—at the least the possession of books. Wordsworth's father gave him the run of a small but choice library—an inestimable gift for an incipient poet. Yet it was also the age of nonconformity, of republicanism, of transcendentalism. Wordsworth when young was a convinced republican, and like every other warm-hearted intelligence welcomed the French Revolution without reserve. But his idealism was bitterly disappointed, almost to the point of trauma, by the excesses he witnessed during his French residence and his subsequent loathing and fear of republicanism seems to date from his return.[6]

Ironically enough he also fell in love with a French girl (a Royalist in politics) by whom he had an illegitimate daughter.[7] Separated by war for many years, he finally decided against marriage to her, but he never wavered as far as his responsibilities were concerned towards the daughter. He acknowledged his paternity, and later sent her money, and visited her on the most affectionate and friendly basis. But his own real interior poetic life unfolded itself when at last he was free to set up house with his beloved sister Dorothy—a dream they had cherished for a long time, and in which she took her natural place as the poet's real Muse. Later he married an old family friend, and collected quite a little harem of eager and affectionate copyists for his work—the "family of Love," as someone called it, impressed by the dignity and harmony of their communal life.

Naturally the psychoanalysts have made Wordsworth, like so many other creative men, a stalking-horse for their theories. I am person-ally sympathetic to Freud's views and believe that Wordsworth himself would have been fascinated by them. But surely it was Freud who once wrote: "Before the mystery of the creative act psychoanalysis lays down its arms"?[8] Yet there is no need for an exaggerated display of clinical tact in this case, if "case" it be, for what is resolved during an analysis of a neurosis is precisely the same sort of tension which is resolved in the act of creation by a major poet. He makes, so to speak, models of his anxieties, and fits them into his life-constellation, submitting himself to the stresses and strains of the business, often risking ill-health or even madness in order to affront and tame them (St. George and the Dragon).

The poetic work, in interpreting these terrors through art, helps him to surmount them in his life. ("The great masters," writes Proust, "are those who master themselves.") Indeed the life-work of a great poet—a Valéry, Rilke, Yeats[9]—should be considered as a long process of triumphantly surmounting his anxieties, his complexes, the wounds which his infantile psyche bears, by the act of exteriorising them, of giving them form. We, his readers, profit vicariously from the transaction of reading and studying such work, for it helps us to do the same with our own stresses. (Each poem is a cry of relief, of victory over the hippogriff). In the case of William Wordsworth, his work might well be likened to the long and horrible self-analysis undertaken by Freud at the beginning of his career as a healer, an operation nobody else was capable of performing for him. "Each original work of art," cries Wordsworth, "must create the taste by which it is to be judged." Read and mark![10]

Of course his beloved sister Dorothy took the place of his dead mother and in the voluptuousness of the transference he was able to feel the comfort and reassurance of his early childhood repeat itself in manhood. Moreover she was no dried-up old maid but a marvellous devoted woman who was the perfect partner in life; in every way sapient enough, intelligent enough, to second his growth. Most of all, it was she who set an exact value on his work, convincing him that it was worth living for and worth starving for. Very well, you may say, it was a surrogate-reassurance to replace what he had lost. But all the more lucky for us that so sensitive and reticent a poet should have such a sister, who demanded nothing of him except love and poetry, and for her part readily supplied the sympathy and the hard work necessary to keep the whole household oriented towards him. It was love all right, but it was a love of a marvellous self-abnegation—the love of Héloïse and Abelard, one might say.[11] So at least says the poet himself in more than one place. It outstripped all thought of real sexuality. (How astonished the brother and sister would be to read this last paragraph!)

> *Then it was*
> *That the belovèd Woman in whose sight*
> *Those days were pass'd, now speaking in a voice*
> *Of sudden admonition, like a brook*

That did but cross a lonely road, and now
Seen, heard and felt, and caught at every turn,
Companion never lost through many a league,
Maintained for me a saving intercourse
With my true self; for, though impair'd and chang'd
Much, as it seem'd, I was no further chang'd
Than as a clouded, not a waning moon:
She, in the midst of all, preserv'd me still
A Poet, made me seek beneath that name
My office upon earth, and nowhere else.[12]

Looked at from this point of view the famous lines written above Tintern Abbey could be considered one of the great love-poems in the language.[13]

The traditional portrait of the poet is drawn for the most part from the synoptic view of his life which tells us, for example, that the revolutionary young man spent 1791–92 in France, watched the first excesses of the revolution, fell in love with Annette Vallon who bore him a daughter, and then returned to England with his head hung low and his revolutionary heart broken by what he regarded not simply as an internal French disaster, but as a betrayal of the hopes for the whole human race. He was not the only one—a whole generation of young freethinkers and utopians all over Europe felt the same. A sick disgust, a heart-wrenching disappointment. Moreover this dark experience mingled with his despair about his French lover; he had every intention of marrying her and bringing her back to England—all this to the delight of Dorothy who at once established friendly and indeed loving contact with the girl. But a mixture of circumstances both personal and international intervened and separated them, not least among them the war with Napoleon, and gradually the marriage prospects faded out of the picture.

Nevertheless, so honest was Wordsworth, that when he fell in love with someone else he insisted on clearing the matter with Annette.

In everything we have to deal with a highly collected man and a high-principled one. He was master of his own ship, however much his infantile poet-side quailed before life and drew strength from the women about him. War put the finishing touches to his French love affair, and he turned away towards his English destiny, with perhaps many regrets and certainly some unjustified self-reproach. It is from this point onward that his life seems to become staider, more orthodox, less colourful. He had been disappointed both in love and in his political visions of human justice. There remained his art. It is worth remembering that later on he married an old family friend, and that for a long time, while he lived with his sister, they took joint charge of a small child which belonged to a widower friend in London who could not meet his responsibilities towards the infant. In other words the household structure was a real one, a homelike one in the real sense of the word. It did not lack a domestic shape capable of engendering for the Wordsworths real human contact, warmth, and responsibility.

Moreover they were all happily devotees of country life, and adept at facing the rigours of climate and the boredom of long winters in the north. To them their native landscape was a Paradise, an Eden, and they never, like other Romantics, hankered for Italy or Greece. Switzerland represented something more real for Wordsworth, not only because it was scenically grandiose but also because it embodied the highest expression of democratic values. When Napoleon invaded it Wordsworth became his implacable enemy, and his sonnets were clarion-calls to rouse the English to their responsibilities towards the rights of man and the freedom of states—and the defeat of tyrants. As time went on Wordsworth may be represented as shifting his allegiances from republicanism to high toryism; was this the inevitable hardening of the arteries which comes after forty or was it based on a measured view of man and his capacities—his ability to deal rationally and sensibly with freedom? I like to presume the latter, though the evidence goes against me.[14] One wonders where he would stand today amidst so many conflicting issues? One is reminded of a jotting by the indefatigable Crabb Robinson:[15]

Wordsworth spoke with great feeling of the present state of the country. He considers the combinations among journeymen, and even the Benefit Societies and all associations of men, apparently for the best purposes, as very alarming: he contemplates the renovation of all the horrors of a war between the poor and the rich, a conflict of property with no property. The memories of the French terror, and the reign of Robespierre, had left their mark.[16]

Young De Quincey has noted somewhere the rate of growth of Wordsworth's reputation. "Up to 1820," he writes, "the name of Wordsworth was trampled underfoot; from 1820 to 1830 it was militant; from 1830 to 1835 it has been triumphant."[17] There is something almost irresistible in the steady deliberate advance of the poet, not simply upon his public, but upon the sentiment of the whole nation. He gradually expanded into a grave public figure, a symbol of the vigour and maturity of English literature. Perhaps even a graven image to some, or a sacred cow. To continue the story, in 1839 Oxford honoured him with a DCL.[18] In 1842 he was accorded a civil list pension which enabled him to resign his sinecure as a Distributor of Stamps which he had held, discharging his duties aptly and faithfully, since 1813. He succeeded, finally, Southey[19] as Poet Laureate in 1843. In 1850, at the ripe age of eighty, Wordsworth died. He was the father of five children, and his wife lived on for another nine years after his death. His renown was nation-wide.

Side by side with his poetic life Wordsworth lived a fruitful and purposeful private life of a family man, passed for the most part in the most quiet and beautiful part of the one countryside which he loved above all others and to which he belonged. In many ways, if one adds up the debit and credit, he was almost supernaturally lucky. To live, first of all, exactly where he wished to; then to devote his whole time, his whole spirit, to his vocation. Poetry was both his life and his *business*. There were moments of hesitation when during his youth he was threatened with having to take a job—becoming a parson or a tutor—and then he felt his poetic independence threatened. But each time the clouds passed and the future allowed him to set his feet upon the path to selfhood, and with it to fame. Has there ever been a poet (without a private income) half as lucky as he? And then, Dorothy Wordsworth—what a gift from the Gods this sister turned out to be.[20] Her invincible devotion to him—and not only to him, but to his work—made a shelter in which his mind could take refuge. The little harem of copyists existed only to further his aims, to make life easy for him.

With such an ambience it would have been impossible not to make the best of one's art. No wonder Wordsworth did his work entirely without the use of drugs, or even the abuse of alcohol. He was perhaps the only poet of his age to manage to work thus. Of course so sensitive a man could not expect to be free from the strains and stresses of creative unhappiness—he would have been exceptional indeed had he never shown a sign of distress or anxiety. One remembers the pain in his side which often prevented him working, and which he outfaced; one remembers the eye-trouble; and also the periods of nervous stress which gave the attentive Dorothy so much cause for alarm and misgiving. But in the end it was Dorothy and not William who suffered a mental overthrow.

Yes, there were occasional money troubles too, and the need to secure himself a sinecure from the distribution of stamps arose in middle life. But this involved only local travelling. He was never forced to leave his own countryside. He always found admirers to let him rent or borrow congenial places to live with his family. Moreover his calculated frugality put him beyond the scope of those to whom he might have found himself indebted had he been a borrower or a spendthrift. If his luck was good, his credit was also, and in money matters he showed conspicuous good sense.

The existence of a definitive text of the poetry, and of more than one comprehensive biography of the poet, gives one the courage if not the right to pick about in the record of his long life in order to isolate if possible the high spots and the low, the miracles of good luck and the calamities which beset him—no poet can hope to side step Nemesis entirely; and Wordsworth the family man, the husband and father, had many sorrows to contend with on his line of march. They temper the rather austere after-image he has left us, and point to a man capable of deep passionate feeling underneath his proud reticence—and most of all where his children were concerned.

I am thinking most particularly of the year 1812 which was a particularly bitter one for the Wordsworth family, for two of the small children died during the course of it—little four year old Catherine first, and then Tom some six months later. Wordsworth's own grief transmuted itself into one of his loveliest poems for the child, though it was not published until much later.

Surprised by joy—impatient as the Wind
I turned to share the transport—Oh! with whom
But Thee, deep buried in the silent tomb,
That spot which no vicissitude can find?
Love, faithful love, recalled thee to my mind—[21]

But there were other bitternesses almost as hard to surmount, such as the unexpected loss of his adored brother John, the sea captain, who went down with the wreck of his ship. This cruel calamity cast a shadow over the hearts of William and Dorothy, for John had been closest to them, and was planning to come one day and share their lives.

Dorothy's own gradual collapse and the gradual foundering of her reason must also have weighed on him a great deal—she was so much his alter ego that it must have seemed like the loss of half of his own mind to watch her slowly descending the long slopes of unreason, to end up as a total mental wreck. All these tragedies he faced with fierce pride and responsibility. Perhaps there were others of which we know nothing, but if his later poetry is coloured by an ever deepening melancholy, a deep gathering pessimism, we might suspect that it was not only due to a gradual loss of faith in man's ability to restore to himself the shattered Paradise which had once seemed (to Wordsworth) within his reach; these private blows of fate must also have helped to charge his poetry with an autumnal sadness, a resignation, perhaps the vibration of his own approaching death. And then the death of his elder married daughter Dora was the final twist of the knife.

Two meetings of a professional kind might be accounted as of capital importance to Wordsworth's thinking. The most important is of course his encounter with the greatest thinker of the age, Coleridge— that unselfish, wayward, haphazard, and eccentric genius who rushed into Wordsworth's life like a whirlwind. Never could the poet have hoped for so profound an understanding of his work; but Coleridge brought even more than sympathetic appreciation. He approved the basic principles upon which Wordsworth had founded his poetic style. How moving is this great encounter; and how tragic that this literary friendship (which gave us the *Lyrical Ballads*) was clouded for so long by a silly misunderstanding which both men were big enough to have surmounted.[22] Never mind. Their association fecundated a whole period of our literature.

To this momentous friendship I would add another meeting, perhaps of less consequence in terms of friendship, but of great importance to the poet's intellectual make-up—the meeting with Hamilton, the Irish mathematical genius.[23] Through him Wordsworth learned all that was to be known about modern science—though of course he was getting on in years while Hamilton was still a young man. But he had always had an aptitude for, a fondness for, mathematics.

Another point is worth mentioning. In spite of the somewhat static picture his life gives, Wordsworth's mind was always open to Europe through its aptitudes. By education he was a classicist and humanist, but he also adventured in Italian and German as well as French. He also travelled in Europe increasingly after the wars subsided and the frontiers opened for travellers. His sympathies were generous and universal even if sometimes hidden under a dry and restrained exterior.

The reader should also bear in mind that this poet composed aloud, testing out his verses on the ear, not only on the eye. To do him justice he should be tested on the inner ear, or frankly, aloud. It will serve no purpose to hint at a certain metrical lack of variety in his work, and perhaps a touch of humourlessness. People of this calibre must be judged by their best qualities, and Wordsworth is no exception as he steers his verse around the rocks and shoals which lay in wait for it—over-meekness, sententiousness, too much austerity, too great a rectitude—towards the open sea of English poetry. He knew full well that the reality he sought lay beyond life, and that life was a very fragile and provisional matter.

The poem is an act of affirmation—one dares to make such a statement feeling that Wordsworth would have quietly agreed.

NOTES

1. Hartley Coleridge (1796–1849) was the eldest son of Samuel Taylor Coleridge (1772–1834) and was also a poet and biographer.
2. Coleridge 93.
3. This verse by J.K. Stephen (1859–1892) is itself a parody of Wordsworth's own "Thought of a Briton on the Subjugation of Switzerland." Durrell appears to be quoting from memory a compressed version of Stephen's "A Sonnet":

   Two voices are there: one is of the deep;
   It learns the storm-cloud's thunderous melody,
   Now roars, now murmurs with the changing sea,
   Now bird-like pipes, now closes soft in sleep:
   And one is of an old half-witted sheep
   Which bleats articulate monotony,
   And indicates that two and one are three,

> *That grass is green, lakes damp, and mountains steep:*
> *And, Wordsworth, both are thine: at certain times*
> *Forth from the heart of thy melodious rhymes,*
> *The form and pressure of high thoughts will burst:*
> *At other times—good Lord! I'd rather be*
> *Quite unacquainted with the A.B.C.*
> *Than write such hopeless rubbish as thy worst.*

4. Durrell is likely referring to Mary Moorman's two-volume *William Wordsworth: A Biography*.

5. This comment, and a good deal of the Introduction, speaks as much to Durrell's wishes for his own works as it does to Wordsworth.

6. Wordsworth visited France during the Revolution and felt a strong attachment to the Republican movement; however, he was highly distressed during the Reign of Terror when he left France.

7. Annette Vallon, who bore their child Caroline Vallon in 1792.

8. A common paraphrase from Freud's "Dostoevsky and Parricide" in *The Future of an Illusion*, in which he writes, "*The Brothers Karamazov* is the most magnificent novel ever written; the episode of the Grand Inquisitor, one of the peaks in the literature of the world, can hardly be valued too highly. Before the problem of the creative artist analysis must, alas, lay down its arms" (177).

9. Paul Valéry (1871–1945) was a French poet whose works Durrell was very familiar with. Rainer Maria Rilke (1875–1926) was an Austrian poet whose works Durrell wrote on and helped to publish in the 1940s in English translations. Durrell refers to W.B. Yeats's (1865–1939) poetic works frequently.

10. Durrell used a paraphrase of the same quotation as the epigraph to the final novel of his career, *Quinx*. This often misquoted passage derives from Wordsworth's May 21, 1807 letter to Lady Beaumont: "Every great and original writer, in proportion as he is great and original, must himself create the taste by which he is to be relished."

11. Famously chaste lovers. Héloïse d'Argenteuil (1101–1164) was a highly learned French nun and Pierre Abélard (1079–1142) was a French philosopher and theologian. They had a love affair, a child, and married, but when Héloïse's uncle Fulbert discovered it, he became abusive to her and eventually had Abélard castrated. Their subsequent love letters ultimately lead to a resignation and acceptance of love as a brother and sister.

12. Wordsworth's *The Prelude* (10:908–21).

13. John Willinsky makes a similar argument based on the same lines from *The Prelude* as a way of reading the scene of instruction in "Tintern Abbey" (Willinsky 47).

14. It is difficult to not regard this as Durrell commenting on himself rather than Wordsworth, as often seems the case in this essay. Durrell's early works from the 1930s to 1948 frequently aligned with the anarchist trends in his contemporaries and most notably through Henry Miller, but after his time in Yugoslavia from 1949 to 1952 followed by four years on Cyprus during the Enosis struggle, he began to adopt more conservative rhetoric, even though his 1968 *Tunc* and 1970 *Nunquam* are strongly anti-corporate and critique cultural hegemony. This relationship between revolution or rebellion and later conservatism is an unresolved conflict in Durrell's career.

15. Henry Crabb Robinson (1775–1867) was a diarist whose posthumous *Diary, Reminiscences and Correspondence* (1869) is an important source of information on many Romantic English writers.

16. From a letter by Robinson to Sir George Beaumont, May 29, 1812 (Batho 169).

17. De Quincey 117. Since Thomas de Quincey's (1785–1859) *Recollections* was republished by Penguin in 1970, and Durrell organized this collection of Wordsworth's poetry for Penguin in 1973, it is likely he has drawn on the De Quincey collection in the 1970 printing. De Quincey is best known for his auto-biographical *Confessions of an English Opium Eater* (1821).

18. Wordsworth was granted a Doctor of Civil Law from Durham University in 1838 and from the University of Oxford in 1839.

19. Robert Southey (1774–1843) was another English Romantic poet and a "Lake Poet" like Wordsworth.

20. The name Dorothy (as with Theodora) is literally gift of the gods.

21. The first several lines of Wordsworth's "Surprised by Joy."

22. Wordsworth and Coleridge were estranged in 1810 due to Coleridge's addiction to opium.

23. Sir William Rowan Hamilton (1805–1865), the Irish mathematician, physicist, and astronomer. The two corresponded for many years. Durrell notes their meeting and friendship in his "The Poetic Obsession of Dublin" in 1972 as well, the year before this work.

L'amour, Clef du Mystère?[1]

I HOPE YOU ARE STILL PREPARED to hear about Shakespeare. I ought to begin by confessing that centenaries and anniversaries, celebrations of national genius always seem to me to savour a little of corpse-eating. But it is true that we, writers, do live on the corpses of our ancestors in the strictly anthropological sense and we are so very much their children, their creations, both physical and intellectual, that it is perhaps poetic justice that we should be dug out from time to time to make a public confession of a debt to them, and to make a standard genuflection to any of the great images of our great ancestors. In the case of Shakespeare, what I found bizarre was the choice of a date like Friday the thirteenth which is considered a very unlucky day. It seemed to me that it was going to clash with my theme, because I wanted to present a portrait of an extremely lucky man. I don't mean by that a man who did not have personal private tragedy in his life, but from the point of view of his gifts, from his genius, it seems to me that the goddess luck was perpetually at his elbow. He had to invent absolutely nothing, the machinery was all lying ready, he simply had to manifest himself and be himself. To begin with, I think we often forget that he was saved from education by the fact that he got married far too early, at the age of eighteen, and already when he went to London to make a living, he had three small children. While he himself always felt somehow dishonoured by the fact that he was not a university man

149

(his use of the word "gentleman" simply means university man), nevertheless when we compare his imagery, in his work, with that of all his contemporaries, we see to what a degree the rather bad form of university of that day, what a bad effect it had on their work. The best of them, Chapman,[2] and almost anybody else one could name of that period, who suffered from a university education, his verse had become encrusted with Latin and Greek allusions with the result that it is virtually unreadable now. In Shakespeare's case, I don't think it was really lack of education. He was just every bit as much of a gentleman as Marlowe who was also a cobbler's son. It was just the small difference of the university education, I think. It was not that he could not throw gods and goddesses into his work just as liberally as anyone else, but that his *métier* made him very much more sensitive to the people he was talking to. I think perhaps half his audience would not have understood a reference to Venus or Aphrodite thrown off like that, and consequently his choice of imagery was limited very strictly to an audience.

Now, I spoke of him as a lucky man and I really believe that good luck did follow him all the way through from the very beginning, first of all in his job. The scholars try and tell us that the Elizabethan stage evolved out of the morality play, but in fact I think that we would be right in considering it a really new invention; it leaped pristine onto the scene thanks to Marlowe and Kyd[3] and perhaps some unnamed other playwrights too. The ordinary dramatic structure of the morality play is so totally different from a play which has character motivation, has plot, and has pace, that I think we would really be right in thinking that someone like Marlowe had placed in Shakespeare's hands the equivalent of a movie camera. I think personally of the Elizabethan stage as a creation to compare with the creation of the cinema of our own epoch. Incidentally, the conditions of writing for the stage were not very dissimilar from the conditions that are obtained today in a modern film studio. It was all team work and done at a terrific pace and very carelessly, and the miracle is that Shakespeare again had the extraordinary luck to work for the same company through his life. Many of the others changed, they were all selling their plays to different companies, and many of them were too gentlemanly to see them performed. He was the only one inside the theatre, and he was actually engaged in the work of mounting them; but he was also able to write them himself and this gave him a stranglehold on the Elizabethan theatre. In fact, on his arrival, at the age of about twenty-eight in London, he is first announced to us by a terrific attack by another dramatist called Greene, who calls him the "upstart crow":[4] the upstart crow beautified without feathers, who thinks that he can bump us out blank verse with the best of them. The considered "upstart crow" at this moment was doing something rather wicked. Up to now these young gentlemen were from the university, and I am not trying to be satirical; the distinction is a terribly important one in the sociological sense. The players were really considered vagabonds and any transgression of the law put them in a very awkward position, whereas the gentleman could recite his neat verse, and he who has been to the university did not have to be a noble's son. None of the others were. Ben Jonson was a bricklayer's son, and Marlowe was a cobbler's son, but he did not happen to have the university education. From the point of view of the law, it put them in a much stronger position than an ordinary player who was classed socially with a footpad or a vagabond. And I think this is really the reason, not snobbery, that we find these complaints in Shakespeare. I think he wanted to have the security of the added gentlemanly position, because Ben Jonson nearly went to the gallows and the penalties were extreme; Nashe had his ears cropped. It did not pay to have opinions; the list of people who suffered for one reason or another, or the list of people who were imprisoned, is quite impressive, and there were even more savage sentences. There was a gentleman called Stubbs who had some opinions about the French marriage; they were quite sound opinions, but it is a fact that he had opinions and they objected to them. His sentence was an extremely severe one. He was sentenced to have his right arm cut off, on the block, at Smithfield, by the public hangman, with the hangman's knife. He submitted to it quite calmly, and when it was over he raised his hat with the other hand and said "God save the Queen." At which point the reporter says: "The multitude was strangely silent"; but you see it was not all that easy. Now in Shakespeare's case, he was almost the only dramatist (I cannot think, in fact, of another off-hand) who did not even *seem* to get into trouble with the authorities. I suspect that he learnt his lesson very rapidly. We must imagine the London of that epoch as being something about the size of a park, perhaps 250,000 people, or Aix-en-Provence or Arles say. If he seems a bit of an enigma to us, he was certainly of flesh and blood to his contemporaries, and they saw him not only on the stage but walking about this town. One of the architectural features of this town was a row of rotting heads on pikes, along the walls, and this was a permanent reminder that opinions were dangerous and could land one in awful trouble.[5]

This sounds like a *boutade* but in fact what would be horrifying to writers today is the state of Elizabethan censorship, and yet, I am not sure that it was not precisely the narrowness and censoriousness of the Elizabethan in general that assisted Shakespeare. It prevented him from becoming either a sociologist, a politician, or a prophet. Now if we could do that for Sartre![6] Well, I think the theme of luck runs all the way to the trough. Few of the people of that period had the luck, for example, to find a livelihood and not to be obliged to adopt an ignominious begging position in front of a noble Lord for trivial presents or perhaps a tiny job as a tutor. While he bemoaned his social status, the fact that he was an ordinary player put the machinery into his hands to earn a livelihood and he seems to care about that very much. I think perhaps independent spirits do not like to beg and borrow, and they must prefer to earn their keep. At any rate, one would not classify as anything but a successful life that of a man who at the age of thirty-five already had money invested in Stratford and who was able to retire to the best house at forty-five or thereabout and live the rest of his short life spending very large sums of money and enjoying himself not with the nobility, because the last drinking bout that he had where he caught the fever that carried him off was with fellow-poets. Every attestation by his contemporaries suggests not only a brilliant actor but a very good-tempered, even, smooth-witted and pleasant person and a humorist. Well, if this distinct pattern is right, as I see it, and luck was the basic thing, he had nothing to do but be himself, and this of course is the hardest thing for any writer to be. It is hard to take time off to be yourself when you have all sorts of other preoccupations. I suspect that now we don't really talk about Shakespeare when we are talking about Shakespeare. For example he must have judged his work by the really acid test of theatrical effi-cacy, and I think we tend to see him more or less as a novelist because I have only seen about eight of his plays in my life, and I am perfectly sure that is about average for most people. To talk fully about his complete canon I think actors and *metteurs en scène*[7] would be the people who are always more fruitful in discussions on Shakespeare because they see more of him.

Incidentally, another point which I have overlooked terribly, and which is important is that despite the fact that he was in the public eye and always acting and so on, he lived a life of relative anonymity. You see, of his plays there were sixteen piracies during his life-time and many of them very corrupt; there was no copyright, so the printer could print anything that he picked up, and the author could say nothing about it; that is how the sonnets got out. In the obvious sixteen piracies there were perhaps four or five plays which were toler-ably accurate, but we had to wait, the world had to wait, until seven years after his death before the big Folio came out, done by his friends, and in that Folio, which had been lying in the strong rooms of the company all these years, there were twenty-one plays that we would not have got if his friends had not put them together. Those plays were not for publication. They were the property of a company of actors, and they were religiously locked up at night after the show. Of course, occasionally, an impecunious actor sold one, or a company went broke, or one was stolen, and they even ingeniously invented two types of shorthand to try to take down plays, so that they would send a spy, and we suspect that the first version of *Hamlet* that we have was a bad stenographic copy taken by someone who went into the theatre and whose shorthand was not up to UNESCO standards.

I don't want to play with the obvious because to place him is not necessary, he placed himself so very squarely all over the world, but if there is an enigma about him, and we seem to feel there is, I think it is created by ourselves. He really was flesh and blood to the contemporaries who saw him walk about, who heard him act, and we know more about him than we know about any other playwright. There does not seem to me to be any mystery, and the materials we have in the form of gossips and anecdotes about him add up to quite an effective picture of temperament. If his life seems a little too uneventful, it is because the Romantics put it into our heads that artists must have dramatic lives in order to be artists at all. I suspect that the reason we find him delineated so vaguely today is because he has become half a god and half a heavy industry. The titles to godship were supplied largely by Coleridge with help of German critics, who were very romantic, and that side of him is rather cloudy. The heavy industry is being supplied by the Americans, in terms of doctorates and scholarships, and in justice to the Americans, we must say, and this is very important, that in the last twenty-five years, all the best scholarship, the most acute work and the most profound work on the Elizabethans has been done by them and they are clearly leading the field in Elizabethan studies. You cannot move without falling in something really critical by an American scholar. As I say, this part-deity part-machine for producing doctorates and theses was apparently a man walking about in the streets of a small town of 250,000 inhabitants, well-known as an actor. The panoramic view he had is also quite explicable I think; he did not have a life as limited as a modern novelist does, who has very little chance, unless he is taken up by society, of seeing the nobility, of meeting people of cultural or any kind of consequence. Though this tiny little world of London of Shakespeare's time was in some ways very small, from the point of view of population, it was an extremely cosmopolitan world; it was open wide to all continents through the river, and it did centre on the whole Court. I don't know how many times an actor in his career today can count upon going to a command performance; I think probably twice or three times if he is lucky. There, they were called to court every week, every ten days, every month for a celebration, and they were quite used to it; it was rather a villagy atmosphere, you must imagine, and they were allowed on equal terms: all the noble people in the land as well as the most sensitive, youthful members of the nobility of that period and the inordinately rich. The suggestion is that it was due to him: the goddess luck again who made Shakespeare a loan and enabled him to buy a share in the company, because Shakespeare's money was made from the company and it came from the public. It was not just handouts from peers and exchanges with dedications. Then, finally, of course, the mystery of why in his will there were no books. And this is rather a mystery. It has been presumed that he bought the best house in Stratford as a sort of status symbol, the poor boy who wants to come back and show that he is a person of distinction now. But I wonder whether he could have been that. At any rate there are no books listed in the will; it is possible he did not like literature.

The scholars are right, of course, when they warn us against the danger of trying to deduce biographical facts about Shakespeare from stray hints in his plays—for despite the ardent and painstaking work of generations of experts, the canon is still in a state of inextricable confusion, not only as regards accurate chronology but also concerning the actual extent of his collaboration with others.

When he died, no less that twenty-one plays were still in manuscript, locked up presumably as part of the property of the playhouse in which he was a partner. The first complete collection was issued seven years after his death by two of his stage associates. He did not supervise this great Folio volume.[8] Many of these plays are retouched versions of old plays by other men which have now disappeared. All save two are based on plots taken from others' books. He was a great borrower, imitator, copier, and collaborator. He appears not to have been at all inventive. Yet in the midst of all this confusion and doubt there is a...something, a Voice which is completely and authentically his own. In poetic range, melody, and orchestration his work is unique, unequalled even in that age of giants.

Who was he? It is strange to know so much about him and yet to find him an enigma. We do in fact know more about him than about any other Elizabethan writer, yet we do not know the interesting things. It is rather like trying to study the destiny of someone from the stubs in his cheque-book. He has successfully buried himself under the immense reticence of his art. Even the world-weary smiling face of the only certain portrait gives little away; in colour he suggests someone who had perhaps some Welsh blood in his veins. Perhaps like his admired Montaigne[9] he had a Jewish strain in him? We cannot be certain. Everything is surmise, every new portrait must be, in the nature of things, a personal adventure.

But though the plays are not the happiest of hunting grounds for clues as to what he was really like, the poetic productions might seem safer ground, since at least we can be certain that these are all his own work. The two long verse-narratives, *Venus and Adonis* and *Lucrece*, show signs of careful preparation for the press. The first came out when he was twenty-nine, the second a year later; they were both best-sellers and established his poetic reputation once and for all. Moreover they went on selling all through his life and beyond it—the first passing through seventeen editions between 1593 and 1675. But it was the stage that made him rich, not poetry; starting from humble origins, the son of a wool merchant in Stratford, he enjoyed a meteoric career both as an actor and as a playwright.

We can be less certain of the famous sonnets which were pirated and yet…nobody reading them could believe they were not by Shakespeare; moreover, even in an age of sonnet sequences, they are extraordinarily unlike any other production. Whatever the scholars say, they are not just exercises in a form or poems written to secure a needed patronage. Finally, it is quite impossible to believe that they do not refer to actual people and events, though who the people may have been and when the events took place is another matter. It is as well to take up a definite position on this vexing matter right away so that those who reject this view of them may be spared the trouble of reading further.

And the young man who wrote them? At eighteen he had married in haste to a woman eight years his senior; she bore him three children, two girls and a boy. At the age of twenty-nine he emerges in London as an actor and a writer of fame. At thirty-three he was rich enough to indulge in what appears to have been a ruling passion—he began to invest in property in and around Stratford. At thirty-four he bought one of the largest houses in Stratford.[10] His father died when he was thirty-eight, his mother when he was forty-five. His twelve-year-old son died when he was thirty-three. He is presumed to have retired to Stratford about the age of forty-five to live the life of a country gentleman and supply the stage with two plays a year. It is clear that we are dealing with a genius who is at the same time gifted with a streak of peasant tenacity and a sound business instinct. This, then, is the bare frame of the picture. What of the subject?

I would like to try and sketch the probable temperament of this young countryman in terms which Dr. John Dee[11] (the eminent astrologer and alchemist of the day) might have found reasonable and plausible. The scholar will smile at the mention of the word "astrology," as he has every right to do; but would Shakespeare have smiled? Despite the skepticism of many of the intelligent men on the subject, the age itself was deeply permeated by a belief in the stars. Shakespeare's own plays illustrate the point. Moreover even Elizabeth herself had no hesitation in consulting Dr. John Dee about such matters. It is not impossible that at some time the young Shakespeare might have had his chart drawn for him, and heard his character discussed. What would the venerable doctor have told him?

He was born in Taurus, most probably on St. George's Day, that of the patron saint of England. The general characteristics of the sign, according to this regretfully imprecise pseudo-science would certainly square with everything we know about Shakespeare's habits and temperament. The dominating factors (Dr. Dee might have remarked) were intensely practical ones; a tremendous passion for ownership of lands and goods, a keen eye for material gain, and excellent judgement in everything to do with material advancement, and inexhaustible industry and application, and a strong fidelity to old ties. Shakespeare's ruling planet was Venus, and the good goddess must have brought him the gifts of charm and physical beauty, mixed perhaps with a troubling sensuality, perhaps even uxoriousness. Altogether a formidable combination of positive qualities for a young man starting a career in an entirely new industry—which is what the Elizabethan stage was in 1590. But on the debit side of the account would be other compensating defects; social timidity and a vein of native obtuseness, of stupidity. Taurus, so entirely free of capriciousness, replaces intuition and imaginative power by obdurate industry. He was obviously not a clever man; he invented nothing, borrowed everything. But whatever this great Original touched turned to magic. He was a sort of sorcerer.

It is in the sonnets that I believe we can come closest to him, can actually overlook a situation in the language. It is clear that they were not intended for publication. They were pirated when he was forty-six and probably issued when he was away from London. He would never have let them go to press with a semi-literate dedication signed by a book-seller's jackal. Moreover while there is much to support the theory that they are addressed to the Earl of Southampton[12] (patron of the two early verse-narratives) the whole case comes apart when we are faced with this obscure dedication, for nobody would address an eminent nobleman publicly in this way, either in Shakespeare's day or in our own.

TO. THE. ONLIE. BEGETTER. OF.

THESE. ENSVING. SONNETS. MR. W.H. ALL. HAPPINESS.

AND. THAT. ETERNITIE.

PROMISED.

BY.

OVR. EVERLIVING. POET.

WISHETH.

THE. WELL-WISHING.

ADVENTVRER. IN.

SETTING.

FORTH.

T.T.

It seems gibberish, and many brilliant theories have been advanced to explain it. In my view the original dedication is the first three lines. The rest was added by the pirate. The word "begetter" suggests Shakespeare very strongly. It chimes with the main theme of the sonnets themselves, and one could also point out in passing that he describes *Venus and Adonis* in his dedication to Southampton as "the first heir" of his invention. Shakespeare seems to have quite a strong obsession about "begetting"; it is a good Taurine trait. Indeed in these passionate sonnets to the "fair youth" he seems far more concerned to see him become the "onlie begetter" of a child than actually to possess him: just as he seems in his life to have been far more concerned to establish himself and his family in Stratford than to bicker over literary honours.

Neither the identity of W.H. nor that of the dark lady has been discovered, despite the numerous hints and clues contained in the poems. Scholarship has tended to excessive reserve about the question of Shakespeare's apparent homosexuality as betrayed by the first group of sonnets to the "fair youth," though the poet himself does not bother to equivocate when he comes to describe his friend.

A woman's face with Nature's own hand painted
Hast thou, the master-mistress of my passion;
A woman's gentle heart, but not acquainted
With shifting change, as is false woman's fashion;
An eye more bright than theirs, less false in rolling,
Gilding the object where upon it gazeth;
A man in hue, all hues in his controlling,
Which steals men's eyes and womans' souls amazeth;
And for a woman wert thou first created;[13]
Till Nature, as she wroght thee, fell a-doting,
And by addition me of thee defeated,
By adding one thing to my purpose nothing.
But since she pricked thee out for womens' pleasure,
Mine be thy love, and thy love's use their treasure.[14]

The truth is that we are facing this great poet not only across a gulf of years but also across a gulf in our national *moeurs*, for though the suppurating sore of Puritanism-Protestantism dribbled on all through the reigns of Elizabeth and James, these people were still by heritage Renaissance men. Passion was an absolute value for them, they respected its laws; and side by side with it they accorded full value to extremes of idealism which today would seem exaggerated. Since Cromwell[15] both passion and love have been more or less relegated to the domain of pathology or the police-court. Certainly in our age a sonnet as passionate and apparently as explicit as the one quoted above would have excited the gravest suspicions of homosexuality in its author. But if the passion expressed appears unequivocal so also does the self-abnegation of it in the last few lines. An Elizabethan would have been puzzled by our angle of vision—which is indeed a profane one; he lived in an age when men were as finely dressed as women, experts in rings, perfume, and brilliant clothes. Marlowe, for example, was almost aggressively homosexual in his attitude if we are to believe (not only the subject-matter of a play or two) the scraps of his tavern-conversation transcribed by two Government spies. "All who care not for tobacco and boys are fools," he says in good round Elizabethan.[16] These words ring sourly in the ear of the prude. They excite a timid prurience all too characteristic of the age, but one which has nothing to do with Elizabethan values. Spenser, in the notes to his "Shepherd's Calendar" supplies an interesting defense of boy-love on the Greek pattern, but he expressly denies that sensual passion plays any part in it.[17] In the case of the sonnets we could easily make a fair case both for and against the theory of Shakespeare's apparent homosexuality in the matter of Mr. W.H. But surely this has no meaning for those who are concerned with the values of art. The Elizabethans excelled in grotesque exaggerations of the sensibility; they ranged heroically between extremes of the idealism in which they believed and the realism of their daily lives. The sonnets are touching reminders from a forgotten age that to love someone deeply—to love them, as it were, beyond the grave while you are still alive with them—is also, in a paradoxical sort of way to try and free them from love, from the shackles of love's particularity, its greed and exclusiveness. The true lover, in this extreme sense, tries to encompass everything, even the betrayals (which are no betrayals at all) in order to give the psyche of the beloved person a chance to grow its own bright phoenix plumage. Real love, whether mixed with passional love or not, has this quality of selflessness. That is why we love women, for they embody it; and Shakespeare's women are full of it. It surely is a wicked limitation in our view of art to spend our time pondering about the sexual relations of Petrarch and Laura, wondering whether Emily Brontë was led astray by a clergyman, or speculating whether Dante would have been better advised to imitate Humbert Humbert with his Lolita.[18] Moreover in the case of the great artist, the artist of the universal scale, we are dealing with someone who was extending the range of his human understanding and insight to a point where he might be considered as much a woman as a man. His bisexual psyche[19] has been allowed to exfoliate, to extend itself abnormally to the very limits of his capacity for human sympathy. In terms of ordinary life this immense range of psycho-sexual sympathy might turn out in the virtual impotence of a Kierkegaard.[20] But let us leave the field of conduct to the moralists and consider only, in this sonnet, the passionate self-abnegation of the poet towards his friend; his recognition that Mr. W.H. must one day find himself as a man through "women's" pleasure. Indeed in the whole of the sequence devoted to W.H. he is urged to create a boy-child in his own likeness; this is held up to him as an ideal which must be fulfilled if he is to justify his own exceptional beauty. And how touchingly naïve is the poet's punning use of the word "prick"—for the Elizabethans "pricked" their signs, and the word is still slang for "penis" with us today. But it is worth pointing out that in the long sequence addressed to the fair youth this obsession with "begetting" is, ironically enough, very typical of the Taurine temperament; the poet was wishing for W.H. the very best that a Taurus could imagine for himself—an heir!

If we dare to imagine that actual events are described in the sonnets, the story they hold for us is a strange one indeed; the first sequence traces out an intimate, perhaps passional, relationship between the poet and a young man, which appears to have lasted for some time; in the second sequence a mysterious dark lady appears on the scene and disturbs this happy state of affairs, first by seducing the young man away from the poet, and finally in making the poet himself fall helplessly in love with her. As far as we can judge this irresistibly attractive female vampire not only shared her favours with both men, but succeeded in completely captivating and subjugating them. It is an extraordinary situation, and one which might have made the subject of one of his greatest plays had he used it; the poems trace out the whole fever-chart of this mysterious three-cornered love-affair with the most moving candour. The poet is cornered by his double passion for a fair man and a female demon. Instructive, too, is the contrast between the pure idealism of the sonnets addressed to the man, and the fiercely realistic sequence addressed to the woman. The fair youth is a pattern of honesty and fidelity while the dark woman is hopelessly profligate, a specialist in every sort of treachery. But neither the poet nor his friend can resist her. Indeed one wonders whether perhaps the unfortunate Shakespeare by insisting so much on the hypothetical heir of Mr. W.H. did not himself finally push him into the arms of this female cormorant, and so become the unwitting cause of his own sufferings. That would be poetic justice indeed!

If we accept the recent dating of the sonnets by Dr. Leslie Hotson,[21] and his case seems a firm one, we can assume that the first batch to the young man were written between the age of twenty-two (when Shakespeare first met Mr. W.H.) and twenty-nine. In other words, when the pirate first produced them in book form, they referred to events which lay far back, nearly twenty years, in the poet's early youth. Perhaps by then the principals were dead, or the subject-matter so obscured by the passage of time that the piracy called forth no protest from the poet. At any rate Shakespeare does not seem to have protested against it.

What can we learn about the fair youth and the dark lady from the sonnets, if we follow up the enigmatic hints with which the text abounds? Mr. W.H. was fair, truthful, faithful, and young—indeed a paragon of virtue. He was rather better bred than the poet, who seems to have been indebted to him both intellectually as well as socially. Shakespeare represents himself as a somewhat rough and gauche country boy whose "rude ignorance" profits from this acquaintance, as do his "untutored" poems. He is also conscious of his low social position and hopes to better his fortunes in order to be more worthy of his friendship for W.H. who incidentally is likened in beauty to Adonis (mark this) as well as Helen and Sappho. Among the images, the "phoenix" and the "tiger" also put in a brief appearance. The sonnets record several partings, several betrayals, several quarrels and reconciliations. Shakespeare seems conscious of his greater age, and of what he calls his "tanned antiquity." He is perhaps somewhat shy of his baldness—at any rate he hates wigs, "the spoils of sepulchers." There are also hints of some scandal which caused the poet unhappiness. Worse still there is a rival for the affections of W.H. who is a poet—a much greater poet than Shakespeare himself: or so he says. Among the key-images which occur more than once is the word "hue" (which meant both complexion and beauty); and pouncing on this, Oscar Wilde[22] developed his theory of the young actor Will Hughes whom Shakespeare is supposed to have loved. It is ingenious as a theory, and may not have been far from the truth. There are some punning sonnets addressed to the dark lady which do lead one to believe that Mr. W.H.'s first name, like Shakespeare's, was "William." And as a matter of fact Sir Sidney Lee[23] does mention that there was a musician called William Hughes at this time; but unfortunately we know nothing about him. To this theory we must concede quite a number of references in the sonnets to music which might indeed suggest that the boy was a musician. But in the light of our present knowledge all is surmise. On the other hand it is worth bearing in mind that all Shakespeare's women were played by boys on the stage, even Juliet and Cleopatra, and also that (faithful Taurus) he belonged to the same company throughout his whole professional career, so that he was, to a certain extent, nearly always writing with his actors in mind—a luck that only dramatists attached to a particular company can enjoy. If only we had a firm text upon which to work we might be bolder in our analysis of his women but alas: from day to day the scholars are making new discoveries. We still do not know how much of Kyd's work is buried in Hamlet, nor how much of Lear has remained from the older version which Shakespeare retouched. This is why I am trying to keep, as far as is possible, to the text of the poems which seem relatively reliable.

The points which seem of most importance in the sonnets do not seem to me to be those which are concerned with the actual identity of the subjects—though of course they provide most of the detective-story interest for the scholar. The insistence on certain lines of thought like W.H.'s hypothetical child and his fairness compared to the darkness and wickedness of his seducer seem to me more fruitful. Indeed as far as the imagery goes the counterpoint between "fair" and "dark," as well as its secondary moral undertone in "fair" and "foul" seem to me to be as important as anything else; they seem, so to speak, the obsessional points in this long sequence of marvelous love-poems. To extend the associations even further would be to counterpoint the "ideal" love of W.H. against the harsher "real" love of the dark woman. Certainly the sonnets to her seem permeated with a *strangely* sexual flavor, full as they are of doubts, recoils, disgust....Even, one might say, insults. If the first love-relationship is an idyll, the second triangular one is an inferno.

Now at some time during—even perhaps while—these sonnets were taking form in Shakespeare's private notebooks, to which presumably only W.H. had access,[24] he constructed, polished, and published the two long narrative poems which he dedicated to the Earl of Southampton, and on which his public fame as a poet was first based. These we may fairly take as being aimed to secure patronage. They say so in their dedications. Indeed from the dedication to *Lucrece* it would already seem that with the first poem Shakespeare has secured the attention of his patron. He promises him all his future work, as every good Taurus would! But what of the themes of these two public poems? Would it be permissible to consider their general plots in the light of what we know, in this century, about the analysis of dreams? I think it would; but it would also be as well to remind the reader who finds a Freudian paper-chase through the images and allegories of our poet either distasteful or ridiculous that Freud himself, that modest genius, presented his findings in the most tentative way, as fruitful hypotheses merely, not as cast iron facts. Moreover it was he who, writing of Shakespeare and Dostoyevsky, said: "Before the mystery of the creative act psychoanalysis lays down her arms";[25] and indeed in later years when Thornton Wilder[26] told him that many of his discoveries had been anticipated by the poets he replied: "But of course. The poets have always known them." This said, let us turn to *Venus and Adonis*.

But of course the first thing to be said is that Shakespeare took his idea from Lodge's *Glaucus and Scilla*,[27] and once again this illustrates a fundamental point about his work. He regarded it much as an actor regards his own, in the sense that the actor is only concerned with his execution, his performance of a part. He is content if "his" Hamlet is the greatest one; he does not ask for a new Hamlet every time. So Shakespeare behaves much more like an interpreter than a creator; if dissatisfied with an existing play he re-wrote it, improved on it. He did not bother to try and invent new themes—a Taurus cannot anyway. He took an existing idea and transformed it, impregnated it with his own genius.

What is interesting about his version of *Venus and Adonis* is not only the choice of title but also the fact that it so closely echoes many of the themes contained in the first sequence of the sonnets—those addressed to W.H. In fact Adonis himself is described in roughly the same terms by Shakespeare's tutelary goddess, Venus, as the male subject of the sonnets.

Stain to all nymphs, more lovely than a man,
More white and red than doves or roses are.[28]

All the way through this rather long-winded attempt to seduce the youth we come upon the same basic themes with which the sonnets have acquainted us. Venus keeps reminding Adonis that "By law of Nature thou art bound to breed." One of the main themes of the W.H. poems is once more reworked here, and with many echoes from the sonnets. But poor Venus can make little headway against the youth. She describes herself thus:

Poor queen of love, in thine own law forlorn,
To love a cheek that smiles at thee in scorn.[29]

In other words the poem is a sort of allegorized version of the first half of the sonnets; the goddess uses all the same blandishments, including the central *leitmotiv* which concerns procreation as being the only justification of physical beauty. It is not hard to be convinced that we have here a stilted and formalized statement of the same situation, only this time presented in terms of a conscious poetic effort. It is a brilliantly cold exteriorization of the old theme, but this time aimed at a public patron. I do not think it too far fetched to suspect this protean artist of being able to present both subjective and objective views of his central preoccupations at this time, and to write these two narrative-poems about problems with which he had dealt privately in the sonnets. There is a very strong similarity between Venus invoking Adonis and Shakespeare invoking Mr. W.H. But here, incidentally, the Freudian could bring some solace to the quivering puritan, for as far as we can see the blandishments of Venus have no effect at all on Adonis, who like a healthy British boy much prefers hunting, shooting, and fishing to more specialized amatory exploits. In fact the goddess is left holding the anemone which sprang from his blood. Shakespeare's reputation has been saved by psychoanalysis. As for the anemone there is some confusion among Elizabethan writers, including Shakespeare. In some places the flower is described as a "rose." (One is instantly reminded of Hamlet, who is described as "the expectancy and *rose*..."[30])

But if this narrative poem represents in my view an extension and elaboration of the situation concerning W.H., where does the dark lady come in? She is certainly not present here. Perhaps it would be worth turning our attention to the poem which immediately followed *Venus and Adonis*? Dare we suspect that the situation described here— the rape of a "fond fair and true" woman by the ravisher Tarquin[31] has any bearing on the second sequence of sonnets. Only if we accept the fact that in dream analysis we should keep an eye out for material which has been displaced as well as for the ordinary substitution of opposites; Lucrece, treated in this context would yield both, for the fair youth, the paragon of all the virtues appears now to have become a fair Roman matron, ravished by the dark ("foul") Tarquin, the embodiment of dreadful lust. How could a Roman matron become fair? Nevertheless...

> This heraldry in Lucrece' face was seen
> Argued by beauty's red and virtue's white:
> Of either colour was the other queen...[32]

It is not the only reference but it will serve. As for Tarquin the references to "blackness" in the moral sense are too numerous not to be noticed. "Black lust, dishonour, shame, misgoverning" cries Lucrece: and after the dark deed has been committed she adds: "My sable ground of sin I will not paint."[33] In other words Lucrece has now usurped the colours of Adonis, and Tarquin those of the dark lady of the sonnets who ravishes her against her will!

Of the dark lady herself, as portrayed in the sonnets, we know very little indeed beyond the fact that her darkness impressed Shakespeare and that she was hopelessly unfaithful to both men. Some scholars, impressed by the references to her colouring, have even gone as far as to suggest that she may actually have been a negress. This is largely due I think to the line. "If wires be black, black wires grow on thy head." Myself I think this is a misunderstanding based on the word "wires" which meant musical strings to the Elizabethan. In Spenser you find, for example, blonde hair described as "golden wyre."[34] As for the darkness of the lady, we do know that darkness of colouring was unfashionable in Elizabethan times, and that gentlemen appeared, then as now, to prefer blondes. It does not even seem to matter what sort of blondes. Sidney addresses two poetic heroines with black eyes and gold hair, though he does not tell us how this was achieved without the aid of science. This may be what Shakespeare means when he writes to the dark lady: "I never saw that you did painting need."

But dark the lady certainly was, and Shakespeare unluckily does not specify how this came to be; he didn't use, like Marston,[35] the early form of our "brunette"; nor does he seem to distinguish clearly between a negro darkness and the tawny colour of the Arab or Gypsy type. Of his dark lady he says mockingly: "If snow be white why then her breasts are dun." But this is not very helpful; it is curious too that he shows no partiality for the words "sooty" and "dusky" which were in common poetic usage, nor for "tawny" which I have found applied to gypsies, and also to the colour of leather and tobacco. Needless to say the scholars have made numberless attempts to penetrate the mystery of the dark lady; some have unearthed a real negress called Lucy Negro, others have suggested a real gypsy—and London abounded in those brilliant magpies during this period. They were known as "Egyptians" because they were believed to come from Egypt. The vagaries and instabilities of Cleopatra show that in creating her character Shakespeare had a gypsy in mind and not a negress.

But if we must abandon the attempt to discover the identity of W.H. and the dark lady (for here scholarship must have the last word) there is no need to dismiss the fair-dark counterpoint which enables us, in terms of the imagery, to look a little way into the story behind the sonnets. It does seem clear that Shakespeare had some special reason to be interested in the darkness of skin, and certainly in some of his plays one finds references which awaken our interest, particularly of course, in those in which he was dealing with dark characters, as for example the two Moors Othello and Aaron. In the case of Othello there is the faintest echo of the Lucrece-Tarquin situation—this time with Desdemona (fair fond and true) playing the role once allotted to Lucrece. Iago calls Othello "old black ram" and "the lascivious Moor," while Brabantio mentions

the sooty bosom
O such a thing as though, to fear, not to delight.[36]

Aaron, in *Titus Andronicus*, offers an equally interesting set of references in the context of colour; for he, a swarthy Moor like Othello, finds no more impediment to his love on the grounds of colour than this coeval. Both Desdemona and Queen Tamora accept their swarthy husbands without demur; but the latter is troubled by the colour of Aaron's child! When she asks him to make away with it this hardened brute behaves with much nobility. The nurse who brings him the child thinks it "loathesome as a toad," but Aaron calls it "sweet blossom" and asks "Is black so base a hue?" Indeed he defends dark skin in lines which are virtually echoes from the sonnets.

> *Coal black is better than another hue,*
> *In that it scorns to bear another hue.*[37]

People with dark skins cannot blush! This appears to be the poet's impression, and he mentions the fact more than once.

The plays, though they are so rich in references, do not of course allow us to carry this kind of enquiry very far. Few of Shakespeare's characters are his own; most are projections of himself based upon existing creations. "By Heavens!" says the King in *Love's Labours Lost* to Biron, "Thy love is black as ebony!" The knight's response is interesting, though spoken half in jest:

> *Is ebony like her? Oh wood divine!*
> *A wife of such wood were felicity...*
> *No face is fair that is not full so black.*[38]

I believe that a careful study of the key images from the sonnets could present us with many fruitful hypotheses about our poet; and if I were a scholar I should hunt down many of these tantalising metaphors—crow, dove, phoenix, lily, rose, anemone, tiger—and follow my enquiry through to the plays. But there is no space to provide more than a tentative sketch of my imagined subject, and I would prefer to revert to yet another poem—this time *The Phoenix and The Turtle*, which appeared in print when the poet was thirty-eight years old, that is to say already in mid-career.

One of the things we know as being characteristic of him was a disinclination to write *vers de société* in an age when almost every poet felt his duty to write odes, dedicatory verses, epithalamia, and so on, in order to curry favour with the great. Today publishers ask writers to give them a "blurb" for the cover of a new book; the Elizabethan version of a "blurb" was a set of commendatory verses affixed to the front of a new book. Poets regarded this as quite normal, but apart from a lovely sonnet printed before a book by his friend Florio,[39] Shakespeare does not seem to have followed tradition; in fact he wrote nothing on the death of Elizabeth or the accession of James. Now this was remarked by this contemporaries, and he was even mildly reproved in print for it.

This strange poem which he contributed to an anthology by invitation is not a piracy; presumably, then, he found the theme a congenial one upon which to work. Certainly there was no money to be made out of *Love's Martyr*, as the anthology was called. The compiler, Robert Chester,[40] invited a number of poets to write on the same theme, and several famous Elizabethans contributed to the compilation. The title poems by Chester himself is too obscure and rambling to yield anything but insoluble mysteries, but the subject matter of this verse-contest is most interesting. The poets were asked to treat the chaste love of a phoenix, which represented a woman, for a turtle, representing a man; they are consumed in the flames of the Arabian pyre, and from their ashes arises a new phoenix—perfect love.

Shakespeare's contribution, like many of the others in this book has been found extremely obscure and the scholars hardly mention it any more, despairing of finding its true meaning. But it seems to me that here once more I find echoes of the subject-matter of the sonnets, the counterpoint of W.H. and the dark lady—only now they are transmuted into metaphysical creatures, no longer man and woman so much as female phoenix and male turtle. Shakespeare calls them, magnificently the "Co-supreme and stars of love." He describes their obsequies.

> So they loved as loved in twain
> Had the essence but in one;
> Two distincts, divisions none;
> Number there in love was slain.

> So between them love did shine,
> That the turtle saw his right
> Flaming in the phoenix' sight;
> Either was the other's mine.

> Property was thus appalled
> That the self was not the same;
> Single nature's double name,
> Neither two nor one was called.[41]

Here too we will find a reference to the "treble-dated" crow (perhaps a misprint for "fated"?) And for my part the famous "death-divining swan" calls up the memory of Lucrece once more:

> And now this pale swan in her watery nest
> Begins the sad dirge of her certain ending.
> "Few words" quoth she "shall fit the trespass best,
> Where no excuse can give the fault amending."[42]

Lucrece also refers to the phoenix when she declares: "So of fame's ashes shall my fame be bred." If one can broadly accept this rather daring identification of the short Threnos for the dead lovers which closes, The Phoenix and The Turtle is doubly moving, particularly with is reference (once more!) to posterity.

Death is now the phoenix nest
And the turtle's loyal breast
To eternity doth rest.

Leaving no posterity;
'Twas not their infirmity,
It was married chastity.

Truth may seem but cannot be;
Beauty brag but 'tis not she;
Truth and beauty buried.

To this urn let those repair
That are either true or fair;
For these dead birds sigh a prayer.[43]

Did he perhaps mean that by this time his two "Co-supremes" were dead—or simply that he had surmounted the wounds they had inflicted on him and was able to transmute the experience into imperishable poetry: and incidentally to recognize the dark lady for the great phoenix, the paragon, and "nonpareil" that she had been? We cannot be sure. My own personal inclination would be to suspect her of being a gypsy in colour and a courtesan by profession. Alas! I cannot prove that Mr. W.H. picked her up in a brothel, or that he paid the price for his "sensual fault" as the poet describes it or something like it. Yet one is free to surmise. And despite the express statement of Aubrey that Shakespeare was "the more to be admired as he would not be debauched, and if invited to court was ill."[44] There is no reason to imagine him as a prude. His plays are pleasingly full of good bawdry, and his references to the Elizabethan stews are many and pointed. There may well be some truth in the contemporary anecdotes about him and his amatory exploits which has come down to us—though I fear it sounds very like the kind of gossip which is invented about famous people the world over. I repeat it for what it is worth. Burbage,[45] the famous star who acted the hero in most of the company's plays had an assignation with a girl; but when he knocked at her door and was asked who was without he replied (it was a pardonable piece of complacency, for he had been a hit in the part) "Richard the Second"; whereupon the voice of his friend Shakespeare was heard within saying: "Tell him that William the Conqueror is here already—and he comes long before Richard." True? False? We do not know.

Psychologists have already pointed out the poet's partiality towards substitution in the early comedies: girls are disguised as pages, brothers as sisters, and so on. This is regarded as a sign of sexual ambivalence; but I am not sure that this is very certain ground. The tradition from which he was borrowing was Italian, and here we may have simply a stage convention of the day and not a clue to psychological predispositions. I am, of course, prepared to concede that Rosalind says of herself that she would be "changeable, longing, and liking...full of tears, full of smiles...as boys and women are."[46] But Rosalind is a renaissance woman. We might find more material in *Two Gentlemen of Verona*, where Proteus loves both Silvia and Julia, and where the latter says of the former: "Her hair is auburn, mine a perfect yellow."[47] But there is not the space to deal exhaustively with such hints. Certainly all such tentative explanations must halt before the magnitude of his female creations, starting with those lovely and spirited girls in the comedies, and gradually gathering breadth and depth and tragic sense in a Cordelia, a Lady MacBeth, and Ophelia. On one score we can reassure ourselves; Shakespeare was not a woman, for no woman has ever or could ever, create beings like these! But perhaps it would be politer to say only that up to today no woman has done so.

All great experiences are a challenge to the artist. They are to be surmounted and transformed, and their precious essence must be distilled and turned to use—for in art lies the justification for reality (from the artist's point of view). I am prepared to presume that this early and seminal experience which marked and formed young Shakespeare finally dispersed itself into the rest of his work, enriching it even as it slowly faded—or was superseded by experiences more wounding, more damaging, more useful. We know almost nothing about the middle period of the great tragedies, except for fragmentary data of little interest. Freudians have done a systematic treatment of *Hamlet* in terms of the Oedipus complex which is extremely brilliant as far as it goes; and Freud, in trying to date *Hamlet*, has suggested that the death of the poet's mother might have set into train the emotions which led to the writing of the play. I would myself be inclined to favour an earlier date connected with the death of his son.

We speak of the artist and tend rather to forget the somewhat grasping peasant Shakespeare was; undeflected in his career he succeeded in making a comfortable fortune which was directed (one might say) obsessively towards re-establishing his family in Stratford. He bought a family coat of arms. Always the faithful Taurus, he kept in touch with his town, visiting it every year, according to Aubrey. He did not want the kind of honours London could have offered him—he left those for Ben Jonson. What he wanted for himself (what he wanted for W.H.) was to found a solid yeoman family with plenty of land. Nothing could turn him from this purpose and nothing did.

So we come to his last work—one which no biographer can afford to overlook though Shakespeare did not actually write it himself; his will. When he came to dictate it a little while before he died there still remained the old active peasant streak. What the death of his son cost him we shall never know; but his two daughters were still alive and suitably married. Either might bear him a male child to continue the succession. So the will was planned; on the surface it may appear a somewhat confusing document but there is no mistaking the central driving purpose to it. It was designed in such a way that the property would find itself intact in the hands of a male descendant—*a male heir*!

From fairest creatures we desire increase
That thereby beauty's rose may never die.[48]

How touching the sonnets are when read in the light of this central dominating purpose of our gentle poet. Alas! his hopes died with his son Hamnet, though he did not live to know it. Within two generations the male side of the family was extinct, and the land for which he had struggled, plotted, and saved, had been slowly dispersed among the families of his daughters. The mainspring of his working life failed him in the last resort, and all his sacrifices were wasted.[49]

We have, then, here the portrait of an exceptionally faithful man, true to old friends and old business ties, true to his own peasant origins and their attitudes, true to his own character with all its mutinous impulses. It would not be too much to suggest that he was also a faithful and truthful lover, and though time has covered up the record of later loves, we have in the sonnets at any rate the record of one great experience which formed him. Perhaps he did not entirely forget the dark lady and the fair youth? Perhaps echoes of them came back sometimes, faded like perfume in a room a long time uninhabited, among the images of his later plays? It is a pardonable sentimentality to imagine so. Here, for example, is one from his last play: *The Tempest.*

Gon: *What marvelous sweet music!*
Alon: *Give us kind keepers, heavens! What were these?*
Seb: *A living drollery. Now I will believe*
      That there are unicorns; that in Arabia
      There is one tree, the phoenix throne; one phoenix
      At this hour reigning there![50]

1. This title is taken from Durrell's publication of an eclectic, partial version of this piece in French translation. The return of the essay to English here is reconstructed from his original English typescript of his UNESCO lectures, which are held at the Bibliothèque Lawrence Durrell, l'Université Paris Ouest, Nanterre. These contain more errors and the repetitions more typical of a spoken presentation than the partial publication in French. The second portion is much cleaner work than the first, but they are presented together here for the sake of completeness. The lecture was given on November 13, 1964 but is based on his draft in 1962 (MacNiven 542). I have taken liberties with punctuation to clarify what would have read aloud well but would cause confusion to the eye. Spelling is also corrected throughout. Most repetitions have been retained from the manuscript of the speech, but those most obviously for spoken presentation are silently elided.

2. George Chapman (1559–1634) was a playwright contemporary with Shakespeare who is best known for his translations of Homer, which inspired John Keats's famous sonnet "On First Looking into Chapman's Homer."

3. Thomas Kyd (1558–1594) was an Elizabethan playwright whose *Spanish Tragedy* is one of Shakespeare's sources for *Hamlet*. There is also much speculation that Kyd wrote a play titled *Hamlet* prior to Shakespeare's.

4. Greene's 1592 pamphlet *Groats-worth of Witte*.

5. Famously, heads decorated the posts of London Bridge as well. It is worth comparing this political discussion with that adopted by Durrell two years earlier in his essay "No Clue to Living" included in this volume (37–46).

6. Jean-Paul Sartre (1905–1980) was a French writer and philosopher who represented Marxism and existentialism in France. Sartre later became explicitly anarchist but at this time was Marxist (though he never belonged to the Communist Party). He also had a long-running public dispute with the French critic Louis Althusser in the 1960s. Althusser held an anti-humanist Marxist position whereas Sartre was adamantly humanist.

7. A film director.

8. This repetition from the previous section likely reflects the structural division of the lecture given in two parts, hence this reminds the audience of what the previous section had covered.

9. Michel de Montaigne (1533–1592) is a French Renaissance writer most famous for his essays.

10. As above, these repetitions appear designed to remind the audience in this second part of the lecture of the concepts and content discussed in the first.

11. Dee (1527–1608) was a mathematician and occultist who tutored Elizabeth I and acquired the largest library in England, perhaps all of Europe at the time.

12. Henry Wriothesley (1573–1624). Shakespeare's first poetic works were dedicated to Wriothesley, and hence speculation leads many to posit his role in the sonnets.

13. Durrell's typescript omits the ninth line.

14. Shakespeare, Sonnet XX. Oscar Wilde famously uses the same sonnet for the same evidence in his novella "The Portrait of Mr. W.H."

15. Oliver Cromwell (1599–1658) was a military leader in the English Civil War and was Lord Protector of the United Kingdom during the Interregnum.

16. As reported by Richard Baines in "the Baines Note," which contains many varied claims about Marlowe (Hopkins 15–17).

17. Edmund Spenser's (1552–1599) *The Shepheardes Calender*, first published in 1579. This refers to the January eclogue in which Hobbinol loves Colin Clout who loves Alexis; however, the anonymous commentary by "E.K." in the poem denies a sexual component (Fone 158–61).

18. An allusion to Vladimir Nabokov's famous pedophiliac novel *Lolita*, in which his narrator, Humbert Humbert, falls in love with a "nymphet" approximately the same age as Dante's Beatrice.

19. Durrell also used the same phrase a few years earlier in the opening note to his novel *Balthazar*. He had wanted *Justine* described as "an investigation of bisexual love," but this was not suitable for publication and reappears in his drafts for the prefatory "Note" to *Balthazar* only as "My topic is a[n] investigation of modern love; the bisexual psyche." I am indebted to Charles Sligh of the University of Tennessee, Chattanooga for further archival evidence—these materials appear in the Durrell fonds in the Morris Library of Southern Illinois University, ICarbS 42/12/1 (enumerated by MacNiven as A.44—A.47). A.44 reads as I have quoted, A.45 is a typed duplicate, A.46 is a typed copy revised in pencil that adds "of Freud" to "the bisexual psyche," and A.47 is then a typed copy identical to the final published Note, which reads, "The central topic of the book is an investigation of modern love" (*Balthazar* 9). The lateness of this revision is further demonstrated by the proof copy of the novel, which is held at the University of Victoria, in which the A.44–A.47 materials from Carbondale are finalized in typescript and then pasted into the proofs for the novel, placed directly over a previous and entirely different version of the same Note (see item 2.3 in the Durrell fonds).

20. Søren Kierkegaard (1813–1855) was a Danish philosopher often seen in the existentialist school. He questioned the importance of non-being and impotence to the notion of the self. Durrell referred to Kierkegaard's works as early as the 1930s.

21. John Leslie Hotson (1897–1992) advances this theory in *Shakespeare's Sonnets Dated and Other Essays* (1949). Durrell's earlier comments on Shakespeare being the son of a wool dealer also derive from Hotson. Hotson did not publish his famous *Mr WH* (1964) until two years after Durrell's piece appeared in print. Durrell follows Wilde closely here.

22. See Wilde's novella "The Portrait of Mr. W.H.," first published in 1889 but expanded for publication in *Lord Arthur Savile's Crime and Other Stories* in 1891.

23. Lee (1859–1926) was a major Shakespeare scholar and biographer. He taught at Balliol College, Oxford, and edited Oxford University Press's facsimile of the First Folio. Durrell is likely referring to his 1904 book *Great Englishmen of the Sixteenth Century*.

24. This is speculative and relates to Durrell's own working method with his notebooks.

25. Durrell refers to this passage several times (Freud, *Future* 177).

26. Wilder (1897–1975) was an American playwright and novelist most famous for his play *Our Town*. He met with Freud in 1935.

27. Thomas Lodge (1558–1625) published this collection of poems in 1580, and it is generally believed that Shakespeare is indebted to him for *Venus and Adonis*.

28. Shakespeare, *Venus and Adonis* 9–10.

29. Shakespeare, *Venus and Adonis* 251–52.

30. *Hamlet* III.i.161.

31. Durrell is referring to Shakespeare's poem "The Rape of Lucrece," which is drawn from Ovid's *Fasti*. Sextus Tarquinius, the son of King Tarquin of Rome, rapes Lucrece, who commits suicide, which ultimately leads to revolt against the Tarquins and the creation of the Roman Republic. Durrell uses the name Tarquin for a major character in his *The Black Book* as well as *Panic Spring*.

32. Shakespeare, *Rape of Lucrece* 115–17.

33. Shakespeare, *Rape of Lucrece* 1074.

34. For instance, see Spenser's *The Faerie Queen*, canto 8, stanza 7.

35. William Moulton Marston (1893–1947) was a comic book writer who created the famous brunette Wonder Woman.

36. Shakespeare, *Othello* I.ii.288–89.

37. This section derives from *Titus Andronicus* IV.ii.1750–85.

38. Shakespeare, *Love's Labor's Lost* IV.iii.1597–99.

39. John Florio (1553–1625) was best known for translating Montaigne into English.

40. Beyond this collection and his contribution to it, very little is known of Chester.

41. Shakespeare, *The Phoenix and the Turtle* 25–40.

42. Shakespeare, *The Rape of Lucrece* 1611–14.

43. Shakespeare, *The Phoenix and the Turtle* 56–67.

44. Originally from a note in the Aubrey manuscript (Chambers 252).

45. Richard Burbage (1568–1619) was the star of Shakespeare's company and a major actor of the period.

46. Shakespeare, *As You Like It* III.ii.1589–93.

47. Shakespeare, *Two Gentlemen of Verona* IV.iv.2007.

48. Shakespeare, *Sonnets* I.1–2.

49. Durrell also had only two daughters, neither of whom had children.

50. Shakespeare, *The Tempest* III.iii.1541–46.

Eternal
Contemporaries

Theatre
Sense and Sensibility

1939

HEAVEN AND CHARING CROSS
by A. Danvers-Walker—St. Martin's Theatre[1]
FAMILY REUNION
by T.S. Eliot—Westminster Theatre

THOSE WHO WERE BAFFLED by the dark spiritual implications of blood-guilt in T.S. Eliot's recent play will be able to turn with composure and pleasure to this human drama, in which every element that goes to make a murderer is psychologically apparent. It is a kind of behaviourist play,[2] written extremely well, articulated clearly and smoothly, and acted brilliantly by a good cast. Indeed, it is crashingly mediocre in conception; and only the marvellous interpretation of the players prevents one noticing the fact until the morning after.[3]

Love, in the case of Charlie Norman, was blind; blind with rage. He loved Bella Wilson[4] with an adolescent lack of control; but even he did not plan the murder which came upon them all so suddenly, and which is the crux of the drama. The ingredients have been well mixed and served: several excellent cockney studies by Mary Clare, Alban Blakelock, Cyril Smith; a few morsels of shrewd and salty human philosophy delivered by George Carney; an extremely fine study of the murderer son by Frederick Peisley; and the best performance of all for balance and sureness of touch—that of Jean Shepheard as Lily, the hunchback.[5] It is a great pity that the solid workmanship and dramatic execution should not have been lit up by one internal spark. After all, drama is not merely events, but the transformation of people's souls in front of one's eyes. If the play of T.S. Eliot (which is by far the most effective comparison to a play of this kind) could be described as all sensibility and no sense, *Heaven and Charing Cross* could be as certainly described as all sense and no sensibility. The people do not move except in time and events; suffering does not alter them. Dramatic inevitability, which is the essence of form in drama becomes here a mere mechanical pattern which is fulfilled. It is a great pity because the acting is really magnificent throughout.

If it is not a winner it will be through no fault of the cast.

Turn to *The Family Reunion*,[6] however, and you are faced by dramatic entertainment of another order, presented every bit as brilliantly by a superb cast. This is a dire parable complicated enough in theme to sound aboriginal to the mind of Mr. Agate; but which the average playgoer should find enthralling, because he will get from it not only drama, but also a good moral judgement on life and destiny. The guilt from which Harry suffers, and which is personified by the Furies who appear so dramatically to him in the family mansion, is caused by more than murder. The murder itself was the result of the guilt—otherwise why so pointless, the pushing of a woman from the boat-deck of a liner? Why did Harry feel what he felt? Above all, exactly how did he feel? The poetry has some great moments in it: and the questions posed here could really only be answered by Hamlet, whose ghost haunts the wings of this play.[7]

One cannot see this play without being convinced that it is a really noble statement on life; and that a great step has been made in verse drama—because the characters for the first time act and interact, not merely emote and mime. In fact this is true drama as opposed to pageant or Camden Town recitative by the waterproof boys' brigade. It shows up the shabby tinfoil conceptions of the other dramatic poets' writing; and reaches behind the shell of events towards the deep symbolic meanings of our actions and our feelings. It contains some of the best and most personal work of T.S. Eliot;[8] and a first class cast to interpret it including Catherine Lacey, who exploits her crooked Brontesque spirit to the full, and Michael Redgrave who does a weird and Hamletesque study of Harry.[9] This is the only play on at the moment that is not only intelligent and beautifully produced, but also poetic as well. This notice of it ends with an unequivocal categoric imperative. See it!

NOTES

1. This relatively obscure play was printed several times and was well-known at the time, but Danvers-Walker does not appear to have had other productions, apart from acting roles. It concerns a working-class youth who strangles his sweetheart, and several reviewers note the play's maudlin nature and comic wit are mismatched with its class orientation (Agate 85–86).
2. Durrell was reading John B. Watson's behaviourist psychology at the time.
3. The high performance standard is noted by other reviewers at the time as well.
4. Norman and Wilson are the play's protagonists.
5. This play went through a large number of productions, during which the cast continued to change. This particular cast cannot be traced back to a specific production date.
6. Eliot's play *The Family Reunion* was not successful during this first production, which ran from March 21 to April 22, 1939. Durrell attended the opening with his wife Nancy and lunched with Eliot on March 25 before travelling to Stratford-upon-Avon to review productions of Shakespeare's *Othello* and *A Comedy of Errors* (Chamberlin 24).
7. Durrell may be pointing to Eliot's essay "Hamlet and His Problems," first published in 1920.
8. Many critics argue the moral struggles in the play reflect Eliot's difficulties in his first marriage to Vivienne Haigh-Wood Eliot, from whom he separated in 1933. She was committed to the Northumberland House asylum in 1938 by her brother.

9. This opening production featured Michael Redgrave as Harry, Helen Haye as Lady Monchensey, and Catherine Lacey as Agatha.

The Happy Rock

1945

HENRY MILLER is still more or less unknown to the general public of England and America. It is not entirely his fault in spite of the fact that the proportion of so-called "unprintable" words employed in the construction of his three great books (*Tropic of Cancer, Black Spring, Tropic of Capricorn*) is fairly high.[1] It is, in fact, due entirely to the power and vehemence of his purely descriptive writing that he is as well known as he is. The abashed literary gents of the thirties who turned in horror from brutal descriptions of Parisian brothel life in *Tropic of Cancer* suddenly found themselves impaled upon passages of miraculous prose about subjects dearer to them—Matisse, Proust, the Seine: flights of prose which seemed incontestably the work of a genius. Thus it is that Miller has got two distinct publics—those who deplore his Brooklyn predilections in subject but feel that he cannot be ignored without loss of literary face; and those few who can see him in the round as a figure in American literature who steps straight up beside Whitman and Melville.[2] Certainly there is no doubt that this towering, shapeless, sometimes comic figure completely overtops the glazed reflections cast by those waxworks of contemporary American fiction—Hemingway, Dos Passos, Faulkner.[3] In Miller you have someone who has crossed the dividing line between art and *kitsch* once and for all.

Tropic of Cancer first came into my hands in 1938 in the island of Corfu.[4] It was not a novel. It was not completely an autobiography. It was a piece of self-evisceration written in the purest romance vein.

Formally the book was a chaos. ("Chaos is the score on which reality is written,"[5] says the author somewhere in it). It contained everything, speculations, soliloquies, short stories, strings of images, flights of fancy. It was chaotic in the way that *Leaves of Grass*[6] is chaotic: it dramatised and ranted; it was cold blooded and terrifying and upsetting. It defied every rule of taste and construction. It completely came off. It rang like a bell in every line.

For over a year I corresponded with Henry Miller.[7] His letters were boisterous, friendly, shy, and warming all at once. They were the letters of a man at once self-possessed and timid: they were puzzling. They were not the letters of an Educationed European. He described himself on various occasions as "just a Brooklyn boy," "Someone who had gone off the gold standard of Literature" and "Something quite other—a Patagonian, say."[8] He was something quite new to me at all events—*genus epileptoid*.[9]

It is always difficult to imagine a writer writing in English who has no correspondence with English literature. Miller has never read Milton, Donne, Shakespeare, Marlowe, Pope, Swift, etc. They do not form, as they do with most writers, a kind of invisible chorus in the subconscious—a stratum of derived experience. Poetry bores Miller: what he reads and enjoys above all things is drama based on the anomalies of human behaviour. His deepest literary influences were always translations of foreigners, Dostoevsky above all, Knut Hamsun, Tchekov, Strindberg.[10] And characteristically the form of literature he most cherishes is autobiography.

Born of poor parents in Brooklyn, New York, he began writing late in life: "at the point of madness," he says in a letter. To be rich in emotion and experience, and to have no centre focus for self-expression, is the common lot of writers when they begin. But to be already a grown man, "exhausted by death of many selves," and undertake a task of self expression is far more difficult. Miller began to write badly—but so badly that it is impossible to find any trace of the published Miller in his first two manuscripts.[11] Side by side with his search for himself, his technical deficiencies sent him in search of models: Melville and Whitman seemed to be the answer—though an incomplete answer. He began reading extensively and along haphazard lines: a course in books on history and comparative religion threw up whole pieces— Atlantean chunks like continents—of new ideas: Buddhism, Nietzsche, Confucius, Nostradamus, Elie Faure, Spengler, D.H. Lawrence, Joyce.[12] There was little order and shape to this vegetable accretion of knowledge. He read like a hungry animal. Science promised but bored. Psychology suddenly came in view with Freud, Bleuler, Jung, Rank;[13] and then one day in Paris he came across Dadaism and Breton's manifestoes. He was enslaved: Surrealism seemed to him to offer a means of breaking out of this hypnotic autism.[14] Yet even here he did not succumb because he realised that this barren mechanistic attitude to the sub-conscious,[15] while it gave one a superb critical apparatus, could not teach one to write about the things that mattered—other human beings, death, marriage, sex. He never joined the movement, but admired it, and still admires it, from a distance.[16]

Then one day life provided the key. A personal *chagrin* of some proportions drove him into a book before he was quite ready for it. Nothing was planned. He walked into *Tropic of Cancer* as a man might walk into a darkened operating theatre. The voice he heard talking was his own personal voice, without overtone or affectation. He began to talk, rapidly and confidently, to himself on paper—he began to talk about his own life and friends with complete candour and naturalness. The result was no self-confession or revelation; the result, strangely enough, was a swollen manuscript in which the world around him was reproduced in a totally unclassical, unromantic, un-European way. It was the voice of one of the Dead End Kids,[17] bringing his news of current affairs to the camp-fire. It was the voice of the Patagonian.

To read *Tropic of Cancer* is to understand how shockingly romantic all European writing after Rousseau has become. In Miller's book all the passions are there, stripped of their romantic envelope; it was not a book due to puritanical shock. (The French would say "a great Catholic book.") It was the book of someone whose fidelity to himself had conquered the narrow confines in which we normally hem the range of subjects permissible to art. It was healthy where Céline and Lawrence were sick.[18] It corroded and blistered where Joyce merely divagated and discharged. Into this portmanteau of confused stories, images, and essays Miller poured the better self of a great man. At the time he wrote this book he was all but starving in Paris. Published by the Obelisk Press,[19] it at first passed unnoticed—but not for long. It was too urgent a voice not to catch the ears of those who were alert. Critics wrote about it. Writers began to visit the little studio in Villa Seurat where Miller was living.

Critics should be interested in him, for there is much to pull to pieces—much bad writing and talking; there is too, a complete lack of imposed form. But there is something else in place of it—the organic form which one finds in all documents of the heart. In Miller's books the author has taken himself as the central character, and he is engaged in rewriting his own life in terms of fiction.[20] In every story, in every aside or soliloquy, it is Henry Miller who stands personally responsible for the success or failure of the work.

He revolves on a stage set by himself; and pictures the world as he sees it, through the soft focus of his marvellous gift for creative prose. It is not, in a sense, "art" after all: his books are combed out as if they were written by the Mississippi river, and as if Miller himself had found and preserved these huge weather-beaten rocks of writing among the other treasures of his life, books, water-colours, love letters, train tickets. He reveals himself so completely that he is completely disguised in this giant grape-vine—his life and times. If anywhere the books fail, it is with the failings of Miller the man: the failings, that is, are not those of a work of art as something detached from the author. But they constitute something new in the art of our times: autobiography conceived in terms of fiction, with a living cast, and with the author in the title role. Apart from the three great books in the saga Miller has indulged in endless peripheral activities—letters to friends, comic articles, essays.

Wherein do Miller's books differ from the other great books of the last twenty years? Think of Proust, of Joyce, of Huxley; their art seems to spring out of non-participation. There is, underneath the dead faecal flow, a refusal somehow to surrender to life. Miller is nearer to Lawrence than to anyone else; but in him we find none of the puritan sensitiveness, the recoil, which we find in the uneven author of *Lady Chatterley's Lover*[21]—surely a most disgusting book *because* it is so painfully romantic. In Miller the process is reversed; he goes out so completely into life that he tends to deform it by his excessive love. He can teach us to see the miraculous in the obscene. (Had I been an Englishman and a critic I should have written "*even* the obscene.")

He is not a psychologist but a dramatist; what excites him is the gesture, the mood, the ambience of a person or a place. He does not inform. He reveals.

What is the quality which divides the lesser work of art from the greater? Surely the degree of metaphysical anxiety and incertitude: the germ of discontent, the torment. In Miller you have a writer with the equipment of a romantic and the temperament of an early Church Father; side by side with the buffoonery and laughter that is an undertone of this mystical discontent and fear. His malady is an essentially religious one.

His English critics (I have not read the American) have done him a disservice in being impertinent about his lack of high purpose and moral uplift. The most puerile, George Orwell,[22] finds him the product of a certain social milieu which is on the point of being swept away. These gas-light reformers, finding no mention in his work of better plumbing for the new world have given him up as socially uninteresting; and in the light of their impertinence you would think that poor Henry

Miller was a moribund documentary writer, whose work would date with its epoch—just as Huxley's *Antic Hay*[23] and the amusing Sitwelliana[24] of the twenties has done. I cannot share this opinion. For me, *Tropic of Cancer* stands beside *Moby Dick*.

"Henry Miller's attitude to sex"—what a portentous phrase! How indeed can one write about sex in English today without being (a) repulsive and fishy like Joyce or (b) repulsed and fruity like Lawrence?[25] Sex in Miller coruscates and roars; syphilis, tulips, sonnets, warm thighs, lavatories, carpets stiff with blood—the whole gamut is there; and how nice it is for once to dispense both with the puritans and with the pagans.

If Eliot[26] has got nearest to God, Miller has got farthest from man. When he strips he teases. And when he digs for water he finds it. Let us thank God for a writer who lacks (a) the common room attitude, (b) an interest in literature. Miller is not interested in obscenity. He is like Nelson.[27] He does not know what the word means. He simply refuses to neglect any manifestation of *life* which interests him— not even for Mudie's Circulating Libraries,[28] the Writer's Guild,[29] or English girls under twelve.

Everyone knows that the English and the Americans don't know how to make love; Miller, in his work, lops away the whole super-structure supporting the great Romantic Lie of the West. He puts this twentieth-century torment properly in its place—so that the lovers in his books are connected purely and directly to each other below the belt. They do not depend on artificial and conventional attitudes of mind when they make love; they do it with real passion and cruelty. A course in him would turn us all from Stopes to Stoats[30]—surely an admirable transformation.

There is very little whining in Miller. He has no "Here we go round the prickly pear" complex. He roars like the Metro-Goldwyn-Mayer lion, until *Ars Gratia Artis*[31] appears round his head with a laurel wreath.

If he is against anything it is the world that Andy Hardy[32] stands for—the world of the lowest common denominator which is being so brilliantly explored by our trite reformers on both sides of the

Atlantic. The world of Nature's Middle Man, where security and inanity link arms. The world which would like to abolish daring and the internal adventure. The world which we live in.

What sort of world does he want? The question is as empty as it is stupid. Like all great artists he wants a world where art would become unnecessary; he wants a New Jerusalem.[33] But failing that (and we will go on failing to build our New Jerusalems, unless our technique changes radically) he is determined to like the world as it is—with its terrors, obscenities, murders, and loves: the world which can only be changed when there are a few more Henry Millers to spend their love upon it. If "Know Thyself"[34] is a moral injunction, then I think we may call Henry Miller a moralist. Art demands a great degree of cowardice.

Miller is the only contemporary I have met or read who is really enjoying himself—and it seems to us an unpleasant phenomenon. He himself once described History in a letter to me as "an endless repetition of the wrong way of living."[35] I am sure that History itself will have a kinder description of him and his work.

As a person he is interesting because he is uncultured—though not uncultivated. His line of vision is not obstructed by derived canons of art and life. Everything registers with pristine clearness. His interest in films and newspapers strikes a note of refined horror in the literary men who admire him. Yet he sees *Frankenstein*,[36] for example, as a deep symbol drawn from mass psychology, and speaks of it with an almost mediaeval sense of wonder and curiosity, as a great current art-symbol—

The perfected monster of man himself, imperfect, and unpredictable. The subconscious awake and walking. Frankenstein is perfect of his kind.[37]

Among films which have provided him with spring-boards of emotion for his ideas one must list the following: *Broadway Follies of 1943, Quai de Brumes, La Femme de Boulanger, The Lost Horizon, The Phantom President, Orage, Un Chien d'Andalou, Le Sang d'un Poete.*[38]

The three great books of Miller take one on a journey through the ardours and terrors of the flesh to the ardours and terrors of the spirit. In *Tropic of Capricorn* the fleshly battle is resolved into a metaphysical struggle; and Miller has undergone, as a man, a great transformation. The easiest way to reflect this change is by giving a list of books which have suddenly come into full force with him. *Confessions of St. Augustine, Lao-Tse, the Gita*, Balzac's *Seraphita*, Nijinsky's *Diary*, Rozanov, Blake.[39] Where these will lead him as an artist none can say; as a person they indicate the deepest development of the heart and sensibility. Transforming himself thus, he still retains all his own positive American qualities: a wonderful sense of buffoonery, complete lack of interest in "professional literature" as such, fearless ability to tread where angels fear. And the good leavening Rabelaisian quality which preserves all good work—a sense of living.

He calls himself no longer "The Patagonian" or "Caliban,"[40] but "The Happy Rock"—for he begins to feel as securely anchored in himself as we feel him to be anchored in American literature, of which he is the greatest contemporary figure. Bad writer, often awkward, often a bad critic, often inaccurate, often prejudiced—let the critics make their futile subtractions. Here is a very great man.

Alexandria

Egypt

NOTES

1.   Miller's works were frequently banned and went through a range of high-profile trials for obscenity around the world.

2.   Herman Melville (1819–1891) and Walt Whitman (1819–1892), both American writers, are frequent references for Miller.

3.   Ernest Hemingway (1899–1961), John Dos Passos (1896–1970), and William Faulkner (1897–1962) were contemporary novelists who shaped American

Modernism and avant-garde prose. Durrell had few comments and little praise for any of these three authors but does note reading them all in his correspondences.

4. Durrell first read *Tropic of Cancer* in 1935, likely in August, after Barclay Hudson had given him the book on Corfu (Durrell, *Durrell–Miller* 3).

5. Miller, *Tropic* 3.

6. Walt Whitman's 1855 poetic *magnum opus*.

7. The Durrell–Miller correspondence lasted from 1935 to Miller's death in 1980. Two critical editions are published, the first edited by George Wickes and the second by Ian MacNiven.

8. All three are common self-descriptions for Miller found in both his letters and *Tropic of Cancer*. The "gold standard" is a significant theme in the novel and also reflects the financial turbulence of the interwar years.

9. Of epileptic origins in classification. Miller also uses this term to self-describe (*Henry Miller On* 91). Durrell's sense is tied to Kretschmer's types, an early psychological classification system for personalities: normal, hysteroid, cycloid, schizoid, and epileptoid. Also see Durrell's 1937 poem "Ballad of Kretschmer's Types" (253–54).

10. Fyodor Dostoyevsky (1821–1881) and Hamsun (1859–1952) are frequent references in Miller's works. Maria Bloshteyn contends, "the impact of Dostoyevsky on Miller is enormous" (vii), and Miller describes Hamsun as "that Dostoevski of the North" when discussing a letter he received from Hamsun (*Sexus* 367). Anton Chekhov (1860–1904) and August Strindberg (1849–1912) are also frequent references for Miller. In *Tropic of Cancer*, he recounts visiting Strindberg's rooms in the Pension Orfila (180–84),

11. Miller's first two novels were published posthumously as *Moloch* and *Crazy Cock*. As Durrell notes in his letter commenting on the book *The Happy Rock*, "I am probably the only person who has read all the Cancer ones as well as the two early bad novels and the original *Tropic* MSS" (*Durrell–Miller* 200).

12. Miller discusses all these topics in several places as well as in his correspondence with Durrell. Friedrich Nietzsche (1844–1900) was a major influence on Miller (Nandyal 11–14). Oswald Spengler (1880–1936) was largely known for his book *Decline of the West*, which posited a historical process of rising and falling cultures. Miller highly valued Elie Faure's works on art history, and he wrote a lengthy critical reflection on Lawrence, *The World of Lawrence*. Miller was less kind to James Joyce in his comments but did integrate a section of Joyce's *Finnegans Wake* into *Tropic of Cancer* (286).

13. Sigmund Freud, Eugen Bleuler (1857–1939), Carl Jung, and Otto Rank were referred to frequently by both Durrell and Miller. Miller knew Rank personally in Paris and New York.

14. Miller eventually broke from the Surrealists based on their communism, which conflicted with his own anarchism (Gifford, "Surrealism's" 42–45). See Miller's "An Open Letter to Surrealists Everywhere" (151–96).

15. The "mechanistic" approach to the unconscious is typical of critiques of the communist component of Surrealism.

16. Miller's use of Surrealist techniques is well-established, as is his admiration for several Surrealists, but he remained markedly outside of Surrealism as a movement. Miller states, "Surrealism is the secret language of our time, the only spiritual counterpart to the materialist activities of the socialist forces that are now driving us to the wall. The seeming discrepancies between the language of Breton, Lenin, or Marx, are only superficial" ("An Open" 178). This same difference is asserted as "it is a mistake to speak about Surrealism. There is no such thing: there are only Surrealists….The desire to posit an ism, to isolate the germ and cultivate it, is a bad sign. It means impotency" (181). Durrell's position is similar and stated clearly in his letters to Miller (Durrell, *Durrell–Miller* 17–19), but he was more directly involved than Miller with the English Surrealists, many of whom adopted Miller's anarchist revision to Surrealism.

17. A group of young actors known for the 1937 film *Dead End*.

18. Louis-Ferdinand Céline (1894–1961) was the pseudonym of Louis-Ferdinand Destouches, whom Miller admired greatly. Miller also wrote a book on Lawrence, *The World of Lawrence*, but it was only published posthumously.

19. The Obelisk Press was run by Jack Kahane and published several of Miller's works as well as Durrell's *The Black Book*. *Tropic of Cancer* was first published in 1934. Though the Obelisk published pornographic materials, it also included serious literary works by Richard Aldington, James Joyce, Cyril Connolly, and Frank Harris.

20. Although Miller wrote in the first person, in many respects his "Henry Miller" is also a character, and the novels are unreliable as autobiography.

21. D.H. Lawrence. The *Lady Chatterley's Lover*, *Fanny Hill*, and *Tropic of Cancer* trial in England was a landmark legal decision in censorship of obscene materials. Also see Durrell's Preface to *Lady Chatterley's Lover* (vii–xi).

22. Orwell discusses Miller's *Tropic of Cancer* extensively as well as Durrell's *The Black Book* in his famous essay "Inside the Whale" (9–50). Durrell and Orwell disagreed publicly over *The Booster*, the periodical produced through the Villa Seurat by Durrell, Miller, and Perlès (Orwell, "Back" 30–31). Tyrus

Miller identifies Orwell's essay on Miller as the quintessential moment of Late Modernism (1–9, 209–10).

23. Aldous Huxley's (1894–1963) comic novel *Antic Hay* was first published in 1923.

24. A general term for literary work of the Sitwell siblings, Edith (1887–1964), Osbert (1892–1969), and Sacheverell Sitwell (1897–1988). Thomas Balston, in 1928, compiled a list of their works published under this title as well.

25. Both James Joyce (1882–1941) and D.H. Lawrence faced censorship difficulties due to the sexual content of their works.

26. T.S. Eliot (1888–1965) was by this time known for his religious sequence *Four Quartets*.

27. Horatio Nelson (1758–1805) was an English naval officer famous for winning the Battle of Trafalgar. Durrell was fond of using Nelson as a target for critiques of British prudery, such as in his poem "A Ballad of the Good Lord Nelson" (113–14).

28. Charles Edward Mudie's lending library had a strong influence on Victorian fiction by emphasizing a three-volume structure and family values.

29. A generic term for unionized writers groups. This is likely in reference to the Writer's Guild of America, East, which was founded in 1912.

30. Marie Stopes (1880–1958) was a eugenicist and innovator in family planning who wrote the sex manual (while claiming to be a virgin) *Married Love: A New Contribution to the Solution of the Sex Difficulties*. She openly supported forced sterilization and Adolf Hitler during World War II, even sending him poetry. In contrast, stoats are weasel-like animals whose winter coats are used for the royal fur ermine. They are known for their promiscuous breeding, about which Durrell would have likely been aware through his brother Gerald Durrell, who mentions stoats in his animal books and pioneered captive breeding programs for small mammals.

31. "Art for Art's Sake." The notion is often tied to Symbolist literature and Oscar Wilde, but the Latin version appears in MGM's logo with a roaring lion.

32. A character played by Mickey Rooney in a series of sixteen comic films from 1937 to 1958 as well as conservative public service announcements. They promote traditional American values in a small-town environment.

33. In this sense, a utopia.

34. A famous Ancient Greek aphorism inscribed on the Temple of Apollo in Delphi: γνῶθι σεαυτόν.

35. Miller wrote in praise of Durrell's typescript of *The Black Book*, "You can grasp it again when you think of history as quite meaningless—as a repetition ad infinitum of the wrong way of living, which is never overcome on the historical

plane, by new ideologies, new wars, new revolutions, new conversions, etc."
(Durrell and Miller 60).

36. The 1931 film directly by James Whale and starring Boris Karloff as the monster, not Mary Shelley's novel of the same title.

37. Paraphrased (Miller, *Tropic of Capricorn* 322–23).

38. *Broadway Follies of 1943* likely refers to *Ziegried Follies of 1943* on Broadway as well as the 1945 film *Ziegfried Follies*. *Quai de Brumes* (Port of Shadows) is a 1938 French film directed by Marcel Carné considered the best of the Poetic Realism movement. *La Femme de Boulanger* (The Baker's Wife) in a 1938 French film directed by Marcel Pagnol. *The Lost Horizon* is a famous 1937 American film by Frank Capra based on James Hinton's novel of the same name—it is set in Shangri-La amidst highly politicized pre-World War II international tensions. *The Phantom President* is a 1932 American musical film directed by Norman Taurog about a presidential look-alike used to woo voters. *Orage* (Storm) is a 1938 French film by Marc Allégret about infidelity and romantic complications amidst relatively free sensuality. *Un Chien d'Andalou* (An Andalusian Dog) is a very short 1929 French surrealist film directed by Luis Bruñel and co-written with Salvador Dalí—it is probably the most famous of the surrealist film experiments. *Le Sang d'un Poete* (The Blood of a Poet) is Jean Cocteau's 1930 French film and the first part of his Orpheus Trilogy.

39. St. Augustine of Hippo's (354–430) *Confessions* is the first autobiography, as such, and hence influenced Miller's chosen novelistic form significantly. Lao Tse was the central figure of Taoism, and the Gita is the Hindu scripture *Bhagavad Gita*. Honoré de Balzac's (1799–1850) novel *Séraphîta* is based on an androgynous person caught between love relationships with a man and a woman. The Polish ballet dancer and choreographer Vaslav Nijinsky (1890–1950) is referred to several times in works by both Durrell and Miller. In a letter to Miller, Durrell recounts, "I always remember the time I brought you back Nijinsky's letters from London—how you took the book, opened it, and walked out of the room (crowded with merry makers) into the street—*there* you absently leaned against a lamp post and read it from cover to cover—or almost" (*Durrell–Miller* 201). Vasily Rozanov (1856–1919) was a controversial Russian writer who focused on sexuality. William Blake (1757–1827) was an English Romantic poet often tied to early anarchism, the visual component of his poetic works, and spiritualism. Durrell alludes and refers to Blake frequently in his works.

40. Patagonian is in relation to Ferdinand Magellan's mythic race of giants in South America. Caliban is the monstrous son of the witch Sycorax in Shakespeare's *The Tempest*.

Studies in
Genius VI
Groddeck

1948

IF THE WORK AND TEACHINGS of Georg Walther Groddeck[1]
(1866–1934) are not as well known today as they deserve to be it is
perhaps largely his own fault. His first job, he considered, was to heal;
the writer and the teacher took second place. Over and above this
Groddeck also knew how quickly the disciple can convert the living
word into the dead canon. He knew that the first disciple is also very
often the first perverter of the truth. And this knowledge informs
his written work with that delightful self-deprecating irony which so
many of his readers profess to find out of place; an irony which says
very clearly "I am not inviting you to follow me, but to follow yourself. I am only here to help if you need me."[2] The age does need its
Groddecks, and will continue to need them until it can grasp the full
majesty and terror of the "It" which he has talked so much about in his
various books and particularly in that neglected masterpiece *The Book
of the It*.[3]

   In considering Groddeck's place in psychology, however, there are
one or two current misunderstandings which deserve to be cleared up
for the benefit of those who have mistaken, or continue to mistake,
him for an orthodox disciple of Freud. Groddeck was the only analyst
whose views had some effect on Freud; and Freud's *The Ego and the Id*

is a tribute to, though unfortunately a misinterpretation of, Groddeck's It theory. Yet so great was his admiration for Freud that the reviewer might well be forgiven who once described him as "a populariser of Freudian theory." No statement, however, could be farther from the truth, for Groddeck, while he accepts and employs much of the heavy equipment of the master, is separated forever from Freud by an entirely different conception of the constitution and functioning of the human psyche. His acknowledgements to Freud begin and end with those wonderful discoveries on the nature of the dream, on the meaning of resistance and transference. In his use of these great conceptual instruments, however, Groddeck was as different from Freud as Lao Tzu was from Confucius. He accepted and praised them as great discoveries of the age; he employed them as weapons in his own way upon organic disease; he revered Freud as the greatest genius of the age; but fundamentally he did not share Freud's views upon the nature of the forces within the human organism which make for health or sickness. And this is the domain in which the doctrines of Groddeck and of Freud part company. In this domain, too, Groddeck emerges as a natural philosopher, as incapable of separating body and mind as he is incapable of separating health and disease.

To Freud the psyche of man was made up of two halves, the conscious and the unconscious parts; but for Groddeck the whole psyche with its inevitable dualisms seemed merely a function of something else— an unknown quantity—which he chose to discuss under the name of the "It." "The sum total of an individual human being," he says,

> physical, mental and spiritual, the organism with all its forces,
> the microcosmos, the universe which is a man, I conceive of as a
> self unknown and forever unknowable, and I call this the "It" as the
> most indefinite term available without either emotional or intel-
> lectual associations. The It-hypothesis I regard not as a truth—for
> what do any of us know about absolute truth—but as a useful tool
> in work and in life; it has stood the test of years of medical work and

*experiment and so far nothing has happened which would lead me
to abandon it or even to modify it in any essential degree. I assume
that man is animated by the It which directs what he does and what
he goes through, and that the assertion "I live" only expresses a small
and superficial part of the total experience "I am lived by the It"...* [4]

This fundamental divergence of view concerning the nature of
health and disease, the nature of the psyche's role, is something
which must be grasped at the outset if we are to interpret Groddeck
to ourselves with any accuracy. For Freud, as indeed for the age and
civilisation of which he was both representative and part, the ego is
supreme. There it lies, like an iron-shod box whose compartments are
waiting to be arranged and packed with the terminologies of psychoanalysis. But to Groddeck the ego appeared as a contemptible mask
fathered on us by the intellect, which by imposing upon the human
being, persuaded him that he was motivated by forces within the
control of his conscious mind. "Yet," asks Groddeck, "what decides
how the food which passes into the stomach is subdivided? What is
the nature of the force which decrees the rate of the heart-beat? What
persuaded the original germ to divide and subdivide itself and to form
objects as dissimilar as brain cortex, muscle or mucus?"

*When we occupy ourselves in any way either with ourselves or with
our fellow-man, we think of the ego as the essential thing. Perhaps,
however, for a little time we can set aside the ego and work a little
with this unknown It instead....We know, for instance, that no man's
ego has had anything to do with the fact that he possesses a human
form, that he is a human being. Yet as soon as we perceive in the
distance a being who is walking on two legs we immediately assume
that this being is an ego, that he can be made responsible for what
he is and what he does and, indeed, if we did not do this everything
that is human would disappear from the world. Still we know quite
certainly that the humanity of this being was never willed by his ego;*

he is human through an act of will of the All or, if you go a little
further, of the It. The ego has not the slightest thing to do with it....
What has breathing to do with the will? We have to begin as soon
as we leave the womb, we cannot choose but breathe. "I love you so
dearly, I could do anything for you." *Who has not felt that, heard it,*
or said it? But try to hold your breath for the sake of your love. In ten
seconds or, at most, in a quarter of a minute, the proof of your love
will disappear before the hunger for air. No one has command over
the power to sleep. It will come or it will not. No one can regulate
the beating of the heart...

Man, then, is himself a function of this mysterious force which
expresses itself through him, through his illness no less than his health.
To Groddeck the psychoanalytic equipment was merely a lens by which
one might see a little more deeply than heretofore into the mystery of
the human being—as an It-self. Over the theory of psychoanalysis, as
he used it, therefore, stood the metaphysical principle which expressed
itself through man's behaviour, through his size, shape, beliefs, wants.
And Groddeck set himself up as a watchman, and where possible, as
an interpreter of this mysterious force. The causes of sickness or health
he decided were unknown; he had already remarked in the course of
his long clinical practice that quite often the same disease was overcome by different treatments, and had been finally led to believe that
disease *as an entity* did not exist, except inasmuch as it was an expression of a man's total personality, his It, expressing itself through him.
Disease was a form of self-expression.

However unlikely it may seem, it is nevertheless a fact that any sort
of treatment, scientific or old-wife's poultice, may turn out to be right
for the patient, since the outcome of medical or other treatment is not
determined by the means prescribed but by what the patient's It likes
to make of the prescription. If this were not the case then every broken
limb which had been properly set and bandaged would be bound to

heal, whereas every surgeon knows of obstinate cases which despite all care and attention defy his efforts and refuse to heal. It is my opinion, backed by some experience with cases of this nature, that a beneficent influence may be directed upon the injured parts...by psycho-analysing the general Unconscious, indeed, I believe that every sickness of the organism, whether physical or mental, may be influenced by psychoanalysis....Of itself psychoanalysis can prove its value in every department of medicine, although of course a man with pneumonia must be put immediately to bed and kept warm, a gangrened limb must be amputated, a broken bone set and immobilised. A badly built house may have to be pulled down and reconstructed with all possible speed when no alternative accommodation is available, and the architect who built it so badly must be made to see his mistakes...and an It which has damaged its own work, lung, or bone, or whatever it may be, must learn its lesson and avoid such mistakes in future...

Since everything has at least two sides, however, it can always be considered from two points of view, and so it is my custom to ask a patient who has slipped and broken his arm: "What was your idea in breaking your arm?" whereas if anyone is reported to have had recourse to morphia to get sleep the night before, I ask him: "How was it the idea of morphine became so important yesterday that you make yourself sleepless, in order to have an excuse for taking it?" So far I have never failed to get a useful reply to such questions, and there is nothing extraordinary about that, for if we take the trouble to make the search we can always find an inward and an outward cause for any event in life.

The sciences of the day have devoted almost the whole of their interest to the outward cause; they have not, as yet, succeeded in escaping from the philosophic impasse created by the natural belief in causality, and side by side with this a belief in the ego as being endowed with free will. In all the marvellous pages of Freud we feel the analytical intellect pursing its chain of cause-and-effect; if only the last link can be reached, if only the first cause can be established, the whole pattern will be made clear. Yet for Groddeck such a proposition was false; the Whole was an unknown, a forever unknowable entity, whose shadows and functions we are. Only a very small corner of this territory was free to be explored by the watchful, only the fringes of this universe lay within the comprehension of the finite human mind which is a function of it. Thus while Freud speaks of cure, Groddeck is really talking of something else—liberation through self-knowledge; and his conception of disease is philosophical rather than rational. In the domain of theory and practice he is Freud's grateful and deeply attentive pupil, but he is using Freud for ends far greater than Freud himself could ever perceive. Psychoanalysis has been in danger of devoting itself only to the tailoring of behaviour, too heavily weighted down by its superstructure of clinical terminology it has been in danger of thinking in terms of medical entities rather than patients. This is the secret of Groddeck's aversion to technical phrases, his determination to express himself as simply as possible using only the homely weapons of analogy and comparison to make his points. In *The Book of the It*, which is cast in the form of letters to a friend, he discusses the whole problem of health and disease from a metaphysical point of view, and with an ironic refusal to dogmatise or tidy his views into a system. But the book itself, brimming over with gay irony and poetry, does succeed in circumscribing this territory of experience with remarkable fidelity; and from it Groddeck emerges not only as a great doctor but also as a philosopher whose It-concept is positively ancient Greek in its clarity and depth. "In vain," says Freud somewhere, "does Groddeck protest that he has nothing to do with science."[5] Yes, in vain, for Groddeck's findings are being daily called upon to supplement the mechanical findings of the science which he respected, but of which he refused to consider himself a part. "Health and sickness," he says,

> are among the It's forms of expression, always ready for use.
> Consideration of these two modes of expression reveals the

remarkable fact that the It never uses either of them alone, but
always both at once: that is to say, no one is altogether ill, there is
always some part which remains sound even in the worst illnesses;
and no one is altogether well, there is always something wrong, even
in the perfectly healthy. Perhaps the best comparison we could give
would be a pair of scales. The It toys with the scales, now putting
a weight in the right pan, now in the left, but never leaving either
pan empty; this game, which is often puzzling but always signifi-
cant, never purposeless, is what we know as life. If once the It loses its
interest in the game, it lets go of life and dies. Death is always volun-
tary; no one dies except he has desired death…The It is ambivalent,
making mysterious but deep-meaning play with will and counter-will,
with wish and counter-wish, driving the sick man into a dual relation
with his doctor so that he loves him as his best friend and helper, yet
sees in him a menace to that artistic effort, his illness.

The illness, then, bears the same relation to the patient as does his
handwriting, his ability to write poetry, his ability to make money;
creation, whether in a poem or a cancer, was still creation, for
Groddeck, and the life of the patient betrayed for him the language
of a mysterious force at work under the surface—behind the ideological scaffolding which the ego had run up around itself. Disease, then,
had its own language no less than health, and when the question of
the cure came up, Groddeck insisted on approaching his patient, not
to meddle with his "disease" but to try and interpret what his It might
be trying to express through the disease. The cure, as we have seen
above, is for Groddeck always a result of having influenced the It, of
having taught it a less painful mode of self-expression. The doctor's
role is that of a catalyst, and more often than not his successful intervention is an accident. Thus the art of healing for Groddeck was a sort
of spiritual athletic for both doctor and patient, the one through self-
knowledge learning to cure his It of its maladjustments, the other
learning from the discipline of interpretation how to use what Graham

Howe[6] has so magnificently called "The will-power of desireless": in other words, how to free himself from *the desire to cure.* This will seem a paradox only to those—and today they are very many—who have no inkling of what it is like to become aware of states outside the comfortable and habitual drowsings of the ego. We are still the children of Descartes, and it is only here and there you will find a spirit who dares to replace that inexorable first proposition, with the words "I am, therefore I can love."[7]

It was this dissatisfaction with the current acceptance of disease as clinical entity that drove Groddeck finally to abandon, wherever possible, recourse to the pharmacopoeia or the knife; in his little clinic in Baden-Baden he preferred to work with a combination of diet, deep massage, and analysis as his surest allies. On these years of successful practice his reputation as a doctor was founded, while his writings, with their disturbing, disarming, mocking note, brought him as many pupils as patients, as many enemies as admirers. The majority of his theories and opinions, together with the It-concept on which his philosophy is based, were already worked out before he had read Freud. Yet he gladly and joyfully accepted the Freudian findings in many cases, and never ceased to revere Freud; but whereas the work of Jung, Adler, Rank, Stekel, might well be considered as modifications and riders to basic Freudian theory, Groddeck's case is unique and exceptional. He stands beside Freud as a philosopher and healer in his own true right.

"With Groddeck," wrote Keyserling[8] after his death,

> has gone one of the most remarkable men I have ever met. He is indeed the only man I have known who continually reminded me of Lao-Tzu; his non-action had just the same magical effect. He took the view that the doctor really knows nothing, and of himself can do nothing, that he should therefore interfere as little as possible, for his very presence can invoke to action the patient's own powers of healing. Naturally he could not run his sanatorium at Baden-Baden

purely on this technique of non-intervention, so he healed his patients
by a combination of psychotherapy and massage in which the pain he
inflicted must have played some part in the cure, for in self-protection
they developed the will-to-life, while the searching questions he put in
analysis often touched them on the raw!...In this way Groddeck cured
me in less than a week of a relapsing phlebitis which other doctors
had warned me would keep me an invalid for years, if not for the rest
of my life.[9]

For the patient Groddeck sought to interpret, through the vagaries
of outward symptom and clinical manifestation, the hidden language
of the It; "I do maintain," he writes,

that man creates his own illnesses for a definite purpose, using the
outer world merely as an instrument, finding there an inexhaustible
supply of material which he can use for this purpose, today a piece
of orange peel, tomorrow the spirochete of syphilis, the day after a
draught of cold air, or anything else that will help him pile up his
woes. And always to gain pleasure, no matter how unlikely that may
seem, for every human being experiences something of pleasure in
suffering; every human being has the feeling of guilt and tries to get
rid of it by self-punishment.

To Groddeck plainly the ego is only a reflexive instrument to be
used as a help in interpreting the motive force which lies behind the
actions and reactions of the whole man; it is perhaps this which gives
his philosophy its bracing life-giving quality. It is a philosophy with
a boundless horizon, whereas the current usages of psychoanalysis
plainly show it to have been built upon a cosmogony as limited in
scope as that which bounded the universe of Kelvin or of Huxley.[10]
If Freud gives us a calculus for the examination of behaviour, the
philosophy on which it rests is a philosophy of causes; to Groddeck,
however, all causes derive from an unknowable principle which

animates our lives and actions. So we are saved from the hubris of regarding ourselves as egos and of limiting our view of man to the geography of his reflexes; by regarding the ego as a function we can re-orientate ourselves more easily to the strains and stresses of a reality which too often the ego rejects, because it cannot comprehend, or because it fears it. So much, then, for the basic difference between the philosophies of Freud and Groddeck; it will be evident, if I have stated my case clearly, that they complement one another, that they are not antithetical, as some have believed them to be; for Freud supplies much of the actual heavy machinery of analysis, and Groddeck joyfully accepts it. In return Groddeck offers a philosophy of orientation and humility which justifies the technocratic contributions of Freud, and allows us to understand more clearly the problems and penalties not merely of disease, for that does not exist *per se*—but of suffering itself. With Freud we penetrate more deeply into the cognitive process; with Groddeck we learn the mystery of participation with the world of which we are part, and from which our ego has attempted to amputate us.

And what of the It? Groddeck does not claim that there is any such thing. He is most careful to insist that the It is not a thing-in-itself, but merely a way-of-seeing, a convenient rule-of-thumb method for attacking the real under its many and deceptive masks; indeed in this his philosophy bears a startling resemblance to the Tao-concept of the Chinese. The It is a way, not a thing, not a principle or a conceptual figment. Having accepted so much, Groddeck is prepared to attempt a half-length portrait of it.

Some moment of beginning must be supposed for this hypothetical It, and for my own purposes I quite arbitrarily suppose it to start with fertilisation…and I assume that the It comes to an end with the death of the individual—though the precise moment at which we can say an individual is dead is again not so simple a matter as it seems….Now the hypothetical It-unit, whose origin we have placed at fertilisation, contains within itself two It-units, a male and a female....It is perhaps necessary here to comment upon the extent of our ignorance concerning the further development of the fertilised ovule. For my purposes it is sufficient to say that after fertilisation the egg divides into two separate beings, two cells as science prefers to call them. The two then divide again into four, into eight, into sixteen and so on, until finally there comes to be what we commonly designate a human being....Now in the fertilised ovule, minute as it is, there must be something or other—the It, we have assumed?— which is able to take charge of this multitudinous dividing into cells, to give them all distinctive forms and functions, to induce them to group themselves as skin, bones, eyes, ears, brain, etc. What becomes of the original It in the moment of division? It must obviously impart its powers to the cells into which it divides, since we know that each of them is able to exist and re-divide independently of the other....It must not be forgotten that the brain, and therefore the intellect, is itself created by the It....Long before the brain comes into existence the It of man is already active and "thinking" without the brain, since it must first construct the brain before it can use it to think with. This is a fundamental point and one we are inclined to ignore or forget. In the assumption that one thinks only with the brain is to be found the origin of a thousand and one absurdities, the origin also of many valuable discoveries and inventions, much that adorns life and much that makes it ugly....Over and against the It there stands the ego, the I, which I take to be merely the tool of the It, but which we are forced by nature to regard as the It's master; whatever we say in theory there remains always for us men the final verdict "I am I"....We cannot get away from it, and even while I assert the proposition is false I am obliged to act as if it were true. Yet I am, by no means, I, but only a continuously changing form in which my "It" displays itself, and the "I" feeling is just one of its ways of deceiving the conscious mind and making it a pliant tool....I go so far as to believe that every single separate cell has this consciousness of individuality, every tissue, every organic system. In other words every It-unit can deceive itself, *if it likes, into thinking of itself as an individuality, a person, an I. This is all very confusing but there it is. I believe that the human hand has its I, that it knows what it does, and knows that it knows. And every kidney-cell and every nail-cell has its consciousness just the same...its "I" consciousness. I cannot prove this, of course, but as a doctor I believe it, for I have seen how the stomach can respond to certain amounts of nourishment, how it makes careful use of its secretion according to the nature and quantity of the material supplied to it, how it uses eye, nose and mouth in selecting what it will enjoy. This "I" which I postulate for cells, organs, etc, like the general-I (or the ego-awareness of the whole man) is by no means the same thing as the It, but is produced by the It, as a mode of expression on all fours with a man's gestures, speech, voice, thinking, building, etc...About the It itself we can know nothing.*

At this point the orthodox objections of the Rationalist deserve to be stated and considered. They are questions which Groddeck himself did not bother to answer, believing as he did that no hypothesis could be made to cover all the known facts of a case without special pleading or sophistry, and being unwilling to strain for interpretations which might appear to cover the whole of reality and yet in truth yield only barren formulae. Groddeck believed that whatever was posited as fact could sooner or later be disproved; hence his caution in presenting the It-hypothesis not as a truth, but as a method. Yet a critic of the proof-of-the-pudding school would have every right to ask questions along the following lines:

That a case of inoperable cancer, say, which defies every other form of treatment, can be made to yield before a Groddeckian attack by massage and analysis, is within the bounds of belief. Even the It-hypothesis might be conceded as a useful working tool in this case. Freud has so far altered the boundaries between the conscious and unconscious intention that we are inclined to respond to suggestions

which fifty years ago would have seemed fantastic. But if a thousand
people contract typhoid from a consignment of fruit are we to assume
that the individual It of each and every one of them has chosen this
form of self expression in a desire for self punishment?

It is the sort of question to which you will find no answer in
Groddeck's books; yet if he seems content to present the It as a partial
hypothesis it is because his major interest is in its individual manifestation. Yet there is nothing in the hypothesis as such to preclude
a wider application. Had he addressed himself to such a question
he might very easily have asserted that just as the cell has its It-ego
polarity, and the whole individual his, so also could any body or
community develop its own. The conventions of the logic that we
live by demand that while we credit the individual with his individuality, we deny such a thing to concepts such as "state," "community,"
"nation"—concepts which we daily use as thought-counters. Yet
when our newspapers speak of a "community decimated by plague"
or a "nation convulsed by hysteria" we accept the idea easily enough,
though our consciousness rejects these formations as fictions. Yet in
time of war a nation is treated as an individuality with certain specified characteristics; politicians "go to the nation"; *The Times* discusses
the "Health of the Nation" with the help of relevant statistics. This
unity which we consider a fiction—could it not reflect, in its component parts, the shadows of the individual unity, which is, according
to Groddeck, no less a fiction? If a national ego why not a national
It? But I am aware that in widening the sphere of application for
the It-hypothesis I am perhaps trespassing: for if Groddeck himself
remained silent on the score he no doubt had his reasons.

And what of the domain of pure accident or misadventure? A man
hurt by a falling wall? The victim of a railway accident? Are we to
assume that his It has made him a victim of circumstances? We know
next to nothing about predisposition—yet it is a term much used
by medical men to cover cases where the link of causality appears

obvious, the effect related satisfactorily to the cause; thus the victim of hereditary syphilis satisfies the syntax of our logic, while the victim of a railway accident seems simply the passive object of fate. And yet we do unconsciously recognise predisposition in individuals, in our friends, for how often when the news of the accident reaches us do we exclaim "But it *would* happen to someone like X!"? The truth is that all relations between events and objects in this world partake of the mystery of the unknown, and we are no more justified in covering one set of events with words "disease" or "illness" than we are of dismissing another with words like "accident" or "coincidence." Groddeck himself was too wily a metaphysician to put himself at the mercy of words. "I should tell you something," he writes,

> *of the onset of diseases, but the truth is that on this subject I know nothing. And about their cure…of that, too, I know just nothing at all. I take both of them as given facts. At the utmost I can say something about the treatment, and that I will do now. The aim of the treatment, of all medical treatment, is to gain some influence over the It….Generally speaking, people have been content with the method called "symptomatic treatment" because it deals with the phenomena of disease, the symptoms. And nobody will assert that they were wrong. But we physicians, because we are forced by our calling to play at being God Almighty, and consequently to entertain overwhelming ideas, long to invent a treatment which will do away not with the symptoms but with the cause of the disease. We want to develop causal therapy as we call it. In this attempt we look around for a cause, and first theoretically establish…that there are apparently two essentially different causes, an inner one, causa interna, which the man contributes of himself, and an outer one, causa externa, which springs from his environment. And accepting this clear distinction we have thrown ourselves with raging force upon the external causes, such as bacilli, chills, over-heating, over-drinking, work, and anything else….Nevertheless in every age*

there have always been physicians who raised their voices to declare
that man himself produced his diseases, that in him are to be found
the causae internae. *. . . There I have my jumping-off point. One*
cannot treat in any way but causally. For both ideas are the same;
no difference exists between them. . . . In truth I am convinced that
in analysing I do no differently than I did before when I ordered hot
baths, gave massage, issued masterful commands, all of which I still
do. The new thing is merely the point of attack in the treatment,
the one symptom which appears to me to be there in all circumstances, the "I". *. . . My treatment . . . consists of the attempt to make*
conscious the unconscious complexes of the "I". . . . That is certainly
something new but it originated not with me, but with Freud; all that
I have done in this matter is to apply the method to organic diseases,
because I hold the view that the object of all medical treatment is the
It: and I believe the It can be influenced as deeply by psychoanalysis
as It can by a surgical operation.

If we have spent much time and space in letting Groddeck, as far
as possible in his own words, define and demarcate the territory of
the It, the reason should by now be apparent. Not only is the ego-It
polarity the foundation-stone upon which his philosophy is built,
but without an understanding of it we cannot proceed to frame the
portrait of this poet-philosopher-doctor with any adequacy; since his
views concerning the function and place of the ego in the world are
carried right through, not only in his study of health and disease, but
also into the realms of art-criticism and cosmology, where his contri-
butions are no less original and beautiful. Groddeck, like Rank,[11] began
as a poet and writer, only to turn aside in middle life and embrace the
role of healer; lack of first-hand acquaintance with Groddeck's poetry,
his one novel, and what his translator describes as "an epic," prevents
me from saying anything about this side of his activities;[12] but in his
one incomplete volume of art-criticism, published here under the
title of *The World of Man*, the reader will be able to follow Groddeck's

study of painting in terms of the It-process—for he believed that man creates the world in his own image, that all his inventions and activities, his science, art, behaviour, language, and so on, reflect very clearly the nature of his primitive experience, no less than the confusion between the ego and the It which rules his thoughts and actions. Unfortunately, his death in 1934 prevented him from carrying out more than the groundwork of his plan, which was to review every department of science and knowledge in terms of this hypothesis; but in the fragments he has left us on art, language, and poetry, the metaphysical basis of his philosophy is carefully illustrated and discussed. The humour, the disarming simplicity and poetry of his writing cannot be commented upon by one who has not read his books in the original German, but it is sufficient to say that enough of Groddeck's personality comes through in translation to make the adventure of reading him well worthwhile, both for the doctor and for the contemporary artist—for the knowledge and practice of the one supplements the ardours and defeats of the other; and art and science are linked more closely than ever today by the very terms of the basic metaphysical dilemma which they both face. All paths end in the metaphysics.

Groddeck was often approached for permission to set up a society in England bearing his name, on the lines of the Freudian and Adlerian Societies; but he always laughed away the suggestion with the words "Pupils always want their teacher to stay put." He was determined that his work should not settle and rigidify into a barren canon of law; that his writings should not become molehills for industrious systematisers, who might pay only lip-service to his theories, respecting the letter of his work at the expense of the spirit. In a way this has been a pity, for it has led to an undeserved neglect—not to mention the downright ignominy of being produced here in a dust-jacket bearing the fatal words, "Issued in sealed glacine wrapper to medical and psychological students only." And this for *The Book of the It*, which should be on every bookshelf!

There has been no space in this study to quote the many clinical case-histories with which Groddeck illustrates his thesis as he goes along; I have been forced to extract, as it were, the hard capsules of theory, and offer them up without their riders and illustrations. But it is sufficient to say that no analyst can afford to disregard Groddeck's views about such matters as resistance and transference any more than they can afford to disregard him on questions like the duration of analysis, the relation of analysis to organic disorders, and the uses of massage. If he wholeheartedly accepted many of Freud's views there were many reservations, many amendments which he did not hesitate to express. For if Freud's is a philosophy of knowledge, Groddeck's is one of acceptance through understanding.

Another fundamental difference deserves to be underlined—a difference which illustrates the temperamental divergence between Freud and Groddeck as clearly as it does the divergence between the two attitudes to medicine which have persisted, often in opposition, from the time of Hippocrates until today. While Groddeck is campaigning wholeheartedly for the philosophy of non-attachment, he refuses to relinquish his heritage as a European in favour of what he considers an Asiatic philosophy. In his view the European is too heavily influenced by the Christian myth to be capable of really comprehending any other; so it is that his interpretation of the religious attitude to life refers us back to Christ, and if he accepts the Oedipus proposition of Freud, he does not hesitate to say that it seems to him a partial explanation. But Groddeck's Christ differs, radically from the attenuated portraits which have been so much in favour with the dreary puritan theologians of our age and time.

Christ was not, neither will he be; He is. He is not real. He is true. It
is not within my power to put all this into words; indeed I believe it
is impossible for anyone to express truth of this sort in words, for it is
imagery, symbol, and the symbol cannot be spoken. It lives and we

are lived by it. One can only use words that are indeterminate and
vague—that it why the term It, completely neutral, was so quickly
caught up—for any definite description destroys the symbol.

And man, by the terms of Groddeck's psychology, lives by the
perpetual symbolisation of his It, through art, music, disease, language.
The process of his growth—his gradual freeing of himself from disease,
which is malorientation towards his true nature, can only come about
by a prolonged and patient self-study; but the study not of the ego
in him so much as of the Prime Mover, the It which manifests itself
through a multiplicity of idiosyncrasies, preferences, attitudes, and
occupations. It is this thorough-going philosophic surrender of
Groddeck's to the It which makes his philosophy relevant both to
patient, to artist, and to the ordinary man. Thus the symbol of the
mother on which he lays such stress in his marvellous essay on childhood fuses into the symbol of the crucifixion, which expresses in
artistic terms this profound and tragic preoccupation.

The cross, too, is a symbol of unimaginable antiquity…and if you ask
anyone to tell you what the Christian cross may seem to him to resemble,
he will most invariably answer "A figure with outstretched arms."
Ask why the arms are outstretched and he will say they are ready to
embrace. But the cross has no power to embrace, since it is made of
wood, nor yet the man who hangs upon it, for he is kept rigid by the
nails; moreover he has his back turned to the cross….What may that
cross be to which man is nailed, upon which he must die in order to
redeem the world? The Romans use the terms os sacrum[13] for the
bone which is over the spot where the birth-pangs start, and in
German it is named the cross-bone, Kreuzbein. The mother-cross
longs to embrace, but cannot, for the arms are inflexible, yet the
longing is there and never ceases….Christ hangs upon the cross, the
Son of Man, the man as Son. The yearning arms which yet may not
embrace are to me the mother's arms. Mother and son are nailed

together, but can never draw near to each other. For the mother there
is no way of escape from her longing than to become dead wood...but
the Son, whose words "Woman, what have I to do with thee?" gave
utterance to the deepest mystery of our human world, dies of his own
Will and in full consciousness upon that cross...

It is in his writings on the nature of art and myths that we can
see, most clearly revealed, the kernel of his thought concerning the
nature of symbolism and the relation of man to the ideological web
he has built about himself; it is here too that one will see how clearly
and brilliantly Groddeck interpreted the role of art in society. He is the
only psychoanalyst for whom the artist is not an interesting cripple
but someone who has, by the surrender of his ego to the flux of the
It, become the agent and translator of the extra-causal forces which
rule us. That he fully appreciated the terrible, ambivalent forces to
which the artist is so often a prey is clear; but he also sees that the
artist's dilemma is also that of everyman, and that this dilemma is
being perpetually restated in art, just as it is being restated in terms
of disease or language. We live (perhaps I should paraphrase the verb
as Groddeck does), we are lived by a symbolic process, for which our
lives provide merely a polished surface on which it may reflect itself.
Just as linguistic relations appear as "effective beliefs" in the dreams
of Groddeck's patients, so the linguistic relations of symbolism,
expressed in art, place before the world a perpetual picture of the
penalties, the terror, and magnificence of living—or of being lived
by this extra-causal reality whose identity we cannot guess. "However
learned and critical we may be," writes Groddeck, "something within
us persists in seeing a window as an eye, a cave as a mother, a staff
as the father." Traced back along the web of affective relations these
symbols yield, in art, a calculus of primitive preoccupation, and
become part of the language of the It; and the nature of man, seen
by the light of them, becomes something more than a barren ego
with its dualistic conflicts between black and white. Indeed the story

of the Gospels, as reinterpreted in the light of Groddeck's non-attach-ment, yields a far more fruitful crop of meanings than is possible if we are to judge it by the dualistic terms of the ego, which is to say, of the will. "Only in the form of Irony can the deepest things of life be uttered, for they lie always outside morality; moreover truth itself is always ambivalent, both sides are true. Whoever wants to understand the Gospel teachings would do well to bear these things in mind." And Groddeck's Christ, interpreted as an Ironist, is perhaps the Christ we are striving to reinterpret to ourselves today. There is no room here for the long-visaged, long-suffering historical Christ of the contempo-rary interpretation, but a Christ capable of symbolising and fulfilling his artistic role, his artistic sacrifice, against the backcloth of a history which, while it can never be fully understood, yet carries for us a deliberate and inexorable meaning disguised in its symbolism.

If we have insisted, in the course of this essay, on the presenta-tion of Groddeck as a philosopher it is because what he has to say has something more than a medical application. In medicine he might be considered simply another heretical Vitalist, for whom the whole is something more than the sum of its parts: certainly he has often been dismissed as a doctor "who applied psycho-analysis to organic disease with remarkable results." While one cannot deny his contri-butions to psychoanalysis, it would not be fair to limit his researches to this particular domain, although the whole of his working life was spent in the clinic, and although he himself threw off his writings without much concern for their fate. Yet it would also be unjust to represent him as a philosopher with a foot-rule by which he measured every human activity. The common factor in all his work is the atti-tude and the It-precept which was sufficiently large as to include all manifestations of human life; it does not delimit, or demarcate, or rigidify the objects upon which it gazes. In other words he refused the temptations of an artificial morality in his dealings with life, and preferred to accord it full rights as an Unknown[14] from which it might be possible for the individual to extract an equation for ordinary living; in so doing he has a message not only for doctors but for artists as well, for the sick no less than for the sound. And one can interpret him best by accepting his It-concept (under the terms of the true-false ambivalence on which he insisted so much) both as truth and as poetic figment. And since Groddeck preferred to consider himself a European and a Christian it would be equally unjust to harp on the eastern religious systems from which the It may seem to derive, or to which it may seem related. ("The power of the eye to see depends entirely on the power of vision inherent in that Light which sees through the eye but which the eye does not see; which hears through the ear, but which the ear does not hear; which thinks through the mind but which the mind does not think. It is the unseen Seer, the unheard Hearer, the unthought Thinker. Other than It there is no seer, hearer, thinker." *Shri Krishna Prem.*[15])

Groddeck would have smiled and agreed, for the principle of non-attachment is certainly the kernel of his philosophy; but the temper of his mind is far more Greek than Indian. And his method of exposition combines hard sane clinical fact with theory in exactly balanced quantities. One has the feeling in reading him that however fantastic a proposition may seem it has come out of the workshop and not out of an ideological hothouse.

Four books bearing his name have been published in England. Of these the only one which pretends to completeness is *The Book of the It;*[16] the three other titles are composed of essays and various papers, strung together by his translator. They are *The World of Man, The Unknown Self,* and *Exploring the Unconscious.* At the time of writing they are all unfortunately out of print. The first and third volumes contain a thorough exposition of his views on the nature of health and disease; *The World of Man* contains the unfinished groundwork of his projected study on the nature of pictorial art. The last volume also contains some general art-criticism, but is chiefly remarkable for an essay entitled *Unconscious Factors in Organic Process* which sets out his views on massage, and contains a sort of new anatomy of the body in terms of psychological processes.[17] Despite the fearfully muddled arrangement of these papers, not to mention a translation which confessedly misses half the poetry and style of the original, these books should all be read if we are to get any kind of full picture of Groddeck's mind at work.

Even Groddeck's greatest opponents in Germany could not but admit to his genius, and to the wealth of brilliant medical observations contained in his books; it is to be sincerely hoped that he will soon occupy his true place in England as a thinker of importance and a doctor with something important to say. It is fourteen years since Groddeck's death and his complete work is still not available to the general public in England. Why?

For the purposes of this brief essay, however, I have struck as far as possible to the philosophy behind his practice, and have not entered into a detailed exposition of his medical beliefs and their clinical application; with a writer as lucid and brilliant as Groddeck one is always in danger of muddying the clear waters of his exposition with top heavy glozes and turbid commentaries. In his work, theory and fact are so skillfully woven up that one is always in danger of damaging the tissue of his thoughts in attempting to take it to pieces. I am content if I have managed to capture the ego-It polarity of his philosophy, and his conception of man as an organic whole. But as with everything in Groddeck one feels that manner and matter are so well-married in him that any attempt to explain him in different words must read as clumsily as a schoolboy's paraphrase of *Hamlet*. This fear must excuse my ending here with a final quotation.

Every observation is necessarily one-sided, every opinion a falsification. The act of observing disintegrates a whole into different fields of observation, whilst in order to arrive at an opinion one must first dissect a whole and then disregard certain of its parts....At the present time we are trying to recover the earlier conception of a unit, the body-mind, and make it the foundation of our theory and action. My own opinion is that this assumption is one we all naturally make and

never entirely abandon and, furthermore, that by our heritage of
thought, we Europeans are all led to trace a relationship between the
individuum and the cosmos....We understand man better when we
see the whole in each of his parts, and we get nearer to a conception
of the universe when we look upon him as part of the whole.

NOTES

1. Durrell first encountered Groddeck's *Book of the It* while in Alexandria and wrote to Miller about it in September 1944: "I'm absolutely bowled over by Groddeck's *Book of the It*—it's simply terrific. I have written England to send you a copy" (Durrell, *Durrell–Miller* 175). Groddeck was also greatly admired by W.H. Auden (Mengham 165) who would inscribe and send copies of *The Book of the It* to friends. Since *Horizon* originally published this essay and was co-edited by Auden's close friend Stephen Spender, who was with Auden during the time he discovered Groddeck, it is likely this essay would have been known to him. This essay has also appeared as the introduction to Groddeck's *The Book of the It*, and it refers to Groddeck's other works, from which Durrell borrowed plots for *The Alexandria Quartet*, such as Semira's nose from *The Unknown Self* (Gifford, "Noses" 2–4), and in it Clea discovers with her new hand, "IT can *paint!*" (Durrell, *Alexandria* 874). Groddeck is explicitly mentioned in *The Avignon Quintet*. Groddeck is out of favour in psychoanalytic communities and was discounted by Carl Jung (1875–1961) in his brief correspondence with Durrell. For more on Durrell's use of Groddeck, see Christensen's "An Overenthusiastic Response" (63–94) and Sobhy's "Alexandria as Groddeck's It" (26–39).

2. Most quotations from Groddeck have not been identified. This anti-authoritarian theme in Groddeck may have been a significant part of his appeal to Durrell at this time, which coincides with his publishing several works through anarchist presses, most notably "Elegy on the Closing of the French Brothels" (30–32) in George Woodcock's NOW in 1947, *Zero and Asylum in the Snow* through Circle Editions 1947, "Eight Aspects of Melissa" (1–8) in *Circle* in 1946, and many poems in the second and third issues of Robert Duncan's *Experimental Review* in 1940–1941.

3. First published as *Das Buch vom Es* in 1923. Durrell's copy would have been the 1923 printing by Funk & Wagnalls. Durrell's annotated copy of Groddeck's *The*

Unknown Self is held by the McPherson Library at the University of Victoria. A
later copy, the 1951 Vision printing, is also held by the Morris Library, Southern
Illinois University, Carbondale, as well as seven other volumes of Groddeck's
work. However, the Morris Library's holdings are mainly in French, and only
Exploring the Unconcsious predates this article in printing (1933). Durrell's first
copies appear lost during his travels after Egypt.

4. Groddeck, *Book of the It* 15–16. Durrell quotes this passage in a letter to Henry
    Miller, February 28, 1946 (*Miller–Durrell* 195).

5. "A writer who, from personal motives, vainly asserts that he has nothing to do
    with the rigours of pure science. I am speaking of George Groddeck....We need
    feel no hesitation in finding a place for Groddeck's discovery in the structure of
    science" (Freud, *The Ego* 23).

6. E. Graham Howe (1896–1975) was a theosophist and psychoanalyst whose works
    Durrell had reviewed in the 1930s.

7. René Descartes (1596–1650) famously proposed "cogito ergo sum" (I think
    therefore I am).

8. Hermann Graf Keyserling (1880–1946) was a German philosopher who studied
    under and was treated by Groddeck.

9. Keyserling 12.

10. William Thomson, 1st Baron Kelvin (1824–1907) and Thomas Henry Huxley
    (1825–1895), both scientists, are held up as examples of determinism and
    Victorian scientific rationalism.

11. Otto Rank (1884–1939) was a psychoanalyst close to Freud whom Henry Miller
    and Anaïs Nin knew well. Durrell first read Rank's *The Trauma of Birth* in 1938
    and wrote an essay on Rank that year—it was declined by *Purpose*, which later
    published his essay on Howe, "The Simple Art of Truth" (MacNiven 201).
    Purpose also published Groddeck's essays in the 1920s.

12. Groddeck's novel *Thomas Weltlein* was published in 1919 and translated into
    English as *The Seeker of Souls*. Freud had significant praise for this novel.

13. The Latin term for the triangular bone at the base of the spine and back of the
    pelvis.

14. Freud derived the term for the Id from Groddeck (*das Es*, literally "the It" in
    English). Likewise, "Unknown" is *Unbewusst* in psychoanalytic terminology, typi-
    cally rendered in English as "Unconscious."

15. Shri Krishna Prem in *The Yoga of the Bhagavad Gita* quoting Srimad Bhagavada
    (167). Shri Krishna Prem was born Ronald Henry Nixon and taught English
    at Lucknow University but changed his name when he studied under the
    university's vice-chancellor, Yashoda Ma. The two founded an Ashram at the

Radha-Krishna temple they built in Mirtola, India. He was the first Westerner to practice Vaishnavism.

16. The English version of *The Book of the It* has been cut; it is not the full text of the original German edition.

17. This chapter is divided into subsections on "Massage and Psychotherapy," "The Body's Middleman," and "Bowel Function."

Constant Zarian

Triple Exile

1952

SOME ACCOUNT OF THE WRITINGS of Constant Zarian[1] is long
overdue—and would no doubt have long since been given had not the
general inaccessibility of his writings in the Armenian language left
the common reader in Europe with only a slender sheaf of poems and
essays in French by which to judge him. Now, in his sixty-third year,
however, he is within striking distance of the European reputation
which must follow the forthcoming translation of his books into French
and German—and as such he commands the attention of the serious
reader in England.

But fame—or even for that matter recognition—are matters of
indifference to this much travelled man of letters who now lives quietly
on the island of his choice in the Gulf of Naples, happy in the memory
of a long life well spent in travel and friendship, in good living and
good writing.

Zarian was born in the Caucasus, in the province of Shirvan, which,
he says somewhere in a biographical note, was "well-known for its poets,
roses, nightingales and its periodical earthquakes." He adds: "So at the
very start I absorbed poetry and a certain anxiety from my natal place."
Poetry and anxiety! An auspicious conjunction of qualities for a twentieth-century man! He attended a local school for some years before

his parents, who were people of substance and position, decided to send him to France to be educated.

Paris provided the school, and Brussels the university—but the results of a Western education were to be quite unforeseen by his parents. Zarian emerged from his studies as a promising poet. He joined the group of flourishing young Belgian poets who at this time gathered round Emil Verhaeren,[2] and his first essays in poetry marked him as a young man of determined and forcible talent.

By now his writings had reached Russia and the Czarist authorities responded to them by forbidding his return; his disgusted family repudiated him; henceforth poetry was to become both a fatherland and a family. At this time his work in French had already earned him a deserved reputation as a writer to be watched. But now came a change.

He had by this time all but forgotten his native language; "only some of my prayers, learned during childhood, clung with obstinacy to me." One night after a memorable conversation with Verhaeren he took, on the advice of the elder poet, the decision to re-learn Armenian, and henceforth only to write in his native tongue. At this time the theories about the "autochthonous artist" were very much in the air, and Verhaeren assured him that however well he wrote in French he would always remain a deraciné, a rootless emigrant in French literature. Why should he not become, although an exile, a mouthpiece for his own people? The artist should accept the responsibilities conferred upon him by the native ties of birth and tongue—and by his stars.

Zarian went to Venice where, on the island of San Lazaro, the monks of the Armenian monastery undertook to teach him his native language and (almost more important) gave him enough work as a translator to enable him to live. In the room, at the very table, where once Byron[3] had started to study Armenian, Zarian undertook this rediscovery of himself. "I realised now," he writes, "that language is simply part of the blood that circulates throughout one's body; one doesn't learn it, but simply discovers it." For several years, absorbed in this self-discovery, he remained in Venice perfecting the instrument which he was henceforth to use.

But it was not enough simply to reclaim the lost power of his native language; as an active and energetic writer with a mission, his duty was to turn his talents towards his own people. But how could he reach them—since he was now a political exile? In 1912 he was to be found in Constantinople, living in the greatest poverty, and gathering round him a group of exiled talents to help him with the foundation of a free literary newspaper written in Armenian. He recognised clearly that a writer's duty is to devote himself to the field of human values and not to waste his talent on ephemeral political polemic. Politics change; values—the true workshop of the poet—have to be perpetually examined and recreated from new points of view. Their basic substance is unchanged, however, since they deal not with the temporal condition of man but with his unchanging inner disposition. They have to be reworked in every generation—"as bread is always the same but has to be kneaded and composed afresh every day if it is to be palatable."

But the outbreak of the First World War put an abrupt end to these considerations; the little band of intellectuals was abruptly dispersed. Escaping arrest by the Turks, Zarian crossed the boarder into Bulgaria and thence made his way to Italy. Here he composed his "Three Mysteries," a pantheistic poem of great force and beauty which, in Italian translation, earned him immediate recognition and which was put to music by Ottorino Respighi.[4]

At the end of the war Zarian returned to Constantinople to continue his literary work, and in 1920 accepted an invitation by the Soviet authorities to return to Armenia with full honours. He was to have a chair founded for him at the University of Erevan.[5] He accepted the invitation and returned. He determined to stay and help the revolutionaries to found their promised Utopia. It took him two years to understand finally the full horror of the system that had been imposed upon his own people. In 1924 he fled.

To those who come back, he will tell you, after having fully tasted the fruits of Communism in Russia, Europe seems a strangely unreal thing; and the values of Europe acquire all of a sudden a new perspective. What are all these people talking about, the traveller asks himself, as everywhere around him he sees traces of a moral order, a coherence in values, a *culture* which has been systematically extirpated behind the curtain? The virtues so far outweigh the defects that it seems incredible to him that he himself was once among those sentimental believers who wished for a new Marxist Utopia and the end of capitalism. To those who have the chance fully to compare the two systems the shock is a very profound one. Not only does capitalism offer the worker a far better chance of ameliorating his lot, *but in every way and from every point of view* it is superior to the paltry materialistic inventions of that dated humbug, the Communist, whose politics are based upon a pipe-dream which in turn is based upon a social grudge.[6] It was from this new angle of vision that the disappointed poet saw Europe on his return.

Many people since Zarian have learned the lesson, too; but for him the shock was perhaps greater, since it concerned his own country and his own people. He had always been disposed to listen openly to criticisms of Communism; no doubt he had always agreed the earlier stages were clumsy, crude, and mistaken. Nevertheless, it offered hopes of equality and justice. But after an exposure to it at first hand he realised with alarm that the system itself did not work (regardless of whether it were to be applied by angels or gangsters). Based on a futile actuary's view of the universe, it laid low every seed of culture and growth that a thousand years of Christian humanism had offered to the Western European. It was the deliberate enemy of the imagination, of love, of every faculty and grace that one could prize as a human being. And here was another paradox; he had expected to find that the Communist state was truly a worker's state and found that it was, in the most precise sense of the word, a state run by the failures of Bloomsbury.[7] Marxism was the bin into which every *manqué* poured the talents he could not exercise in the arts and sciences.

To return then, like Lazarus risen from the grave, and to find the currents still running strongly leftward in Europe, was something which made his blood run cold. Fifty years of sentimental agitation, of barren provincial Utopianism, had produced this attitude in public opinion. To read the utterances of a Shaw, a Haldane,[8] after leaving Armenia was almost to despair of the fate of Western Europe as such— for never had so gigantic and palpable a fraud, so hideous a tyranny ever been supported by so many men of apparent distinction and eminence.

Zarian has never ceased to believe in the artist as the responsible factor in human affairs; and the blame for this situation he laid, and still lays, at the door of the Western artist. The utter *irresponsibility* in human affairs which has characterised the artists of the last fifty years, he often insists, is something that can only be appreciated in all its richness by someone who has enjoyed the fruits of their agitation—a worker's state: at least so Zarian thought when, once more in France, he tried to assemble his ideas of the two years he had passed in his country. He was consumed by anxiety that Europe, with all its remediable faults, should be destroyed by the tyranny he saw approaching in so many seductive guises.

Marxism, he recognised, was itself the enemy, whether in the mild form of humanistic socialism advocated by the sentimental agitators of the west, or in its complete Soviet form; indeed one could only be a stepping stone to the other. What could he do to atone for his mistake? What kind of artist could he become without falling into the camp of the clericals, or the duller ranks of the quasi-reactionaries? How best could he contribute to the twentieth-century symposium?[9]

It was these considerations that were finally to determine the shape and magnitude of the writings which, for the next twenty years and more, were to pour from his pen. It was no conscious choice that made Zarian a classical man—it was the development of a natural style of mind, founded in bitter experience and in a tenacious belief that if man was to be saved from destruction he stood in need of major artists of a new type—*responsible men*. His own task was no longer to reject, to criticise, to whine—but, in the deepest sense of the word, to submerge in the swift currents of history and to give their impulse direction and form. "To endure and contribute"—that was the new motto: and he has never deviated by a hairsbreadth from it in his attitude to his work and his people.

He was by now a triple exile: exiled by both Czarist and Bolshevik; and doubly exiled from the current of European thought by his choice of language. After what he had seen he recognised that the Fabians[10] and their followers, though they were striking many a shrewd blow for justice in social affairs, were still hypnotised by the corpus of belief derived out of Marxism. They constituted nothing less than an intellectual fifth column situated at the heart of European life. The very science upon which their belief in a new social order was founded had become obsolete with the relativity principle.[11] There was a real danger that they would succeed in destroying the old culture and finding themselves with nothing to put in its place. Could they not recognise that cultures were born and died like organisms? That they could not be forced and shaped only by the human powers of a fallible logic?

Zarian addressed himself to the social problem not by entering the arena as a man of politics or of science but simply as an artist devoted to the responsibilities which his country and language had put upon him. He dealt with Soviet Armenia in the way that one would deal with the phenomenon of, say, first love—artistically. His "Impressions of Soviet Life" and "The Co-operative and the Bones of the Mammoth"[12] recreated the atmosphere and flavour of the submerged life that human beings live when their hearts have been conscripted under the flag of the false god, Matter. The emphasis was on the pity and the comedy, and his best effects have some of the simplicity and grotesque humour of Gogol.[13]

For the rest, his work belongs to the main current of European thought, and his books from 1930 onwards were milestones set up along the winding roads of his journeys, both physical and spiritual, in the Europe he had come to love. His *Philosophical Studies* and the two fat *Notebooks* (1946) contain not only his impressions of Spain, Italy, and Holland but, in a sense, a study of the philosophic background

which makes or unmakes nations; yet these studies were free from
a false professionalism in that they were at all points derived, not
from abstractions, but from the landscape, wine, food, people, and
languages he encountered.

He spent the Second World War in America and published there
what he regards as his greatest novel, *The Ship Upon The Mountain*. So
much for the prose of this formidable poet, the appearance of whose
prose work has been punctuated through the years by the publication
of many books of verse. This year his *Collected Poems* are in the press
and contain all the work that he wishes to preserve in this medium.[14]

"As a classical man," Zarian is fond of saying, "I am either out of
date or else I belong to a type of artist who has not yet emerged but
whom the future will bring us: the artist who belongs to his people."
It is perhaps easier to be this type of artist if one belongs to a small
people whose literature is as yet not significant in the way that, say,
German or French literature is. Certainly our own native genius seems
to be bred out of revolt, out of a refusal to conform or belong (Shelley,
Byron, Lawrence, Blake,[15] etc.). It is characteristic also that in English
it is the rebels that Zarian most admires...Nevertheless he feels that
the future will bring us artists who belong without being tame or
toothless, without being a Southey or Rogers.[16] "They will not stop
being exiles, of course," adds Zarian, "because it seems that one has
to be an exile in order to belong to the world." The translation of his
work into two European languages will, we believe, qualify him for
admission into this class.

NOTES

1.   Zarian (1885–1969) was an Armenian poet and writer whom Durrell first met
      on Corfu in the 1930s. He escaped the Armenian Genocide by fleeing to Bulgaria
      but later returned to Istanbul. He taught at Yerevan State University (1922–
      1925), Columbia University at the same time as the Frankfurt School in exile

(1944–1946), and the American University of Beirut (1952–1954). Zarian knew Vladimir Lenin in Geneva, where both lectured, and he befriended Apollinaire, Pablo Picasso, Céline, and Paul Éluard, among other artists and writers. His autobiography, *Countries and Gods*, covers the period when he was on Corfu in Durrell's company. Also see Vartan Matiossian's "Kostan Zarian and Lawrence Durrell: A Correspondence" (75–101).

2. Emile Verhaeren (1855–1916) was a Symbolist Belgian poet.

3. George Gordon Byron (1788–1824) was a passionate supporter of the Armenian cause and the Armenian language. He also wrote *English Grammar and Armenian* and *Armenian Grammar and English*, and he continued to translate Armenian materials until his death.

4. Respighi (1879–1936) was a famous Italian composer who set several of Zarian's texts to music, though he does not appear to have ever set this specific work.

5. Zarian was a professor of comparative literature at this time.

6. Durrell's anti-communist sentiments were already well-established in the 1930s and intensified after his residence in Yugoslavia. Whether this derived from conservative inclinations or his associations with anarchist authors remains a critical debate.

7. Bloomsbury is an area of London but also identifies a literary group that dominated British Modernism. It was strongly associated with the Fabian Socialists, though it was not as strongly tied to communism, per se.

8. George Bernard Shaw and J.B.S. Haldane (1892–1964) were both prominent socialists, and Haldane eventually became an outspoken communist, though professionally he was a geneticist.

9. Again, the uncertainty over Durrell's own politics is important here. Durrell often voiced his resentment for socialist, Marxist, as well as conservative and retrograde values. The conflict in which he places Zarian between socialist and reactionary politics suggests an anti-authoritarian, personalist third option. At the time Durrell wrote this article, he was completing four years of service for the British Council in Belgrade, Yugoslavia, following Josip Broz Tito's break with Joseph Stalin and the Cominform in 1948.

10. The Fabian Society is a British Socialist movement famously associated with the Bloomsbury circle of writers and intellectuals. It is closely tied to the Labour Party.

11. Durrell employed these terms in his own work, *The Alexandria Quartet*, only a few years later, such as in the introductory note to *Balthazar*. This suggests he is articulating his own notions here rather than Zarian's.

12. Both works are from the early 1930s. Nearly all the texts by Zarian to which Durrell refers were originally published in Boston in the periodical *Hairenik*.

13. Nikolai Gogol (1809–1852) was a Russian novelist best known for his satiric work.

14. See Zarian, *Girk' diwts'aznergut'eants'* (1978).

15. Given the political nature of Durrell's discussion of Zarian, his alignment with Percy Bysshe Shelley, Lord Byron, D.H. Lawrence, and William Blake is telling. Blake is often regarded, with William Godwin, as a forerunner to modern anti-authoritarian anarchism, as is Shelley, who married Godwin's daughter Mary. Simon Casey has established the link between Lawrence, who was deeply sympathetic to Blake and Godwin, and anarchism (2–12). Byron is the most suitable alignment based on his deep ties to Armenian literature and culture as well as his involvement in revolutionary movements of independence.

16. Robert Southey (1774–1843) and Samuel Rogers (1763–1855) were both English Romantic poets with early ties to supporting the radicalism of the French Revolution but who quickly became conservative Tories with little rebellion to incite their works. Southey was poet laureate for thirty years, and Rogers was vital for supporting other writers, including securing William Wordsworth's sinecure as distributor of stamps and recommending Alfred Lord Tennyson for the position of poet laureate, succeeding Wordsworth in the position, who had succeeded Southey.

Enigma
Variations

1957

MR. EZRA POUND'S POETRY has so secure a place in the canon of
modern literature that there can be no harm in a reviewer admitting
that his huge work-in-progress, *The Cantos*,[1] presents the reader with
a series of insurmountable difficulties, not the least of which is the
apparent lack of a discernable architectural pattern shaping towards
a whole. Is it because the poem is as yet incomplete? I would like to
think so. Yet this new volume,[2] which seems full of the chips and fragments thrown off by a giant rock-drill at work upon a statue, is just as
baffling as its predecessor; for the statue itself is still not visible to the
naked eye. I personally am beginning to wonder whether it is there
at all.

Presumably this work will take its place among those great unfinished enigmas of art which tease the mind by their incompleteness,
their hostility to form and the rights of communication between poets
and their readers; their surrender to the Platonic daemon. Somewhere
there is a special shelf reserved for them—Mallarmé's *Igitur*, Smart's
Song of David, Rimbaud's *Season in Hell*, Solomos's *Woman of Xante*:
Blake, Hölderlin, Nijinksy...[3] they shade insensibly into the poets of
mysticism, of alchemy, like Nostradamus and Dr. John Dee. They
belong to the irrational twilight world where the symbol prime is king
and where the experience it mirrors is incommunicable save in these

mutterings and groanings, frenzied prayers uttered in the complete loneliness of the poet's workshop. Mr. Pound has every right to demand sympathy and suspend judgement of his critics. He is writing an *agon*.[4]

But...if one removed all the verbs and nouns from a volume of Spengler[5] and then interspersed what was left with a few Chinese characters from Fenellosa's book[6] and some hieroglyphs from Budge's *Egyptian Book of the Dead*[7] one could, by synthetic means, produce roughly the sort of effects achieved by Mr. Pound in this poem. I am speaking only of the form. If Joyce ran pun-mad in *Finnegans Wake*[8] Mr. Pound has run quotation-mad here, though he has successfully disguised most of his quotations by cutting them into pieces. One recognizes only the quotation marks, as it were. What is he getting at?

The whole momentum of his work seems to derive, as well as to rest upon, an obsessive preoccupation with human history. Indeed the central intention of the *Cantos*—if one can dare to be so precise about so inchoate a production—seems to be to erect a great rubbish heap of cultural fragments,[9] a giant word-tumulus in which the spades of future archaeologists will turn up something of everything—a fragment (incomplete) of every known culture. In this sense the poem is in the direct line of descent from the great cultural jumble-sales already organized by Eliot in *The Waste Land* and Joyce in *Finnegan*. These works illustrate the twentieth-century psyche at dispersal points—dispersal into a series of component parts or states—literary spectrum analysis. One reads them as one might read the brilliant and baffling annotations of a great scholar to a text which has been lost but which—to judge by the quotations cited—was of heart-breaking beauty. But there is one point upon which I cannot make up my mind. Is there in Mr. Pound's poem any trace of the conscious deliberation, the purpose and regulation of means, which irradiate the works of Eliot and Joyce, and which in fact constitute their real claim to be regarded as works of art rather than hoaxes? I can as yet find none. But perhaps the outlines will emerge in time and supply the huge cumbersome, indeed gruesome, piece of contrivance with a fulcrum, a point of intention.

I know the poetic symbol is not rational and didactic so much as initiatory, and when faced with a work like the Chinese *Book of Changes* I realized that it is meaningless to me because I haven't really mastered its metaphysic; I am quite prepared to believe that I am encountering the same trouble with Mr. Pound's poem. The only trouble is that I am beginning to wonder whether there is, at the bottom of it, something like the same informing seed which, when I grasp it, will enable me to enter the poem quietly and shut the door behind me. If this is so I shall be delighted, for I have always loved the early Pound and no writer of my generation can fail to acknowledge the debt he owes to so brilliant an innovator and exploiter of metrical forms.[10] We, his readers, must keep trying and wait patiently for the conclusion of this poem. But I can't disguise the fact that so far these oracular discharges afflict me like the message of a teleprinter in need of mechanical attention.

NOTES

1.   Pound (1885–1972) was a major American Modernist poet most famous for his epic poem *The Cantos*. By 1957, his reputation had been seriously damaged by his promotion of fascism, anti-Semitism, and charges of treason against him, which led to his incarceration in St. Elizabeths Hospital after an insanity plea. He remained there until 1958. Durrell's wife in 1957 was Claude Vincedon, a Zionist Jew of the Menasce family who wrote a Zionist novel, *A Chair for the Prophet*, which bears many similarities to Durrell's works. That Durrell reviewed Pound at this time, prior to Pound's recanting of his anti-Semitism and while still incarcerated, is striking.

2.   Ezra Pound, *Section: Rock-Drill. Cantos lxxxv–xcv*, Faber, 12s.

3.   Stéphane Mallarmé (1842–1898) was a French Symbolist poet, though *Igitur: ou, la Folie d'Elbehnon* is an unfinished collection of experimental short prose pieces that he began in 1869. Christopher Smart (1722–1771) wrote his poem "Song of David," which attempts to meld human poetry with divinely inspired scriptures, while incarcerated in an asylum. Rimbaud's "A Season in Hell" influenced the Surrealists through its experimentation. Solomos's prose work "The Woman of Zante" is also experimental. For all these authors, influence on the Surrealists is

the common thread as well as their blending of stylistic experimentation with idiosyncratic quasi-mysticism.

4. Notably, in 1938 Durrell began his third novel, *The Black Book*, with the phrase "The *agon* then, it begins" (1).

5. Oswald Spengler (1880–1936) was most famous for *The Decline of the West*.

6. Ernest Fenellosa (1853–1908) was an American professor in Japan whose work on Chinese language and literature was most famously promoted by Pound, who inherited his papers. The book is certainly *The Chinese Written Character as a Medium for Poetry* first published in 1919. See Haun Saussy's 2009 critical edition through Fordham University Press.

7. E.A. Wallace Budge (1857–1934) was a prolific British Egyptologist. Durrell titled several drafts of novels *Book of the Dead* and had read Budge closely.

8. James Joyce's (1882–1941) final novel, which is characterized by complex and lengthy multilingual puns and wordplays.

9. Durrell may be suggesting a parallel to the closing scene of Eliot's *The Waste Land*, which is also a "quotation-mad" text.

10. Durrell's debt is clear at this time as well. In the closing words of his 1962 revised version of his 1957 novel, *Justine*, for the omnibus edition of *The Alexandria Quartet*, he ends the book with the final words of Pound's first Canto "So that…" (195).

The Shades of
Dylan Thomas

1957

MUCH WAS WRITTEN ABOUT THOMAS immediately after his
untimely death, but for the most part it took the form of obituary,
eulogy, and criticism.[1] Fifty years from now his readers will want to
know other things, about the way he looked and talked and wrote—
for these are the little things which bring a poet alive to his readers;
they are perhaps worth jotting down, even though I was not a close
friend of his and my memories of him are of an early period, when
18 Poems[2] had woken the world of poetry up to the fact that a new
and original poet had sprung out of Wales. Others will have better
stories of his latest period. It is to be hoped that they won't be lost,
or snowed under by anecdotes of his wildness and improvidence
only. For he was an original in his way.

I first met him quite by chance; on a flying visit to England I had
been commissioned by Henry Miller to investigate the story that Anna
Wickham,[3] the poetess, had a large private diary for publication, parts
of which might be regarded as actionable if produced in England itself.
I called on her to see if there was any truth in the story. She was a rather
formidable person, of intimidating size and forthrightness—and I soon
found out that her diary was a myth. (She afterwards hanged herself
from the window-sash of her house because cigarettes went up in
price—a noble protest at the English way of life.) While I was talking

to her, Thomas came into the room and introduced himself. He had caught the name of Henry Miller—whom he deeply admired—and wanted to know what was going forward. He was then a slim, neat young man with well-trimmed hair and a well-cut suit—anything less like the sublunary golliwog I was to meet years later cannot be imagined.

His voice was low and musical, his smile ready. Since he wanted to know more about the Paris Group,[4] as he called it, I was delighted that he should elect to share a long bus ride back to Notting Hill Gate with me; we talked and became good friends. He was full of eager questions about Miller, most of which I was able to answer; and in return I questioned him about his own work which he took seriously but not too seriously. He was particularly amused by our attempts to revitalise *The Booster* (official publication of the American Country Club, Paris, France). By some stroke of fate this periodical, so like *The Hairdresser* in format, had come into the possession of Alfred Perlès who had been instructed to turn it into a Paris version of the *New Yorker*. As Perlès cordially detested the paper's owner, he decided to make it really good; and this is where we came in. *The Booster* became so good so quickly that within three numbers it had not only lost all its advertising but had provoked the President to the Club to threaten us with an action under French laws of obscenity. It became an act of wisdom to transfer *The Booster* to London where it lived on for two numbers under the incognito of *Delta*, before dying.[5] Some of Thomas's work was first printed here.[6] It is worth mentioning, perhaps, that today bound sets fetch up to sixty pounds second-hand!

All this gossip seemed to delight Thomas, who confessed that he found the English literary scene rather dull and he promised us contributions, which he duly sent so long as we were in Paris. I found him then very self-possessed and single-minded and with a marvellous sense of the comic. He was not, I thought, very widely read—indeed, reading bored him somewhat. He liked some novels, and mentioned Dickens and Lawrence with enthusiasm. But though he had heard of Freud and Jung, he had not at this time read either. He listened with attention to what one had to say but gave the impression of knowing exactly what interested him, and being unwilling to waste energies outside his chosen field. I imagine true poets must be like that, shielding their sensibilities against distracting intrusions from the world of ideas. I liked him awfully, too, because he believed in hard work and said that he never released a poem until he had tested every nut and bolt in its body. We drank a farewell beer at the local and promised to keep in touch, which we did for years, exchanging vigorous and jolly messages whenever I happened to be in England but too far away perhaps to reach him.

I tried, I remember, to persuade him to come back to Paris with us and then on to Corfu for a summer. I thought the Mediterranean would blind him with its colours and perhaps help him dig new veins for his verse—the image is a happy one, for his poems rattled and banged away in the darkness like convoys of coal-trucks. And you could always hear the sound of the rock-drill[7] in the best of them. But he sheered away from France and Greece—and wrote saying he preferred to mix his colours from the greys and browns of Wales. He couldn't be budged on this.

Later that year (1937, I think) when the editorial staff of *The Booster* took incontinently to its heels and fled from the threat of persecution by the French to the more liberal atmosphere of London, I found myself piloting Miller (trembling and swearing) past the Customs at Dover. (He had been turned back once before and had developed a formidable phobia of English Customs officials).[8] Furtively in another part of the crowd came Alfred Perlès wearing dark glasses which would have deceived nobody—so like an illegal psychoanalyst did he look at the best of times. We joined forces on the train and there was much rejoicing. We had a bottle of beer and an editorial conference in which we decided to change *Booster* to *Delta* and see just how much English printers could be made to stand.

Miller had compiled a list of people he wanted to meet, at the head of which stood the name D. Thomas, followed in brackets by the words "crazy Welsh poet."

Anaïs Nin's husband, Hugo Guiler the painter, also happened to be Hugo Guiler the banker and patron of the arts;[9] he allowed us to make his London flat our headquarters and thoughtfully furnished it with six cases of a good Bordeaux against such entertaining as we might have to do. And here we organised a few dinner parties which would enable Henry Miller to meet writers of his own calibre. They were good evenings. For a while it was hard to locate Thomas, and then I ran him down. He was living in Hammersmith and was delighted at a chance to meet Miller. But, alas! on the evening in question he kept us waiting hours and we were on the point of giving him up for lost when the telephone rang. He said in hollow, muffled tones: "I can't find the flat so I'm not coming." He wasn't tipsy. He just sounded terribly nervous and ill at ease. "Where are you now?" I said. "Because I'll get a taxi and fetch you." That startled him. "As a matter of fact," he said, "I'm just too afraid to come. You'll have to excuse me." He then told me that he was telephoning from the pub immediately opposite the house. "Stay there," I said, and ran out across the road to meet him and lay hands on him.

I hadn't seen him for some time and he had altered a good deal. He was the golliwog poet of the later portraits—there is one of him by that marvellous photographer, Bill Brandt,[10] which should by now be on every bottle of stout in the kingdom. He was ruffled and tousled and looked as if he had been sleeping in a haystack. He had a huge muffler round his throat. He was also extremely jumpy and touchy and said he was too frightened to move from the pub and that I should stay there and have a drink with him. This I did, and after a bit his nervous aggressiveness died down and I was able to suggest dinner. I painted a ludicrous picture of poor Henry Miller walking round and round the dinner-table cursing him until I prevailed upon him to come with me. Once we left the pub he completely changed, became absolutely himself, and took the whole thing with complete assurance and *sang-froid*. Within ten minutes the nervous man was teasing Miller and enjoying Hugo Guiler's good wine—and indeed offering to read us his latest poems, which he did there and then. Miller was delighted, too, and Thomas thereupon launched into a fragment of poetic prose with his curious pulpiteer's thrasonical voice; I didn't awfully like the way he read—and only when I heard him on the radio did I realise the full power and beauty of his voice.

We talked and drank late into the night and altogether it was a splendid evening; and from then on we met fairly frequently, though he would never come direct to the house. He always rang up from the pub and forced me to have a drink with him there before he would come into the house. I don't know why.[11]

I had several chances of discussing poetic theory with him then, and he answered questions with complete certitude, honestly and quickly. He had few preconceived views about what poetry should or shouldn't be. He wrote slowly, I found to my surprise, and with difficulty, in that small square hand—I always imagined his work falling out red-hot into the mould. He also mutated adjectives and nouns until he squeezed them into the right shape to suit his theme. He went on worrying them for ages before he was satisfied. I saw one phrase which filled a whole exercise book, repeated over and over again in different ways.

We argued a good deal, too, and I remember accusing him of being more interested in sound than in meaning—which he denied. But he agreed that he played all his shots, so to speak, from up at the net: every one was a smash-hit. He liked the simile and said with approval: "That's it. No mercy on the reader." But he was robust and without any self-importance and rejoiced in a laugh.

I was reading a good deal in the Museum[12] at this time, and used to spend my lunch hours drifting about the manuscript room. It is always thrilling to see a page of the original Don Juan, or something in Keats's own handwriting.[13] I never tired of it. One day, in an unfrequented corner of the room, I saw what I took to be a page of Dylan Thomas. I was surprised to find it was a page of an Emily Brontë MS, and I was so struck with the similarity that I bought a sixpenny facsimile and posted it to Thomas. The next day he wrote: "Strange that facsimile by E.B. I thought it was a rejected poem of mine when I opened it. Yes, it's my handwriting, and I can read every word of it." A day or two after this I happened on a picture of the three Brontë girls (is it by Bramwell, unfinished?) and I was struck by a resemblance between Emily and Dylan Thomas. The dark, slightly popping eye, the toneless skin and dark hair....I told him about it, and he was amused and delighted; and when I accused him of being a reincarnation of her he agreed at once and added: "And what is so strange about that? She's the only woman I've ever loved!"

I remember several meetings that Spring, before I went abroad again; not all are worth writing about—for some were boisterous and silly, and some unproductive of anything but good-natured noise. Thomas, under the physical and mental robustness, was quite a sensitive person and rather tended to use his boisterousness as a defence against people who might bore him and make demands on him. He did not care for conversation about writing, and was not really interested enough in ideas to give much thought to them. These things invaded the privacy he felt he needed for his work. He wanted to make himself more sensitive and less conscious. "You know," he once said, "when I'm in company which contains admirers or fans or fellow-writers, I begin to feel I'm under false pretences. That is why I act the clown." And he could be a splendid clown. When he was in a rip-roaring mood he seemed to attract to him everything that was fantastic and unreal in the air around him.

I went for one pub-crawl with him which was as full of comic and unreal incidents as an Irish novel. Indeed the grotesque and unreal in events and people always stepped to Thomas's elbow when he started clowning. It was as if he had touched off a secret spring of lunacy in reality itself. It was a splendid form of safety, I suppose, to move in a coloured cloud of real-life fantasies. Once I visited thirteen drinking clubs in an afternoon with him in an attempt to trace a pair of shoes which he had absently taken off in one of them—he did not remember which. The types of people we met, and the hallucinating conversations which ramified around these shoes would have made a whole novel. In one place three old men helped him crawl under a bar to see if they were there, and one of them got stuck and couldn't be got out; in another he nearly got tattooed by an elderly Indian; in a third... It was like a Joyce Cary[14] novel. And finally, he told me, that when he got home he found the shoes standing beside his bed. He had simply forgotten to put them on....

Yes, a splendid clown and a splendid poet. But under the clowning and the planned appearances of this wild and woolly public figure there was somebody quieter, somebody very much harassed by a gift; and I like to think of him in those early days. I am sure others who knew him well will have more interesting memories of him. I hope these lines may persuade his friends to write them down before they fade.

NOTES

1. Two versions of this commentary were published. The first, much shorter, version was published a year earlier in Tambimuttu's *Poetry London–New York* as "Correspondence" (34–35), the manuscript for which is held in the McPherson Library, University of Victoria. Thomas died in 1953.

2. Thomas's first collection of poetry, *18 Poems*, was published on December 18, 1934 and was highly acclaimed by critics, including Edith Sitwell.

3. The pseudonym for Edith Alice Mary Harper (1884–1947). Her autobiographical essay "Prelude to a Spring Clean" dates from this time and is likely Durrell's reference here, though it is more likely he was sent to Wickham by John Gawsworth than Miller. Wickham financially supported Thomas and his new wife in 1935.

4. The group of authors associated with the Villa Seurat.

5. Durrell edited the three issues of *Delta*, the last of which was dedicated to poetry and was co-edited with David Gascoyne. Several of Thomas's works appear across both *The Booster* and *Delta*. For the most thorough survey of this network, see Von Richthofen's exhaustive unpublished dissertation, "The Booster/Delta Nexus."

6. This includes Thomas's final version of "Prologue to an Adventure," which has never been reprinted in this corrected form. The timelines for Thomas's works and the dating of the Durrell–Thomas correspondence are conflicting in much of the critical work on Thomas, often dating their friendship later and overlooking the importance of the versions of Thomas's works published in *Delta* (Gifford, "Durrell's *Delta*" 19–23). Thomas also comments on the important influence Durrell's *The Black Book* (1938) had on him.

7. Durrell reviewed Ezra Pound's "rock-drill" Cantos in the same year as publishing this piece, so this is more than a casual description. See his "Enigma Variations" in this volume (235–38).

8. Miller includes an extended account of being turned back in his collection *The Cosmological Eye* (Miller, "Via Dieppe-Newhaven" 197–228).

9. This fact was generally kept private and not printed until after Guiler's death in 1985, after which unexpurgated version of Nin's famous diary appeared that corrected previous omissions of references to Guiler. Durrell originally spelled Guiler as "Guyler" in this piece.

10. Brandt (1904–1983) was also familiar to Durrell, and he wrote an introduction to Brandt's 1983 book *Nudes*.

11. Thomas's account of some of this period appear in his letters to Durrell, published in *Two Cities* three years after this article ("Letters to Lawrence" 1–5).

12. The British Museum. Durrell describes his semi-autobiographical alter ego, Walsh, in *Pied Piper of Lovers* as also reading extensively in the British Library.

13. George Gordon Byron's (1788–1824) epic poem "Don Juan." Durrell refers to John Keats (1795–1821) extensively across both his poetry and prose.

14. Cary (1888–1957) was an Irish novelist who died in March of the same year as Durrell published this work on Thomas. This was likely Durrell's reason for the comparison.

Bernard
Spencer

1964

BERNARD SPENCER'S[1] SUDDEN DEATH recently snapped a link
which was first forged in 1938 when he arrived in Greece to work for
the British Council in Salonika. We met first in Athens; and later, when
the Germans attacked Greece, we found ourselves fellow-refugees in
Egypt together with Robin Fedden and George Seferis and many other
poets and writers, some in uniform and others in civilian service like
ourselves.[2] In Egypt we saw a great deal of each other, collaborated on
a poetry magazine called *Personal Landscape,* and for some time shared
a flat on the first floor opposite the Mohammed Ali Club. It was a strange
period, full of a kind of tragic euphoria. Cairo at this time was buzzing
with poets.

Our headquarters then was the Anglo-Egyptian Union, where in our
time off we played billiards endlessly and drank beer, criticising each
other's work with merciless candour, and arguing hotly about the make-up
of each number of our little paper. There was so much material to choose
from, and so many people from whom to solicit verse; the trouble was
that we were short of money and paper and were forced to limit ourselves
strictly to what we thought was the very best work. As it was we found
excellent material to hand in poetry by Terence Tiller, George Seferis,
G.S. Fraser, Gwyn Williams, and many others; and translations of major
European-work hitherto not available in English—Rilke by Ruth Speirs

and Cavafy by Amy Nimr. Nor must I forget to include the satire and the essays of Robert Liddell and Diana Gould.[3]

In all this Bernard played an attentive if somewhat lackadaisical part; he was a man impossible to harry or fluster. Nor was this mere laziness; it was a kind of inherent belief that if you hurried things too much you couldn't observe them with the necessary attention and extract from them their vital juices. He was always reproving me for my lack of what he called "a respect for the Object" and I accepted his mild reproofs with attention. I had discovered something in his poetry and his conversation which interested me and fired me—because it was a quality I felt I lacked. He had a sort of piercing yet undogmatic irony of approach to people and things; as if he had taken up some sort of quiet vantage-point inside himself from which with unerring fidelity he pronounced upon the world—not in the form of grandiose generalisations, aphorisms or epigrams, but in small strict pronouncements which hit home.[4] His best poetry is like that—a succession of plain, almost nude, statements which somehow give one the feeling of incontrovertibility. The feeling, the tenderness is all the purer for not being orchestrated too richly; in the fine grain of his poetry there is much that reminds me of Edward Thomas,[5] and his best poems will certainly live as long as the best of Thomas.

I told him this once; he neither agreed nor disagreed. He put on his most quizzical expression and said, "Have a beer." The real truth was, I think, that his poetry was so bracketed to his private vision that he didn't care whether it *was* better or worse than Thomas or Keats or anyone else....It was good Spencer, that was what mattered. Later, when that blond vagabond, Keith Douglas,[6] strayed into our midst, fresh from a desert battle, with a pocketful of fine poems, he and Bernard made common cause and became great friends. I understood this because they had the same sort of poetic frequency and the same lucid approach to words. But I don't want to give the impression that we talked much theory; neither poets nor dentists talk shop for preference out of hours. But we talked about it in the context of our editing and the work submitted by our fellow writers. Each weekend was spent in a struggle to shape up the next number. (Terence was being too bloody metaphysical, Robin's last lines lacked bowstring...and so on.)

Nevertheless our paper (five-hundred copies) was over-subscribed from the first number onwards and I still think that the little anthology of selections from it chosen by Robin Fedden, which Tambimuttu was to father after the war, is something more than a period piece.[7] It is only when I think of all the contributors on whom we did not levy a claim that my heart sinks....What a paper we could have made in Cairo at that time had we had world enough and time, not to mention money and paper! Freya Stark, Georges Henein, Albert Cossery, P.H. Newby[8]....So many writers we knew; writers, so to speak, within our editorial grasp! Alas! We had not enough money to launch anything on a large scale. We paid for our paper out of our own pockets, and from the first number it covered costs. Contributors were paid only in glory.

In all this whirl of movement I seem to see the tall, rather saturnine, figure of Bernard moving about his tasks with a quiet yet purposeful energy. Physically he was tallish, extremely good looking, and of slender build; his expression was usually one of quizzical amusement. He was shy, and one had to prise a laugh out of him, but when it arrived it was quite disarming. He was reticent without being in any way reserved, and to such good purpose that I, who feel that I knew him so well, would be hard put to it to fill in a detailed questionnaire about his life. He never spoke about his family or friends. I gathered they were Indian Army, or something of the kind. He had been sent to Marlborough, where he was neither happy nor unhappy; to Oxford, which he had enjoyed mildly; to Greece, which woke him up. Once in Greece he started to carve out quite new kinds of poem, and indeed it is within the context of Greece that his work is best judged.

It sounds unreasonable, perhaps, but I think in order to criticise his work one does have to know the Mediterranean a little, and especially Greece; just as Seferis's poetry and my own can only be truly judged within the frame of reference created by its point of impulse:

Greece. Indeed, our sense of exile from Greece was a very real thing and has been very well summed up by Robin Fedden in the brilliant little preface which he wrote for the Tambimuttu anthology.[9] I think that what I shared with Bernard Spencer was the knowledge that for both of us Greece had acted like some terrific drug—a tonic. We had sloughed a youthful skin there and grown a new one. But, of course, we were not the only poets suddenly to get penetrated by the Attic light…I am thinking of Rex Warner, Henry Miller, Patrick Leigh-Fermor, Robert Liddell, Francis King, among others.

I think it is too early to attempt a detailed portrait of Bernard Spencer; his work must be collected and be given time to find its roots. It is small in both scale and in production. Once when I tried to prod him into producing more work he said: "I was never one for the long haul." One of the reasons he found it so hard to find a publisher was that he could seldom muster more than fifteen poems at a given time. But the fifteen were all sound as a nut. He did not labour his work like Dylan Thomas, who went backwards and forwards over the words like a spider, re-weaving them, re-ordering them, testing them; Bernard tried to re-feel weak passages and correct whole phrases rather than single adjectives or nouns. "Ah! You phrase-makers!" he once said to me. "Your trouble is that you are insanely ambitious!" Of course I used to respond by attacking his laziness, though I knew his slowness to kindle wasn't laziness but a special pace he had set himself. When his eye was in, the result was something very special. Spencer saw things in a particular way; the surface description of person or place always led to a poetic judgement which hit one squarely. One turned back to read the poem again because, though deceptively simple, it had a kind of weird specific density of its own. Yes, he is very much a poet of place and mood—that is why he should be read in the context of his Greece, his Spain, his Austria.

By now the war had begun to narrow to a close: history was being changed around us. We were to find ourselves being gradually dispersed by circumstance, thrown on to new trajectories by the vagaries of private destiny or by the work we were doing. Seferis, Spencer, Dorian Cooke, Gwyn Williams, G.S. Fraser, Terence Tiller[10]....It was clear that if the magazine were to survive us it would lack both contributors and the impulse and freshness which had first created it. Besides, we were jealous of it, and did not want to confide it to other hands. The preface to our last issue, a joint one, read as follows:

A CHANGE OF LANDSCAPE

When we were relatively cut off from England and the term of our stay in the Middle East seemed likely to be indefinite, there was an evident place for a local verse periodical. Personal Landscape was accordingly started in January 1942. For three years it has provided a vehicle, the only one available in English, for serious poets and critics in the Middle East. It has also, at a time when propaganda colours all perspectives, emphasized those "personal landscapes" which lie obstinately outside national and political frontiers.[11] Today, with the end of the European war almost in sight, poets, like others, are beginning to leave the Middle East, and for those who remain there is no longer literary isolation. With the improvement in communications a manuscript reaches London in a week and periodicals come out here in roughly the same time. Soon, in fact, there will no longer be any need for an English verse periodical in this part of the world. For this reason the present number is to be the last. We prefer to die at meridian.

This last issue contained Spencer's fine poem "Auction Room," together with poems by Tiller, Hugh Gordon Porteus, and some translations from Cavafy by Amy Nimr (Lady Smart). It also contained a brief obituary note on Keith Douglas, who had been killed in the Normandy landings.[12] The news of his death saddened and infuriated us all, but I think Spencer, who had known him best, felt worst about it. It was ominous for it somehow underlined all the other partings which were in the air. We had begun to disperse to different places— Athens, Madrid, Belgrade....

In my own case the future landscapes were to be Rhodes, Buenos Aires, Belgrade, Cyprus, Provence. Spencer's trajectory took him to Greece, Madrid, London and, lastly, Vienna.[13] We kept, so to speak, a mental image of each other's whereabouts and often, in our long journeys round the globe, managed to spend a few hours in each other's company. The *Personal Landscape* period constituted a sort of extra personal link, a private geography almost; a place-name was subtly altered by the mere knowledge that one or other of our friends— our *Personal Landscape* friends—was there *en poste*. So it was that I managed to spend time ashore at Lisbon to meet Harold Edwards, the Skelton specialist, who first translated the novels of Albert Cossery into English. (He and his wife committed suicide under mysterious circumstances some years later.)[14] He was a very close friend of Spencer and the news of his death came as a shock to us all. But the winds of chance which carried Seferis to Cape Town and Ankara, Dorian Cooke to Serbia, Patrick Leigh-Fermor from Crete to Hamburg and back to Greece, carried Spencer himself back briefly to his beloved Athens for a while and then to Madrid.[15]

We met occasionally in odd places, usually unexpectedly; once with Roy Campbell at the Black Swan in Notting Hill Gate, once in a lift in the Colonial Office, once at Oxford. Last of all it was at Edinburgh. Henry Miller and I were preparing to do battle with the infidel in the Mackewan Hall when the phone rang and David Abercrombie's[16] voice said: "Would you like the phone number of Bernard Spencer? He is leaving for Vienna tonight. You might just catch him." It was in keeping with all the other meetings, what Bernard called "a swift glancing blow." We sat round a kitchen table for an all too brief hour and exchanged all the gossip of the day. He was in sparkling form and full of plans for future work. He had recently married a beautiful young Scots girl and she had changed his luck for it. At least he had managed to find a publisher for his poems. I have seldom seen him so gay.

I think he tended to see us rather as a band of intellectual merce-
naries, being pushed about all over the globe at the behest of invisible
powers, but remaining always united in a curious sort of way—bound
together by this war-period and by the fact that we were all case-
hardened travellers, in a way displaced persons; too much travel had
turned us into professional ex-patriates, restless for the flavour of foreign
cities, and who would never (it was too late) settle down again except
in some remote place—a Greek island, Lisbon, Toledo, Alexandria.
But the rallying point of predilection would always be Athens and if
ever we could manage to get posted there....Yes, these meetings always
began by an exchange of news. Where was Bernard, Ines, Robin, Gwyn,
Dorian, Keith, Harold?[17] It was a sort of litany of the Cairo period; we
were a band of migrants maintaining in this way a tenuous hold on each
other's affections, unchanged by time and distance. I think this, too,
was what we had in mind in choosing an epigraph for the last number
of *Personal Landscape*; it was a comic quotation from the diary of an
Elizabethan merchant traveller called John Sanderson who had spent
the years 1585–86 in Egypt. In a passage he recalls his somewhat
colourful Middle East acquaintance in the following terms:

*Gobo Garaway died with wenching at Scio. Charles Merrell, the
whore-monger, shott dead throughe the head in the way to Alepo by a
janesary shutinge at a pigion. Envious Barli died a begar at the Grange;
Lumbard at London, no lesse; Harman, a knave and a roge; Tient, a
knave graver. Midnall the cocould, alive at the Indies. Pate dead at
Sidon; W. Aldrich at Modon; Field in the West Contry with his froward
wife is fadlinge; and Bourne (Davi) with marchandisinge makes
much peddling, and now is bankrout and (some say) a cockold.*[18]

It carries the compound ring of distance, nostalgia, and personal
loneliness which is, I think, the occupational disease of the poet and
traveller alike.

1. Spencer (1909–1963) was a British poet arising from the same network of authors that later became known as the Auden generation. He was, like Durrell, born in India, though he went on to an Oxford education where he knew W.H. Auden (1907–1973), Louis MacNeice (1907–1963), and Stephen Spender (1909–1995). He also co-edited *Oxford Poetry* for two years, first with Spender and then with Spender's cousin Richard Goodman, the former just one year after the journal had been edited by Auden and Cecil Day Lewis (1904–1972).

2. Durrell was active in anti-fascism activities prior to the Nazi invasion of Greece, and his characterization of their group as refugees is accurate with other contemporary descriptions. Durrell had begun working for the British Council on an interim basis during the Italian invasion of Greece, but this would have followed after Spencer's arrival.

3. This is an illustrious list. Amy Nimr became Lady Amy Smart; Diana Gould married the violin virtuoso, perhaps the greatest of the twentieth century, Yehudi Menuhin. They all remained close for the rest of their lives. Tiller, Seferis, Fraser, and Williams were closely linked with Durrell during this period. All contributed to *Personal Landscape* in the terms described here.

4. Spencer's "Ideas About Poetry" in *Personal Landscape* is a good instance of such specific pronouncements that would have impacted Durrell's work (2).

5. Thomas (1878–1917) was a World War I poet commemorated in Westminster Abbey's Poet's Corner.

6. Douglas (1920–1944) was a major poet of World War II and was well known by most of the North African poets in *Personal Landscape*.

7. Fedden selected from the journal *Personal Landscape* for an anthology of the same title published under Tambimuttu's Poetry London imprint in 1945. Durrell is listed as the editor in a portion of the advertising materials.

8. None of these four authors appear in *Personal Landscape*. Durrell later wrote the introduction to Stark's *The Journey's Echo* (xi–xii) and the two wrote mutually supportive pieces for a variety of venues. Newby went on to anthologize Durrell's works as well. Cossery was first published in English in part through Durrell's connections to the anarchist Circle Editions series of publications in California, which was produced by George Leite, Kenneth Rexroth, and Robert Duncan (all of whom also published Durrell's works). Henein was published by the same group.

9. "Introduction: An Anatomy of Exile" (7–15). Also see Fedden's "Personal Landscape" (63–65).

10. Many of these poets also became government officials. All were published in *Personal Landscape*.

11. This extra-national and anti-propaganda perspective is not simply apolitical. In many respects, it reflects the anti-authoritarian emphases of the networks from which *Personal Landscape* was built, which had developed via the Villa Seurat and was reflected in the journal's ties to the expressly anarchist *Circle* and *Transformation* publications.

12. See Spencer's "In an Auction Room" (12). The issue also includes Terence Tiller's "Roman Portraits" (4), Porteus's "Phoenician Images" (13), and Nimr's "The Poetry of Cavafy" (14–20), which translates Cavafy's "In the Same Space," "The God Abandons Anthony," "The Ides of March," "Without Heed," "Those Who Risk," "Return," "To Ammonis Who Died at 29 Years Old in 610 A.D.," "The Afternoon Sun," and "So That it May Survive." Nimr also refers to Valassopoulo's translations included in Forster's *Pharos and Pharillon*. The obituary on Douglas closed the issue and was written by Bernard Spencer himself.

13. Spencer relocated several times, like Durrell, due to his work in the British Council.

14. Edwards was a faculty member at Farouk I University in Alexandria with Gwyn Williams during World War II, and was hence close to Durrell. Edwards translated Cossery's *Les hommes oubliés de Dieu* as *Men God Forgot*, which was published in 1946 by George Leite's Circle Editions in Berkeley, through Henry Miller's influence and Durrell's involvement. Leite also published Durrell's *Zero and Asylum in the Snow* the next year and had advanced plans and a contract to publish Durrell's *The Black Book*, likely up to the production of page proofs, perhaps abandoned over financial difficulties or fears of censorship. A portion of Edwards's translation of Cossery was also published in 1943 in the Cairo-based journal *Orientations*, which was edited by G.S. Fraser. In addition to his ongoing ties to Durrell, Cossery was also close friends with Albert Camus and Jean Genet.

15. All of their relocations were as a result of government service.

16. Abercrombie (1909–1992) was a professor of phonetics at the University of Edinburgh where he established the Department of Phonetics.

17. Bernard Spencer, Lady Ines Burrows (née Walter), Robin Fedden, Gwyn Williams, Dorian Cooke, Keith Bullen, and Harold Edwards were all close friends in Alexandria during the war. Cooke, Williams, and Edwards were all at Farouk I University, Bullen was headmaster of the Gezira Preparatory School (which hosted the Salamander Club, later the Salamander Trust that published much war poetry), and Burrows married the British diplomat Bernard Burrows, with

whom Durrell remained close long after his work with the British Council ended.

18. See Sanderson's *Travels of John Sanderson in the Levant, 1584–1602*. Durrell was also a long-time reader of Elizabethan literary materials of all forms.

The
Other
Eliot

1965

WHEN I GREW TO KNOW HIM a little better and to value his own
creative richness at its true worth I took the liberty of arranging the
letters of his name thus, Tse-Lio-t,[1] to suggest that there was a Chinese
Taoist sage lurking under the sober cloak of his Anglo-Catholicism: the
change amused him, and he did not demur. I think he probably felt that,
dogmatic theology aside, there was a suitable kind of root relationship
between the rarest and ripest experience in both ways of viewing the
world—the Eastern and the Western. There was such breadth and scope
to his mind that it was possible to elicit an unusual range of sympathies from him for matters which lay far outside the range of his own
personal preoccupations. That is why I feel that I knew him quite well,
though in fact I know nothing about him; I know no more about his
life than *Who's Who* can tell me. The hazards of literary business threw
him in my path in my early twenties as a publisher of my poems, and
as one of the most truthful and gentle critics I have ever met.

The literary eminence of the house of Faber & Faber[2] today always
gives one the impression that it is much older than it in fact is; one
thinks of it as a sort of Murray[3] hallowed by several generations of fine
publishing and resonant with great names like Byron or Moore. It enjoys

this sort of status despite the fact that it is an extremely young firm; I remember its being founded in the twenties under the name of Faber & Gwyer. The point of these remarks is to suggest that much of its present eminence is due to Eliot's work; to his farseeing advisory work, which led to the publication of all the best poetry and critical work of the time. No, not all; but very nearly.

If this was for me a fruitful and rewarding relationship, it was entirely due to this painstaking and gentle man whose mind had so fine a cutting edge, and who undertook his duties so seriously and with such method that he went far beyond them in his dealings with the young writers of the house. I cannot believe that my experiences with Eliot the publisher were any different from those enjoyed by other poets and writers from the same stable. The real mystery is where the devil he found time to deal with us all in such detail, criticising, consoling, and encouraging. In my case it can only be accounted for by suggesting that he was some sort of saint; poor man, he had to deal with an argumentative, combative, opinionated young man—a self-inflated ego betraying all the marks of insecurity and vanity. At times it was necessary to cut me down to size, and whenever I succeeded in irritating him too much, he would do it with such breathtaking elegance and style that it left me gasping. But always without heat, without vanity, charitably. It was unpardonable! Moreover, his views were backed up by accurate and factual work, incredibly detailed and pondered, so that I was torn between exasperation at the justice of his remarks and shame at having driven him to waste so much time explaining things so painstakingly to the refractory child he must have assumed me to be.

A wicked man indeed, for he was seldom wrong, and what is worse, he was never splenetic or small-minded. Happily I have preserved all the letters he wrote me, in which business affairs are often tempered by a witty aside or a penetrating judgement, and they make excellent reading today.[4] From them I can judge how formative an influence he was upon me, not as a writer so much but as a friendly counsellor of letters.[5] The public image of him at that time was of a rather humourless literary bonze of the Sainte-Beuve type. (It should be remembered that at the period of which I am writing he had not yet published his plays and his *Four Quartets*. His fame, which, was considerable, rested upon some criticism and upon poems like *The Waste Land* and *Ash Wednesday*.) Needless to say he did not correspond at all to this literary image. When first I met him I found his gravity rather intimidating; but as I saw more of him I found that laughter was very near the surface. It came in sudden little flashes.

Henry Miller, who said that he always visualised Eliot as a "lean-faced Calvinist," was most astonished and intrigued when I returned to Paris with an account of my first two meetings with him. So much so, in fact, that he started reading him with attention and prevailed upon me to engineer a meeting with him in London, a meeting which duly took place in a little flat in Notting Hill Gate, loaned to me by Anaïs Nin's husband, Hugh Guiler, the painter.[6] I think Eliot himself was a little intimidated by the thought of meeting the renegade hero of *Tropic of Cancer* in the flesh, while Miller was still half convinced that Eliot would be dressed like a Swiss pastor. At any rate, the relief on both sides was very apparent, and I remember a great deal of laughter. They got on famously; and it was now that Eliot made one of those gestures which displayed not only his kindness but the unswerving, uncompromising truthfulness which from then on was to characterise for me everything he did and thought. He offered Miller a blurb for his book, and myself a prefatory note for *The Black Book*.[7] This could have compromised his reputation somewhat, for by the standards of the day both of us were "unsavoury writers" (choice phrase), while Eliot's own great reputation was tremendously respectable. But no; he liked the books, and without thought to himself offered us his help. He always had this unfaltering honesty in his dealings. From this delightful evening one small scrap of conversation comes back.

ELIOT: Of course there is more than one kind of pornography; often it has nothing to do with four-letter words.[8]

MILLER: Who are you thinking of?
ELIOT [with immense seraphic gravity]: Actually, Charles
 Morgan.[9]

"My dear Durrell, I'm sorry that you found my letter acid;
I thought it was perfectly sweet myself. But if you like the acid
I shall see what I can do…" (1937)

But he was too much of an aristocrat of letters not to scorn the
sitting duck, and even at his most acid he remained kind without
indulgence. Intellectually, he was not a boxer but a judo expert.

5 Nov. 1937

*Dear Durrell; I have read the "Poet's Horn Book" with interest and
with some apprehension. Let me say at once that for reasons which
have nothing to do with its merit I don't think the* Criterion *is quite
the place for it. I don't like to publish articles in the* Criterion *in which
my own work is one of the subjects discussed, and on the other hand,
if you cut me out of this article it would not only mutilate the article
but would in a way have as bad an effect as if you left me in. That is
to say, it might give the impression that I liked to publish articles
which criticised several of my contemporaries but left me alone. So if
you publish it I think it had better appear elsewhere.*

*Now first considering the article without relation to yourself. It
seems to me that you make out an admirable case if the presuppositions are admitted. But these presuppositions are very great and it
would indeed take a good deal of study to find out exactly what they
are, as I am not sure that they are all quite conscious. But one can use
as some test of the validity of the premises one's instinctive feeling
about the conclusions. It seems to me that there must be something
wrong about the presumptions behind a course of reasoning which*

leads you to dismiss Ezra Pound in a phrase, and to deal with
Wyndham Lewis, one of the most living of living writers, in the same
category as—and indeed as somewhat less significant than—Aldous
Huxley who is one of the deadest. Surely the fact that Lewis writes
good English and the fact that Aldous Huxley does not are relevant?

Secondly, as for this kind of critical activity as an occupation for
yourself, which is the cause of my apprehension. There seems to me to
lie a danger for you as a creative writer in critical work which is
particularly concerned with making conscious the activity of your
creative mind. If you were concerned with building theories which had
nothing to do with, or conflicted with, your creative activity, I should
consider this sort of writing a healthy outlet, and also desirable for
bringing in a little money. You will doubtless remark that this point of
mine is a bit of disingenuous apologetics, to which I will only say that
the opinion crossed my mind before it crossed yours. But I have lately
had to give a couple of lectures on Shakespeare, without having realised
in advance what it was going to let me in for, and I am so alarmed at
finding that my interpretation of Shakespeare was really concerned
with what I myself am interested in doing in the theatre, that I think
I had better leave Shakespeare alone for some time to come. If I am
writing a play I think I am better concerned with becoming conscious
of how to do it rather than in becoming conscious of what I am trying
to do. All this could be elaborated at considerable length but I know
that you are quite capable of doing that for yourself whether you
agree with my point or not. I have certain opinions which you will
no doubt discount; I think, for instance, that you and Miller make
far too much fuss about D.H. Lawrence; but that has nothing to do
with it....

July 1949

Dear Larry,

*Your undated letter is a masterpiece. In future, when your letters are
undated (as they usually are) I propose to date them a week earlier
than my reply, which will therefore always be immediate; and when
in future they are also unsigned (as they have sometimes been in the
past) I hold myself free not to answer them at all without blame. But,
as I say, it was a good letter and I approve it. I always believe it is a
good thing to encourage authors to believe that their work is a little
better than it is—not much better than it is, but a little. It is normal
and proper that authors should consider their publisher not quite
up to their latest work; it is only a grievous error, sometimes leading
to calamity, when they cherish the illusion that there may be some
other publisher more intelligent, more alert, more understanding of
his own interests even (in the long run, the very long run) than the
publisher they have. However, this leads to a further consideration of
Sappho,[10] which I have not neglected, but have re-perused from time
to time ever since. (You must remember that your letter was written
only a week ago: the transatlantic air-mail is very quick nowadays.)
Now, I still don't see how it could be produced without a surgical
operation; and I am sure that the surgical operation by a good
producer would be so beneficial that I had rather print the play after
than before. Nevertheless I think it a good piece of work; not quite so
good as you try to persuade yourself (for the first paragraph of your
letter was addressed to yourself, not to me) but still good. The author
is a little pretentious, and sometimes makes the mistake of trying to
emulate Shakespeare in gnomic utterances put in a queer way, but
on the whole he does know his onions, and plants them right side up.
And it is refreshing always to find a poet who does understand that
prose sense comes first, and that poetry is merely prose developed by
a knowledge of aeronautics. So, even if it isn't produced, I want to
publish it.*

But this is only the beginning. First we must see how On Seeming
to Presume[11] *does: and in the present state of the poetry market (the
bottom of which has fallen out) (I could quote you some amazing figures
of three digits) you are not to expect anything but misery. Nevertheless
I shall try to persuade my board to publish* Sappho. *But, my dear
Larry, do you realise what that means? This is an enormous book of
179 pages, far bigger than any poetry volume; nowadays, what with
the wages the printers and binders get, much more than authors, that
is a price of* at least 10/6 per copy;[12] *which reduces the market to
wealthy poetry lovers—and of course poetry lovers are not wealthy.
Do you see now why I should like to hold forth some promise of stage
production? Few people buy poetry; fewer still buy poetic drama—
unless it has had such a* succès d'estime *on the stage that they think
they ought to seem to know about it. The money we shall lose by
publishing* Sappho....*Meanwhile a few points of detail, assuming
that you have a carbon copy of the text in my hands.*

Here follow two pages of detailed corrections and queries which
could not have cost him less than two hours to elaborate. The letter
ends as follows:

Read Antony and Cleopatra *and simplify. Shakespeare was lucky
in his time, as all great dramatists have been: and we are unlucky.
We have got to make plays in which the mental movements cannot
find physical equivalents. But when one comes to the big moment
(and if we can't get it we can't do drama) there must be some simple
fundamental emotion (expressed, of course, in deathless verse) which
everybody can understand.*

Yours in haste
T.S. Eliot

"Yours in haste!" But he never appeared to be hurrying about anything: his pace was slow and thorough, vegetative, ruminative. And being the very type of the leptosome—in the classification of Kretschmer[13]—he shared some of the mental habits of the ilk. A slight tendency to think twice before making a decision, to ponder, to list all the reasons why not—in fact, the complete opposite to his client. At first I found this most provoking, but gradually, as I began to understand the sort of man I was dealing with, I grew ashamed of pestering him and making him waste so much of his time on me. I allowed him to wrestle me down, confident that his judgement was nearly always sounder than mine. The result was that everything of mine, by the time it reached the press, was all the better for having passed through those skillful hands. I often tried to get a poor poem past him, but if I did do so, I was left in no doubt about his own reservations.

Now, if he did all this for me, what did he not do for the other and better poets on the Faber list? One shudders to think what he would have earned in overtime today.

Our actual meetings in the flesh over twenty years were few and far between, and I began to regret not being able to see more of him. However brief, there was no occasion when he did not leave me some small fragment of conversation to think over. He never "made conversation"; he always talked. The idlest and silliest question always produced a deeply deliberated answer. He did not turn things aside and take refuge in persiflage as most of us do. Even sometimes when I was teasing him he riposted very neatly in tones of perfect sobriety. "Though your writing betrays great intelligence," I once said, "there is a mystery in it for me. How can an intelligent man be a Christian, much less a Catholic?" He gazed smilingly at me for a moment. I went on. "After all, if you examine Christianity from the historical point of view, you come out somewhere among the Eleusinian mysteries, no?" He sighed and agreed, still smiling. "And then," I went on, warming to my task, "how suspect your poems are, littered with Buddhist references and snatches of Heraclitus and so on. I can't think how they let you into the Church."

Eliot put on a very sober expression and said: "Perhaps they haven't found out about me yet?"

On another occasion I had spent the whole morning trying to get a biography of Giordano Bruno, and my reception at a famous Catholic bookshop had been so equivocal and frightened that it put me in a rage. I had to see Eliot directly afterward and said: "There, you see your blasted Catholics. I go down to try and find something about Bruno, and they behave as if I had asked for the Marquis de Sade." He grinned and said: "Perfectly right and proper." I said, "But Eliot, they were Catholics, and he is a very important figure!" He nodded. "I agree about that," he said, "but I think you are very lucky they didn't take your name and address. Now you try going to the ------- Bookshop"[14] (a Communist bookshop) "and ask them for a little book about Trotsky...."

About poetry, his own and other people's, he often had striking things to say; things which lodged in my mind because they explained his own working stance. For example: "A poet must be deliberately lazy" and "One should write as little as one possibly can" and "I always try to make the whole business seem as unimportant as I can."

I tried to lure him to Greece, but he said that he preferred gloomy places to write in, and added: "Now *The Waste Land* I wrote in a rainy pension in Geneva."[15] He warmly agreed with Dylan Thomas's views about the dangers of lotus-eating and too much sun.[16] And once when I was moaning about having no time to write, he asked quietly whether I hadn't discovered that the early morning was the best time. He said that when he had had to work as a bank clerk he got up two hours earlier and spent a good hour working for himself before going to his job. Later I discovered that Valéry used the same working pattern when he was employed by Havas.[17]

The only time that I have ever seen Eliot put out of countenance was after he had discovered that I had spent a whole winter in Rhodes[18] with nothing to read except Sherlock Holmes. At the mention of the name he lit up like a torch. He, it seemed, was a tremendous fan of Holmes and could quote at length from the saga. "I flatter myself," he said—and this is the nearest to an immodesty that I had ever heard him go—"that I know the names of everyone, even the smallest character." Two minutes afterward he found he could not recall the name of one of Doyle's puppets. His annoyance was comical. He struck his knee with irritation and concentrated. It would not come. Then he burst out laughing at himself. While we were still on the subject of Holmes that evening the conversation turned sideways toward his own Quartets,[19] which had just come out and had created a great impression. Many were the complicated exegeses being published tracing his debts to people as various as Lao-tse and Saint Augustine, and goodness knows who else. "By the way," he said anxiously, "I trust that you, as a genuine Holmes fan, noticed the reference to him in Burnt Norton?" I had not. He looked shocked and pained. "Really not?" he said. "You do disappoint me deeply. A clear reference to The Hound of the Baskervilles. I refer to the 'great Grimpen Marsh,' do you recall?" Yes, then I remembered; but I had forgotten that it features in the Holmes story. "But listen, Eliot, with all this critical work on your sources, has nobody mentioned it?" His eye lit up like the eye of a zealot. "Not yet," he said under his breath. "They haven't twigged it. But please don't tell anyone, will you?"[20] I promised to keep his secret.

These few notes are intended only to serve as a short personal sketch of the Eliot I knew, the publisher and critic and warm-hearted acquaintance. It will remain for others to do the serious tasks of assessment, if indeed they have not already been done. Anyway, I am no critic, as Eliot himself warned me, and have learned my lesson. Our views often diverged radically—about playwriting for example; I accused him of writing masques, not plays. He thought that plays about people were not of much interest to a poet. But he always listened and brooded heavily before starting one of his Socratic excursions with an "if" or a "but."

As far as I understood the artist Eliot, I should say that he differed very greatly from others I have known, in the qualities of self-abnegation and a sense of responsibility to the culture of his time. He was a responsible man, who felt that his words were acting as a formative influence on the age and that it was necessary to use them creatively, to further insight. He could not stand displays of temperament and talent devoted to inferior ends like glory. He could not, for example, support Lawrence:[21] he admired his gifts; indeed, admitted his genius; but insisted that his ideas were "clap-trap." He forced himself to be a conscious artist and wasted no efforts to examine and test his own workshop ideas so that his own gift might be directed. It will be understood that I am not talking about dogmatic assumptions of any sort, but simply an orientation toward what he believed to be the sources of our culture and its insights. He wanted to help and not hinder self-understanding. Both his critical and poetic work are securely anchored in a notion of gradual self-definition by the ego; what is defined as easier to master, and easier to shed. At any rate, that is how I see him.

But I was lucky that the hazards of chance enabled me to catch sight of the human being, who is often hidden in his work. The sober and cautious and humble man could also laugh; and it is his laughter that I best remember.

NOTES

1. "T.S. Eliot," Durrell's poetry editor at Faber & Faber. The French translation of this piece was published as "Tse-lio-t" (3–8) in the same year.
2. Faber & Faber is now a famous British publishing house, but it originated in the Scientific Press, run by Sir Maurice Gwyer. Gwyer and Geoffrey Faber founded Gwyer and Faber in 1925, and when they dissolved the enterprise in 1929, Faber created Faber & Faber, though he had no partner. The publishing house became known for its extensive poetry offerings, and its publications include the most eminent authors of the twentieth century.
3. John Murray was an English publisher founded in 1768, and it has perhaps the most illustrious "stable" of authors for any press, ranging from Jane Austen and Queen Victoria to Charles Darwin and Lord Byron.

4. A portion of Durrell's letters to Eliot are published as "Letters to T.S. Eliot" (348–58). Eliot's letters to Durrell remain in the Durrell Collection of the Morris Library, Southern Illinois University, Carbondale.

5. Durrell was often keen to avoid showing Eliot's influence, and his positioning of Cavafy in *The Alexandria Quartet* is likely a way of displacing attention from the book's extensive allusions to Eliot's poetry.

6. This relationship was not normally acknowledged in print until after Guiler's death in 1985, though Durrell also refers to it in his "Shades of Dylan Thomas."

7. Eliot's comments were used for the flyleaf of the Obelisk Press edition of Durrell's *The Black Book*. Since both books were banned, this was a significant risk for Eliot.

8. Eliot's own bawdy and semi-pornographic writings were only published in 1996, long after his death, in *Inventions of the March Hare*.

9. Morgan (1894–1958) was a highly successful though now overlooked British novelist and critic.

10. Durrell's first published and performed play, which Eliot published through Faber & Faber.

11. First published by Faber & Faber in 1948. Apart from edited collections, Durrell did not publish another book of poetry with Faber & Faber until *The Ikons* in 1966, after Eliot's death.

12. 10/6 is a pre-decimalization price of a half guinea or ten shillings and six pence. Counting in guineas traditionally indicates a higher class affiliation; hence, pricing to 10/6 would be posh and reflects the target audience of "wealthy poetry lovers."

13. Ernst Kretschmer was a German psychiatrist who established a typology of human bodies and personalities. The leptosomic is small and weak and prone to fastidiousness.

14. Likely Colletts or Central Books, which would then have been the Worker's Bookshop.

15. For a detailed survey of the composition of *The Waste Land*, see Lawrence Rainey (27–84).

16. This remark by Thomas is included in his letters to Durrell (2–5).

17. The French poet, Paul Valéry (1871–1945), was employed by the Havas news agency for twenty years and only began his writing career after having taken up this flexible position.

18. Durrell resided on Rhodes from 1945 to 1947 while he was director of public relations. He describes this period in *Reflections on a Marine Venus* and this particular winter in "From a Winter Journal" (252–60).

19. Eliot's *Four Quartets* is a set of four poems first published from 1935 to 1942. They were only published as a set in 1943 and 1944 in Britain.

20. Eliot only mentions a grimpen (a term etymologically uncertain but generally seen as invented by Sir Arthur Conan Doyle) in the second section of "East Coker," the second poem of the *Four Quartets*. The *Oxford English Dictionary* lists both Eliot and Doyle as its only examples of the word in use.

21. D.H. Lawrence (1885–1930) was a British novelist and poet who is often regarded as given to peculiar or unusual views on sexuality, psychology, and instinct.

Richard
Aldington

1965

ALDINGTON'S WORK meant a great deal to me as a young man and I
was heartily glad to have the opportunity of trying to repay my debt to
him by friendship and literary support during the last few years of his
life when his fortunes had failed him and his career had virtually come
to an end. I owed him much. Long before I could limp in French, his
fine translations gave me a passport to French literature; his own war
poetry and vivid satirical novels delighted me; it was in his pages that
I first read serious praise of Eliot, Proust, and Joyce as the true creative
spirits of our time. He had not waited until Lady Chatterley set the
world by the ears to acclaim Lawrence; but had long since defended
The Rainbow and *Sons and Lovers* in brilliant fashion. Pound and Lewis
and Campbell also benefitted by his strong sword-arm at a time when
the general public looked upon them as noisy freaks or intellectual
perverts, or worse.

All this was of the greatest importance to a writer in the bud. His
lively and compassionate views on literature were expressed in admirably fashioned prose, full of a fierce generosity which gave the lie to
humbug and sterile pedantry. He occupied, from quite an early age, a
well-merited position of importance in English writing and a thoroughly
well-earned financial success with work on several fronts at once. All

this is forgotten today but will soon be remembered when his books once more come into print.

At the time when I met him, disaster had overtaken him and financial distress stared him in the face—a serious matter for a man in his sixties, born and bred to literature, and who knew no other trade. He could not cheerfully turn to grave digging or teaching as I could— he had never been forced to do anything but write. His books on T.E. Lawrence and Norman Douglas[1] were responsible for this state of affairs; they had not only damaged him critically but had alienated him from the common reader, from his own public, from the libraries. With the trouble caused by these two volumes the whole of the rest of his admirable life work went out of print and out of public demand— some seventy titles in all! This was, of course, catastrophic for a man living on his books, and he was facing up to it gamely; but the tide had turned against him. Publishers would not reprint him, booksellers would not stock him; but worst of all his public had deserted him. If his last few years were made tolerable and even happy ones it was due to the timely help of a fellow writer who also admired him and who set him on his feet financially.

He was a difficult, touchy, strange, lonely, shy, aggravating, and utterly delightful man. I was very much honoured to enjoy his friendship and an intimacy which permitted me frequently to disagree with him. Curiously enough he enjoyed this very much. It never affected our firm friendship; and in fact he positively reveled in the title we (my wife[2] and I) bestowed upon him—that of "Top Grumpy." He sometimes put on special performances of outrageous grumpiness especially for us, for the pleasure of making us laugh. And we tried more than once to coax him into some public field where his truly endearing grumpiness could cause sympathy and not distaste. Aldington would certainly have won both sympathy and attention had he attacked such a public medium. One could not help seeing the heart of gold underneath the surface explosions of temper; the generosity hidden under the snappy tone of voice. None of this, alas, can be done for one by cold print in default of the author's tone of voice, the connotation, the attitude of mind expressed by feature. Aldington with his striking good looks and gentle address would have been a winner. But he was too shy, and considered it "infra dig to make a mountebank of himself"—so I could only murmur "Touché" and leave it at that.

I have said he was lonely, and this is true; while he knew and loved Europe, spoke excellent French and Italian, one always thought of him rather as a British exile than as of a European of British *souche*. He had cut himself off in some indefinable way from the current of British life, and in my view this isolation was harmful to this most British of authors. But here I stumble upon a field of absolute ignorance, for he was also a reticent man. He never spoke about his private life, his marriages, his personal affairs; indeed to this day I do not know anything about him as a human being, only as a writer. He once or twice hinted that his whole interior affective life had come to a stop in the twenties, and that after that epoch "everything seemed finished." Europe, he said, had committed suicide in 1914. I reminded myself that his first visit to Europe had been around 1905—an epoch which I have great difficulty in visualizing.

Another factor which came into play due to his isolation was a curious though intermittent faulting of judgement in literary matters; of course he was deeply embittered by the collapse of his career. But he persisted in attributing it entirely to the fact that he had been ambushed by the critics and not cold-shouldered by the public. Nothing I could say would convince him that in the case of his Lawrence and Douglas books it was more his manner than his matter which caused so much offence, which had indeed damaged the public image of this fine poet and man of letters. No. He would not have it. It was "The Cockney Commorra." The late Wyndham Lewis also suffered from this "secret enemy" complex— perhaps we all do to various degrees?

His death came as a great blow to us; there was nothing to predict it in his magnificent physique and his robust good health. I am inclined to attribute it simply to the fact that he felt there was nothing more to live for; he despaired of regaining the lost ground. For the last few years he had been living up in the Cher as the guest of a firm friend, admirer, and fine writer, who had put his house at Aldington's disposal. But most of the time he was alone, doing his own cooking. But he was proud as well as reticent and in all the long letters we got from him there is plenty of grumpiness but never a complaint. He went down with all guns firing, and his last letter which I received twenty-four hours before he died is full of rogue elephant fireworks; a specially grumpy performance deliberately calculated to make my wife exclaim: "Ah, that wrong-headed old grumpy up there in the Cher." I can hear his burst of laughter at the familiar phrase!

It was ironic that shortly before his death he was invited to spend his seventieth birthday in Russia and meet his Soviet readers. He went with a number of prepared grumpinesses and some specially tailored clothes designed to show that while he loved Russian literature and the Russian people he was Richard Aldington, Esq., British and Conservative to the core. But the warmth of his reception quite won his heart; readers from all over Russia slogged up to Moscow to shake his hand. I think in his heart of hearts he must have compared this reception to the grim silence of London—not one telegram of congratulations, not one line from the press!

Well, he is dead, this old British grumpy; subtract what you will on the account of wrong-headedness, of intemperateness of judgement, and so on. There remains a good deal which those who knew him will always remember with affection: great generosities, great quixotries, great gallantries. And when the smoke of battle has died down around his name, his books will win him back his true place among the important writers of our time.

NOTES

1. Aldington's two books from 1954, *Pinorman: Personal Recollections of Norman Douglas, Pino Orioli and Charles Prentice* and his more contentious *Lawrence L'Imposteur: T.E. Lawrence, The Legend and the Man* (1954), which was retitled the next year for its British publication with the more neutral *Lawrence of Arabia: A Biographical Enquiry*. Douglas (1868–1952) is largely remembered for his novel *South Wind*, to which Durrell alludes in several of his own novels.

2. Claude Vincedon.

On
George
Seferis

1975

THE NOBEL PRIZE was a most appropriate prize to salute the work of
George Seferis,[1] for with him Greek Literature crossed the great divide
into Europe, and laid its firm claim upon the European consciousness,
becoming a part of it. This is not to decry the great Greek poets of the
last fifty years—far from it. But their sensibility remains Greek in the
Balkan sense, and their work, while brilliant, is metropolitan Greek in
spirit. They were not, as he was, essentially cosmopolitan souls (Cavafy
is the one exception), and one wonders whether Seferis's Smyrniot
connections did not give him the same angle of vision as Alexandria's
did for Cavafy. That, and the roving life of a diplomat. He himself always
ironised over himself as a wanderer, and the *persona* or double he chose
for himself (just as his admired friend Eliot chose "Prufrock," just as
Pound chose "Mauberley") was "Stratis Thalassinos,"[2] an ironic seaman-
traveller. He looked upon the impermanence and folly of life with the
detached eye of a man who knows that he is leaving it, for his ship will
be sailing in a few hours. He did not worry much about death—it was
a voyage like any other; he was living in the midst of it! But he felt
how provisional life was, and how absurd.

His temperamental relationship with T.S. Eliot will strike anyone who knew them both, for they had much in common. They were both great critics, and they both worked coolly and quietly like great surgeons ("hastening slowly"). Both were mystics, and savants. When Eliot speaks of "getting every ounce of tradition behind each word"[3] one thinks of Seferis, so deeply steeped in the ancient Greek tragedy, and yet so modern in his approach. As a young consul in London, Seferis announced to a friend in Athens: "There is a chap here who must have read my poems, at any rate he is influenced by them. He is called T.S. Eliot."[4] At any rate he used to tell this anecdote against himself; later he explained to me why he had been right in one sense. Both poets felt that their point of departure had been the French Symbolists, and particularly Laforgue and Rimbaud;[5] the later theoretical work of the surrealists meant less to them. They were both clear-headed enough to recognise that that movement, however fruitful, would end in politics.[6] Seferis was lucky in his translators both English and French; to have Jacques La Carrière and Yves Bonnefoy to introduce one in Paris, and Rex Warner[7] in London—this was a great help both to him and to us, his readers.

Another faculty the two great poets shared was the ability to let drop observations about life and poetry which tumbled into the mind like pebbles down an empty well, and echoed on for years. Seferis once said that, in a sense, poetry was the complete life of the poet, the inner life, and that the mere biography was a shadow play. He added that if he were stopped after his death at the Heavenly Gates by Peter and asked to justify the time spent on earth, he could only point to his poetry in order to plead that he had not wasted his life in unliving!

Shortly before the news of the prize came through, I visited Seferis in Athens to renew a friendship which had started to fall into disrepair owing to too long separations.[8] He was already ill but as always resigned and brave-hearted. He said something about having to economise a bit because he was retired now and even an Ambassador's pension was relatively modest. However he knew that in Greece there would always be some corner of an island with a few black olives and a can of retsina. I tried to cheer him by saying: "Don't worry; one of these fine years Greece will be given the Nobel—and there is only you. You will get it on the grounds of your whole work. Of its stature." He groaned and said: "Don't wish me that, my dear Larry. I feel that I am going on more and more towards anonymity!" A little while after that came the great prize.

He also said to me once: "We Greek poets have one problem more than you or the French; we have a language almost as broken up into shards as the remains of Troy. Half our vocabulary goes back to Homer, half to Byzance. We have to select and shape it, and as the peasant language is the purest, and has guarded intact so many of the ancient Greek words, using them so naturally, we must try and make the demotic our foundation in the teeth of the professors and the journalists." He went on with a smile: "But she is such a firebrand, this damned tongue of ours." He used the lovely word "Pismatara!"[9]

All honour to this great poet and the old-new Greek tradition he has helped to shape.

NOTES

1. Seferis was granted the Nobel Prize in Literature in 1963.
2. Prufrock appears in Eliot's famous "The Love Song of J. Alfred Prufrock" (1915) and Mauberley in Pound's long poem "Hugh Selwyn Mauberley" (1920), which is in many ways akin to Eliot's poem, though more overtly autobiographical. Seferis's poem "Stratis Thalassinos among the Agapanthi" is focused largely on exile, but the characters appears across several of his works from 1940 to 1965. Durrell's juxtaposition of Seferis and Eliot shows how he regarded the two poets.
3. See Eliot's "Tradition and the Individual Talent," 13–22.
4. Eliot had a significant impact on Seferis's works, and he was familiar with at least a little of Eliot's work as early as 1931 (Beaton 107–09).
5. Jules Laforgue (1860–1887) was an important French Symbolist poet who influenced English literary Modernism, T.S. Eliot and Ezra Pound in particular.

Arthur Rimbaud (1854–1891) was also a profoundly influential French poet, though he gave up writing by the time he was twenty-one. Durrell mentions Rimbaud and his lover Paul Verlaine in his first novel, *Pied Piper of Lovers* (190).

6. Durrell spoke out against the communist politics of Surrealism during and after the 1936 London International Surrealist exhibition and was closely tied to its anarchist revisions in English Surrealism.

7. All three did significant work as translators. La Carrière (1925–2005) was a writer and translator as well as a personal friend of Durrell's, Bonnefoy (1923–) is a French poet and essayist, and Warner (1905–1986) was a major translator of Greek materials whom Durrell knew well and who introduced Durrell's co-translated edition of Seferis's poetry.

8. Durrell and Seferis's friendship was particularly strained by Durrell's service to the British on Cyprus during the Enosis struggle. The two, however, maintained friendly correspondences with each other even during the periods in which most critics describe their relationship as having failed. This part of their correspondence is held in the Durrell Library in l'Univesité Paris Ouest, Nanterre, and the Gennadius Library, Athens.

9. Though Durrell translates the adjective πεισματαρα as "damned," its meaning is often closer to "stubborn."

Poets
Under
the Bed

1989

THE POETRY PUBLISHING WORLD is going to suffer deeply at the
passing of M.J.T. Tambimuttu, who, for some forty years, has occupied
a curiously commanding position in the London world of letters, as
friend, guide, and publisher of so many poets of the first rank. We all
know what quarrelsome and unstable people artists are, yet their affection for and trust in Tambi and his doings were unbounded, even among
those who might have had most to criticise about his work. They spoke
of him always with a loving and humorous concern, through which
shone affection and admiration.[1]

I am thinking of Eliot, who spoke of him in a wondering whisper,
and described him as the most courageous of the younger publishers.[2]
And even those he might exasperate by one of his manoeuvres never
for a moment lost their basic affection for him. We need this sort
of living reminder in a philistine and positivistic civilisation, and if
Tambi could claim anything it would be that he won the affection of
souls so different as, say, Henry Moore, Graham Sutherland, David
Gascoyne, Henry Miller, Anaïs Nin, and scores of others.[3]

He could also be careless and irritating. Our moments of exasperation with him were real ones, but it was always a loving and concerned

281

exasperation, and I do not think he lost a friend ever, despite divergences of policy or practice.

My own memories of him go back to before the war and before he had made his mark on the London scene.[4] Some of the sites from which he elected to operate were fairly bizarre—like the steam-room of the Russell Square public baths, which he adopted as a head office for a brief period. Indeed, if he finally left the baths it was with reluctance, and because of the deleterious effect of the steam on his manuscripts.

My very first meeting with him was at a rendezvous off Tottenham Court Road, where he had rented a room in a cheap boarding-house and lay in bed late of a morning, going over his plans to bring poetry to the public at large. It was my first interview with him and I saw with amusement that the entire contents of his first number reposed under his bed in an enormous Victorian chamber-pot. It was into this that he dipped for his authors.[5]

Of course there were later and more affluent times and more up-to-date offices, but like a true lover of art and literature Tambi had a great affection for the seedier side of his adored London. Many a pub taproom earned his allegiance as a boardroom, and for a while he could not be prised away from the Hog in the Pound in Oxford Street, a most uncomfortable venue in which to discuss literature.[6]

He leaves the general state of poetry publishing much improved for his presence and happy activity, and he himself felt that he had scored a praiseworthy success in his efforts to found and organise an Indian Arts Council in London which might arrange exhibitions of Indian treasures already in our collections but which never see the light of day.[7] It is to be hoped that this activity will continue after he has gone; it would be his most effective memorial.

NOTES

1. Through Poetry London, Meary James Thurairajah Tambimuttu (1915–1983) published several of Durrell's works as well as those of his close friends. Many of the poets involved with *The Booster* and *Delta*, the journals published via the Villa Seurat in Paris in the 1930s, went on to publish through Poetry London. This includes Elizabeth Smart's *By Grand Central Station I Sat Down and Wept*, which recounts her relationship with George Barker, whom she met through Durrell. Many of the poets associated with the wartime *Personal Landscape* in North Africa and the New Apocalypse in London were similarly involved.

2. T.S. Eliot was, by this time, an important editor at Faber & Faber.

3. All of these writers were tied to either the New Apocalypse in London or the Villa Seurat in Paris.

4. Tambimuttu became important during World War II as a publisher of poetry and literature. He was perhaps the most dedicated publisher of the works of younger poets during the war when such poets were otherwise often excluded from the mainstream. Tambimuttu included several works by Durrell in his periodical *Poetry London* as well as his novel *Cefalû* in the Editions Poetry London book series. Durrell also published Tambimuttu's "Ceylonese Lovesong" in *Delta* in 1939 (14).

5. This would have been approximately 1939 though perhaps earlier since Durrell first met with Tambimuttu very shortly after his arrival in London.

6. This is now a high-end pub on 28 South Molton Street, London. Tambimuttu also frequented the Fitzroy Tavern, which is likely where he and Durrell met.

7. Tambimuttu founded the Indian Arts Council in May 1983 with a grant of £20,000 from Indira Gandhi (Ranasinha 136).

Spirit of
Place
Travel Writing

Corfu
Isle of Legend

1939

IT LIES IN THE SHADOW of the Albanian snows, its yellow sickle dim in this late spring haze, as a vessel lies at anchor;[1] northward looms the snout of Pantocratoras,[2] like the eroded sutures of a skull; southward the more kindly landscape slides downhill, dappled with cultivation to Lefkimi,[3] the flat Calabrian-looking plateau inhabited only by deep-sea squills. Strictly speaking, it gives the impression of two islands, not one; the metamorphic northern balconies of stone, habitation only for the monk and the eagle, welded to the sleepy lowlands facing the mainland. To the north and west, vertebrae of stone, the unmistakable Grecian flavour; to the east, in the rich moist acres of cultivation, a polyglot, confusing atmosphere—Byzance, Venice, Turkey, Russia.[4]

The town itself is enigmatic, various—some have said characterless; the architecture Venetian, confused by British Victorian monuments, French adaptations, modern Greek scenic effects.[5] The people shiftless, lazy, not to be trusted; all the vices and none of the virtues of six occupations. The Ghetto still speaks a private argot which has been identified with a Venetian dialect of the Middle Ages;[6] the British have left behind them their traditional game, cricket,[7] whose terminology has become with time nothing less than fantastic; the French a tradition for sparkle and gallantry; the Turks a hatred and fear which nothing will ever dispel.

287

But apart from these urban manifestations, the character of the Corfiots has remained a well-defined constant; since the Corinthian wars they have remained a contentious, difficult people: wrong-headed, insular. If their island is Homeric, the fishermen of the northern coasts live up to the reputation history has given them; do not forget that Ulysses was washed up in the great bay at Paleocastrizza.[8] The whole impetus of the island's history is contained in a phrase like that. At the mouth of Lake Halkiopolous you can still see the fate of the boat that took him home—spars, rigging, men, all turned to stone. The women still wash their clothes in the little stream that flows down by the hillock still called Atona, where the temple stood; the cypresses still arch in the wind by the deserted temple of Artemis.[9]

The ancient pantheon still exists, through it has suffered a sea change. Charondas the ferryman has become Lord of Death in the place of Pluto; and in some of the mountain villages he has been turned into "the black cavalier," the night-rider, who comes down from the sky, gathering little children at his saddle and trailing the old men after him into his kingdom—by the hair! In some places, however, the obol is still placed between the lips of the corpse before burial, indicating that the Ferryman has perhaps not altered his occupation, and still demands the fee for the crossing.[10]

The Black Rider probably dates from the time of the Klephts, those doughty ruffians to whom Greece owes her present independence; the legends lie like geological formations in the people's consciousness, difficult to disentangle, difficult to assign to their correct period. The overlapping occupations have left behind them their debris of super-stition; for example, the Venetians left behind them a headless negro to haunt the scorching swamps by Govina;[11] the Turks, the ghosts of an eunuch and a young girl who walk by the full moon among the cypresses near Ypso,[12] wringing their hands and moaning.

The patron saint of the island himself (Saint Spiridion) has a formidable reputation for miracles; during the Turkish invasions he performed innumerable feats of divine daring, stamping out armies, sinking flotillas, and decoying a grain-fleet to the island once when the inhabitants were on the point of starvation; the peasants cherish a unique faith in him, taking their diseases to the church, their hopes, their problems, more readily than to the doctors. Every year the wizened little mummy of the saint is carried in a progress round the town, bobbing and twitching, through the glass windows of his sedan-chair. To swear by his name is to swear the most solemn of oaths; to touch him is to be healed of the most intractable disease; to renounce him would be to become tied suddenly in knots by the four agues. But since the good saint is a busy man, and cannot be everywhere at once, complimentary charms against fate are favoured; the cart-horses wear a necklet of beads as a protection against the evil eye; the priest confers a more orthodox blessing at certain times of the year, splashing the house with holy water from a cypress-twig; amulets of terrific efficacy are bartered in the town.

Possession by devils is a phenomenon to be met with also; by great luck I was able to witness the possession of an old lady by the Fiend, a sight not only convincing and frightening, but one which did not seem to answer any medical descriptions of suggestive hysteria or epilepsy. The subject collapsed on the deck of a sailing-boat (she was on her way to the town), and became absolutely rigid, her features drained of blood until the flesh took on a strange mud colour. A moment of this rigidity and she began to tremble convulsively, and to utter the strangest of sounds—the hoarse, muffled barking of a dog. The fit lasted perhaps five minutes, perhaps slightly more.

Other cases of demoniacal possession have been recorded in which the Fiend spoke from the mouth of the subject in an unknown language (analogous to the "pneumatic tongues" mentioned by St. Paul).[13] The exorcism service in Alexandrine Greek, chanted by an unlettered priest, however, is apt to be almost as bizarre as the phenomenon it is intended to destroy. Possession by devils is second only to possession by nereids; the penalties are not specified but they are grave ones. To a woman one can lose one's heart, but to a nereid a man will lose his soul.

On the deserted sand-beaches of the west coast at the full moon strange ceremonies are supposed to take place. The man who sleeps by the surf will be woken at midnight to see the salt-dripping figure of a woman standing ankle-deep in the foam. What they will say to one another is not told; but he will bring her back by morning to his village where he will marry her. Beautiful she will be, but dumb; and barren also. But should anyone by chance ask her the fatal question "What is your name?" she will disappear down to the sea by night, leaving behind her a curse on the husband's family and on his descendants.

Midday and midnight are the two fatal times for charms to taken effect; sleep in the shadow of a cypress at either time and you will awake mad: a tonic madness which will give you the second sight necessary to see goblins, the nereids who sit and watch by the deserted springs, and the great god Pan, who is by no means dead.

For the mountains there is one set of legends; for the lowlands another; and for the sailor his own nostrums against evil at sea.

The patron saint presides over all of them. With his image nailed to the prow a man can be sure of a smooth journey across these blue waters, among the islands where the cypresses nod. Nicholas the old sailor (whose portrait appears here)[14] declares that when he puts out with his amulet, the good saint locks up the narrow seas and chains up the north wind. He considers himself personally favoured.

But there are other eventualities to be considered, such as water-spouts. A very special technique has been invented for dealing with these. Each craft carries on board a black-handled knife: and when a waterspout has been sighted the captain sends below for it. Seizing it in his right hand he carves on the deck a sacred pentacle; and then, aiming the blade of the knife, like a revolver, at the middle of the column of water, he intones the first phrases of the Demotic Bible:

Έις την αρχην εταν ο Λογος
Και ο Λογος εταν ο θεος[15]

The desired effect is produced; the waterspout breaks, and the ship can run safely to her harbour.

To sail at the full moon also demands a measure of caution; the Ionian is haunted by the unknown goddess, who rises like a serpent beside a boat and calls out, in fearful tones: "And how goes it with Alexander?"[16] Should she receive no reply. She is liable to overturn the boat with a gesture of rage; the only answer which will avert tragedy is: "He lives and reigns still." For the benefit of fair-weather Ionian sailors, the Demotic text of the formula is appended.

Q: Τι γινεται ο Αλεξανδρος;
A: Ζει και βασιλευει[17]

Nicholas the sailor insists on the necessity of learning this charm. "Because," says he, "an angry sea is simply water—but an angry goddess is a woman." No-one who has sailed by moonlight under the Venetian forts, on a sea like silk, would ever disbelieve him. Charms against fate are necessary here in a landscape where the harbours are few, and the villages perched on the ribs of the mountain inaccessible; where a journey of twenty miles by sea seems equal to a journey across a continent.

At Kassope in the north the ruins of the Tiberian fort are overgrown with arbutus and asphodel; the walls gnawed by the weather.[18] At dawn on certain days, however, the inhabitants of the little town, huddled beneath, have heard the hobnailed tread of roman centurions and seen the flash of bronze at the fents and loopholes; at Halkiopolous in the south (the Phaecian port, the γλυκυς λιμην[19] of Dion Cassius) the petrified barque of Ulysses has been known to move: oars have been seen beating: and the whole island, impelled by them, has started out for Ithaca with its royal guest. By morning the tragedy has happened again. The cypresses sprout from the broken walls of the monastery; the rats scuttle in the dark outhouses. Masts, rigging, shields, men they have been turned back to stone again.

On the long white road which skirts the Venetian salt-pans and leads to the town, the man who walks in the siesta-hour runs the risk of a meeting with the Three Women; if their beauty is not enough to move him they will try other means of getting him to speak to them. They will even take up sticks and belabour him silently where he stands: and if he should so much as open his mouth and speak a syllable he will be struck dumb for the rest of his life. Pan himself has a private dancing-glade above Cannone,[20] deep among the cypress and olive trees, where the peasants do not dare to venture; it gushes out of an apparently blank rockface and dribbles down towards the sea. Drink of this water and return, they tell you; for once having drunk of it you will always come back to the island. The charm is on you.

In the spring the turtle-doves arrive,[21] and the hills echo with their plaintive, insistent note, whereby hangs a legend perhaps the most beautiful of all of them.

In some of the remoter parts of the island these are known as *deka'ktures*, which means literally "eighteeners" (δεκα'κτο). They say that when Christ was on His way to the Cross, a certain soldier in the crowd, seeing His distress and pitying Him, tried to buy a bowl of milk from a woman standing nearby. Now she was crying at the top of her voice, "Eighteen a bowl." And the soldier when he came up to her was met by this same insistent cry; and on searching about he could only muster seventeen coins to pay for the milk he wished to buy. All attempts to bargain with the woman failed; to his entreaties she only returned the harsh cry "deka'kto, deka'kto." Accordingly she was changed into a turtle-dove, to cry her wares forever, in a lower and more melodious key, to be sure, but just as insistently as ever, among the fields. That is the legend; and to it they add, with perhaps just a touch of malice, the belief that should the turtle-dove ever, by mistake, cry "seventeen" instead of her customary "eighteen," the end of the world would be at hand.

The legends are alive here because they form an intimate part of the Greek peasant's daily life; and not merely alive but necessary to a people which lives in a world so violent in its colour, so terribly lonely in its scenery—a world in which a belief in God is as imperative as a belief in His dark opposite, the Devil. Among these long olive-glades anything is possible; and if it has been said that the ancient Greek legend is dead, it is only because it is almost unrecognisable under its patina. But legend itself lives; and by it the people themselves no less than their scenery become legendary, fabulous.

Here is an island where garlic is still prophylactic against the evil eye, the fingers of the toad against possession by demons; and super-imposed upon these folk-superstitions are the lovely aerial sculptures of the ancient world; the mother of Gorgons with her belt of snakes from the temple of Artemis (now alas! A museum piece);[22] the deserted bays were Nausicaa played with the court maidens; the long yellow coastline stretching down into the blue towards Xante and Crete, alive under this sky as flesh is alive.

The traveller who climbs the Corfiot olive-groves to drink from the Traveller's Spring must find out sooner or later the uselessness of the act; the difficulty is not to return to Corfu, but to leave it.

NOTES

1. An anonymous editorial introduction originally prefaced this article: "Familiar in tourist itineraries, not long ago a British possession, Corfu remains little known to the English public. Nor would many English visitors succeed in capturing, as Mr. Durrell does, those varied essences of the Greek mystery which Corfu distils—groves that are yet nymph-haunted, bays that resound with Homeric echoes, sailors for whom magic lurks in every wave, sibyls whose pronounce-ments can bind and loose the hearts of men."

2. The largest mountain on Corfu. It dominates the landscape of the north of the island.

3. A village on the southern end of Corfu.

4. Corfu was never formally controlled by Turkey, though it was by the Byzantine Empire, the Venetian Empire, and Russia. Due to Turkish domination of the

Greek mainland, Turkish influences are still significant, though much less so than in the rest of Greece.

5. The British Government House was built with stone from Malta, an imitation of the Rue de Rivoli from Paris runs beside it, and Corfu Town itself is Venetian in construction. Its hybridity is unmistakable.

6. The Jewish population of Corfu was largely removed four years later to Nazi extermination camps during World War II, and the ghetto of the town (from Venice's original) was bombed. The Jewish Quarter of Corfu Town still contains many dilapidated buildings that remain uninhabited but were part of the Jewish community. A distinct dialect did exist, and rural communities on the island still integrate elements of Italian into Modern Greek.

7. A cricket green is still active beside the Liston in the Old Town.

8. A variety of stories and locations relating to Ulysses are associated with and circulated on the island.

9. These locations are in modern Kanoni, South of Corfu Town. Durrell's family lived near to Kanoni in Perama. These sites are now in Paleopolis, the old city, and the pediment for the Temple of Artemis is in the Archaeological Museum, though it was housed in the Palace of Saint Michael beside the Pension Suisse in which Durrell first resided.

10. Compare to Durrell's short story "Down the Styx" (417–22).

11. Govia, Gouvia, or Govino Bay is a village north of Corfu Town in an area Durrell would have passed regularly. Though they are not now swampy, this may have been the case at the time. More likely, however, is that he meant the area around Lake Korisia on the southwest of the island. He was well acquainted with both locations.

12. Ipsos is a coastal village north of Gouvia but still southwest of Kalami, where Durrell lived.

13. 1 Corinthians 12:14.

14. The photograph by Nancy Myers was originally included here.

15. John 1.1: "In the beginning was the Word, and the Word was with God."

16. Alexander the Great (356–323 BCE) was a Greek king and highly successful conqueror.

17. As Durrell renders it above, "How is Alexander?" "He lives and stills reigns."

18. The Castle at Kassope on the north of Corfu. It was destroyed by the Venetians and would have been in ruins at Durrell's time, though it was restored in the early 2000s.

19. The sweet lemon.

20. Typically Kanoni, south of Corfu Town in the ancient city centre.

21. Notably, Durrell prepared a typescript entitled "A Village of the Turtle-Doves" set on a Greek island. Kanoni, immediately south of Corfu Town and near to his family in Perama, is likely the setting.

22. The original temple is in ruins, but the pediment is in good condition and on display in the Archaeological Museum in Corfu Town. During Durrell's time on the island, it would have been in the Palace of Saint Michael. The same pediment appears to have influenced the American poet H.D.'s experience of "the writing on the wall" while she was on Corfu, as recorded in her *Tribute to Freud* (52–53).

The Island
of the Rose

1947

IF YOU SHOULD HAVE THE LUCK to approach it, as perhaps one
should, through the soft mist of a June nightfall, you would undoubtedly imagine it some great sea-animal asleep on the water. The eastern
spit of sand upon which both the ancient and the modern town were
built shelves slowly down into the channel from the slopes of Monte
Smith, so called because Sir Sidney Smith,[1] the conqueror of Napoleon
at Acre, once set up his battle headquarters here. This would constitute the hump of your whale. Eastward loom the weather-worn Carian
mountains, casting shadows so dense that the sea is stained saffron by
the last rays of the sinking sun. Nestling in the natural amphitheatre
where once stood the dazzling buildings and temples of the ancient
town, the Crusader fortress[2] with its encircling walls and crumbling
turrets looks for all the world like a town in pen and ink, situated upon
the margins of some illuminated manuscript: a mediaeval dream of
an island fortress called Rhodes which the mist has invented for you,
and which will dissolve as you enter the tiny harbour of Mandraccio to
anchor under the fort of St. Nicholas where once, it is suggested, the
famous Colossus stood.[3]

   To the traveller familiar with the Rhodes of pre-war years much will
seem different;[4] yet the medieval town may still be considered one of
the best-preserved monuments to the architecture of the Middle Ages

297

extant in Europe. The walls have escaped save for one large breach. An extensive area of the Jewish quarter, however, has disappeared into a heap of rubble and plaster. Of the pre-war Jewish community, which numbered three thousand souls, only some thirty have managed to survive the rigors of the concentration camp and find their way back to the desolate Hebraica.[5] A few of the smaller treasures have disappeared, but in the main the Italians succeeded in storing the contents of their museums safely; and though seriously bombarded more than once, Rhodes suffered, as it were, little more than contemporary damage. Her Middle Ages remains with all its somber beauty. And it is for this, no less than for her landscape, that the traveller of the future will brave the sea-journey from Piraeus or Alexandria.[6]

The history of Rhodes presents a picture so highly coloured and so packed with detail that it would be a daring thing to attempt to compress it within the confines of so short a study as this must be; yet the visitor is, so to speak, always within range of its beckonings. One cannot escape it. Each walk through the old town will throw up historical reminiscences so rich in their content that one is forced to halt, to speculate, to imagine. Hard by the ugly modern cinema bequeathed to the Rhodians by their last Governor,[7] the traces of a Hellenic wall will remind one that somewhere here Caesar and Pompey struggled under Rhodian rhetoricians for mastery over the art of speechmaking.[8] Here the exiled Tiberius,[9] in his short cloak, walked among the temples, happy to have been granted Rhodes as a place of exile. Strolling beside the mirror-calm waters of Mandraccio harbour, in which one can see the little fort of St. Nicholas reflected, who can help trying to imagine the Colossus of Rhodes which earned, by its prodigious size, a place in the catalogue of the Wonders? If, then, these notes are to be of service to the visitors of the future they should surely touch and illuminate those parts of Rhodian history which lie, so to speak, outside the covers of books, embodied in a building or a legend whose reference is contemporary and immediate. How much of the orthodox chronology does the traveller of today need to enjoy this lovely and mysterious island? Let us be bold.

Before Rhodes came into being, the power of the island was vested in three ancient cities—Lindos, Kameiros, and Ialysos (modern Phileremo). No one can claim to know Rhodes who has not visited them, for they are still there today; Lindos blazing upon its stony promontory, Kameiros tucked into the limestone hollows of the landscape like a letter into an envelope, and Phileremo stately and remote among its nursery pines. Each has its peculiar flavour, its peculiar evocations; though all are different, one cannot but describe them as evoking something common to the broad placid tone of the island as a whole. They are different features of the same lovely face.

From the Lindean acropolis, where once the goddess Athena accepted the flameless sacrifices of the ancients, one can stare down a sheer five hundred feet at the summer sea, motionless now and drowsy. It is like staring into the lens of a peacock's eye enormously magnified. Eastward lies the landlocked harbour with the little stone igloo which is today known as the tomb of the philosopher Cleobulus,[10] one of the Seven Wise Men of the ancient world. In the summer sunshine the white-washed houses of the town and the steep walls of the acropolis blaze like a diamond.

Cross to the opposite side of the island and see Kameiros. Here the archaeologist's spade has exposed the dazzling slender columns and walls of the Hellenic town. It lies in the honey-gold afternoon light, listening to the melodious ringing of water in its own deep cisterns. The light has a peculiar density and weight, as if the blue sea had stained it with some of its own troubled dyes. The amphitheatre is littered with chipped inscriptions. One can make out the names of some of the city fathers: Solon, Aristides, Aristomachos.[11]

Phileremo lies inland, behind the modern village of Trianda. Standing on its now desolate and empty acropolis, one can look out towards the sea across the delightful green countryside that Timocreon[12] knew as a child. From the inner terraces the ground slopes clear away to Maritza, where the gutted modern Italian aerodrome lies.[13] Phileremo is within walking distance of the modern town.

At some time before 408 BC disaster overtook the three ancient cities. A great earthquake tore them to pieces. It was then that the inhabitants decided to move eastward and found a joint town which would offer them safety against the hazards of nature. The flat-ended promontory may have suggested a building-site which would prove earthquake-proof. At all events Grecian Rhodes was built in 408. It was perhaps the earliest example of over-all town-planning, for it was designed by the famous Hippodamus[14] who was responsible for the harbour of ancient Piraeus. The city that he created was, by all accounts, staggering in its simplicity and beauty. So selective a judge as Strabo[15] himself preferred it even to Alexandria and Rome. Its length is given as eighty stades,[16] and its inhabitants numbered some two hundred thousand. The carefully grouped buildings and temples ran round the semicircle of the natural amphitheatre, leading down to the three harbours. At their back, on the little hillock today known as Monte Smith, stood a temple and acropolis encircled by a sacred wood. Pliny[17] states that the town was decorated by some three thousand lovely statues of which one hundred were colossi.

What remains today? Apart from the ancient stadium where the flocks of goats still idly browse, scarcely anything, to remind one of Rhodes' ancient splendour. On the crown of Monte Smith a few emplacements cut in the rock; towards Simbuli on the western side of the town, some shallow graves. In the centre of the old walled town one stumbles upon some broken drums belonging to an unknown temple. Hard by the Gate of St. Paul a few stone ramps remain to recall the famous Rhodian shipyards which turned out those marvellous triremes. Everything else has been swallowed in the slow succession of earthquakes which began some fifty years after the setting up of the great sun-god, the statue to Helios which we know as the Colossus. Today as one stands above the little theatre which is let into the walls of the stadium and looks down the softly inclining planes of orchard and meadow, it is the mediaeval town alone that one sees: the windmills softly turning against the sky, the great buttresses of the Crusader outworks—and the slender minatory fingers of the mosques which finally triumphed over it all. It is the Rhodes that Richard the Lionheart saw in 1191, when his fleet put into the harbour for a ten-day spell, en route for the shores of Cyprus.[18]

But what of the more recent history of Rhodes? For three hundred years the island endured the kindly but negligent rule of the Ottoman Turks. Yet it says something for the tenacious nationalism of the Greeks that they retained, and retain to this day, their distinction of tongue, creed, and costume. Throughout the centuries the vague and shifting shape of a possible Union remained with them—a Union which today has become fact and not fancy.[19] Today there are some forty thousand Greeks on Rhodes and some six thousand Turks; though these figures will be altered when all the refugees have returned, the proportions will still be representative. Greek island culture remains predominant throughout the Dodecanese.[20]

In 1912 the Italians annexed Rhodes, together with some fourteen other islands of the group,[21] and for a while the island remained merely a political counter for the Great Powers to bargain with. As late as 1923, however, an Italian governor of the island (more or less exiled there for his republican sympathies) saw its possibilities as a tourist resort, and started restorations side by side with modern developments. The island was encircled with some 150 kilometres of first-class motor-road which is today intact. Extensive reforestation was begun to check the soil-erosion which has destroyed the productivity of nearly every Aegean island. The ancient monuments were carefully and lovingly restored. Local production was increased by the development of state-subsidized farms. Though the local Greeks suffered from expropriation and petty despotism, the island itself became extremely rich and beautiful. A handsome modern town sprang up outside the mediaeval walled town; and these labours were crowned by the building of a great hotel which even today must rank among the best in Europe.

The name of the Governor responsible for much of this labour was Mario Lago.[22] His successor,[23] who replaced him in 1936, managed within a comparatively short time to ruin more than half of the town by tasteless and vulgar restoration, and to exhaust the flourishing revenues of the island. Yet despite the handiwork of this parvenu (who was a close personal friend of Mussolini) the island today retains enough of its natural loveliness to delight the eye and mind of the traveller in search of Mediterranean beauties; and more than its fair share of creature comforts to humour the exacting. Even the wartime invasion of the German and Italian armies—when the island became simply a cupboard for the hungry soldiery—did not completely ruin Rhodes. After a two-year interim spell of patient if often improvised work under the British Military Administration the Rhodians today feel confident that before long the normal life of the island will have recovered from the rigours and ravages of war. Much of the damage to buildings and monuments has been repaired. Deforestation has been halted. It remains to be seen whether the incoming Greek administration will be given the necessary budget to guarantee the upkeep of the island. The existing works and amenities of the town, however, make it the fourth or fifth town of Greece now that the Dodecanese are being incorporated into the Aegean group of islands.

A subject of frequent and admiring comment is the Rhodian character itself, which for gentleness, hospitality, and moderation is a model that might profitably be followed by the rest of the Balkans. The metropolitan Greeks themselves have been amazed at the absence of party strife on the political plane, and at the high degree of public order and civic responsibility apparent in the behaviour of the islanders. Cynics have been apt to suggest that Italian rule was harsh enough to break the natural Greek ebullience of the native character; while politicians point out that the long divorce from metropolitan affairs has made the Rhodian ill-informed about home issues. In justice to Rhodes it should be pointed out that moderation and poise was a remarked characteristic of the ancient Rhodians; while on behalf of the modern one might with justice quote the opinion of Newton, that garrulous English archaeologist and consul whose

Travels and Discoveries in the Levant makes an ideal companion for the
modern traveller.[24] In 1865 he was able to write: "The Rhodian peasant
does not fatigue his guest with cumbrous hospitality as the Greek
bourgeois does; he does not poison him with raki, clog him with
sweetmeats, cram him with pilaff and sicken him with *narguilehs*...I
have generally found them thrifty, gentle and obliging in their intercourse with strangers and with one another, and far more truthful and
honest than any Greeks I have ever had to deal with."[25] It would be
impossible to contest the truth of that judgement even today.

To the scholar Rhodes offers a variety of instruction; for the Hellenist,
Kameiros (Homer's "golden Kameiros"[26]), Lindos and Phileremo, for
the student of Byzance the almost inaccessible churches of Funtocli
and Alaerma, for the mediaevalist the incomparably rich material in
Rhodes town, and in the frowning Crusader forts with which the long ·
green coastline of Rhodes is studded—Pheraclea, dour Monolithos,
Castello, and Villanova. The abundance of material precludes any
general view of the island to all who cannot spare six months of study:
for the different periods overlap each other closely, and the historical
events seem at first inextricably entangled. The student of church
architecture will be able to study the mosques which rise from the
foundations of Byzantine churches, or to read of the Ottoman sieges
from the illuminated Arabic texts in the Turkish library. A bowshot
from where Demetrius of Macedonia[27] launched in 304 BC the attack
which gained him the appellation Poliorcetes ("Besieger")—the site
was subsequently the Grand Master's[28] garden, and after that the
cemetery of the Murad Reis mosque—he will be able, in the cool deep
shade of the courtyard, to speculate on the fate of the exiled satiric
poet Hascmet, who lies buried there: for Rhodes was also a place of
exile for the Turks as it had once been for the Romans.[29]

Much good paper and ink have been employed by the historians
in describing the famous Colossus of Rhodes; the curious traveller
who attempts to find his way through the subject by visiting the excellent archaeological library of Rhodes may well be forgiven if he comes

away with rather a headache, for the subject has been one of violent controversy among specialists. Perhaps a brief summary of known facts, shorn of conjecture, would be of service to him. The Colossus was designed to commemorate the tremendous siege of antiquity when the Rhodians repulsed the forces of Demetrius Poliorcetes. It took twelve years to design and mount and it was finally thrown down by an earthquake which demolished Rhodes (c. 222 BC). The statue was about 105 feet in height. Its position is not known with any certainty, but the story that it "straddled the harbour" is a medieval concoction. No ancient authority makes this allegation. One of the most popular sites suggested is the present site of the tower of St. Nicholas fronting Mandraccio harbour. After its fall the great statue lay on the ground for some nine centuries. It was finally broken up by the Arabs in the seventh century AD and the metal carried off to Syria where it was put up to auction and knocked down to a Jew from Ur.[30] The amount of the successful bid is unrecorded. It is recorded that several hundreds of camels were needed to load the scrap. Torr,[31] by far the best historian who has written about Rhodes, is inclined to the idea that the Colossus occupied a site somewhere within the Deigma, the oriental bazaar with which Hippodamus beautified the ancient town. The field of conjecture is, however, open to everyone who dares to venture into it.

Nor will the student of folk-lore be disappointed, for the peasant-lore of Rhodes does not seem to have suffered from the exile endured by the Dodecanese. Rather one might imagine that the long seclusion has caused the legends and proverbs of the Rhodians, as it were, to ferment—for solitude and separation quicken memory. Certain it is that whoever hunts for a continuity of culture between Rhodes and Greece will find not an element missing; the nereids, for example, which haunt the springs and waterfalls of Greece, also exist here in great abundance. Everywhere in the long verdant valleys behind Monte Smith one stumbles upon the daisy-starred glades which are their dancing-floors, and every village has some tale to tell about them. Once in Aphando, for example, a shepherdess who had lately borne a child was walking up the hill to her fold when she fell in with a body of nereids. She began to run but they chased and easily overtook her. She was in mortal terror—and with good reason; for whoever gets dragged into a nereid's dance will not be allowed to stop until she falls dead from exhaustion. However, it so happened that the shepherdess was carrying on her back an embroidered mule-bag with some of the baby's swaddling clothes in it. This saved her, for when the nereids laid hands upon her they recoiled, screaming: "It burns, how it burns!"[32]

Among the other tenacious peasant survivals which argue an ancient Greek origin is the modern Pan, who under the name of *kallikanzaros* makes life a misery for the housewife by his tricks no less in Rhodes than elsewhere in Greece. Here, however, he is often known as the Kaous, a word which seems to derive from the Modern Greek verb meaning "to burn," and which conveys a pleasing evocation of brimstone and saltpetre. The Kaous is usually encountered at lonely crossroads, or late at night on dark footpaths. Everyone dreads such encounters, for the Kaous is as malicious as he is powerful. Usually he sneaks up behind you and asks hoarsely "Feathers or lead?" You must reply with the greatest circumspection. If you say "Feathers" you may escape, but if you say "Lead" he will leap on your back and throttle you, or ride you all over the landscape like a horse, thrashing you with a stick. In general there is nothing you can do about it; though it is recorded that once a particularly wide-awake villager from Alaerma managed to catch a Kaous by its two pointed ears. Holding it thus he took it home and burnt a hole in its hairy leg with a red-hot iron. The Kaous shrieked and fainted, while out of the wound crawled a mass of small snakes which were killed one by one. This treatment proved beneficial, for the Kaous awoke towards morning healed from its insanity, and muttered: "Deeply, deeply I slept; and lightly, lightly I've woken."

Some idea of the continuity of myth and belief may be gathered from the story of Helen of Troy and the peasant legend which preserves it to this day. According to one version Helen survived her husband

and was driven from her home by her stepsons. It was in Rhodes that she took refuge, where, the story goes on, Polyxo found and hanged her from a tree to avenge himself for the loss of Tlepolemos during the Trojan War. History records a grove of trees at Lindos which were held sacred to "Helen Dendritis" and which preserved the memory of this beautiful and ill-fated woman as a tree goddess. But today Helen Dendritis has disappeared, together with her grove of trees. Instead the modern peasant tells the story of how once a great queen called Helen hung herself because she was unhappy. She hung herself from the tall branches of a pine, using a rainbow for a cord. And to this day the rainbow in some parts of the island is called "Helen's Cord"— surely a beautiful transition from one myth to another.

I have quoted these examples of folk-lore to indicate that despite its long separation from Greece, Rhodes may still fairly claim to be within the main current of Greek peasant culture. The songs and legends of the island have never been fully harvested though several industrious workers in this field have made a start, and the average traveller who knows a little modern Greek will have no difficulty in unearthing new ones. The stronghold of Greek lore and habit is undoubtedly the mountain village of Embona which lies at the foot of Mount Atabyron. Here the girls wear a distinctive dress which recalls Crete more than anything else, for their legs are cased in soft jack-boots which guard them against the dense and prickly scrub of their native highlands. On the slopes of the mountain which was once sacred to Taurine Zeus they farm their orchards and rocky hold-ings. The natives of Embona are celebrated for their dancing and no local fiesta is deemed complete unless a visiting body of *Emboniatisses*, as they are called, put in an appearance and dance the native dance known as the *sousta*. This is a sight not easily forgotten; for the tradi-tional costume, with its violent colours, and the speed of the dance produce the most delightful kaleidoscopic effects, as of a great multi-coloured fan opening and shutting. Several villages of Rhodes are celebrated for their dancers, but Embona above any other; and the cry that goes up when the mountain dancers arrive at any lowland fiesta proves conclusively enough that the Rhodians willingly concede the highest honours to them. "The Embona girls have arrived," cry the peasants; "now we shall see some dancing."

The only other mountain of any size apart from Mount Atabyron is the easily accessible and now rather domesticated Profeta. The modern road-system has made it so easy of access that here in spring one may wander for hours through the scented pine-glades, or lie upon a dazzling carpet of anemones and peonies. But its peculiar atmosphere has already been recorded in the beautiful poem of Mr. Sacheverell Sitwell[33] which the curious reader will stumble upon in *Canons of Giant Art*.[34] The evocation of Profeta and its goddess is far more complete and moving than it could ever be in prose:

It was her sacred mountain, in the heart of mist,
A wood of wild rocks where every echo called,
Where words bent back at you as soon as spoken
From rocks like houses or like sudden islands;
Here stags wandered,...

Indeed the stags still wander on Profeta, though their numbers have been sadly depleted by the Germans and by neglect during the war years.

These notes have hinted at the enjoyment that Rhodes offers to the scholar and to the student of folk-lore. Another kind of traveller will no doubt be as interested in the wild flowers which star the green slopes of the hills in spring—the sheets of narcissus and anemone; he will prefer to see contemporary Rhodes, with the whitewashed villages whose orchards and gardens are everywhere stabbed with the scarlet dots of the hibiscus. It is for him that we should record the existence of nearly a hundred different varieties of orchid, and of a rare black peony which may be seen occasionally on the topmost slopes of Monte Profeta. And it is for him also that we should record the existence of a spring at Salaco whose waters exercise a magnetic charm over the wayfarers who quench their thirst at it. The legend says that whoever drinks at Salaco is bound to return to Rhodes, marry a Rhodian girl and spend his life in the island.

Sea-communication with Alexandria and Beirut has already been restored; a regular air-service from Athens was opened in June of this year. Rhodes, then, is going to be easily accessible both from Egypt and from metropolitan Greece. There could be no lovelier place to spend the cool Mediterranean spring, or the parched and sunny August weather which ushers in the Day of St. Demetrius, upon which the casks of village wine are broached according to custom. The Emperor Tiberius, whose judgement in so many things was at fault, never hesitated when it came to the choice of Rhodes as a place of exile. The contemporary traveller will have no difficulty in endorsing his judgement when he visits this paragon among the islands of the Levant.

NOTES

1. Smith (1764–1840) was a British admiral who successfully fought the Siege of Acre in 1799 (now Akko in Israel) and turned Napoleon back from his conquest of Syria.
2. This is still a well-preserved fortress in Rhodes.
3. The Colossus of Rhodes was one of the Seven Wonders of the Ancient World. It was a large statue of the god Helios, stood over thirty metres, and was constructed of iron and bronze between 292 and 280 BCE.
4. Prior to World War II. Durrell lived on Rhodes following the war and leading up to the accretion of the Dodecanese Islands to Greece. *Reflections on a Marine Venus*, his longest work about Rhodes, was editorially cut to remove most references to the war (Roessel, "'Cut'" 64–77), so its appearance here and in his other shorter writings shows that, for Durrell, the effect of the Second World War on the local population was important.
5. Durrell notes this with regard to Jewish populations in other publications from this period, but it is largely absent from *Reflections on a Marine Venus* due to editorial excisions by Anne Ridler at Faber & Faber (Roessel, "'Cut'" 64–77). His partner at this time (and second wife), Eve Cohen, was a Zionist Jew, as was his

third wife, Claude Marie Vincedon, from the Menasce family. Claude wrote a Zionist novel, *A Chair for the Prophet*, during her relationship with Durrell.

6. Piraeus is the major port of Athens. Durrell arrived on Rhodes from Alexandria, Egypt.

7. Mario de Vecchi was the fascist governor of Rhodes under Italian rule. He imposed anti-Semitic laws, and many Jews fled Rhodes prior to the German arrival in 1943. Durrell also comments on the oppression and transportation of Rhodes' Jewish population in "Letter in the Sofa" in this volume (325–29).

8. Both Cicero and Pompey attended Posidonius's lectures on Rhodes. Although Julius Caesar extensively quotes Posidonius, Durrell likely means Cicero here.

9. Tiberius (42 BCE–37 CE) was the second Roman Emperor. He retired to Rhodes in 6 BCE.

10. Cleobulus was a citizen of Lindos on Rhodes and Plutarch calls him their King. Durrell lived in the Villa Cleobulus while on Rhodes.

11. Kameiros is an ancient city of Rhodes noted by Homer in *The Iliad*. Durrell is likely referring to real inscriptions, though all three were significant Athenians.

12. A Greek poet of 480 BCE. Plutarch quotes Timocrean in chapter 21 of *Themistocles* and is likely Durrell's source here.

13. These World War II images are cut from Durrell's *Reflections on a Marine Venus*, so their presence here indicates his first intentions for that book.

14. Hippodamus of Miletus (498–408 BCE) is described by Aristotle as the first man to plan a city in order to shape society. Durrell's interest in city structures here foreshadows his later work in *The Alexandria Quartet* and *The Revolt of Aphrodite*, both of which are concerned with how urban space influences its residents.

15. Strabo (63 BCE–24 CE) is known primarily for his seventeen-volume work, *Geographica*.

16. Stadia are an ancient measurement of length. Approximately 14,800 metres or nine miles.

17. Pliny the Elder (23–79 CE) wrote of Rhodes in his *Natural History*.

18. King Richard I (1157–1199) resided briefly in Byzantine Rhodes during the Third Crusade before continuing to Cyprus.

19. The accretion of the Dodecanese Islands to Greece was completed in 1947 with the Peace Treaty with Italy, and union was formalized in 1948.

20. Mussolini imposed a formal program of Italianization on the island, but it did not succeed.

21. Although the Dodecanese are literally "twelve islands," they include 150 smaller islands.

22. Lago was governor from 1923 to 1936. In contrast to his successor, his term is seen as harmonious and peaceful.

23. Cesare Maria De Vecchi (1884–1959) was a lifelong fascist. He is also responsible for much of the oppression of Rhodes' Jewish population prior to their removal to concentration camps by the Nazis.

24. Charles Thomas Newton (1816–1894) published this work in 1865 while professor of archaeology at University College, London.

25. Newton 207.

26. The Homeric epithet in *The Iliad* is actually "white-gleaming" αργινοεις (2.656), often translated as "chalky."

27. Demetrius I (337–283 BCE) unsuccessfully besieged Rhodes and invented several new siege engines to do so. Durrell's source is Plutarch's *Life of Demetrius*.

28. The Knights Hospitaller built the Palace of the Grand Master of the Knights of Rhodes in the fourteenth century, after 1309.

29. This garden is where Durrell lived in the Villa Cleobolus during his time on Rhodes.

30. Durrell is drawing from the *Chronicle* of Theophanes the Confessor (758–818) in which the remains of the Colossus are reported as sold by Turkish conquerors to a Jew from Edessa.

31. Cecil Torr (1857–1928) wrote both *Rhodes in Ancient Times* (Cambridge: Cambridge UP, 1885) and *Rhodes in Modern Times* (Cambridge: Cambridge UP, 1887). Durrell also refers to Torr several times in *Reflections on a Marine Venus*.

32. In Ancient Greek materials, nereids are water nymphs who are typically helpful to sailors. In Modern Greek myths, they are any form of nymph or fairy, typically quasi-demonic.

33. Sir Sacheverell Sitwell, 6th Baronet CH (November 15, 1897–October 1, 1988) was an English writer, best known as an art critic and writer on architecture, particularly the baroque. He was the younger brother of Dame Edith Sitwell and Sir Osbert Sitwell.

34. Sitwell's collection, *Canons of Giant Art: Twenty Torsos in Heroic Landscapes* (1933).

Can Dreams Live on When Dreamers Die?

1947

IN THE ANCIENT WORLD they set great store by dreams. One ancient author[1] divides them into five classes of which the fifth is dreams of divination, or oracles. People practiced what is known as incubation— that is to say, sleeping within the precincts of a temple—in order to have the dreams they felt would yield useful interpretations, the dreams which might give them guidance in their lives or settle problems for them. When the great cult of Aesculapius[2] arose, dreams played a great part in the technique of healing the sick; there is still a good deal we do not know about ancient medicine, but what we do indicates that those who were sick travelled to one of the many temples where they entered a special building and spent the first night in incubation. There were hundreds of temples all over Greece, and today we think that those which we have unearthed at Epidaurus and Cos[3] must have been the most famous. On arrival the suppliant made his sacrifices and performed some sort of ritual whose details are not known to us today; then he slept in the special dormitory set aside for him, and during his sleep the god appeared and either healed him outright or prescribed a course of treatment for him to follow. So you see dreams were a form of diag- nosis, just as for the psychoanalyst today the patient's dreams give a kind of symbolic picture of his subconscious preoccupations and his problems. But they were far more important in the ancient world because everybody believed they came directly from the god himself.

I was thinking along these lines one hot August day in 1939 when some friends suggested a trip to Epidaurus in southern Greece.[4] I had never seen the temple and very much wanted to go, so we set off. It did not take long from Corinth, where we were then staying, and as the car bumped down the shallow gradient into the valley I could quite understand how not only the temple but the whole of the territory of Epidaurus was considered sacred to the god. The plain is very green and encircled by wooded mountains, and gives one the strangest impression: as if, not only the temple, but the whole landscape had been designed deliberately by men. There was something at once intimate and healing about it all. A light wind ruffled the arbutus and holm-oak; the sea was just out of sight but one heard it, like the whispering in a sea-shell; above us in that shattering blue silence of the Greek sky, two eagles sat, almost motionless. We spent the whole day wandering about the theatre and the temple, and looking at the treasures in the little museum.

The guide was an amiable fellow, a typical Greek peasant, and while I was talking to him he told me that he had managed to get a transfer to another place—Mycaenae.[5] As this is rather a bleak fortress perched on a hill I asked him jokingly why he was so silly as to get transferred from this peaceful valley with its silence and greenness: and to exchange it for a place like Mycaenae. "If I told you why," he said, "you would think me mad. It is because of the dreams. I can't bear the dreams we have in this valley." This, in a fantastic sort of way, was interesting. "What dreams?" I said. "Everybody in this valley has dreams," he said. "Some people don't mind, but as for me I'm off." I was, I suppose, rather skeptical about the whole thing, because he looked at me and made a face as much as to say: "Yes, you think I'm mad like the others."

I asked him to tell me some of the dreams but he seemed reluctant to do so. "They're a lot of rubbish," he said: and then, as an afterthought, "But I'll tell you one thing: the old man in the fresco appears frequently in them." The fresco in the museum showed a grave Assyrian-looking face with dense ringlets falling down to the shoulders. I cannot remember now if it represented Aesculapius or not: at any rate it is an extraordinary piece of stone-carving. The guide went on: "Now you'll perhaps imagine that it's natural enough, when I spend almost every day in the museum, that the old man makes an impression on my mind; but tell me one thing. Why should my two kids dream about him when they have never set foot in the museum?"[6] The two children were sitting under a tree playing and I tried to question them. The boy was too shy to talk and hung his head, but the little girl was made of sterner stuff; she was about twelve. I asked her if she dreamed about an old man and if she could describe him. I cannot say that she said anything of great interest, but one little gesture she made was curious. She spread her fingers and drew them down from her ears to her shoulders as she described the old man's hair. By this time the rest of the party wanted to move off, so I had no chance of pursuing the matter further. As I was leaving the guide said, in rather a cynical or sardonic way: "If you don't believe me, ask any of the peasants who live in this valley. They all have dreams. The valley is full of dreams."

As we bumped back to Nauplia in the twilight, through the enchanted Greek landscape, I could not help wondering whether the dreams of those countless thousands of suppliants had stayed behind in this valley; whether they were the dreams of the ancient Greeks which had lingered on there. Naturally enough, I tried the subject out over dinner and got heartily laughed at for my pains; but sometimes these odd ideas prove to have something in them. However, we were then on the point of war with Germany and the whole thing slipped out of my mind. It was not indeed until 1945 that it all came back to me.

I was on the island of Cos at that time, and was working for the British administration that took over the Dodecanese Islands. In Cos, you will remember, there is a centre of the Aesculapian cult which was as famous in ancient times as that of Epidaurus. The archaeologists have located the place and dug out most of the temple. I decided to have a look at it. So I borrowed a three-tonner from a charitable UNRRA[7] official and drove out along the dusty summer roads to the shoulder of hillside where the Aesculapium stands. The site itself is enough to take your breath away; the temple is laid out on the slopes of a green hill, and standing at the top you look down across the flat and verdant plains of Cos to the blue sea.

I was drifting about in the silence and heat of this summer afternoon when I caught sight of a tent top sticking out of a dip in the ground and I walked towards it. A couple of soldiers were lying reading yellowbacks[8] and I passed the time of day with them. They were both red-faced Yorkshiremen, and I think they belonged to some Ordnance unit which was clearing up the German and Italian ammunition which littered the island. We sat and had a yarn, our voices sounding thin and clear in that rare atmosphere. They asked about the "blinking temple," as they called it, and I gave them all the blinking information I could muster up about it. I told them about the cult of Aesculapius and what I knew of healing technique employed by the god. When I got to the dreams I noted they exchanged glances, and I was suddenly reminded of my encounter years before with the guide at Epidaurus.

Almost before I know what I was saying I had asked them whether they had noticed anything peculiar about their dreams up here on the hill. They both looked rather startled and embarrassed but finally the elder of the two piped up and said: "Well, as a matter of fact, we used to camp up there inside the blinking temple, but we didn't like it, so we came down here. Better atmosphere, ain't it, Charlie?" Charlie said it was. They were not very communicative—Yorkshiremen aren't. But as far as I could make out they had spent several very disturbed night within the temple precincts, and Charlie had had one or two nightmares. "And when you think of the beer ration," he said plaintively, "you can't put it down to that." No, there was something queer about the place itself; and though they could not describe their dreams very clearly, I was reminded very forcibly of the guide's little daughter at Epidaurus as she combed out imaginary ringlets with her fingers. It was somehow odd to come across the same sort of evidence in two different places, and from two different sources; yet both places were sacred to Aesculapius and in both of them the same sort of ceremonies and practices took place. Was it possible, I found myself wondering again, that dreams do not disappear? That long after we are dead our dreams remain behind us? And especially in a place like this which must have been charged with hundreds of thousands of dreams, and with the fervent beliefs of the dreamers, the ancient Greek dreamers; had Charlie, that red-faced, unimaginative British soldier somehow made a contact with the ancient Greeks by letting their dreams invade his sleeping mind?

I said nothing of this to the two soldiers. They stood politely by the temple and waved goodbye to me as the truck rattled down the road to Cos. But I resolved there and then to visit the Aesculapium and sleep in the suppliant's corner of the temple; and to record any dreams I might have in a notebook. I'm afraid there is not time to give you the results of this experiment; or rather this series of experiments. In the first place, they are not complete and it may be years before I have time to visit Greece again and do some more work on them. But the material I have to date is interesting enough to suggest that dreams do perhaps live on in these ancient centres of healing, and can tell one things of great esoteric significance.[9]

NOTES

1. Ambrosius Theodosius Macrobius (395–423), a Roman philosopher, wrote two books on *The Dream of Scipio* that make this stratification of dreams, as did Calcidius, a fourth-century translator of Plato from whom Chaucer drew materials. Durrell may also be referring to Artemidorus, a Greek geographer of the second and first centuries BCE who wrote the five-volume *Oneirocritica*,

or *The Interpretation of Dreams*, though he does not expressly make this same classification.

2. Asclepius is the Greek god of medicine and healing. In the Cult of Asclepius, the injured or sick would make a pilgrimage to the temple where they would undergo a variety of cleansing rituals followed by spending the night in the sanctuary, after which they would report their dreams to the priest for interpretation and prescription. The god would visit the pilgrims during sleep to prescribe or carry out healing. Epidaurus was the most famous asclepieion, but there were many others, including Butrint in Albania, a short journey by boat from where Durrell had lived in Kalami.

3. Both sites are well preserved, and Epidaurus is famous for the astonishing acoustics of its theatre. Kos is near to the Dodecanese, where Durrell served at this time, and was home to Hippocrates (460–370 BCE), from whom we derive the Hippocratic Oath.

4. Durrell later returned to Epidaurus with his wife Nancy after parting ways with Henry Miller en route, who was planning to return to America for fear of the impending invasion of Greece. This previous 1939 visit is not otherwise recorded.

5. Henry Miller describes a visit to Mycenae with George Katsimbalis in his 1941 book *The Colossus of Maroussi*, which Durrell had read by this time.

6. In the Cult of Asclepius, the god might appear to the pilgrims during their night in the temple.

7. The United Nations Relief and Rehabilitation Administration, which organized relief for the victims of World War II.

8. Like penny dreadfuls, yellowbacks were inexpensive sensational or adventure novels.

9. Carl Jung (1875–1961), the famous Swiss psychiatrist, wrote to Durrell on December 15, 1947 via the BBC after reading this piece. Jung notes, "Having had some experience of a similar kind I should very much like to know in what your further observations consist" as he was keen "to learn about your hellenic dreams" (Jung n. pag.). Only two letters are extant from Jung, the second sent directly to Durrell in Argentina, in which he responds to Durrell's comments on Georg Groddeck. Jung's interest focuses on Durrell's dream experiences during travel with the implication that these express the "extraordinary relations between our unconscious mind and what one calls time and space" (n. pag.).

Family Portrait

1952

THOSE WHO REJOICE in the easy generalizations about national character should never visit Yugoslavia,[1] for no country I know presents quite so bewildering a mixture of races, creeds, and landscapes. Even on the map it presents a forbidding picture to those who study the complex crosshatching of mountain ranges, the ragged seams of frontier which mark off the six republics and the two autonomous areas. Six republics, four languages, and three religions. The vertebral column of the country is starred with towns each possessing different cultural characteristics—Ljubljana, Zagreb, Belgrade, Skoplje. How to bring them within the scope of the same focus—that is the problem.[2]

The various national characters are so sharply defined that for a time one is disposed to regard the country as a parcel of irreconcilable states. Only when one has travelled backwards and forwards a good deal over these invisible frontiers of tongue and temperament does one begin to see the total pattern of the Yugoslav temperament, which borrows a contribution from all of these various characteristics. Above all, one must see the Slovenes not only in Slovenia but also out of it; one must meet Serbs not only in Serbia but also in the other republics in order for one's observation to condense.

Yugoslavia is still young; it is like an oil painting which has not quite dried yet—hence the difficulty of framing it. The various characters which are depicted are still, so to speak, fermenting. What are they?

Slovenia's inheritance is religious and scholastic. Ljubljana expresses some of the poetry and piety of its character, which carries overtones of clericalism. A passion for order and principle is its chief gift to the nation. The tempo of life is smooth, orderly, for the Slovenes were born to organize. But underneath their temperament lies something deeper, a poetry which is expressed in the wild hinterland of snow-crowned mountains and vivid lakes: a landscape which for us seems to be peopled with witches in conical hats, with gnomes and other inhabitants of the fairy tales. Slovenia is the Scotland of Yugoslavia, and the Slovenes share many of the characteristics of the Scots— sobriety, Presbyterianism, a passion for ruled margins—and one can never see Ljubljana without feeling that it is somehow a compromise between Edinburgh and some Gothic Central European town.

Pleasure-loving Zagreb lies further south with its talkative mercuric Croats, whose character flowers, so to speak, along the banks of the wide rivers and green fields. There is little that is rocky about the Croats; their humor and self-possession gives them a particular warmth, while the very curiosity of their temperament contributes speed and movement to their talk and gestures. They are eager for new experiences; social life is a passion with them, almost an art. They are quick to make friends and they exhaust friendships quickly. The Croats are impatient not for pleasure—that shallow object—but for happiness; unless life is actively happy, incandescent with happiness, the good Croat feels that he is wasting time. "When I am not actively happy," says a Croat friend of mine, "when things are just normal it is awful. I feel as if I have toothache." This eagerness makes them stimulating company.

Between Zagreb and Belgrade another invisible frontier must be crossed to come to terms with the Serbian character with its curious yet delightful mixture of pride and gentleness. The Serb has still some of the pastoral virtues of the clan and family about him—one thinks of the landed farmer described in Hesiod. His vision of life is simple, straightforward, and aristocratic in the best sense. His character lacks any betraying sophistication; it would be hard to think of a better friend or a more implacable enemy. He is slow to kindle, sometimes a little pedantic, but his warmth and generosity live longer than that of other peoples.

Yet side by side with this there is a curious, unexpectedly Irish delight in disorder. The Serb likes to take life easily. He is happy-go-lucky. He gives with both hands not only because he is generous but also because possessions mean little to him. His is a character made for the open air—scaling those razorbacked mountains and grassy uplands of his country, or swimming happily in the dense swift rivers like the Danube and Sava. Where the Croat will spend all day exploring ideas in a coffee shop, the Serb will spend his time exploring nature. He is more physical than mental. He doubts less and enjoys more. But he is never garrulous or hysterical. His temperament is based on reticence rather than on a troubled reserve. But once you discover him and prove your worth as a companion, the Serb uncorks himself. (I choose the metaphor advisedly since Serbian hospitality is inseparable from the thought of plum brandy in my mind.) At first he seems too serious, almost taciturn; but buried in every Serbian soul there is a touch of Falstaff.[3] This is what makes him so rewarding a friend.

Leaving Belgrade you must choose for yourself whether you will hobble southward along bad roads to Skoplje, or scale the mountain bastions which separate you from Sarajevo and the coast. If you are hunting character, then continue southward through the Ebar Valley; but if the Bosnian and Dalmatian intrigue you, then turn off and cross the mountains to the west.

Sarajevo lies in the lap of the mountains, brilliant as a jewel. A quiet dark-eyed people, gentle voiced and friendly, dreaming away their life behind these stony ramparts. In Bosnia you will discover men whose ancestors were obviously eagles; but on the coast, with its relaxing

Mediterranean breezes, its olives and blue coves you will feel the
Dalmatian character, supple, resilient, and with more than a touch of
familiar *far niente* about it. For the Dalmatian, one feels, the proper
occupation is lying in the sun and writing poetry; it is a surprise to
find that they are good executives and administrators as well.

But the reader will forgive me if I drag him unwillingly back from
the coast to Belgrade in order to follow out the journey southward.
The Dalmatian coast is justly celebrated for its charms; but they are
insidious. Once let a visitor sun his bones along this beautiful coast,
and he becomes unwilling to face the mountain passes and the craggy
roads back to the capital. After three days he finds that he has become
a complete Dalmation, incapable of mustering his sun-drenched senses
for the physical exertion of the journey back to Belgrade. Force must
be used. Argument is not enough because this is the graveyard of those
unwary souls who plan to spend a month in Yugoslavia and "see everything." Northern visitors would be well advised to leave Dalmatia for
the end of their visit, when all their work is done. This is particularly
necessary for writers and journalists. How many have returned to
their northern homes with nothing more to show for their visit than
an empty notebook, a royal coat of tan, and an incoherent desire to
return one day and "settle down for good in Dubrovnik"?[4]

The wise man will press on through the dusty roads of southern Serbia
towards Skoplje, and surrender himself to the charms of a landscape
whose extremes are not sudden and harsh. The scale grows larger. When
there are mountains they stand far back against the sky; the valleys fan
away into panoramas of richness. The rivers have all the space they
need in which to deploy. They are not pressed for time. Nor dare the
traveller hurry, for the road surfaces become wicked after Kragujevac.[5]

Macedonia is the most withdrawn of the republics and lies within
the orbit of Oriental Yugoslavia, so to speak; one feels the cultural
currents setting eastward in the music and costume of the place. Its
poetry still carries the inherited flavors of Turkey, and the inhabitants

of the republic are proud of their own language which they wear like a pair of new shoes. Macedonia has always been a *point névralgique*[6] from the political and strategic point of view, and this has contributed a certain sharpness and over-sensitiveness to the character of the people. Their generosity is tempered by suspicion. The Macedonian is always on guard. But once reassured, he is hospitable and friendly as only an inhabitant of the Balkans can be. From Skoplje the lines of communications thin away towards Greece and Bulgaria. We have travelled some seven hundred miles across the country, through one of the most beautiful and varied landscapes in the world.

These, then, are roughly the components out of which the national character of the future will be composed. How rich and how complex it already is I have tried to indicate. To the three chief religions, Catholic, Orthodox, and Moslem, I am tempted, quite seriously, to add a fourth: Marxism. This is not a joke, for Marxism is much more than a social theory. It is a cosmology which makes exclusive claims upon belief just as Catholicism does. It has its own world view, and to its adherents it has much of the force and coherence of a religion.[7]

The unification of the Yugoslav peoples is one of the strongest and best-based planks in the government platform. A truce has been made, a unity created between these different republics which has been designed to hold them together until all the memories of past troubles, bitter quarrels, temperamental differences, have become reconciled and unified by time. Whatever reservations a Yugoslav might have on political affairs, it would be difficult to find one who would not agree to the tremendous value of this unifying ideal, and to those of us who have spent any time here, the fruits of this policy are already becoming clear. A new, a tangible unity is becoming apparent in every corner of social life, whether it be in the army or in a state enterprise. The administrative and technical skill of the Slovene, the drive of the Croat, the purposeful resourcefulness of the Serb—they are all finding their place and beginning to make their contribution felt. All that the new Yugoslavia hopes to be must depend on the fruits of that co-operation.

Nations, like individuals, grow slowly, and the harder the struggle the richer the experience upon which character is founded. Yugoslavia has struggled out of the mists of foreign oppression and has gathered itself together. But it is so various and so brightly coloured (I am thinking of the patchwork quilts that one sees in illustrations to Grimm[8]) that sometimes the Yugoslavs themselves are bewildered by the multiplicity of colours and patterns.

Out of all this confused colouring, however, their national character is beginning to emerge, and there is little doubt that when it does it is in the arts that it will leave the first imprint of its unique temperament. Their self-interpretation will come in sculpture, poetry, and music. Already there are the first signs on the horizon. No one can see these first fruits of unity without a feeling of hope for the future.

NOTES

1. Modern day Serbia, Montenegro, Macedonia, Kosovo, Slovenia, and Croatia in the Balkans. Durrell served in communist Yugoslavia from 1948 to 1952 while Josip Broz Tito was in power. He was first posted there when Tito broke ties with Stalin's Cominform.

2. This plurality of cultures, ethnicities, and politics was always "the problem" and has ultimately led to the dissolution of the state. Ljubljana is now the capital of Slovenia; Zagreb is the capital of Croatia; Belgrade is the capital of Serbia; and Skoplje is the capital of Macedonia.

3. Sir John Falstaff is a comic yet complex character in Shakespeare's *Henry IV, Part I*, *Henry IV, Part II*, and *The Merry Wives of Windsor*.

4. Dubrovnik is a UNESCO World Heritage Site and idyllic city on the coast of Croatia.

5. A major city in Serbia known for construction and industry.

6. The nerve centre.

7. Durrell voiced his dislike of Marxism beginning in the 1930s, despite its fashionable nature among poetry circles of the time. Despite his anti-establishment pose and critique of social norms, as well as his critique of consumerism and capitalism, Durrell never voiced support or serious interest in Marxism. This is most

likely due to his alignment with a variety of anti-authoritarian views (Gifford, "Anarchist" 57–71; Gifford, "Surrealism's" 36–64) until his posting to Yugoslavia, after which a tone of conservatism entered his public comments, though his fiercest critiques of consumerism and cultural hegemony were in the novels of *The Revolt of Aphrodite* (*Tunc* and *Nunquam*), published in 1968 and 1970.

8. *Grimm's Fairy Tales*, which are German but richly illustrated in many editions.

Letter in
the Sofa

1957

IT WAS A YOUNG SAPPER MAJOR who found the love-letter while
he was combing through the villa his unit had inherited from the
Germans, on the look-out for booby-traps—though I must confess this
seemed to me an unnecessary operation, for we had moved swiftly
into the Island of Rhodes to find its starving garrison only too glad to
welcome us.

The Germans were literally starving; there were two hundred
deaths a day from sheer malnutrition among forces and civilians alike.
The place was a shambles.

I still retain an image of destroyers drawn up in the harbor feeding
out biscuits from the great broken boxes by searchlight, tossing them
into the forest of waving hands in great packets.

Unit for unit, the incoming administration took over the offices
and billets of the military garrison, and the sappers inherited a rather
pleasant villa on the hill from some German sapper unit. While I was
only a civilian, I had arranged to mess with them as my printing-press
was near by.

It was odd that, just as I was calling on them to make my number,
their major should hand me a love-letter in Italian. He had been
groping in the bowels of the big, ugly Second Empire sofa which
stood in the window, with its incomparable view over the sea and

325

the Anatolian hills. I translated a few lines for him, and he grunted contemptuously.

"A love-letter," he said. "I suppose these Huns had girl-friends up here of a night."

I put it in my pocket and forgot all about it; but later that evening I remembered it over my solitary dinner in the town (my work kept me late) and I read it again in full.

It was rather a remarkable letter to find in a sofa, and as I read it I became interested, for it was written in the most touching and spirited style. There was nothing mawkish or silly about it at all.

It was signed Rebecca Monteverdi and addressed to someone called Wilhelm-Maria.

It was a long letter, almost valedictory, for the writer had been surprised by the dreadful news that Wilhelm-Maria had been posted back to Germany: she did not know whether he would find this letter in its hiding-place or have time to leave one for her. (Apparently he had neither been able to claim her letter nor deposit his own.)

She spoke also of the Italian lessons, and "other officers."

It seems as if she had been giving the unit Italian lessons.

But why the sofa, then, and the secrecy?

Then the truth suddenly dawned. Her name was a Jewish one, a typical Spanish-Levantine name, Monteverdi! This explained the secrecy, at least, the hidden exchange of letters via the sofa on which she sat to give her lessons.

I thought no more of the matter until one day, quite by accident, the intelligence people who were fussing through the garrison muster rolls produced some information about the original inhabitants of the mess.

There was only one Wilhelm-Maria on it: Rowohlt.

Then there came another small coincidence—a party in the mess during which I met the grave, sad Mr. Silvani, President of the Jewish Committee of the island, and learned some distasteful things about what the Germans had done.

"Out of a population of seven thousand Jews," he told me quietly, "they took away three thousand, mostly women, among them my own daughter."[1]

He paused and drank his cocktail with an air of great deliberation. Then he went on steadily: "Up to now, we have located about 1,500 through the Red Cross. They are all over the place."

I said: "Well, that's something—I suppose they will be coming back."

He looked at me quietly with the muscles tightened in his jaw. Yet his voice was mild.

"Most of the women," he said, "were sent to officers' brothels on the Russian front, and many, some…well they don't want to come back. Out of shame."

I don't know what prompted me to say: "Do you know anything of a girl called Rebecca Monteverdi?"

He nodded slowly and put his glass down. "Of course. She was taken among the last lot. A brilliant girl. Doctor of Law at the University of Rome. She was caught here on holiday by the war and stayed on with her mother, dead now. She gave Italian lessons to the Germans. But that did not save her."

All of a sudden I felt that I could see her very clearly, her dark head bent to her lesson-books, seated before the window with its marvelous panorama of water and mountains.

"Did you know her?" asked Mr. Silvani, and again to my surprise I found myself answering: "Not personally. She is a friend of my sister."

He could not tell me whether she was among the 1,500 persons located who might be expected to return. The war was over, but there was a good deal of chaos everywhere. You never knew.

And if she did, Wilhelm-Maria, if he was not dead, was somewhere in the tangle and confusion of a disrupted Germany. If she did return, could she find him? Would she want to? Or perhaps…There I let speculation rest.

But good stories don't let one rest. Two months later I met a don engaged on the undonish work of going through the German archives on the island, sorting out the papers to check the names of the prisoners we held in the desert pens in Egypt.

I asked him to keep an eye open for a German sapper officer called Wilhelm-Maria Rowohlt, as I would like his address.

Trust an Oxford don! Within three weeks I had a note from him on my desk at the office, telling me that he had turned up information on Wilhelm-Maria and giving me an address in Bavaria—a little village of sorts, full of timber mills. He had even discovered that Wilhelm-Maria was a Doctor of Philology from Dresden.

I wrote him gratefully, though of course all this was purely gratuitous curiosity; I felt I was prying into something which was hardly my own affair. After all, if Rebecca Monteverdi came back, and Wilhelm-Maria wanted to reach her...

Then my own posting came through and I packed my affairs, sad to leave this beautiful island. To my surprise, I found the crumpled love-letter among my papers. I can't think why it had not been destroyed.

I sat and read it again right through, seeing the whole story quite clearly now in my own mind. What is more commonplace in a war than the human love story?

Then on a pure impulse, I took the love-letter and scribbled a few lines on the back of it—I didn't know quite how to put it—giving Wilhelm-Maria's address, and hoping that she would once more get in touch with him. (We writers are sentimental people at heart.)

In the morning I took the letter round to Mr. Silvani. I had to pay a courtesy call to say goodbye anyway.

"May I leave this for Rebecca Monteverdi?" I asked him, "I mean in case she should come back to the island. I expect that sooner or later she will be located and brought back. It is rather an important message. It contains my sister's address."

He assured me that it would remain to await her arrival among his archives.

The next day I left the island, and have never been back. And that is the end of the story. It is years ago now. I have never had the courage to write back and find out whether she got back and found my letter—her letter. I feel superstitious about these things. It is better to let destiny take its own course not to try and be a *deus ex machina*.

After all, suppose she did get back and get in touch; she might have found him married already, or legless, or a tramp in the new Germany. Life finds a thousand ways to cheat lovers.

I personally don't want to know the answer to the story. I know that in life it is always a thousand to one against the Happy Ending. For life is not like a short story. Or is it?

NOTE

1. Rhodes had been hard pressed under a fascist and anti-Semitic Italian governor and then the Nazi occupation. In 1944, 1,673 Jews were taken from Rhodes and transported to Auschwitz where approximately 150 survived. A Rebecca Capelouto was among the survivors, and she may be Durrell's inspiration in this text.

The Moonlight
of Your Smile

1960

THERE WERE MANY MEMORABLE, delightful or just sinister aspects
of life in Cyprus which I was not able to investigate for myself during
my stay there.[1] But my sharpest regret is that I never managed to visit
the factory in Larnaca which manufactures black false teeth. I know.
I know. I too could hardly believe my ears when first I was told of its
existence. "Black false teeth?" I said. The Colonial Secretary of the day
was a master of anecdote, and I suspected him of pulling my leg when
he mentioned the place.

"Did you say black teeth?" I echoed. He enjoyed my obvious incre-
dulity for a whole second before reassuring me that he had intended
no joke. "Apparently," he said (and he was always glad to illustrate that
truth was stranger than fiction). "Apparently, all over the Far East,
where people chew betel nut, black false teeth are as much in demand
as white ones with us. The Larnaca factory here is the sole manufac-
turer and exporter of black artificial smiles in the whole world. Why
don't you visit it?"

I determined to do so, but somehow I never got around to it. We
were in the middle of political crises[2] of varying intensity and the pressure of events always prevented me. But I never forgot about it, and
later that year, when I became a Government Press Officer, I sent a

reporter down to Larnaca with instructions to write a feature on the factory for the *Cyprus Review*.[3]

He came back looking thoughtful and said plaintively that he had not been able to get inside the factory. He had telephoned the manager twice and had told that the makers were averse to all publicity about the black teeth. He asked why, it was feared the lucrative Far East market would be impaired if the world got to know about the black teeth. Apparently, Asians were rather sensitive about false teeth in general, even white ones. Publicity about the black teeth might have unforeseen results on sales.

There the matter rested for some months. God knows, I did not wish to harm the island's industries in any way, yet I confess to a feeling that there was something rather curious, perhaps even a bit sinister, about it all.

INFORMATION

After a year, a visiting reporter in search of colour material came to my office and asked me for some information about the black false teeth. This gave me an opportunity of pressing the matter officially, so to speak, and I wrote twice to the factory asking for permission to report on its wares, but neither letter was answered.

Then one day a highly nervous businessman called at my office and left me a fat brochure and a single tooth (but a white one) mounted in some unlovely pinkish material. I was out at the time, and my secretary received this. When I got back, she was looking rather faint. Perhaps she had feared it was an EOKA[4] bomb, wrapped up so neatly in tissue paper. But even the fact that it was a tooth did little to reassure her.

There was not a scrap of information about the black teeth. The businessman who wore black gloves (a sinister touch, this) had told her that I could only publicise the exploits of the firm as and where they concerned white false teeth. Blacks were on the secret list. It seemed to me that the directors were obviously under some frightful misapprehension—or in the grip of an inexplicable pudeur. I let the matter slide once more.

Then, some months later, during the riots and upheavals, I ran into an officer I knew in charge of search parties in the Larnaca district. His job was, as he put it, to "unstitch" places where the illicit manufacture of grenades might be taking place. At once I implored him to lead his men to the false teeth factory and examine the whole question of its products with an unclouded eye. I felt I simply must know. Did they or did they not manufacture black false teeth? By this time the thing was rather preying on my mind.

I could see he didn't believe my story, but he made a note of the factory's name and promised to look into the matter in the normal course of his duties.

"YOU WERE RIGHT"

A month later he walked slowly into my office and lowered himself into the armchair, breathing heavily. "By gad, you were right," he said in a low voice. "I thought you were pulling my leg at first. Upon my soul, they do make black false teeth. It gave the men quite a turn to see these rows and rows of black snappers hanging on the walls. Ugh!" and he shuddered. "But there were not bombs, alas!" He smiled. "And I brought you a little souvenir to set your mind at rest."

He placed a set of black false teeth on my desk. I slumped in my chair with relief. At last! The teeth were rather smaller than I had expected and appeared to be made of black liquorice. But the set was complete. I thanked him profusely. I suddenly felt ten years younger and liberated from an obsession. After washing them in the lavatory I tried them on. I was due to leave Cyprus the next day[5] so I wore them back into my office and gave my secretary a fright by smiling at her with them in. They were a success.

Ah well, I hope these notes do the tooth industry no harm. I had some difficulties in getting the black teeth through the customs at that end and was finally forced to sign a document attesting that they were the used personal effects of a Government official returning to UK on termination of contract.[6]

At London Airport, too, there was a little feeling about them. It was suggested that I should pay duty on them as works of native art, but I successfully evaded all charges and signed another document attesting that they were purely for personal use.

They lie before me now as I write. I don't suppose they could be considered either very useful or very beautiful. But they prop up a burning cigarette quite well as I type and next week, when I go up for my Foreign Service interview and ask for another foreign posting, they may just do the trick.[7]

NOTES

1. Durrell initially moved to Cyprus as an English teacher at the Pancyprean Gymnasium in order to spend his time writing, but he was drawn into public relations work for the British government and editorship of the *Cyprus Review* during Greek agitation for union with Greece and independence from British rule.

2. Ultimately, these crises included the planting of an incendiary bomb in Durrell's garage and his flight from the island after having been informed he had become a target (MacNiven 439). This was during the struggle for Enosis, union with Greece.

3. Durrell edited the *Cyprus Review* from 1954 to 1956. It had been run as a vehicle for British propaganda since 1942 but was meant to become a vehicle for Cypriot pride as well as literary and artistic materials (MacNiven 418). It is unrelated to the modern journal *Cyprus Review*.

4. The National Organization of Cypriot Fighters who fought for union of Cyprus with Greece.

5. Durrell left Cyrpus under much different circumstances, and his comments here minimize the desperation of the situation and his personal fears of assassination after an incendiary bomb was left in his garage and Greek friends told him he was a potential target. Durrell fled Cyprus quickly on August 26, 1956.

6. After fleeing Cyprus and leaving his house in Bellapaix, Durrell returned to London in August 1956 with little money and lived with Claude, who would become his third wife, in friends' homes and with his mother for a time. It was

a poor homecoming after so many years in service abroad, and they moved to France little more than four months later, very early in 1957.

7. At this point in 1960, after four years out of British government work, it was unlikely Durrell would accept another posting for any reason, but the text may date to the period prior to his publication of *Bitter Lemons* and *Justine* in 1957 when the financial necessity would likely have been stronger, and it is possible this was initially meant to form a scene in *Bitter Lemons*.

The Poetic
Obsession
of Dublin

1972

IN AN ERA when there are societies for the suppression of almost
everyone and everything it is surprising that there is not one devoted
to the total suppression of Duffy.[1] He has caused so much trouble
to his friends…his search for the Holy Grail in the back parlour of
Mooney's; his address to the nation (fell into the docks); his guide to
Irish sentiment (one shilling). Yes, if there were a Nobel for Utter
Awfulness, Duffy would get it. Yet, in spite of this, when chance sent
me to Dublin I discovered that he had gone back home for a visit and
asked him to show me round. In Dublin he was O'Duffy. In England,
where he lived precariously off bookmaking, he was simple Duffy—
he dropped the particle. I sent him a telegram care of Duggan's, which
I knew from his conversation was his favourite haunt after Neary's.
I made my need quite clear. I said: "Please no folklore, no Irish eyes
are smiling stuff, no feckless charm. Just want to see the city with calm
detachment." His answer was characteristic. "Try and come during
Ramadan and share a glass of ruby porter." Was I to presume from
this that the Irish had suddenly gone Moslem?

However, I swallowed my misgivings and took a plane which lofted
me into the warm pearly sunlight of a precocious spring morning, high

over the Irish Channel with its criss-crossed vortices of wind hither-and-thithering. Tilted up against the sky-ceiling we could look down upon the islands which lay about like cattle in a field, while the glittering sea flared back at the windows of the aircraft like a shield of bronze. Ireland slid towards us silently, looking somehow frail and vulnerable with its soft curves—not craggy and beetling like Scotland or Wales. We hovered, we circled, coming down lower and lower until at last the pilot made a short run in and rolled us towards the small compact building of the airport. Dublin Airport—its homely size gives one a premonition about the capital—perhaps even the secret of its charm, namely size, that vital key to living values. All the cities which haunt one are life-size, built to human scale. Once they grow beyond a certain size their cohesion gets swallowed up and it's no longer possible to be haunted by them in quite the same way. London and Paris have grown this way—out of affection and intimacy: one loves little pieces of them now, not the whole. But Edinburgh, Zagreb, Lucca, Geneva—it is still possible to centre a poetic obsession around them. A fine poetic city should be walkable across and should not have more than a quarter of a million inhabitants living in it. I felt Dublin would be this way, and it was.

Duffy was waiting for me, talking to a pretty Customs Officer in uniform; she had blue eyes and a cowslip complexion. I thanked him for his presence. "Nothing is too much for a friend one distrusts," he replied, lighting up his pipe. Nobody could have minded his luggage being searched by such a girl but she simply smiled and waved us through, so that Duffy led me out into the blue-violet air of an Irish spring. He himself looked as if he had slept in his clothes, and he was rapturously unshaven—presumably because it was Ramadan. In the taxi he appeared to drowse as we sauntered and bumbled on our way. He had become very much stouter since last we had met, and when I commented on the fact he said it was a "phantom pregnancy," whatever that might be—he had read about it in a woman's paper. Everything smelt marvellous out here: wet earth, glimmer of streams,

larks rising from dewy ground. And Green! That was the code word—
Irish green. I told him that the philosophic society of the University
had invited me over to hear a paper read on my work and to take
part in a discussion on it with the students.[2] It had been a marvellous
chance to visit the island and correct the impressions I had gathered
from my readings. "Sinister impressions, about the Liffey running dark
with Guinness, about Saturday night being folklore night, and so on."[3]
Duffy puffed and wagged his head. "I fear that mostly your impressions are well founded. Why even the damned island is shaped like a
diseased liver."

The earliest impression one gets on the way into the city is one of
amazement at the number and height of the television aerials. It's as if
the people were dying of news-hunger, as if the houses were reaching
up to drink the sky empty of information. Reception was bad, said the
chauffeur, and now with the troubles on the northern border people
wanted to get the English channels. He was a mine of essential information but I have forgotten most of the things he told me—all except
one. He said that Guinness was not fattening if you drank enough of it.
I made a mental note of the fact.

I was deposited at the old Shelbourne hotel,[4] which appeared to
have as many bars as bedrooms—comfortable old-fashioned bars with
good service, where hunting men could gather round a tall glass in the
intervals of riding to hounds. Here there was a good deal of damning
of England's eyes—always a pleasant occupation—but not so much
serious politics was talked. I had agreed to meet Duffy later in the day,
and to deliver myself to the student representative who would meet
me in the bar. This pleasant and serious young man, by name Richard
Pine,[5] was waiting for me already, and Duffy, who had a terror of intellectuals, fled with a murmured goodbye.

Pine and I shared a precious glass of smoky whiskey while we talked
about the paper he was to read to the society that evening, and then
when I had washed and brushed up, he took me for my first leisurely
stroll about the city, up and down the little streets made world famous

by the writers who have lavished their poetry on them. Was ever a city—apart perhaps from Paris—so beloved of its artists? The net result, of course, is that when one gets there one is continually shocked into surprised recognition of its features. One knows the place already. The streets wiggle and wander in real life as they do in Irish fiction. The worlds of Joyce, Beckett, Yeats, and Synge[6] leap out at one in isolated vignettes, or merge into a spectrum of colours illustrated everywhere by that soft, bitter-sweet accent with its sensual lilt. One realises the charm and strength of intimacy. Why, running like a *leitmotiv* under the soft buzz of traffic, one hears the crying of seagulls as they hover over the main street. One is aware of the sea always and of the Liffey, which puffs and stumbles and bumps its way through the streets like some tiny locomotive. Grafton Street down to O'Connell was not a long way in miles, but it spanned centuries of Ireland's confused but magical history, and once one hit the river one was seduced along its quays towards venerable pubs like the Brazen Head[7] where ragged gentlemen of the most absurd respectability wagered mind over porter in huge glasses full of the foaming ruby brew. One recalls E.M. Forster's advice to the visitor to Alexandria. "The best way to see the city is to walk about aimlessly,"[8] he says. Same goes for Dublin. But your journey will be punctuated at every turn by a pub of charm. My hosts informed me that there were over a thousand places where one could drink— a large number for a population of six hundred thousand souls. Consequently, it is safe to say that that little puddle of soapsuds at the bottom of the Irish soul is composed of the "heads" of thousands of demolished Guinnesses.

But that night it was Trinity,[9] and here I was received for dinner in Hall with the philosophic society whose members were all very young but conscious of forming part of a venerable tradition. The surround- ings too—the Elizabethan college with its world famous library and its clattery courts of cobbles linking the lecture rooms and residences softly lit in the evening mist (a feeling of gaslight): the imposing back- cloth of the place was a fitting match for the dignity and sobriety of my hosts. The great Hall with its portraits has been so often described and I will not attempt yet another picture. Two pretty blonde girls—scholars of the college—opened and closed the proceedings with a Latin grace. I felt relaxed and happy, surrounded by these young philosophers of Ireland. I recalled Hamilton of Trinity[10]—practically the Einstein of his day—who so entranced Wordsworth by his conversation that the old poet became a firm friend of his. These younglings were fitting successors to that great man, who was still practically a babe in arms when he became Astronomer Royal of the United Kingdom. After dinner we retired for coffee before the lecture, and here my host disappeared for a moment to consult his notes.

It will be enough to say that young Pine's dismantling of my ideas and intentions was brilliantly done and was one of the best close-ups of the work—such as it is—I have heard. He was a skillful and persuasive lecturer, and not at all deaf to the ironies and comedies which form so large a part of my literary baggage. The hall filled up, and the philosophic proceedings which followed allowed everyone to fire an arrow into the target area which Pine had labelled "Sexual curiosity and metaphysical speculation in the work of." It was a treat to see with what interest and vivacity these young men and women skirted the minefields of modern ideas, and with what idealism they tackled our contemporary problems from permissiveness to pollution. The young today are touching in their concern; they are young and fresh of course, and not worn down to the lining as we old buffers are—disgusted at the behaviour of man after having lived out a long lifetime of wars and catastrophes and big disappointments. They are more idealistic than I was at their age, and I give them a sincere *chapeau* in the French sense. I can well understand why my daughters think I am a damned old reactionary corpse-watcher. It's just that I have run out of oxygen and adrenaline.

It was a fine Irish gift to me this evening with the students of Trinity, and it formed so to speak one leg of my Irish see-saw. While I was in Dublin I spent half my time with Richard and his friends, being guided

and coaxed and instructed by (what better?) undergraduates with
their sharp and special knowledge of ways and means and their *sang
froid* which reminded me of my own student days. The energy one
had! I doubt if I slept more than a few hours between my seventeenth
and twenty-third year. As I remember too, I lived on beer and Smith's
Potato Crisps with an occasional watered gin to make the mortar set.

The other leg of my see-saw was, of course, Duffy, who awaited me
at strategic points, strategic pubs where he crouched against the bar in
the attitude of a mental defective, and in between, in gulps of ruby beer,
addressed himself to a fearful drink called Dog's Nose (invented by the
Liverpool Irish). To watch this thing being made up before him was
horrifying—all the customers including myself turned pale to the gums.
Unless I am wrong, it is equal parts of gin, whiskey, rum, cognac, and
Liffey water with a touch of lemon and an aspirin.[11] I didn't dare to try
it. I stayed with the ruby which was dense and powerful and kept me
getting thinner and thinner or so I hoped devoutly. Thus gradually under
the tutelage of these people I assembled my impressions of this charming
and seductive capital. With the students I explored the river line with
its fine landmarks—St. Paul's, or Four Courts, or the ravishing Customs
House. Softly puffing ran the Liffey, softly whewing wheeled the gulls
in the high grey air where snatches of blue showed through. The
spring was hesitant, still hovering on the edge of snow.

Faithfully after every such outing my undergraduate hosts would
deliver me to pubs like Mooney's or Kehoe's[12] in South Anne Street
where Duffy would be waiting with his hat pulled down over his nose
like the original Informer, drawing softly on his pipe. "Sure 'tis the
drinking keeps me in a state of candour," he admitted. Yet it was with
Duffy I enjoyed the life of the open street; he had no eye or feel for
literature or architecture but he had the innate taste to take me to the
open markets in Moore and Thomas Streets where fruit and vegetables
are sold to a background of scabrous back-chat worthy of Aristophanes.
At every street corner practically he would introduce me to large fully-
fashioned and loquacious bodies selling flowers from dilapidated prams.

Whether they made any money is questionable as they seemed always ready to give away their stock to passers-by. Duffy never failed to earn a button-hole as he passed, exchanging growls of welcome and warm shoulder-thumps with these steatopygous[13] mamas. When he did not know their names he called them "Mrs. O,"[14] which is apparently the usual form of address when such a case arises. With Duffy I walked the slums as well as the docks. We went right down to the harbour mouth one day to a pub he wished to revisit for sentimental reasons. The girl behind the bar used to be "kind as a Christian to him." But, alas, she had gone and nobody knew where, and the bar was full of rowdy French fishermen whose trawler had just put into harbour for refitting. They were huge crumbling men with the strong accents of Brittany. Nor need I fear to add that it was with Duffy that we made a deeply reverent visit to the giant Guinness factory on the southern bank of the river— probably the greatest religious edifice in the country, speaking purely in the anthropological sense. Even Duffy, for whom nothing was sacred, lowered his voice when he spoke of it. He almost took off his hat and genuflected when we entered the gates for the grand tour of the place. For miles around spreads the rich thick smell of heated barley. Like grave scientists we enrolled ourselves for the guided tour which we knew would entail a great deal of free sipping, tasting, and perhaps at the end (if our control broke loose) actually paddling in the stuff. There were about a dozen other tourists full of scientific curiosity like ourselves. Inevitably after this protracted tour we hit the evening air again and felt everything bending backwards. There was nothing for it but to rush down to O'Connell Street and restore the equilibrium of the universe with a more pointed drink—like Jameson's brown whiskey in small compact doses. But what happy memories of the factory I would take away with me! If ever I had to write about Ireland I would write a long mood-piece redolent of blarney, barley, and silky blackness: of Guinness, God, and whatever else begins with a G.

It was singular, too, how little time and thought people spent on the troubles in the black north; the situation went up and down like the temperature of a fevered patient. But in between its high points it could fall to sub-normal. One cheerful undergraduate spoke of an inevitable civil war. But there had been a long lull in the north and the mercuric Irish temperament could not sustain a high pitch of feeling unless it was perpetually being fed by bloody incidents. Thoughts turned elsewhere. Duffy admitted that everyone was behaving like cannibals. Nevertheless, he added, since the troubles began the suicide rate had dropped to zero. It was confusing, these sudden outbursts of blind hate followed by long sunny Guinness-golden periods when the troubles didn't seem to exist. For the sake of the record I note that we were ten days off the Londonderry incident when Dublin retaliated by burning down the Embassy in Merrion Square.[15]

I am glad to have got in a visit with Pine to this gracious and evocative square. It wasn't only to visit Oscar Wilde but also to say hullo to Sheridan Le Fanu and Maturin.[16] By the time they fired the lovely building where the British Embassy was housed I was back in London. But I didn't neglect to pay my respects to Swift also as he lay buried beside Stella in echoing St. Patrick's. I dragged the reluctant Duffy with me this time and succeeded in mildly interesting him in the fact that Swift had endowed the first lunatic asylum in Dublin. According to the rhyme it was a very necessary act.

He gave the little wealth he had
To build a house for fools and mad
And show by one satyric touch
No nation needed it so much.[17]

But now my visit was drawing to a close and Duffy said: "Sure, I guess you've just about inhaled the place." Yes, that was it. Soft powder of snowfall on the Wicklow hills next day turned all the pleasant landscapes around Dublin into a Chinese watercolour. Then rain came, a soft grey rain falling across the long tender sweeps of Georgian building, ruffling the plumes of the river and making the seagulls plaintive as they wheeled over O'Connell Street and Halfpenny Bridge. Everything was sinking back into the mist and silence of winter again, after a few days of false spring. I went to kiss Anna Livia goodbye—her head is a keystone on the Customs House.[18] I wished her many more poets and drunkards to celebrate her charms. She is the symbol of the Liffey. Duffy was too sad to accompany me to the airport and I was glad. I hate goodbyes. It had been a good trip but too short. "Come again, sir," said the girl with the cowslip complexion. "Come back for longer." As the plane lifted and careened I saw that the grey mist had seized the island and blotted out its soft outlines. The sea looked black and cruel as we sped back to England.

NOTES

1. As Richard Pine has pointed out, Duffy and the pub Duggans are fictional. This article is loosely based on Durrell's visit to Dublin with Margaret McCall in 1972. Conversations with Pine have been particularly helpful for annotating this chapter.

2. This paper was by Pine.

3. The Liffey is the river running through Dublin.

4. A luxury hotel in Dublin facing into St. Stephen's Green.

5. Pine is the author of several critical works on Lawrence Durrell, most notably *Lawrence Durrell: The Mindscape*. He also founded and directed the Durrell School of Corfu. This incident is also described in MacNiven's biography (590) and in Durrell's letters to Henry Miller, *The Durrell–Miller Letters, 1935–80* (453).

6. Joyce and Yeats are frequent references for Durrell. Samuel Beckett (1906–1989) and J.M. Synge (1871–1909) are far less common, though Durrell first learned of Beckett in the 1930s from Henry Miller. All four are major Irish authors.

7. The Brazen Head is Ireland's oldest pub, dating to 1198, at 20 Lower Bridge Street.

8. Forster 134. Durrell was particularly fond of quoting this passage.

9. Trinity College Dublin.

10. Sir William Rowan Hamilton (1805–1865), an Irish physicist, astronomer, and mathematician at Trinity College Dublin, and he was also a close friend to the poets William Wordsworth (1770–1850) and Samuel Taylor Coleridge (1772–1834).

11. A Dog's Nose is typically gin and stout (Guinness), but there are several variations. The description of the drink first appeared in Charles Dickens's *Pickwick Papers*: "H. Walker, tailor, wife, and two children. When in better circumstances, owns to having been in the constant habit of drinking ale and beer; says he is not certain whether he did not twice a week, for twenty years, taste 'dog's nose,' which your committee find upon inquiry, to be composed of warm porter, moist sugar, gin, and nutmeg" (412).

12. Both pubs are on South Anne Street.

13. Extreme accumulation of fat on the posterior.

14. Durrell's third wife, Claude, wrote a memoir about running a pub in Cork, *Mrs. O'* (1957).

15. On February 2, 1972, crowds destroyed the British embassy in retaliation to the Bloody Sunday Bogside Massacre in Derry (Northern Ireland) on January 30, in which twenty-six unarmed civil rights protestors were shot by the British Army, and thirteen were killed. Several were shot in the back.

16. Durrell had a long-term attachment to Oscar Wilde's (1854–1900) works. Le Fanu (1814–1873) was most famous for writing ghost stories, of which "Carmilla," the story of a lesbian vampire in the collection *In A Glass Darkly*, is the most famous. Le Fanu is a likely influence on Durrell's references in poetry and prose to vampires, such as in *The Alexandria Quartet*, *The Avignon Quintet*, and *The Red Limbo Lingo*. Charles Maturin (1782–1824) wrote Gothic plays and novels, most famously *Melmoth the Wanderer*—his sister-in-law was Oscar Wilde's grandmother, and Wilde refers to *Melmoth the Wanderer* in *The Picture of Dorian Gray*. All three authors lived in Merrion Square, and a statue of Wilde sits there.

17. From Jonathan Swift's poem *On The Death of Dr. Swift* (1731).

18. Anna Livia Plurabella is a famous embodiment of the River Liffey, and Durrell is surely thinking of James Joyce's *Finnegans Wake*. The keystones in the Customs House include the images of heads representing bodies of water.

Borromean
Isles

1973

SOMETHING IN THE NAME has always set up a sympathetic echo in my head—a hint of an Edward Lear[1] invention, a hint of *Through The Looking Glass*;[2] and while many years ago I caught a glimpse of them from the deck of a small boat wrapped in lake mist, it was only enough to whet my curiosity. Yet the idea of them stayed on tenaciously in my memory over the years. Borromean! Were the islands perhaps inhabited by Lewis Carroll's "borogoves?"[3] The word echoed on in my head, and then, at long last, came the chance to revisit them, the invitation I waited for.

Instead of fighting my way to the sea, I was to turn inland at Genoa and ramble across the midriff of Italy until I came to that corner of Lake Maggiore, with its twisting mountain ranges and shifting lake mists, its mauve and yellow sunsets wrapped in huge skeins about the sky. Italy is so shamelessly beautiful that one is constantly forgetting the fact of its beauty. As for the Borromean Islands, their romantic celebrity has always put them on a par with Capri or Corfu. For my part I found them so wonderfully, outrageously soft on the eye as to invite other, more symbolic associations—an Eden dreamed up by Blake or Poussin.[4]

Part of the dream music of the name was connected with the story of the three little deserted islands that got somehow woven into the life history of the Borromeo family.[5] Gradually, over very many generations,

347

the family secured one part and then another, thinking first of summer houses or country residences. The mad dream of the palace of Isola Bella was slow in forming. But it came, and when it did its conception was breathtaking in its grandeur, for it was to be the real family seat of the illustrious house of Borromeo. This was a family that had given so many brilliant sons to the science and the arts, to the church and to the law. Under Charles Borromeo III the central idea found root, and the grand design of Isola Bella took shape. It was named after his wife Isabella D'Adda, though neither he nor she lived to see it completed. But the divided motif was there, for it was to be their family seat, yes, but it was also to be a palace of pleasure shaped into the design of a huge green ship, lying at anchor on the azure waters of the great lake. Ideas were taken from everywhere. There is even a hanging garden of Babylonian provenance. But, as the family was forever running out of money, the work proceeded by fits and starts and remains incomplete in some details to this very day. This is romantic sugar-icing architecture of an outrageous kind, offset by the luxuriance of lake greenery that is almost tropical in its profusion.

But first I lay at Novara, the fine little town that gives its name to the whole province. Moreover I was travelling rather late in the season, which is always wise when one has to deal with a very popular tourist place. Italy cannot be all that different, I thought to myself.[6] To my delight I was not wrong; the last days of September were placid and autumnal-sweet, and everybody who didn't live there was starting to pack up. Hotels were slacking off, and the lake campgrounds were already deserted. Winter and mist lay ahead. But meanwhile the cafés basked in sunshine, their coloured awnings spread out like sails. The graceful gardens of the little town were drifted up with the first fallen leaves.[7] Plump horse chestnuts crashed through the trees, falling from their spiky green purses and bumping on the roof of my little camping car. Old pensioners swept away at them so that children or old ladies would not turn an ankle walking on them. In the public garden there is a ghastly statue of nymphs in attitudes of supplication, invoking the sky for rain, perhaps, or the gods for husbands. I have forgotten the inscription.

Novara, too, I had almost forgotten, but not quite. I remember the queer red tessellated streets with their strips of gray concrete stretching down the middle for rubber wheels to grip. And the lovely duomo rearing up in the same shredded red brickwork, so fragile.

I am a literary tourist, which is the worst kind of globetrotter. For example, I spent ten minutes in Novara station. Why? When Nietzsche went mad, his two closest friends went to his aid and took him back to the lunatic asylum at Jena from Turin.[8] There was a three-hour wait in bitter weather here, the silent madman standing between his two sad friends. Indeed the whole of Novara smells of Nietzsche, of that marvelous girl Lou Andreas-Salomé.[9]

These literary memories were only strengthened when next morning very early I took the road to Orta, that little kidney-shaped lake of quite special beauty where they spent a summer, and where Nietzsche outlined to the eager and sympathetic Lou (he was thirty-eight and she twenty-four) the plot of *Zarathustra*.[10] In the dense warm mist I did a little pilgrimage to the Sacro Monte with its twenty little chapels, each with a group of statuary illustrating the vicissitudes of St. Francis's life.[11]

Then on I went to Stresa nearby at a single bound. By now the morning mists had cleared, and the whole clear-scooped foreshore of the great lake opened in front of me like a seashell. Stresa with its tiny railway station emphasizes the Victorian storybook atmosphere. A sign said TO THE ENGLISH CHURCH, which gave one an instant feeling of security. There would be sure to be a branch of Barclays Bank at Stresa.

And then the islands—they came sailing unselfconsciously out of the mist and into the warm orbit of the sun, sure of the visitor's approbation, like great film stars. Could one not echo Napoleon and Josephine's admiration? And who would want to cross swords with Flaubert and Stendhal?[12] Not me.

And these great rambling hotels left over from a forgotten age of opulence, inhabited now by the ghosts of long dead millionaires and frail English nannies. Each hotel had its vast library of tall glass-fronted bookcases full of yellowing Tauchnitz editions of Conrad and Dickens and Kipling. How beautiful it was.

And the food, too, was fine lake food, without the intricacy and tetchiness of the French cuisine. Good stable wines, red and white, many smoked mountain delicacies like sausage and *viande de Grison*[13] but, on the whole, matter of fact.

The fine red wine of Stresa is just right for what we English call "elevenses," namely, a midmorning snort to keep the soul sharply attuned to nature's beauties, to keep the fantasy booted and spurred. Such was the charm of that sunlight I found myself gracefully polishing off a whole bottle while I scouted the little harbor for a boatman to carry me over the water to Isola Bella.

I supposed that a good deal of hard bargaining would be in order, and I thought of Mark Twain in the Holy Land: the passage where he says that when he heard the prices the boatmen charged on Galilee he was not surprised that Jesus walked on the water rather than pay them.[14] But I was wrong about it all. My boatman turned out to be a mild ex-schoolmaster who was kindly as well as knowledgeable, and the price was fixed by law. So over the still pearly water we went puttering in his launch, to make a leisurely circuit of the two smaller islands before turning our prow in the direction of the finest. The last groups of tourists were arriving from several points on the mainland: peasants from the Italian Tyrol. Milanese families and even some Swabian Germans with folklore wives in bonnets and aprons and starched kerchiefs. The men wore dark brown medieval dress such as one sees in the paintings of Brueghel.[15]

I climbed the staircase to the palace entrance where the group of uniformed guides lounged in the sunlight like gun dogs. Business was slack. I fell upon a pleasant young guide who set me quite a pace around the corkscrew palace with its armories and crypts and chancels, its secret gardens and sweetly curving balustrades and loggias. Considering the relatively small size of the island it is amazing how it gives the feeling of space and grandeur. It conveys harmony and grace, and also operatic fantasy so dear to the Italian heart. There are white peacocks that walk the extraordinary construction known as the Amphitheatre, scolding you with their horrible voices. And the grottoes whose walls are covered in coloured seashells. And a marionette theatre…

Perhaps the most astonishing collection on the island is the plant collection that is unique and deserves a catalog all to itself. It took quite a time to complete a leisurely circuit, but when it was over I bade my boatman come and lunch with me at the little café called the Dolphin, the headquarters of the native fishing colony. We ate excellent lake trout and drank red wine while the sunlight steepened and the afternoon drew slowly on. We spoke of Isola Bella and my boatman said: "It is unfortunately too beautiful. When you make something so beautiful that the whole world must come and see it—why, what happens to your private life? You are overrun." He had something there. Imagine standing on the green bridge of this pleasure ship and suddenly seeing a boat approach with Napoleon sitting in it, or Queen Victoria (for she was also an approving visitor). You could hardly send the butler down to say you were out when it came to guests of such calibre. I suppose this explains why the descendants of the family no longer inhabit this precious place. No doubt they have settled for privacy in Rome or Milan. And so Isola Bella with its cargo of fantasies belongs to the whole world, to us.

NOTES

1. · Lear (1812–1888) was an English poet and artist. His nonsense verse remains popular today, and Durrell wrote an introduction to his letters and engravings from Corfu, *Lear's Corfu*, published in 1965 (7–8).
2. Lewis Carroll's sequel to *Alice's Adventures in Wonderland*.
3. A nonsense word (defined as a bird by Humpty Dumpty) in Carroll's poem "Jabberwocky," which first appeared in *Through the Looking Glass*.

4.   William Blake (1757–1827), the English Romantic poet whom Durrell refers to frequently. Nicolas Poussin (1594–1665) was a major French painter perhaps most famous for his *Et in Arcadia ego*, which is in the Louvre and is Durrell's likely reference here, though Poussin is generally known for his pastoral scenes.

5.   This ancient family still owns some of the islands and was an important political force in the sixteenth and seventeenth centuries.

6.   Durrell took this trip in order to compile his book *Sicilian Carousel* (1976), his only travel book not based on a lengthy residence.

7.   The Castello Visconteo-Sforzesco in Navara is surrounded by the Allea public gardens.

8.   Friedrich Nietzsche (1844–1900) had a mental breakdown in the streets of Turin in 1889, followed by his "Madness Letters," two of which were received by his friends Jacob Burkhardt and Franz Overbeck, who decided Overbeck would travel to Turin and return Nietzsche to Basel and then to Jena.

9.   Nietzsche had an indeterminate relationship with Lou Andreas-Salomé (1861–1937) via Paul Rée, which ended when she believed he had fallen in love with her.

10. Nietzsche travelled to Orta with Andreas-Salomé, her mother, and Rée. Although the nature of their relationship is unclear, they were more intimate here than anywhere else. He had already begun drafting his most famous work, *Thus Spake Zarathustra*.

11. The Sacro Monte di Orta is a Roman Catholic structure first built in 1583 and dedicated to St. Francis of Assisi.

12. Napolean Bonaparte (1769–1821) was the emperor of France and married Joséphine de Beauharnais (1763–1814). Their mythic romance has been developed into many histories and fictions, and some of their love letters survive. The French novelist Gustave Flaubert (1821–1880) is most famous for his novel *Madame Bovary* but also wrote historical fiction. Durrell is likely referring to either *Salammbô* or "The Legend of Saint Julian the Hospitalier." Stendhal is the pen name for Marie-Henri Beyle (1783–1842), whom Durrell admired greatly.

13. A seasoned, salted, and air-dried meat, mainly beef.

14. Mark Twain (1835–1910) was the pseudonym for the American humorist Samuel Clemens. Durrell is referring to his travel narrative, *The Innocents Abroad, or The New Pilgrims' Progress* (1869), which recounts his travel in Europe and with religious pilgrims in the Holy Land in 1867.

15. The Brueghel family had several painters, the most famous of whom was Pieter Bruegel, the only one who spelled his name without the "h." He is Durrell's most likely reference here.

Alexandria
Revisited

1978

IN 1975 THE BBC TOOK ME BACK TO GREECE to make a film called *Spirit of Place*, based on my island books and the memories of the years when I lived there.[1] In between these happy Greek years lay darker ones, marked by war, which I had spent in Cairo and Alexandria. Last year, the film director, Peter Adam, suggested we travel again together, this time to Egypt, to the scenes of *The Alexandria Quartet*, and try to touch all the points which, either from a literary or personal point of view, meant something to me, or marked me or moved me.

Filming is a sort of composite art—one is always manufacturing the work of two or three people and trying to assemble it into a coherent image. The writer is a solitary animal sitting in a garret, and when the stuff comes off his typewriter nobody else interferes with it. So to try and make a film about a subject which was precious and probably, from a general point of view, out of date was a trepidation added to traditional neuroses.

To return to Egypt, to revisit Alexandria in order to see what traces, if any, remained of that extravagantly coloured world I had painted in *The Alexandria Quartet*? The idea filled me with unease. After thirty years or so, the country must have changed. There had been the long post-war reaction to the West and then an eight-year flirtation with Russia—until the abrupt discovery that Marxism spelt materialism. Then, apart from these factors, even the Egypt I had painted—or rather the Alexandria—had itself ceased to exist by the time I got there in the war years. Cavafy was eight years dead; the brothel quarter had moved to Cairo, whence I had brought it back to help me set the stage once more. And I myself? Had I changed also, as Egypt must have? These ideas, together with ancient memories of the place, splashed about in my mind as the plane hovered and sank upon Heliopolis through a sunset more marvellous than any I remember. At least nature was a constant, one could count on her. Or so I hoped.

But we were very late and in the huge pandemonium of the airport, which vibrates still with the old noise and dust and smells, it was easy to think that not so very much had changed. This aspect of daily life, anyway; here we were, limp with fatigue at nine o'clock at night, but the beggars and borrowers, the scroungers and the footpads were still bursting with life. We got out to our bus, yes, but almost left our clothes behind in the process—so many were the imploring hands which plucked at our sleeves, or dived upon our shoes to clean them by main force.

The first, the capital, change became immediately and delightfully plain: the uncovered faces of the Egyptian women. The veil had been set aside. And this was a change to be acclaimed, whatever the conservative elements of the country might say. But then, as if in revenge, they had pronounced against the bare breasts of the famous Egyptian belly-dancer, and forced her to wear an ignoble muslin shift. But this we were to encounter later in the journey. We had decided to motor by night to Alexandria, and once our film gear was loaded we nosed across the dusty rumbling metropolis with here and there a gleam of polished Nile water flowing, it seemed, out of the sky into the earth, and set off down the long road towards the famous old seaport.

One was immediately reminded of the war period because of the long stream of lorries heading the same way, mostly without tail-lights—an endless crocodile bearing bales of dusty cotton towards the ships which would take them across the world. How often I took this night journey during the war; but the convoys then, rustling along in the darkness, bore our tanks and carriers and ammunition and every kind of weapon towards the Eighth Army front.

A very tired file crew arrived in Alexandria in the middle of the night and piled up at the old Cecil Hotel, with its echoes of *Justine*.[2] Here we found that our rooms had been given away because of our lateness. However, after long argument, we recovered them and went piously to bed to awake next day to brilliant sunlight and a fine race of blue sea dashing the spray over the seafront with its aged palm trees clicking in the damp sea wind. Alexandria! Yes, it is shabbier, more unkempt, and it has lost its superficial cosmopolitan society, but some of the old magnetism is still there. The newcomer might just manage to feel some of its ancient charm, some of the attraction which excited the minds of Cavafy, E.M. Forster, and Seferis. And there are still small corners which have not budged—like the quarter where Scobie[3] lived, or the mosque where he worshipped. The markets still pulse and vibrate with their exotic wares, and the fortune-tellers are still in business, as are the tattooers. There are still Greek taverns, like Diamandakis, in full swing, and several new Egyptian ones where one can eat well. But a great deal of the old leisure has gone, indeed there is little feeling of opulence to the place—Nasser[4] discouraged that, as his little blue-trousered university girls will explain to you seriously. Perhaps it is for the better. At any rate, in their blue trousers and unveiled now, one can see Egyptian girls are the most beautiful in the world.

We were sorry to leave them, and they pretended they were sorry to see us go up-river—back across the desert this time, stopping for a brief brush with the Coptic monks of St. Bishoy,[5] whose philosophy and life offered a marvellous austere commentary to the noisy, discordant, and tragic tempo of the towns. The air was like breathing ancient parchment. One was appalled by the harshness of their lives but one wanted to stay forever.

The next stop was Cairo, with its famous pyramids and the whole extraordinary placid life unrolling around them. They form the Hyde

Park Corner of the Middle East. Now they crawl with tourists, but during the war we had them to ourselves—like the hotels, which had been taken over and turned into HQs. You were likely to get caught in the revolving doors of Shepheard's Hotel, because General de Gaulle[6] used to enter at such a rate that if you were light you would get swept round and round. At that time Egypt was neutral, Cairo an open city, and the blackout was something mysterious that had happened over there in Europe. Here we lived in a blaze of light. It was all the more extraordinary because people managed to get back from the line quite often for the weekend, for a drink and a dance, for a cinema or an art show. Fifty miles away the armies gnashed and gnawed at each other. I remember attending a party on a Nile barge which included a belly dancer. The host had invited far too many people, and this boat was badly anchored. The belly dancer rotated like an enormous top— she was one of the big ones—and every time she approached one side the whole boat listed. So we had to try to persuade her to stay in the middle of the floor. Finally she went too near the rails, the entire barge turned over and we all found ourselves in the Nile!

Cairo, of course, is vastly changed. Now five times as many people live in the city as did when I was there. Most of the old places are gone. So we lost little time there and travelled south to Upper Egypt. You feel the river wind at once, and the long muscle of the Nile as you go winding up to Luxor and Aswan. Aswan is a kind of paradise, out of time. You put your feet up, mentally, physically and spiritually. The massive battered remnants of the ancient civilisation which surround you are so different from anything you could imagine down in Cairo: the temples of Abu Simbel and Karnak, the Valley of the Kings. The desert is ever present here, the burning glass of Egypt. Where the water is flowing through your fingers, the desert is flowing through your mind. These barren dunes are the last museum—nothing ever rots; the wind may blow tomorrow and uncover a whole civilisation.[7]

What struck me during the filming (which took us all over Egypt) was that previously I had never seen the country at all. All I had seen then was, literally, Alexandria and Cairo. Working as a press officer at the British embassy, I had no time to register impressions. The war was the most exhausting period, I was really too numb to make a sort of paper model of Egypt. Now, having come back, I can construct it much more happily. I realise now that I must keep a leg in Egypt, because the new novels[8] I am writing span the war period. The war tore a hole in the beginning of my creative life and tore a hole in the lives of my characters at precisely the same point. You can't send people away and have them come back six years later without explaining how or why. Wars are so terribly boring to describe. So Egypt is the answer.

I was relieved to have my feelings reassured by this visit. The terrifying thing about film-making is that one has to work against Egypt, because it is so damned beautiful, so extravagant, that everywhere one puts up a camera one is in danger of the picture postcard. But a film can catch that wonderful feeling of stillness that Egypt always conveys: the slow, green blood-time of the Nile. We have such an album of pictures, and I realise that the still image is not comparable with the moving one, because the camera is actually photographing time passing. All this, of course, constitutes distress which directors must feel, as opposed to what writers feel.

It is very strange to come back to Egypt now, after such a lapse of time, and find it relatively unchanged—because of the emanations of the ground. One verifies them by going from one sacred site to another, in the course of making this film, and they seem to me on the same frequency, with the same vibrations. The landscape is scribbled with the signatures of men and epochs. The changes are simply superficial.

NOTES

1. Peter Adam was responsible for the BBC documentary Durrell describes, and his own "Alexandria Revisited" is very close to this text (395–410). Also see Adam's interviews with Durrell, "Everything Comes Right" (163–72) and "Creating a Delicious Amnesia" (173–81).

2. Durrell used the Cecil Hotel as a setting in his novel *Justine*. He was also very familiar with the hotel itself.

3. A humorous character in Durrell's *Alexandria Quartet* loosely based on Bimbashi McPherson among others. Durrell was fond of pretending that Scobie was a real person in interviews, though he was certainly fictional.

4. Gamal Abdel Nasser (1918–1970) was the president of Egypt and a major force for Pan-Arab nationalism as well as the international promotion of Egyptian culture.

5. The Corptic Orthodox Monestary of St. Bishoy in Wadi El-Natroun, Egypt.

6. Charles de Gaulle (1890–1970) was a French military leader at this time and became prime minister of France in 1958 and then president in 1959.

7. Stephanides reports that, in September 1941, he and Durrell were given a tour of the pyramids by the renowned Egyptologist George Andrew Reisner, including the tomb of Queen Hetepheres I, which Reisner had discovered (81–82).

8. These novels were posthumously collected as *The Avignon Quintet*. At this time, he had completed the first, *Monsieur*, which contains several scenes set in Egypt, as well as the second, *Livia*, which he finalized after returning from this trip to Egypt.

With Durrell
in Egypt

1978

WE WERE STILL HIGH IN THE AIR, enjoying a brilliant sunlight.
The sun had not yet disappeared behind the horizon but was climbing
steadily down through the golden bars of cloud. I did not need to be
reminded that the two royal colours of Egypt, gold and green, were a
kind of symbol of her sunsets, which are almost always the same, hardly
ever differing in their primary colours. But below us the world had
turned on its side and Cairo had foundered into near darkness—a
provisional darkness, because the dust of the desert obscures outlines—
and we were sinking down toward it into a pool of night punctuated
by drifts of stars and the lights of the city just coming on. We could
glimpse the sinuous backbone of the old serpent, the Nile, polished
and gleaming and, strangely enough, giving off steam like a hot flat-
iron. Then darkness closed in abruptly, our own lights came on, and
the capital swam up to meet us.

I was not reassured by Cairo's aerodrome, simply because I am
always thrown into a panic by a great deal of noise and screaming, and
Cairo rather specializes in a state of total pandemonium. This comes
about, I have discovered after long analysis, because the bureaucracy,
which is saddled with rather arduous and meticulous work, is not 100
percent literate, so that most orders are given verbally and there is
no record of their having been carried out or not. As everyone is both

officious and zealous, the resulting pandemonium—there is no other word except a Greek one, though there must have been a hieroglyphic for it in ancient times—has to be seen to be believed.

This creates a terrible state of distress. You find yourself so helpless when someone takes your passport, throws it on a desk in an empty booth and then walks away and is lost in the crowd. Somebody else, meanwhile, is forcibly trying to clean your shoes, holding the ends of your trousers so that you can't move, and screaming at you. Somebody else has stepped forward and is charmingly offering you a rusty syringe, in fact, a free injection of something which you do not need, having been injected with the necessaries before leaving.

It was with great relief that our team—a BBC crew come to make a film about Egypt and about myself—recognized the editor of Le Progès Égyptien,[1] who had so kindly come to meet us. He was waiting at the barrier and he did a great deal to smooth down the overzealous ministrations. I must add, too, that we received very special treatment partly because Dr. Mursi Saad el-Din[2] happened to be an old, old colleague, in the realm of poetry. He had published his first poems in Personal Landscape in 1940 when he was an obscure official. Now he is the important chairman of the State Information Service and he, too, had actually come down himself to meet us, but we were so woefully late that he finally got hungry and went home to dinner, leaving an invitation for us all to come round and share it. But we were in a quandary because we had planned to pick up our little bus as soon as we arrived and drive it straight up to Alexandria that same night. Moreover, the bus was there already, in perfect trim, with all our equipment. What to do? After a moment of scattered debate, Peter Adam, the director of the film, decided that we would go up to Alex by night so that we could start work there the next day.

It was a good decision. In fact, it was a comfort to get into the little van that was to be our transport for some time to come. We did not take the lonely desert road for fear of getting stranded, but decided on the inner one that leads through a straggle of ill-lit villages. This is the road that had been kept open while we supplied the Eighth Army during World War II. It was always a mystery to me how it was never hit, or sabotaged, or damaged. I was excited, and delighted in the darkness as we started to take our place in a long, long convey loaded down with bales of cotton. Cotton, indeed, was drifting everywhere. The whole night was filled with shreds of cotton, instead, of course, of tanks, because every night, all night, during the period when I did this little jaunt during the war, the Eighth Army was being supplied (largely by the Americans at that time) in semisecret with the Shermans and other elaborate tinware that enabled Montgomery to bring off the Alamein victory.[3] But now we were only carrying cotton, yet it was much the same procedure atmospherically, and we went through the various villages. They had not changed at all. The petrol pump is still broken at Damanhur and the man still winds it up by hand and unleashes steams of petrol all over the place. And the desert is always there at your elbow, the dust blows in; it is very, very deserted, the desert. The flesh is sorely tired in Egypt, it becomes desiccated, and the eyes are tired by the dust, and it's such a relief when you clear the last headland and suddenly feel trees and the cool they bring and then, abruptly, sand dunes and the seafront.

We didn't get to the Cecil Hotel in Alexandria until after midnight. The lift didn't work terribly well. It was largely a handheld lift, so to speak, and I could foresee that the man who operated it, who was called Ibrahim, would very shortly be left without a limb because, like a gorilla,[4] he kept putting his hand through the bars to excite knobs and pull switches so that the tenuous electric current would push it. However, in Egypt you learn to cover your ears, mouth and eyes, like those three monkeys in the Indian frescoes, and trust in fate. It hadn't changed all that much after all; not fate, Alexandria.

Lying awake that night in my high-ceilinged room, I tried to recapture old impressions and to square the feeling of this dark Alexandria around me with the old half-forgotten Alexandria that I had once known, and I found that the one constant was the wind. The wind that comes straight out of the Greek Cyclades and invests the entire town. It's a nimble-fingered wind. It strays everywhere. All the flags rattle, the palm leaves rattle. Every time it lets up you feel as though you had suddenly gone deaf, but most of the time it's fingering you all over, even in this huge blank old hotel room. It must, I suppose, have been once a rather opulent Edwardian-type room with large Voltaire chairs and scrolls on the ceiling and white plaster moldings, and now it was simply a shell of its former self, with the wind coming in under those clumsy great doors and shutters and through the bathroom window. There was this constant pressure of wind, and feeling it I was reassured and back in…well, in a Greek island, and I dropped into sleep like a lamb.

On the morrow there was a brilliant ripe sunlight and the whole of the city to explore again. The centre is so small that one can traverse the length and breadth of it during a comfortable morning's shopping. But all the smart shops seemed to have folded up and all the old businesses—the French, the Italian, the Jewish, the Armenian—had vanished. The Arabic language had replaced all the other languages on the medicine bottles, on boardings, on posters, which gives the whole city a feeling of having been plunged into Arabdom. In the old days, a restaurant invited you to six different types of menu, and the whole thing had gaiety and charm. In fact, it's not possible to see the little watercolours of Raoul Dufy of the Cannes waterfront about forty years ago without realizing that that was how Alex used to look. It was a thoroughly cosmopolitan Mediterranean town.

Now, alas or not, the desert had moved in, and the Russians had moved out. The long, eight-year flirtation with Russia had really not been extremely fruitful, though I am not sure about the economic or sociological benefits they might have brought which were invisible to my tourist eye.[5] Perhaps they had brought benefits, I don't know, but what had happened was simply that the dust has got into the town and that everything agreeable, Western, rich, comfortable, capitalist, and easygoing had vanished.

There are no more coloured awnings on the seafront, and while the cafés are still there they're now deserted, and if you ask for a coffee, sometimes there isn't one. Shortage and stress seem to me the two cardinal factors. But, at the same time, very few beggars were to be seen in the streets, and the unveiled women were a treat because the enormous variety and the beauty of the Egyptian face had come out, and with it the wonderful impact of different cultures. You had a face, for example, from the middle of Africa which had impacted on a blond face from the steppes, and the result was honey-gold eyes and the most marvelous complexion, and an extraordinary tilt to the head not to be found anywhere else in the world. And a felucca walk! That's Alexandria! I was glad to discover it anew through a sudden change of political weather in which the veil—that hated veil which reduced one to a pair of twinkling eyes—had at last been abolished.

Yes, the next morning it was sunny and I walked curiously about the town feeling all disembodied, like a ghost, because nearly everyone I had known here was dead. I went and had a look at my old office and I saw how much had changed. Little enough in the sense of the climatic dispositions—the fresh wind blowing through it all the time was still there. But a great deal of the style, the elegance, the sparseness and the richness and the luxuriance had vanished, and with it had come not really a proletarianism, not an aggressive coolie culture, but simply apathy—apathy and dust and, of course, the feeling that nothing worked.

Take the postal service: it is the most extraordinary thing in the world. The British got it to work in a hesitant way for a few years, but something was always going wrong. I don't know what the word for it is in Arabic, a postal service, but it must represent something very strange to them. Most of your letters never arrive and some of them in the same batch arrive within ten minutes of your having written them as if there were a telepathic computer somewhere. Of the hundreds of postcards I've sent from various places in Egypt, only about one-third arrived, and those in such record time as not to be believed by the people who received them. Anyway, these kinds of anomalies are part of the Egyptian scene and you rapidly accustom yourself to them.

Familiarity and sentiment and the sense of leisure and pleasure had led my steps at last toward the Greek quarter and finally toward the Greek library, where I managed to unearth a friend of mine, a poet, Theodore Moschonas,[6] who has been the Greek Patriarchal Secretary for the last half-century, I suppose. He's eighty-seven. It didn't seem to be possible that he was still there, looking as young as ever, as intelligent as ever, with his perfect English. We talked for a little while, talked our way back to the old Alexandria, and I told him that I was being given a "*Justine* party" that evening by a notable Egyptian surgeon, married to an English lady, who had great affection for my books and wished to make it as much the kind of party as I might have described in one of them. He chuckled and said, "I don't know who on earth could arrange that for you today, but I wish you luck." I think he meant by this that the old Greek colony had completely disappeared in the social sense.

In fact, we were only about forty guests, but the party took place in a tremendously smart pavilion just outside the confines of the town. There were four to six languages spoken. The girls wore long dresses. There were German girls, there were British, there were Swedes, there were French and there were Greeks, but not too many diplomats, who always tend to act as wadding in a party, preventing the sincere flow of thought or gaiety. The whole evening was so strikingly in contrast to the rundown town that we all felt how welcome was the elegance, the smartness and the snap of the old Alexandria that had all but vanished. It was a wonderful gift to me—a compliment in the true Alexandrian style.

But there was another pleasure in store for me. Peter Adam had discovered that at the Greek Consulate space had been found for a small Cavafy museum. The poet's work had been with me since I was twenty, I suppose, and since I was first introduced to it in Athens during a momentous evening that was shared by Henry Miller and that he has described a little bit in *The Colossus of Maroussi*.[7] Then C.P. Cavafy was completely unknown.

Well, I did not really expect very much of this museum, but it proved to be quite perfect. The consulate itself is rather a handsome, old-fashioned, Pan-Hellenic building of a style which I would characterize as "gymnasium." Gymnasiums in Greece go in for marble columns and arcades and green lawns, and the museum has a vast courtyard lined with marble columns. The Greek Consulate shares this idiom with them and has a pleasant aura of sunshine, the feeling of being not too far from Plato's Academy.

Moreover, the museum had actually been donated the contents of Cavafy's little flat down in Rue Lepsius, and all the furniture had been arranged in the exact fashion in which he had left it when he died. It reminded me very much of my pious visits to Baker Street at the end of the war, where some bright man had decided to reconstruct, in the most faithful detail, the rooms of Sherlock Holmes with all the mementos of the master and Dr. Watson! But here it was even better because it was more truthful to fact. There was Cavafy's own furniture, which I so well remember as being the kind of furniture of the polite salons of Greece when I first went there. What was more touching, more moving still, was his entire library, the books that had been cherished but well-used.

It seemed to me rather sacrilegious, in fact, to sit at the actual desk of the old poet, uncomfortable as it was, with all his books around me and to read in English, instead of in Greek, for the BBC two of his famous Alexandrian poems. I quickly wrote postcards to the people who had shared that evening in Athens when, for the first time, we heard the great poems "Ithaca," "The Barbarians," and "The City" read in beautiful English translation by George Katsimbalis, the Colossus himself. From this fruitful desk I sent him one, I sent another to Miller in America. I sent one to Theodore Stephanides in London, and one to another friend in Athens who also had been present. I hoped that the cards would bring the perennial message of Cavafy's poetry to them, and a very happy memory of Athens, 1938.

Well, the *Justine* party furnished me with a number of new friends, and on the following two days I wandered around the shops with them to see what sort of things were still available. Not very much I am afraid; it's pretty much a shambles, really. All I found, with interest, that the long flirtation with the Russians had yielded practically no sympathy. It shouldn't have surprised me but it did, because I thought if ever they had had a fitting theatre of operations, a country as poor as Egypt was perfect for their kind of solutions to economic problems. Here they could apply their form of institutionalized poverty with all the sanctimoniousness necessary but I had reckoned without the fact that Moslems still believe in God and Marxists don't. Though an Egyptian may be poor and illiterate, he is still fervently religious. What kind of propaganda is possible against this? On the other hand, one had hoped that the Russians might have found some solution to the great problems in Egypt, such as the perennial food shortages that plague the economy, driving prices up and the citizenry to sometimes violent outbursts, but it didn't seem that they had. All that they had spread was a sense of penury, intellectual and economic.

I suppose their greatest triumph might be considered the High Dam at Aswan, but already there have been second thoughts about it and nobody in Egypt seemed to think that it had really justified itself. There was a kind of ambivalent feeling about it. With reason, for it's a tremendously fragile creation. A Boy Scout with a sack full of gelignite could blow it up and drown everyone in Egypt in a few days, so that one has to think about it in strategic terms also. Then, in ecological terms, the danger of fooling about with the Nile current is that while you might, with luck, increase the amount of land that can be cultivated, you risk tearing the mud out of its bed. The silk sleeve of that delicious black mud which the Nile brings down—mud which provides the soil on which the Egyptian grows his crops—is like the mucous membrane of the Nile, and it would be tragic if fooling about with the dam altered the actual density of the silt. This, too, was a problem that was put to me by journalists, and so on and so forth. I apologize for recording gossip, but I can do no other. I simply can't pronounce on these problems, they're too technical. All I can say is that the Egyptians did seem to me no richer than they had been, but they did seem to me much happier. They felt freerer, they were more independent now the Russians had gone, and it's a country where even poverty has a splendid kind of opulence. Well, the Russians had spent eight years there but, apart from a few windbreaks, I was not shown anything of any special interest, and I had the impression that the basic thing that Russia had done for the Egyptians was to free the lower classes psychologically, because now the old begging whine had been replaced by a much more resilient and independent "Hallo!" which was pleasant to hear.

In Cairo we were able to see, so to speak, more clearly round us, because it is the centre of communications. And here one realizes that it's not the war and the problems of war that have made the country difficult to visit at the moment. What really has created that problem is tourist block-bookings. The hotel arrangements in Egypt are pretty fragile, good at their very best, but, even at the moderate levels, extremely expensive, and they have been literally block-booked so far ahead, perhaps two years ahead, that it is not possible for individuals to set off to look around Egypt, though there is no real official impediment to such a notion. It is simply a question that in doing so, visitors limit themselves to a level of accommodation and sanitation that is worse than medieval. Indeed, in many places it is not possible to get a room at all.

There was a good deal of pictorial work for the camera to do in the mosques and bazaars, and we were glad of our own transport, though I must say nothing was difficult to visit. If there were difficulties of movement it was not due to overofficiousness; it was due, at one point, for example, to a sudden dearth of taxis. All the taxis disappeared for a few days. At another time, all small change seemed to disappear. Successive waves of this sort swept across Cairo, and there didn't seem to be any particular reason. They were just like sudden attacks of dizziness in a social system that was, of course, always pretty precarious. But the overpopulation is something you really do feel in Cairo, where everyone appears to be standing on his neighbour's face, and this creates a frenetic subsistence. I had forgotten how the old beggars, beggars who were really hungry, challenged one in asking for money. It's almost as if they would gouge your eyes out with a pocketknife. But the smallest suggestion of a smile on your face is always enough to break their skull into a million pieces of friendly laughter. The poor in Egypt are perhaps the gayest poor anywhere in the universe.

In Cairo we were lodged in great style at the finest hotel in Egypt, the old Mena House. It has lost its old, rather seedy chic but has gained in Oriental opulence and size, having been taken over by the Indians. Comfortable and spacious as it was, the decor of the bars and public salons suggested something between the Taj Mahal and a Hollywood musical. And with justice, for its patrons were for the most part American travellers intrepidly doing the Egyptian circuit on tours that were pretty efficiently run, as far as I could see. The trip was not too exacting—a visit to the Egyptian Museum, to Sakara, and then the Pyramids was what most programs featured. It is pleasing to record, too, that the Pyramids are much better looked after and much less encumbered than they used to be; there are no more streams of beggars and footpads hanging about whining and plucking your sleeve and quite equal to snatching your wallet in the Grand Corridor! No, it is much better organized, and if you pick your time of day (very early, or late, when the tourists have gone), you can still find yourself alone among the ruins. Tipping the wink to a Sphinx while riding among the Pyramids at sunset still has its old Robert Hichens romantic glow.[8]

I was rather sad that Dr. Mursi was unable to materialize during this period, but as an old press attaché I quite realized what kept him—his President, the gentle Sadat, had just made his astonishing visit to Israel and, of course, the news wires were blocked with messages.[9]

Sadat's amazing leap into the dark was, of course, the subject of every conversation devoted to politics. It had caused both jubilation and consternation; jubilation because the ordinary Egyptian is easygoing and peaceable and hates conscription and war; consternation because the President had consulted nobody in the matter. It was easy to foresee that this gallant initiative would set the other Arab states smoldering with thoughts of treachery and separate negotiations. Qaddafi in Libya,[10] for example, who had shacked-up with the Russians, to use a vulgar phrase, would be furious. And so it turned out; his reaction was immediate and sulfurous. More amusing, though, was the fact that Sadat had unwittingly thrown his own propaganda line into confusion. The old hard Arab line vis-à-vis the Jews was slightly in disarray. It was hardly the moment to keep on calling for a Holy War, for it might prejudice delicate negotiations. But all hearts were really with Sadat, for the Egyptians are fundamentally generous; the trouble is that they are also fickle. Sadat might make agreements that another President, subjected to other forces, might repudiate overnight.

I was curious to see whether Nasser's vaunted claims to have abolished illiteracy were founded on anything more solid than propaganda. There were now five times as many Egyptians as there had been when I was last here, in 1950, yet the shift in newspaper circulation did not reflect a sudden expansion of a reading public. It is a pity, because if one can't read and write, and can't add and subtract, the modern world becomes a tricky place in which to live. Thus Egypt has always been an easy place to exploit, and doubly so now because the foreigners had gone and the Copts were in eclipse. It stood to reason that like Cleopatra of old, a girl with more beauty than brains, Egypt was forced into flirtations of power, playing off her powerful neighbours one against the other in order to balance her budget, depleted from overspending. So she was playing Russia and America now just as once she had played Rome off against Anatolia, France against England. It will always be like this. But the Sadat initiative did not seem to enter into this category of calculated scheming, for he had risked much in letting himself be guided by the generous impulse; he has many enemies and many risks to run, but the gesture was wonderful and well worth them all. It proves that in him Egypt has found not simply another politician but a somewhat saintly statesman. It would be a wonderful breakthrough if this thorny problem could be set aside in favour of a peaceful coexistence. It depends on what role the Russians decide to adopt.

Politics aside, everything else was reassuring. We really did have time for leisurely sessions at the Pyramids with nobody about. Nor were we bothered by officialdom. The team was able to shoot more or less at random along the canals with their dramatic background of desert and pyramid.

The Egyptians were rather astonished by the great age of many of the American tourists, and they marveled at their stamina. I must say, it did seem sometimes as if whole geriatric wards had been swept up and pushed into aeroplanes. It was both touching and amusing to see the rows of stationary camels with their elaborately accoutered drivers waiting on the slope below the pyramids. Everyone just had to have his or her picture taken on a camel, and they were efficiently processed by the guides. The look of beatitude on grandma's face was a delight. You could see how she looked at the age of ten when she first encountered a camel in her picture book. It was most touching. I was glad to overhear conversations which suggested that she wasn't being gypped, that she did feel she was getting her money's worth, despite the almost universal affliction which she called (out of delicacy) "Montezuma's revenge." This, of course, I knew only too well, and we were all to be lightly touched by it before the trip was over. What helped us, perhaps, was our preoccupation with the cholera epidemic, just being brought under control while we were there. Mineral water costs about the same as whisky!

The great souk, the Grand Bazaar, so to speak, still exercises its romantic charm, still swarms with the old inhabitants of Cairo—beggars, soothsayers, sellers of water, musk, perfumes, and spices. It is Aladdin's cave, and the cameraman went suitably mad over it.

But for me the richest moments I spent in Cairo were with that extraordinary being, Hassan Fathy,[11] in his eagle's eyrie high up in the Citadel. I had long known him by name and fame as an architect, and indeed we had common friends. One of them, Dmitri Papadimas, the photographer, was responsible for the precious afternoon with this faunlike old man, who looks a young fifty. Indeed, sometimes he looks a stripling, especially when he bursts out laughing and hugs himself with joy as he recounts some idiocy of the Government or some foolish pronouncement by a Government minister. Fathy's book *Architecture for the Poor* is now world-famous, as, indeed, is his model village, New Gourna, in which he demonstrated, as a pilot scheme, what can be done with the simple, eternal, ancient mud brick of Egypt as a housing tool. Great ideas are often the most simple and his book is much more than an architectural manual; it is also an esthetic autobiography, full of felicitous turns of phrase and penetrating ideas about the relation of happiness to architecture, of insight to good living. But a mud brick? It is everywhere, of course, but what Hassan Fathy discovered when he started working with it was that its cheapness could enable the poor of Egypt to house themselves commodiously, and even harmoniously, for hardly any outlay. Nobody today can provide public housing for under $1,200 a unit, whereas Fathy discovered that with his mud-brick technique he could bring the cost down to as little as $500, including kitchen and bathroom. But more exciting, more poetic still, was the link that this technique provided with ancient Egypt, with that violent young queen, Hatshepsut, who was so enamoured of the beauty and use of mud that she allowed herself to be frescoed making the first mud brick— purely as a promotional stunt, I suppose! Would that Fathy's rediscovery of this ancient building material could receive the blessing of officialdom. As we climbed the last staircase and came out upon the roof balcony of his beautiful house, which is right in the midst of the Citadel mosques, he said: "Look! Two cities, two ways of life, of building."

His gesture took in the warm brown girdle of domes that surrounded his balcony, each with its crescent moon—bubbles of infinity set into the regal coronet of Islamic belief, each radiating the magnetism of its ancient faith. Then, turning toward the desert, he pointed to the skyscrapers of the new Cairo hanging in their clouds of dust over the Nile. The comparison was unfair, and he admitted it; the mosque is not a habitation, and a skyscraper is not a mosque. Nevertheless, the juxtaposition was striking and revealed two ways of thinking about life, of living it.

The occasion was also exciting, for Fathy had just been given an award by the President, and there was some talk of a meeting being arranged between them. There was no doubt that if the Government officially espoused the Fathy plan for rebuilding the villages of Egypt, it could not only prove economically justified by low cost but would actually open a renaissance in peasant architecture that might revolutionize more than Egypt. That night I reread the old architect's book and prayed that such a wonderful thing might come about. And often in the day to come, I thought of him as we wandered through the elegantly decorated Nubian villages whose buildings had first taught him that one can build anything with mud bricks—even domes on squinches! In my sleep, the young Queen Hatshepsut seemed to appear before me holding a mud brick and smiling. I vowed to take one home with me so that I could wish on it for the poor of Egypt each Christmas Day.

So the hours in Cairo passed pleasantly, with the feeling that the camera had had plenty of subject matter. The team at last began to feel its feet, to believe that they were really there, living in the shadow of the ancient Pyramids with nothing to stop them from rising at dawn for a ride through the white sweet desert air. For my part, I had discovered the small haunting call of the rock doves—my room opened on the desert pure—and some of the forgotten rhythm of Egyptian time, which is like no other. One enters the slow blood rhythm of the Nile water flowing softly, unhurriedly down to the sea.

After the frenetic and discordant noises of the capital, Aswan, lying in its quiet shoulder of the great river, seemed as cool to the skin

and the mind as lint or some rare lotion distilled from the green fast-
nesses of this flowing water as it soothes its way down to the sea, its
way studded with islands and villages, with margins of desert and
oases. The feeling of air and space is wonderful. And here, of course,
one makes a really intimate acquaintance with the felucca.[12] Like some
great fashion plate, fully conscious of her beauty, she turns and that
haunted me while I was here and then continued to haunt my writings long after I had left. We were to have three or four stabs at Upper
Egypt before departing. Peter Adam had selected the places where
it was most likely that words and music (images and sound) might
manage to make a marriage. Film is a cursedly fragile medium, and
I was glad that I did not have his worries and preoccupations. But
he was a good surgeon. To wake up in the early morning and find
myself, after a brief air hop, confronted by the gigantic gorgons of
Abu Simbel[13] was rather a clever way of shaking my nerve and seeing
whether I could talk sense or would simply babble to the camera,
however, I found myself babbling to (I beg the reader to believe this)
Mia Farrow under a dusty tamarisk tree, while we both wolfed the
nauseous box lunch that the hotel had provided. We had, in fact, run
across the bow of a very big craft—a big-budget movie based upon a
venerable Agatha Christie novel, and truffled with big stars.[14]

It seemed strange at the time but, actually, given the gigantic and
somewhat horrific sculpture of the Abu Simbel group, the meeting
was most appropriate, for however magnetic the site, the sculpture,
in the esthetic sense, is what Noël Coward[15] would have classified as
Metro-Goldwyn-Mayer. Indeed, there is something about the colossal
effigies of Upper Egypt that fills me with an uneasy sense of…fore-
boding, I might say. One feels they exist in some leaden brooding
dimension full of their own Saturnian weight. They are preoccupied
with the inertia of death, the way the little kings and queens are in
their precious mummy wrappings—cocoons of immortality. In Egypt,
matter counted for little, it was not manipulated with pious lust,
with a sensual feel for its nature. The statues sit there in monolithic

glumness, brooding forever upon the penumbra of death. The occasional human touch is so very welcome—the realization that even great kings, like small children, were allowed to take their toys to bed with them, and thence into the darkness of the grave. But the obsessional preoccupation with non-being is finally wearying—think of the vivid prolixity of Indian or Greek sculptural idioms and then return to these huge glum telamons! Yes, it was appropriate that some of the great public tacks and falters and surges at the behest of the river winds. The tall lateen seems to reach for heaven. As the river winds vary hardly at all in their general pattern, these lovely craft seem to perform simple Euclidean maneuvers on the green water, leaning their cheeks close into the wind. The sunsets, with feluccas moving across them on patrol or tacking into the eye of the sinking sun, are as unforgettable as ever. Even the noisiest of tourists feels a sudden stirring in his spirit as he watches the scene from his balcony or from the little belvedere of the new Cataract Hotel (another disgraceful piece of architecture, by the way).

But another surprise for the newcomer is to encounter the Nubians on their home ground, so different are they from both the Bedouin and the town Egyptians. They are great big brown men and wonderfully beautiful women, who exude a calm and grace that is quite at ease with itself, quite unflurried. Their faces, carved in chocolate, are full of intelligence and, strangely enough, humour; laughter is very near the surface, and the white ivory smile of Nubia is something one does not easily forget. They open their arms to welcome you to their country and say, in a deep rich bass, the word "Hullo!" It means everything connected with welcome, this great big brown "Hullo." You hear it uttered from feluccas that cross you on the river; you hear it in town; everywhere, the brown "Hullo." But apart from this impression of being among intelligent, unflurried human beings, one sees that here the hotels and tourist agencies really work. These people are as intelligent as they are beautiful. How terrible that so many of them have eyes missing—the dreadful scourge of ophthalmia still visits the poor of Egypt. Two of the boatmen who took us for river trips were quite blind, and each had a small boy to help him. But they were efficient and competent and took the wind on their cheeks in a professional way, to gauge its direction and speed. The villages were a delight, and these people reminded me of stories I had read of the South Sea Islanders before the arrival of the missionaries.

But after a few days filming among these poetic islets the producer decided that we must shorten rein. After all, we had not come to Egypt to painstakingly photograph everything but to attempt to trap that elusive wraith, the spirit of place. Images of the silver screen should be wandering about these haunting sites—spitfire Bette Davis, effervescent Peter Ustinov, and David Niven,[16] who was my mother's pinup boy for the last ten years of her life. Indeed, it's to Niven that I owe the fact that she actually read a book by me. She had always found them too dull and heavy going, until one day I showed her a fan letter from the star praising the books and saying that someone else would only play Mountolive over his dead body! That electrified my mother. She read everything, and, seeing Niven in all the roles, she naturally found that it was peerless stuff. Thank you, David Niven!

By now, however, the time had begun to count us down, and, thanks to the good judgement of Adam, we were able to take the pulse beat of Idfu and Kom Ombo during the course of a long and blazing car ride along the steep banks of forgotten canals where the ancient wooden water wheels (the sakieh of Egypt that, in the folklore of the land, always whisper messages to the wind) groaned and creaked and shrieked like banshees. A late descendant of Cleopatra's asp in the form of a toothless cobra obligingly hissed at the camera in the bewitching precincts of Kom Ombo, with its moving and, for once, very human cartoons. Here one felt the spirit lift, for virtue and immortality were being poured out of jars like wine, like nectar! There was faith and gaiety and movement being expressed. What a change from the other sculpture!

The winter sun beats down upon the bronze hills where the great Theban temple of Queen Hatshepsut stands—the mountain shaven like a skull. In this dryness there are no echoes; shout if you will! The universe seems padded like a studio. Another memory: rowing about in the violet ruins of Philae watching the sunset drain out of the sky. One curious water bird watched us, but said nothing. At Idfu, a buzzard flew out of a tower with a terrific flap of wings. These Egyptian moments existed like the wing beats of birds from some forgotten civilisation, from some period existing outside the human imagination. Luxor and the ruins of Karnak strengthened one's attachment to the place, and also one's distrust of the institutionalized monumental masonry devoted to Ramses II. So much banality, so much repetition. Why? I think the answer is, really, to give the artisans something to do. Otherwise they would have caused political mischief, as the unemployed have always done.

The last quiet days at Luxor were a sort of happy fulfillment, for the camera boys pronounced themselves content. In fact, of course, Adam's troubles were only just beginning; on him lay the responsibility for assembling and tailoring all the various elements into something coherent, true to its objective and also easy on the eye. I was glad that I did not share the weight of this responsibility—my part was done. But I had found myself a little Hassan Fathy mud brick from Gourna (the domain of Hatshepsut) and had slipped it into my suitcase. I could always wish him luck on that, I felt.

Cairo awaited us now, and the characteristic pandemonium I have already described, but at the heart of it there were now kindly officials we knew who greeted us warmly. One felt at home.

And so ended the great adventure. At Heathrow, they were curious about my mud brick. "Is it very old?" they asked. When I said no, indeed it was very new, they lost interest. At Orly, on my way home to Sommières, the lively eye of the French customs man gazed at it in a world-weary way. "Was it something to eat?" he asked. When I said no, he waved me through in a resigned sort of way. The little brick lies before me as I write these lines. A tourist souvenir? No, something more.[17]

NOTES

1. A major Egyptian newspaper.

2. El-Din (1921–2013) eventually became the editor-in-chief of *Egypt Today* and was an important translator of modern Egyptian literature into English. He was an important spokesman and advisor to the Egyptian President Anwar El Sadat at this time and was particularly important to him during the secret negotiation of the Camp David Accords in September 1978. Durrell was in Egypt less than a month later in October. El-Din graduated from King Fuad I University's English Department in 1943 where he took Bernard Spencer's criticism tutorial. At this time, the department would have held many of Durrell's good friends on staff, including Gwyn Williams, Herbert Howarth, and Robert Liddell. Durrell may, however, be confused about Mursi's involvement in *Personal Landscape*, despite the very active participation of his professors at the time. The only Egyptian author included is Ibrahim Shukrallah with Howarth translating Shawqy's "To a Late Composer" from Arabic (6–7). El-Din does refer to Durrell teaching and mentoring poetry in the 1940s in several of his articles.

3. The Second Battle of Alamein was a major military victory by General Bernard Montgomery in World War II, November 1942. It ended the threat of Axis occupation of Egypt and the Suez Canal.

4. Durrell also refers to "paws" and other animal images with regard to colonized subjects in other works (Gifford, "Editor's Introduction" xii), though this is widespread enough in his works to avoid being related to racial categories.

5. The USSR developed strong ties with Egypt, despite tensions with Nasser, but in 1972 Anwar Sadat expelled Soviet military forces.

6. Durrell also thanks Moschonas for his advice in *Prospero's Cell* (vii), which he wrote while living in Egypt during World War II.

7. Although this evening did occur, Durrell had already encountered Cavafy's works on Corfu shortly after meeting Stephanides there, likely in 1935 or 1936. He and Stephanides jointly translated "Waiting for the Barbarians" in *The New English Weekly* in 1939 as well (MacNiven, *Lawrence* 242).

8. Robert Smythe Hichens (1864–1950) was an English novelist who wrote several works set in Egypt. He also anonymously wrote *The Green Carnation*, the satire of Oscar Wilde.

9. Mursi was a personal advisor to Sadat, who had just completed the Camp David Accords less than a month earlier. Sadat had visited Israel a year earlier in November 1977.

10. Muammar al-Gaddafi (1942–2011) was the leader of Libya from 1969 to 2011. He founded Islamic Socialism.

11. Fathy (1900–1989) was a major force in Egyptian architecture and influenced architects around the world through his Institute for Appropriate Design and the 1973 translation of his book *Architecture for the Poor*, which emphasized natural resources and environmentally sound materials.

12. A traditional Egyptian sailboat distinct from the Dhow.

13. This entire archaeological site was relocated for the creation of the Aswan Dam.

14. Farrow (1945–) had already been made famous by her roles in *Rosemary's Baby* (1968) and *The Great Gatsby* (1978). She was, at this time, filming an adaptation of Christie's (1890–1976) mystery novel *Murder on the Nile*.

15. Coward (1899–1973) was a famous British playwright and composer known for his wit.

16. Davis (1908–1989), Ustinov (1921–2004), and Niven (1910–1983) all starred in *Death on the Nile*. Durrell's mother died in 1964, and in the preceding decade Niven won the Academy Award for Best Actor and was at the height of his distinguished career.

17. As a metaphor for Egypt and the intense struggles of the period over economic and social forms of organization, "the little brick" is notable for its working-class, anti-capitalist or anti-corporate, and social-levelling associations as well as its relation to indigenous history.

Works Cited

Adam, Peter. "Alexandria Revisited." *Twentieth-Century Literature: A Scholarly and Critical Journal* 33.3 (1987): 395–410. Print.

———. "Creating a Delicious Amnesia." *Lawrence Durrell: Conversations.* Ed. Earl G. Ingersoll. Cranbury, NJ: Associated University Presses, 1998. 173–81. Print.

———. "Everything Comes Right." *Lawrence Durrell: Conversations.* Ed. Earl G. Ingersoll. Cranbury, NJ: Associated University Presses, 1998. 163–72. Print.

Agate, James. "Those Dodsworths." *The Amazing Theatre.* New York: Benjamin Blom, Inc., 1939. 80–86. Print.

Aldington, Richard, and Lawrence Durrell. *Literary Lifelines: The Richard Aldington–Lawrence Durrell Correspondence.* Eds. Ian S. MacNiven and Harry T. Moore. New York: Viking Press, 1981. Print.

Auden, W.H. "Cavafy." *The New York Times* 11 Mar. 1973: 427. Print.

Batho, Edith C. *The Later Wordsworth.* Cambridge: Cambridge UP, 1933. Print.

Beaton, Roderick. *George Seferis: Waiting for the Angel, A Biography.* New Haven: Yale UP, 2003. Print.

Berdyaev, Nikolai. *Solitude and Society.* Trans. George Reavey. London: Geoffrey Bles, 1938. Print.

Bloshteyn, Maria R. *The Making of a Counter-Culture Icon: Henry Miller's Dostoevsky.* Toronto: U of Toronto P, 2007. Print.

Bowen, Roger. *Many Histories Deep: The Personal Landscape Poets in Egypt, 1940–45.* Madison, NJ: Fairleigh Dickinson UP, 1995. Print.

Brassaï. "Chair Prime." *The Booster* 2.7 (1937): 23. Print.

———. *Conversations with Picasso.* Trans. Jane Marie Todd. Chicago: U of Chicago P, 1999. Print.

Byron, George Gordon, Lord. *The Life, Writings, Opinions and Times of the Right Hon. George Gordon Noel Byron, Lord Byron.* London: Matthew Iley, 1825. Print.

———. *Lord Byron: The Major Works*. Ed. Jerome McGann. Oxford: Oxford UP, 2008. Print.

Calochytos, Vangelis. "'Lawrence Durrell, the Bitterest Lemon': Cyps and Brits Loving Each Other to Death in Cyrpus, 1953–57." *Lawrence Durrell and the Greek World*. Ed. Anna Lillios. Selsingrove, PA: Susquehanna UP, 2004. 169–90. Print.

Casey, Simon. *Naked Liberty and the World of Desire: Elements of Anarchism in the Works of D.H. Lawrence*. London: Routledge, 2003. Print.

Chamberlin, Brewster. *A Chronology of the Life and Times of Lawrence Durrell, Homme de Lettres*. Corfu, Greece: Durrell School of Corfu, 2007. Print.

Chambers, E.K. *William Shakespeare: A Study of Facts and Problems*. Vol 2. Oxford: Clarendon, 1930. Print.

Christensen, Peter G. "An Overenthusiastic Response: Lawrence Durrell's Interpretation of Georg Groddeck." *A Café in Space: The Anaïs Nin Literary Journal* 4 (2007): 63–94. Print.

Coleridge, Hartley. *Letters of Hartley Coleridge*. Ed. Grace Evelyn Griggs and Earl Leslie Griggs. London: Oxford UP, 1936. Print.

Confora, Luciano. *The Vanished Library: A Wonder of the Ancient World*. Berkeley: U of California P, 1989. Print.

Coryat, Thomas. *Coryat's Crudities*. London: James MacLehose & Sons, 1905. Print.

Cox, Shelley. "The Island Lover: Lawrence Durrell's 'The Magnetic Island.'" *Deus Loci: The Lawrence Durrell Journal* NS 7 (1999): 45–57. Print.

Darwin, Charles. *On Evolution*. Eds. Thomas F. Glick and David Kohn. Indianapolis: HackPett Publishing Co., 1996. Print.

De Montalk, Stephanie. *Unquiet World: The Life of Count Geoffrey Potocki de Montalk*. Wellington: Victoria UP, 2001. Print.

De Quincey, Thomas. *Recollections of the Lake and the Lake Poets*. Ed. David Wright. Harmondsworth: Penguin, 1970. Print.

Delaney, Paul. *Bill Brandt: A Life*. Palo Alto, CA: Stanford UP, 2004. Print.

Dickens, Charles. *The Pickwick Papers*. Ed. James Kinsley. Oxford: Oxford UP, 2008. Print.

Duncan, Robert. "An Ark for Lawrence Durrell." *The Years as Catches: First Poems (1939–1946)*. Berkeley, CA: Oyez, 1966. 11. Print.

Durrell, Lawrence. "Airgraph on Refugee Poets in Africa." *Poetry London* 2.10 (1944): 212–15. Print.

———. "Alexandria Revisited." *Radio Times* 8–14 Apr. 1978: n. pag. Print.

———. "L'amour, Clef Du Mystère?" Bibliothèque Lawrence Durrell, l'Université Paris Ouest, Nanterre. TS.

———. "Ballad of Kretschmer's Types." *Collected Poems 1931–1974*. Ed. James A. Brigham. London: Faber & Faber, 1985. 253–54. Print.

———. "A Ballad of the Good Lord Nelson." *Collected Poems*. Ed. James Brigham. London: Faber & Faber, 1985. 113–14. Print.

———. *Balthazar*. London: Faber & Faber, 1958. Print.

———. "Bernard Spencer." *The London Magazine* 3.10 (1964): 42–47. Print.

———. "Borromean Isles." *Leisure and Travel* 4.3 (1973): 36–37, 63. Print.

———. "Byron." *Collected Poems 1931–1974*. Ed. James Brigham. London: Faber & Faber, 1980. 120–23. Print.

———. "Can Dreams Live On When Dreamers Die?" *The Listener* 25 Sep. 1947: 52. Print.

———. "A Cavafy Find." *The London Magazine* 3.7 (1956): 11–14. Print.

———. "Commentary." *A Festschrift for Djuna Barnes on Her 80th Birthday*. Ed. Alex Gildzen. Kent, OH: Kent State UP, 1972. n. pag. Print.

———. "Constant Zarian: Triple Exile." *The Poetry Review* 43.1 (1952): 30–34. Print.

———. "Corfu: Isle of Legend." *The Geographical Magazine* 8.5 (1939): 325–34. Print.

———. "Down the Styx." *Spirit of Place: Letters and Essays on Travel*. Ed. Alan G. Thomas. London: Faber & Faber, 1968. 417–22. Print.

———. "Elegy on the Closing of the French Brothels." *NOW* 8 (1947): 30–32. Print.

———. "Endpapers and Inklings." *Antaeus* 61 (1988): 88–95. Print.

———. "Enigma Variations." *Time and Tide* 16 March 1957: 319–20. Print.

———. "Family Portrait." *U.N. World* 6 (1952): 60–63. Print.

———. "From a Winter Journal." *Pleasures of New Writing: An Anthology of Poems, Stories and Other Prose Pieces from the Pages of NEW WRITING*. Ed. John Lehmann. London: John Lehmann Ltd., 1952. 252–60. Print.

———. "From a Writer's Journal." *The Windmill* 2.2 (1947): 50–58. Print.

———. "From the Elephant's Back." *Poetry London–New York* 2 (1982): 1–9. Rpt. in *The Fiction Magazine* 2.3 (1983): 59–64. Print.

———. *From the Greek of Sekilianos and Seferis*. Rhodes: Privately printed, 1946. Print.

———. "Hamlet, Prince of China." *Delta* 2.3 (1938): 38–45. Print.

———. "The Happy Rock." *The Happy Rock: A Book About Henry Miller*. Berkeley, CA: Bern Porter, 1945. 1–6. Print.

———. "Hellene and Philhellene." *Times Literary Supplement* 13 May 1949: 1–2. Print.

———. *Henri Michaux, The Poet of Supreme Solipsism*. Birmingham: Delos Press, 1990. Print.

———. "The Heraldic Universe." *Personal Landscape* 1.4 (1942): 7–8. Print.

———. "Ideas About Poems." *Personal Landscape* 1.1 (1942): 3. Print.

———. "Ideas About Poems [II]." *Personal Landscape* 1.2 (1942): 2. Print.

———. Introduction. *Lear's Corfu: An Anthology Drawn From the Painter's Letters and Prefaced by Lawrence Durrell*. Ed. Marie Aspioti. Corfu, GR: Corfu Travel, 1965. 7–8. Print.

———. Introduction. *Wordsworth; Selected by Lawrence Durrell*. Harmondsworth: Penguin Books, 1973. 9–21. Print.

———. "The Island of the Rose." *The Geographical Magazine* 20.6 (1947): 230–39. Print.

———. "Lamas in a French Forest." *Telegraph Magazine* 18 Nov. 1984: n. pag. Print.

———. "A Letter from the Land of the Gods." *The Right Review* 8 (1939): n. pag. Print.

———. "Letter in the Sofa." *Evening Standard* 22 Nov. 1957: n. pag. Print.

———. "Letters to T.S. Eliot." *Twentieth Century Literature: A Scholarly and Critical Journal* 33.3 (1987): 348–58. Print.

———. *Monsieur or The Prince of Darkness*. London: Faber & Faber, 1974. Print.

———. "The Moonlight of Your Smile." *King's School Review* 1.2 (1960): 3. Print.

———. "No Clue to Living." *Times Literary Supplement* 27 May 1960: 339. Rpt. in *The Writer's Dilemma*. Ed. Stephen Spender. London: Oxford UP, 1961. 17–24. Print.

———. "On George Seferis." *George Seferis 1900–1971*. London: National Book League and the British Council, 1975. 7–8. Print.

———. "The Other Eliot." *The Atlantic Monthly* 215.5 (1965): 60–64. Print.

———. *Panic Spring: A Romance*. 1937. Victoria, BC. ELS Editions, 2008. Print.

———. "Paris Journal—for David Gascoyne." *Collected Poems 1931–1974*. Ed. James Brigham. London: Faber & Faber, 1980. 68. Print.

———. *Pied Piper of Lovers*. 1935. Victoria, BC. ELS Editions, 2008. Print.

———. "The Poetic Obsession of Dublin." *Travel & Leisure* 2.4 (1972): 33–36, 69–70. Print.

———. "Poets Under the Bed." *Tambimuttu: Bridge Between Two Worlds*. Ed. Jane Williams. London: Peter Owen, 1989. n. pag. Print.

———. Preface. *The Black Book*. By Durrell. London: Faber & Faber, 1977. 9–11. Print.

———. Preface. *Lady Chatterley's Lover*. By D.H. Lawrence. New York: Bantam Books, 1968. vii–xi. Print.

———. "The Prince and Hamlet: A Diagnosis." *The New English Weekly* 10.14 (1937): 271–73. Print.

———. "A Propos de Tarr." *Tarr*. Wyndham Lewis. Trans. Bernard Lafourcade. Paris: Christian Bourgois Editeur, 1970. 567–68. Print.

———. *Prospero's Cell: A Guide to the Landscape and Manners of the Island of Corcyra*. Edinburg, VA: Axios Press, 2009. Print.

———. "Prospero's Isle ("to Caliban")." *T'ien Hsia Monthly* 9.2 (1939): 129–39. Print.

——. "A Real Heart Transplant into English." *The New York Times Book Review* 21 Jan. 1973: F2–3. Print.

——. *Reflections on a Marine Venus*. Edinburg, VA: Axios Press, 2009. Print.

——. "Richard Aldington." *Richard Aldington: An Intimate Portrait*. Eds. Alistair Kershaw and Frederic-Jacques Temple. Carbondale: Southern Illinois UP, 1965. 19–23. Print.

——. "The Shades of Dylan Thomas." *Encounter* 9.6 (1957): 56–59. Print.

——. *Sicilian Carousel*. London: Faber & Faber, 1977. Print.

——. "Some Notes on My Friend John Gawsworth." *Spirit of Place: Letters and Essays on Travel*. Ed. Alan G. Thomas. London: Faber and Faber, 1969. 17–70. Print.

——. *Spirit of Place: Letters and Essays on Travel*. London: Faber & Faber, 1969. Print.

——. "Studies in Genius VI: Groddeck." *Horizon* 17 (June 1948): 384–403. Print.

——. "Theatre: Sense and Sensibility." *International Post* 1.1 (1939): 17–19. Print.

——. "This Magnetic, Bedevilled Island that Tugs at my Heart." *Daily Standard* 22 Aug. 1972: 6. Print.

——. "A Traveller in Egypt." *The New York Times* 15 January 1961. Print.

——. "Tse-lio-t." Trans. Jean Blot. *Preuves: Les Idées Qui Changent le Monde* 170 (1965): 3–8. Print.

——. *Tunc*. London: Faber & Faber, 1968. Print.

——. "With Durrell in Egypt." *The New York Times* 11 June 1978: 43–50. Print.

——. "Zero." *Seven* 6 (1939): 8–18. Print.

Durrell, Lawrence, and Henry Miller. *The Durrell–Miller Letters, 1935–80*. Ed. Ian S. MacNiven. London: Faber & Faber, 1988. Print.

Eliot, John. *The Parlement of Pratlers: A Series of Elizabethan Dialogues and Monologues Illustrating Daily Life and the Conduct of a Gentleman on the Grand Tour Extracted from "Ortho-epia gallica," a Book on the Corect Pronunciation of the French Language Written by John Eliot, and Published in the Year 1593*. Ed. Jack Lindsay. London: Fanfrolico Press, 1928. Print.

Eliot, T.S. "Hamlet and His Problems." *The Sacred Wood: Essays on Poetry and Criticism*. 1928. London: Methuen and Co. Ltd., 1960. 95–103. Print.

——. *The Letters of T.S. Eliot: Volume 1, 1898–1921*. Ed. Valerie Eliot. Boston: Houghton Mifflin Harcourt, 1988. Print.

——. "Tradition and the Individual Talent." *Selected Essays*. 1932. London: Faber & Faber, 1999. 13–22. Print.

Fedden, Robin. "Introduction: An Anatomy of Exile." *Personal Landscape: An Anthology of Exile*. London: Poetry London, 1945. 7–15. Print.

——. "Personal Landscape." *The London Magazine* 5.12 (1966): 63–65. Print.

Fone, Byrne R.S. *The Columbia Anthology of Gay Literature: Readings from Western Antiquity to the Present Day*. New York: Columbia UP, 2001. Print.

Forster, E.M. *Alexandria: A History and A Guide*. Ed. Michael Haag. London: Michael Haag Ltd., 1982. Print.

——. *Pharos and Pharillon*. Richmond: Hogarth Press, 1923. Print.

Fraenkel, Michael. *Bastard Death: The Autobiography of an Idea*. Paris: Carrefour, 1936. Print.

Fraser, G.S. "City of Benares." *Personal Landscape* 1.3 (1942): 12. Print.

——. "Ideas About Poetry VI: Mathaios Pascalis His Ideas About Poems." *Personal Landscape* 2.3 (1944): 2. Print.

Freud, Sigmund. *The Ego and the Id*. Trans. James Strachey. London: Hogarth Press, 1923. Print.

——. *The Future of an Illusion*. Trans. James Strachey. London: Hogarth Press, 1968. Print.

Gascoyne, David. "Fellow Bondsmen." *Deus Loci: The Lawrence Durrell Journal* NS 1 (1992): 4–7. Print.

Gibbons, Thomas. "'Allotropic States' and 'Fiddle-bow': D.H. Lawrence's Occult Sources." *Notes and Queries* 35.3 (1988): 338–41. Print.

Gifford, James. "Anarchist Transformations of English Surrealism: The Villa Seurat Network." *jml: Journal of Modern Literature* 33.4 (2010): 57–71. Print.

——. "Durrell's *Delta* and Dylan Thomas' 'Prologue to an Adventure.'" *In-Between: Studies in Literary Criticism* 13.1 (2004): 19–23. Print.

——. "Editor's Introduction." *Pied Piper of Lovers*. Victoria, BC: ELS Editions, 2008. vii–xvii. Print.

——. "Editor's Preface." *Panic Spring: A Romance*. Victoria, BC: ELS Editions, 2008. vii–xiv. Print.

——. "Hellensim/Modernism: Negotiating Modernisms and the Philhellene in Greece." Ed. Tatiani Rapatzikou. *Anglo-American Perceptions of Hellenism*. Newcastle: Cambridge Scholars Publishing, 2006. 82–97. Print.

——. "Noses in *The Alexandria Quartet*." *Notes on Contemporary Literature* 34.1 (2004): 2–4. Print.

——. *Personal Modernisms: Anarchist Networks and the Later Avant-Gardes*. Edmonton: U of Alberta P, 2014. Print.

——. "Surrealism's Anglo-American Afterlife: The Herbert Read and Henry Miller Network." *Nexus: The International Henry Miller Journal* 5 (2008): 36–64. Print.

Gifford, James, and Michael Stevens. "A Variant of Lawrence Durrell's *Livia; or, Buried Alive* and the Composition of *Monsieur; or, the Prince of Darkness*." *Lawrence Durrell at the Crossroads of Arts and Sciences*. Eds. Corinne Alexandre-Garner,

Isabelle Keller-Privat, and Murielle Philippe. Paris: Presses Universitaires de Paris Ouest, 2010. 173–93. Print.

Godshalk, William Leigh. "Some Sources of Durrell's Alexandria Quartet." *Modern Fiction Studies* 13.3 (1967): 361–74. Print.

Green, Roger. "Lawrence Durrell: The Spirit of Winged Words." *Aegean Review* Fall–Winter (1987): 8–25. Print.

Groddeck, Georg. *The Book of the It.* New York: Funk & Wagnalls Company, 1923. Print.

Gwynne, Rosalind. "Islam and Muslims in *The Alexandria Quartet.*" *Deus Loci: The Lawrence Durrell Journal* NS 5 (1997): 90–102. Print.

Haag, Michael. *Alexandria City of Memory.* New Haven: Yale UP, 2004. Print.

Hammond, Andrew. *The Balkans and the West: Constructing the European Other, 1945–2003.* Aldershot: Ashgate, 2004. Print.

H.D. *Tribute to Freud.* New York: New Directions, 1972. Print.

Hepburn, Charles. "The Ironclad." *Personal Landscape* 2.2 (1944): 9. Print.

Herbrechter, Stefan. *Lawrence Durrell, Postmodernism and the Ethics of Alterity.* Amsterdam: Rodopi, 1999. Print.

Hirst, Anthony. "'The Old Poet of the City': Cavafy in Darley's Alexandria." *Deus Loci: The Lawrence Durrell Journal* NS 8 (2001): 69–94. Print.

Hopkins, Lisa. *Christopher Marlowe, Renaissance Dramatist.* Edinburgh: Edinburgh UP, 2008. Print.

Hotson, John Leslie. *Mr. W.H.* London: Alfred A. Knopf, 1964. Print.

——. *Shakespeare's Sonnets Dated and Other Essays.* New York: Oxford UP, 1949. Print.

Howell, James. *Instructions for Forreine Travell.* Ed. Edward Arbor. London: English Reprints, 1889. Print.

Irace, Kathleen O. Introduction. *The First Quarto of Hamlet.* Cambridge: Cambridge UP, 1998. 1–27. Print.

Jones, Ernest. *Hamlet and Oedipus.* New York: W.W. Norton & Co., 1949. Print.

——. "The Oedipus-Complex as An Explanation of Hamlet's Mystery: A Study in Motive." *The American Journal of Psychology* 21.1 (1910): 72–113. Print.

Jung, Carl. Letters to Lawrence Durrell. Undated, circa 1947–1948. Lawrence Durrell Papers. Southern Illinois University Carbondale, Morris Library, Carbondale. TS.

Kaczvinsky, Donald P. "Durrell and the Political Unrest: Paris, May 1968." *In-between: Essays and Studies in Literary Criticism* 11.2 (2002): 171–79. Print.

——. "Memlik's House and Mountolive's Uniform: Orientalism, Ornamentalism, and *The Alexandria Quartet.*" *Contemporary Literature* 48.1 (2007): 93–118. Print.

Keeley, Edmund. *Inventing Paradise: The Greek Journey 1937–47*. Evanston, IL: Northwestern UP, 2002. Print.

———. "T.S. Eliot and the Poetry of George Seferis." *Comparative Literature* 8.3 (1956): 214–26. Print.

Keery, James. "The Apocalypse Poets, 'New Modernism,' and 'The Progressive View of Art' *Poetry London* (1939–51) and *Indian Writing* (1940–2)." *The Oxford Critical and Cultural History of Modernism Magazines, Volume I, Britain and Ireland 1880–1955*. New York: Oxford UP, 2009. 874–97. Print.

Keyserling, Hermann Graf. Foreword. *The World of Man*. George Groddeck. London: Vision Press, 1951. 12–14. Print.

Lawrence, D.H. *The Letters of D.H. Lawrence*. Eds. George J. Zytaruk and James T. Boulton. Cambridge: Cambridge UP, 1981. Print.

Lee, Sir Sidney. *Great Englishmen of the Sixteenth Century*. London: A. Constable and Co., 1904. Print.

Lemon, Lee T. "Durrell, Derrida, and the Heraldic Universe." *Lawrence Durrell: Comprehending the Whole*. Eds. Julius Rowan Raper, Melody L. Enscore, and Paige Matthey Bynum. Columbia: U of Missouri P, 1995. 62–69. Print.

Liddell, Robert. "A Note on Cavafy." *Personal Landscape* 1.3 (1942): 9–10. Print.

———. *Unreal City: A Novel*. London: Jonathan Cape, 1952. Print.

Lorca, Federico García. "O Guitar." *Selected Poems*. Trans. Martin Sorrell. Oxford: Oxford UP, 2007. 49–51. Print.

MacNiven, Ian S. *Lawrence Durrell: A Biography*. London: Faber & Faber, 1998. Print.

Marsh, Janet Zimmerman. "The Influence of Hinduism in William Butler Yeats's 'Meru.'" *The Yeats Eliot Review* 22.4 (2005): 15–18. Print.

Matiossian, Vartan. "Kostan Zarian and Lawrence Durrell: A Correspondence." *Journal of the Society for Armenian Studies* 8 (1995): 75–101. Print.

Mengham, Rod. "Auden, Psychology and Society." *The Cambridge Companion to W.H. Auden*. Ed. Stan Smith. Cambridge: Cambridge UP, 2004. 165–74. Print.

Miller, Henry. "The Angel is My Watermark." *Black Spring*. New York: Grove Press, 1963. 55–76. Print.

———. "The Eye of Paris." *Wisdom of the Heart*. New York: New Directions, 1960. 173–86. Print.

———. *Henry Miller On Writing*. New York: New Directions, 1964. Print.

———. "Henry Miller's Letters to Herbert Read: 1935–1958." *Nexus: The International Henry Miller Journal* 5 (2008): 3–35. Print.

———. *Letters of Henry Miller and Wallace Fowlie*. New York: Grove Press, 1975. Print.

———. *Letters to Emil*. Ed. George Wickes. New York: New Directions, 1989. Print.

———. "The New Instinctivism." *Nexus: The International Henry Miller Journal* 4 (2007): 3–56. Print.

———. "An Open Letter to Surrealists Everywhere." *The Cosmological Eye*. New York: New Directions, 1939. 151–96. Print.

———. *Sexus*. New York: Grove Press, 1987. Print.

———. *The Time of the Assassins: A Study of Rimbaud*. New York: New Directions, 1962. Print.

———. *Tropic of Cancer*. New York: Grove Press, 1961. Print.

———. "Via Dieppe-Newhaven." *The Cosmological Eye*. New York: New Directions, 1939. 197–228. Print.

———. "Wisdom of the Heart." *The Modern Mystic* 2 (April 1939): 31–46. *The Wisdom of the Heart*. New York: New Directions, 1960. 31–46. Print.

Miller, Tyrus. *Late Modernism: Politics, Fiction, and the Arts between the Wars*. Berkeley: U of California P, 1999. Print.

Milton, John. *Areopagitica*. Ed. Sir Richard C. Jebb. Cambridge: Cambridge U P, 1918. Print.

Mollo, Mary. "Larry, My Friend." *Twentieth Century Literature: A Scholarly and Critical Journal* 33.3 (1987): 317–28. Print.

Moorman, Mary. *William Wordsworth: A Biography*. Oxford: Clarendon, 1957–1965. 2 vols. Print.

Morrison, Ray. *A Smile in His Mind's Eye: A Study of the Early Works of Lawrence Durrell*. Toronto: U of Toronto P, 2005. Print.

Mulvihill, James. "Conrad's Accountant and Durrell's *Tunc*." *Notes on Contemporary Literature* 30.3 (2000): 11–12. Print.

Nandyal, Ranganath. "Henry Miller as an Existentialist Outsider." *A Mosaic of Encounters (India & USA: Literature, Society and Politics)*. Eds. A.A. Mutalik-Desai, V.K. Malhotra, T.S. Anand, and Prashant K. Sinha. New Delhi: Creative Books, 1999. 11–14. Print.

Newton, C.T. *Travels and Discoveries in the Levant*. Vol. 1. London: Day & Son, Ltd., 1865. Print.

Nimr [Smart], Amy. "The Poetry of Cavafy." *Personal Landscape* 2.4 (1945): 14–20. Print.

Orend, Karl. "Fucking Your Way to Paradise: An Introduction to Anarchism in the Life and Work of Henry Miller." *Nexus: The International Henry Miller Journal* 6 (2009): 44–77. Print.

———. *Henry Miller's Red Phoenix: A Lawrentian Quest*. Paris: Alyscamps Press, 2006. Print.

Orwell, George. "Back to the Twenties." *New English Weekly* 12.2 (1937): 30–31. Print.

———. "Inside the Whale." *Inside the Whale and Other Essays*. New York: Penguin, 2001. 9–50. Print.

———. "Shooting An Elephant." *The Collected Essays, Journalism and Letters of George Orwell*. Vol. 1. Eds. Sonia Orwell and Ian Angus. London: Secker & Warburg, 1968. 235–42. Print.

Papadimitriou, Elie. "Anatolia: Second Recitative." *Personal Landscape* 2.3 (1944): 3–4. Print.

Papayanis, Marilyn Adler. *Writing in the Margins: The Ethics of Expatriation From Lawrence to Ondaatje*. Nashville: Vanderbilt UP, 2005. Print.

Pine, Richard. *Lawrence Durrell: The Mindscape*. London: Palgrave Macmillan, 1994. Print.

———. "Theodore Stephanides: A Brief Biography." Theodore Stephanides. *Autumn Gleanings: Corfu Memoirs and Poems*. Eds. Richard Pine, Lindsay Parker, James Gifford, and Anthony Hirst. Corfu, GR: Durrell School of Corfu, 2011. 12–18. Print.

Porteus, Hugh Gordon. "Phoenician Images." *Personal Landscape* 2.4 (1945): 13–14. Print.

Prem, Shri Krishna. *The Yoga of the Bhagavad Gita*. Sandpoint, ID: Morning Light Press, 2008. Print.

Rainey, Lawrence S. "Eliot among the Typists: Writing *The Waste Land*." *Modernism/ modernity* 12.1 (2005): 27–84. Print.

Ranasinha, Ruvani. *South Asian Writers in Twentieth-Century Britain*. Oxford: Oxford UP, 2007. Print.

Read, Herbert. "Speech by Herbert Read at the Conway Hall." *The Surrealist Bulletin* 4 (1936): 7–13. Print.

Rodd, James Rennell. *The Customs and Lore of Modern Greece*. London: David Stott, 1892. Print.

Roessel, David. "'Cut in Half as It Was': Editorial Excisions and the Original Shape of Reflections on a Marine Venus." *Deus Loci: The Lawrence Durrell Journal* NS 6 (1998): 64–77. Print.

———. *In Byron's Shadow: Modern Greece in the English and American Imagination*. New York: Oxford UP, 2001. Print.

Sanderson, John. *Travels of John Sanderson in the Levant, 1584–1602*. Vol. 67. London: Hakluyt Society, 1931. Print.

Schimanski, Stefan, and Henry Treece. "Towards A Personalist Attitude: Introduction." *Transformation*. London: Victor Gollancz Ltd., 1943. 13–17. Print.

Schorer, Mark. "*On Lady Chatterley's Lover*." *Evergreen Review* 1 (1957): 149–78. Print.

Secombe, Thomas. *The Age of Shakespeare (1579–1631)*. 1902. London: G. Bell & Sons, 1927. Print.

Seferis, George. "Cavafy and Eliot—A Comparison." *On The Greek Style: Selected Essays on Poetry and Hellenism*. Trans. Rex Warner. London: The Bodley Head, 1967. 121–61. Print.

———. "The King of Asine." *Personal Landscape* 2.3 (1944): 9–10. Print.

———. *The King of Asine and Other Poems*. Trans. Bernard Spencer, Lawrence Durrell, and Nano Valaoritis. London: John Lehmann Ltd., 1948. Print.

———. "Letter from a Greek Poet." *Personal Landscape* 1.1 (1942): 10. Print.

Shakespeare, William. *Hamlet (Folio 1, 1623)*. Ed. David Bevington. *Internet Shakespeare Editions*. University of Victoria, 1 June 2014. Web.

———. *Hamlet (Quarto 1, 1603)*. Ed. David Bevington. *Internet Shakespeare Editions*. University of Victoria, 1 June 2014. Web.

———. *Love's Labour's Lost (Folio 1, 1623)*. Ed. Timothy Billings. *Internet Shakespeare Editions*. University of Victoria, 1 June 2014. Web.

———. *Othello (Folio 1, 1623)*. Eds. Donald L. Bailey and Jessica Slights. *Internet Shakespeare Editions*. University of Victoria, 1 June 2014. Web.

———. *Rape of Lucrece (Modern)*. Ed. Hardy M. Cook. *Internet Shakespeare Editions*. University of Victoria, 1 June 2014. Web.

———. *The Sonnets (Modern)*. Eds. Michael Best, Ian Lancashire, and Hardy M. Cook. *Internet Shakespeare Editions*. University of Victoria, 1 June 2014. Web.

———. *The Tempest (Folio 1, 1623)*. Eds. Brent Whitted and Paul Yachnin. *Internet Shakespeare Editions*. University of Victoria, 1 June 2014. Web.

———. *Titus Andronicus (Folio 1, 1623)*. *Internet Shakespeare Editions*. University of Victoria, 1 June 2014. Web.

———. *Venus and Adonis*. Ed. Hardy M. Cook. *Internet Shakespeare Editions*. University of Victoria, 1 June 2014. Web.

Shawqy. "To a Late Composer." Trans. Herbert Howarth and Ibrahim Shukrallah. *Personal Landscape* 2.1 (1943): 6–7. Print.

Snow, C.P. *The Two Cultures*. Cambridge: Cambridge UP, 1959. Print.

Sobhy, Soad Hussein. "Alexandria As Groddeck's It." *Deus Loci: The Lawrence Durrell Journal* NS 6 (1998): 26–39. Print.

Spencer, Bernard. "Ideas About Poetry." *Personal Landscape* 1.4 (1942): 2. Print.

———. "In an Auction Room." *Personal Landscape* 2.4 (1945): 12. Print.

Stanford, Derek. "Lawrence Durrell." *The Freedom of Poetry: Studies in Contemporary Verse*. London: Falcon Press, 1947. 123–35. Print.

———. "Lawrence Durrell: An Early View of His Poetry." Ed. Harry T. Moore. *The World of Lawrence Durrell*. Carbondale: Southern Illinois UP, 1962. 38–48. Print.

Stephanides, Theodore. *Autumn Gleanings: Corfu Memoirs and Poems*. Eds. Richard
　　Pine, Lindsay Parker, and James Gifford. Corfu, GR: Durrell School of Corfu and
　　the International Lawrence Durrell Society, 2010. Print.

Tambimuttu, James Meary. "Ceylonese Lovesong." *Delta* 3 (1939): 14. Print.

Thomas, Dylan. "Letters to Lawrence Durrell." *Two Cities* 4 (1960): 1–5. Print.

Tiller, Terence. "Roman Portraits." *Personal Landscape* 2.4 (1945): 4. Print.

Tomkinson, Fiona. "Durrell's 'Poem in Space and Time' at the Crossroads of the
　　Arts and Sciences." *Lawrence Durrell at the Crossroads of Arts and Sciences*. Eds.
　　Corinne Alexandre-Garner, Isabelle Keller-Privat, and Murielle Philippe. Paris:
　　Presses Universitaires de Paris Ouest, 2010. 117–32. Print.

Treece, Henry. "Towards a Personalist Literature." *Transformation Four*. London:
　　Lindsay Drummond Ltd., 1945. 217–19. Print.

Trelawny, Edward John. *The Recollections of the Last Days of Shelley and Byron*. New
　　York: Carroll and Graf Publishers, Inc., 2000. Print.

Valaoritis, Nanos. "Remembering the Poets: Translating Seferis with Durrell and
　　Bernard Spencer." *Lawrence Durrell and the Greek World*. Ed. Anna Lillios.
　　London: Associated University Presses, 2004. 46–56. Print.

Von Richthofen, Patrick. "The Booster/Delta Nexus: Henry Miller and His Friends
　　in the Literary World of Paris and London on the Eve of the Second World War."
　　Diss. University of Durham, 1987. Print.

Waller, John. "Lawrence Durrell: A Clever Magician." *The Poetry Review* 38.3 (1947):
　　177–82. Print.

Wilde, Oscar. "Mr. W.H." *Lord Arthur Savile's Crime: The Portrait of Mr. W.H. and Other
　　Stories*. London: Methuen, 1900. Web.

Williams, Raymond. "Advertising: The Magic System." *Culture and Materialism*.
　　London: Verso, 2005. 170–95. Print.

Willinsky, John. "Lessons from the Wordsworths and the Domestic Scene of Writing."
　　The Educational Legacy of Romanticism. Ed. John Willinsky. Waterloo, ON: Wilfrid
　　Laurier UP, 1990. 33–54. Print.

Woolf, Virginia. "On Not Knowing Greek." *The Common Reader*. Ed. Andrew
　　McNeillie. New York: Harcourt, Inc., 1984. 23–38. Print.

Yates, F. "The Importance of John Eliot's *Ortho-Epia Gallica*." *The Review of English
　　Studies* 7.28 (1931): 419–30. Print.

Zarian, Kostan. *Girk' diwts'aznergut'eants'*. Erusaghēm: Tparan Srbots' Hakobeants',
　　1978. Print.

Index

Beirut, 232n1, 308

Bergson, Henri, 21n38

Bermuda, 90, 96n24

Bhagavad Gita, 194, 198n39, 219, 222–23n15. *See also* Hinduism

Bien, Peter, 130, 132n5

Blake, William, 20n27, 193, 194, 198n39, 231, 233n15, 235, 347, 352n4

Blakelock, Alban, 183

Bleuler, Eugen, 189, 196n13

Bloom, Harold, xxii, xxiii

Bloomsbury, 228, 232n7, 232n10

Bloshteyn, Maria, 195n10

Bolero (journal), xiv, xvii

Bonaparte, Napoleon, 140, 141, 297, 308n1, 349, 351, 352n12

Bonnefoy, Yves, 278, 280n7

Book of Changes, 237

Booster (journal), xxxiin9, 196n22, 240, 241, 245n5, 283n1

Borromean Islands, 347–52

Bowra, Cecil Maurice, 115, 120n27

Brandt, Bill, 242, 246n10

Breton, André, 64, 70n6, 189, 196n16. *See also* Surrealism

British Council, 23n54, 232n9, 247, 254n2, 255n13, 255–56n17

British Empire, xxv, 18n13. *See also* colonialism

British Raj, xiv, xviii, xxiv, xxv, xxvi, 1–24. *See also* colonialism

Brontë, Bramwell, 244

Brontë, Emily, 161, 185, 243–44

Bruno, Giordano, 265

Buddhism, 3, 5, 13–15, 24n59, 53–58, 189, 264

Budge, E.A. Wallace, 236, 238n7

Bullen, Keith, 255n17

Burbage, Richard, 174, 180n45

Burrows, Ines, 253, 255n17

Byron, George Gordon, Lord, xxvii, 32, 226, 231, 232n3, 233n15, 243, 246n13, 257, 267n3

and Philhellenism, 109–13, 118, 118n1, 118n3, 118n9–10

Cairo. *See* Egypt

Calder, 13, 56n60

Calotychos, Vangelis, xviii

Calvos, Andreas. *See* Kalvos, Andreas

Campbell, Roy, 252, 271

Campos, Alaro de, 20n30

Camus, Albert, 255n14

Capetanakis, 115, 120n25

capitalism, xix, xviii, 228, 362, 378n17

Caramanlis, 49, 50–51n7

Carney, George, 183

Carroll, Lewis, 11, 347, 351n2–3

Cary, Joyce, 245, 246n14

Cavafy, Aristides, 123, 127n2

Cavafy, C.P., xxii, 36n12, 120n27, 121n29, 268n5, 277, 354–55, 364–65

translations of, 115–16, 120n26, 121n28, 121n30, 123–27, 129–33, 248, 251, 255n12, 377n7

Céline, Louis-Ferdinand, 190, 196n18, 232

Cézanne, Paul, 78

Chamberlin, Brewster, 185n6, ix

Chapman, George, 150, 177n2

Chaucer, Geoffrey, 32, 315n1

Chekhov, Anton, 188, 195n10

Chessman, Caryl, 38, 44n6–7

Chester, Robert, 171, 180n40

China, 12, 58n3, 73–79, 105n3, 208,
    236–37, 238n6, 257, 344
    invasion of Tibet, 54
Christ, 215–18, 292, 350
Christianity, 4–6, 9, 11, 14, 15, 19,
    48–49, 58n3, 76, 80n17, 81n17,
    86, 88, 96n10, 97n33, 126, 127,
    160, 194, 197n26, 215–19, 228,
    257, 259, 264, 265, 292, 294n13,
    294n15, 321, 343, 349. *See also*
    Copts
Christie, Agatha, 373, 378n14
Christmas, 7, 16, 53, 372
Cicero, 309n8
Circle (journal), xiv, xv, xxxin1, xxxin5,
    221n2, 254n8, 255n11, 255n14
Clare, Mary, 183
Cleobulus, 299, 309n10, 310n29
Cocteau, Jean, 198n38
Cohen, Eve, 50n3, 308n5
Coleridge, Hartley, 135, 146n1–2
Coleridge, Samuel Taylor, 135, 145,
    146n1, 148n22, 154, 346n10
colonialism, xiii, xiv, xix, xxi, xxiv, xxv,
    xxvi, xxviii, 1–24, 18n13, 294n5,
    331–35, 377n4
Comfort, Alex, xiv, xxx–xxxin1
communism, xix, xvi, xvii, xviii, xx, 15,
    21n35, 27–28, 39, 45n12, 80n4,
    80n6, 104n2, 177n6, 196n14–16,
    227, 228, 232n6–8, 232n8, 265,
    280n6, 322n1, 362
Confucius, 189, 200
Connolly, Cyril, 196n19
Conrad, Joseph, 350
conservatism, xix, xvii, xviii, xx, 27–28,
    51n8, 111, 112, 133n11, 141,

148n14, 197n32, 229, 232n6,
    232n9, 233n16, 274, 323n7
Cooke, Dorian, 251, 252, 255n17
Cooney, James, xxx–xxxin1
Copts, 355, 369
Corfu, viii, ix, xi, xxvii, xxviii, 20n32,
    20n34, 20n40, 22n42, 22n44,
    23n54, 27, 35n4, 70n5, 80n1,
    80n5, 83–97, 108, 109, 118n6,
    119n18, 120n23, 127n4, 188,
    195n4, 231–32n1, 241, 287–95,
    316n2, 345n5, 347, 351n1, 377n7
    Saint Spiridion, 92, 93, 108, 118n6,
    288, 289
Coryat, Thomas, 85, 86, 89, 95n6,
    96n7, 96n11
Cos, 311, 313, 314, 315, 316n3
Cossery, Albert, xxxin5, 249, 252,
    254n8, 255n14
Coward, Noël, 373, 378n15
Cox, Shelley, 50n1
Croatia. *See* Yugoslavia
Cromwell, Oliver, 160, 178n15
Cuba, 44n7
Curie, Marie, 22n42
Cyprus, xiv, xvii, xviii, xxviii, 22n42, 86,
    92, 121n32, 123, 127n1, 148n14,
    252, 280n8, 301, 309n18
    Durrell's residence, 331–35
    and partition, 47–51
    unification with Greece (*see* Enosis)
Cyprus Review (journal), 332, 334n1,
    334n3

D'Annunzio, Gabriele, 30, 36n6
DADA, 8, 11, 22n45, 189
Dante, 30, 161, 178n18
Danvers-Walker, A., 183–86

French Revolution, 137, 140, 147n6,
233n15
Freud, Sigmund, xviii, 1, 8–13, 20n28,
22n44, 23n47, 23n51, 23n56,
23n57, 138, 139, 147n8, 165, 167,
175, 178n19, 179n25, 179n26,
189, 196n13, 240, 295n22
The Ego and the Id, 199, 204, 222n5
and Groddeck, 199–204, 206-208,
210, 213–15, 222n5, 222n11,
222n12, 222n14
Oedipus complex, 215
See also psychoanalysis

al-Gaddafi, Muammar, 369, 378n10
Gandhi, Indira, 283n7
Gascoyne, David, 21n35, 21n40, 245n5,
281
Gaugin, Paul, 10, 64, 70n4, 75, 78
Gaulle, Charles de, 356, 358n6
Gawsworth, John, 245n3
Genet, Jean, 255n14
Gifford, James, xxxiin9, xxxiin3–4,
17n2, 23n48, 36n12, 44n5, 70n6,
104n2, 196n14, 221n1, 246n6,
323n7, 377n4
Godshalk, William Leigh, 119n15, xii
Godwin, William, 233n15
Gogol, Nikolai, 230, 233n13
Goldman, Emma, xxxin3
Goodland, John, 21n35
Goodman, Richard, 254n1
Gorgon, 293, 373
Gould, Diana. *See* Menuhin, Diana
Gramsci, Antonio, 45n13
Greece, xviii, xxiv, xxvi–xxviii, 9, 10, 12,
21n40, 22n42, 39, 41, 47, 68, 88,

141, 241, 265, 277, 278, 325, 362,
364, 365
Asia Minor disaster, 32–33, 36n8,
36n10, 58n3
and Egypt, 29–35
Elgin Marbles, xix
and Mythologies, 306, 311–16
Philhellenism, xiii, xix, xviii, xxvi,
xxvii, 36n12, 107–21, 249–50,
252–53
and Shakespeare, 287–95
See also Corfu; Rhodes
Green, Peter, xviii
Greene, Robert, 83, 86, 95n1, 96n8,
176n4
Grey Walls Press, xiv, xxxin1
Groddeck, Georg, 12, 23n51, 23n53,
199–223, 316n9
Book of the It, 214, 219
Exploring the Unconscious, 219
The Unknown Self, 219, 221–22n3
The World of Man, 213, 219
See also psychoanalysis
Guiler, Hugo, 242, 246n9, 259, 268n6

H.D., 295n22
Haag, Michael, xii
Haldane, J.B.S., 229, 232n8
Hamilton, William Rowan, 145,
148n23, 341, 346n10
Hammond, Andrew, xvii
Hamsun, Knut, 188, 195n10
Harper, Edith Alice Mary.
See Wickham, Anna
Harris, Frank, 196n19
Harrison, J.B., 64, 70n5
Harvey, Gabriel, 112, 120n20
Hascmet, 303

Elizabethan era, 149, 151–58, 169, 175, 177n5, 253

Macedonia. *See* Yugoslavia

Macmillan, Harold, xix

MacNeice, Louis, 111, 119n16, 254n1

MacNiven, Ian S., 18n8, 18n11, 18n14, 19n22, 22n44, 23n54, 28n1, 59n6, 80n4, 127n4, 177n1, 178n19, 195n7, 222n11, 334n2, 334n3, 345n5, 377n7

Macrobius, Ambrosius Theodosius, 315n1

Magellan, Ferdinand, 198n40

Mailer, Norman, 2, 17n6

Makarios, 48, 49, 50, 50n2, 50n6

Mallarmé, Stéphane, 235, 237n3

Manning, Olivia, 36n13, 120n27

Marlowe, Christopher, 97n32, 150, 151, 161, 178n16, 188

Marston, William Moulton, 169, 179n35

Marx, Karl, 196n16, xvi, xviii

Marxism, 36n8, 40, 177n6, 196n16, 228, 229, 230, 232n9, 321, 322n7, 353, 362, 366, 367, 369, xix
anti-Marxism, xiv, xix, xvii, xx, xxi, 232n6

Matisse, Henri, 187

Maturin, 344, 346n16

Maugham, Somerset, 54, 58n2

McCall, Margaret, 345n1

McPherson, Bimbashi, 358n3

Mediterranean, 47, 96n6, 96n25, 118n2, 241, 249, 302, 308, 320, 362, xiii, xxvi

Melville, Herman, 187, 189, 192, 194n2

Menuhin, Diana, 248, 254n3

Milarepa, Jetsun, 53, 54, 58n1

Miller, Henry, xi, xiv–xvii, xx–xxii, xxvii, xxx, xxxin1, xxxin3, 10, 12, 17n4, 18n13, 20n27, 21n35, 22n42, 22n43, 22n44, 23n48, 23n52, 29, 35n1, 45n14, 63, 69n1–2, 71n13, 73–81, 104n2, 105n4, 130, 148n14, 187–98, 221n1, 222n4, 222n11, 239, 240, 241, 242, 243, 245n3, 246n8, 250, 252, 255n14, 259–61, 281, 316n4–5, 345n5–6, 364–65
Black Spring, 77, 80n9, 187
Colossus of Maroussi, 22n42, 23n52, 29, 35n3, 132n6, 316n5, 365
The Cosmological Eye, 35n1, 246n8
film interests of, 193, 198n38
"An Open Letter to Surrealists Everywhere," xvii, 45n11, 196n14, 196n16
Tropic of Cancer, 77, 80n9, 187–90, 192, 195n4–5, 195n10–12, 196n19, 196n22, 259
Tropic of Capricorn, 187, 194, 198n37

Milton, John, 63, 70n3, 136, 188

Modernism, xiii, xxi, xxii, xxiv, xxvii, xxviii, xxxiin9, 21n38, 22n42, 36n12, 46n18, 70n4, 195n3, 197n22, 232n7, 237n1, 279n5.
See also Eliot, T.S.; Joyce, James; Pound, Ezra

Montaigne, Michel de, 156, 177n9

Montenegro. *See* Yugoslavia

Montgomery, Bernard, 361, 377n3

Moore, Henry, 281

Moorman, Mary, 147

Morgan, Charles, 260, 268n9

Morrison, Ray, 46n17